PARAMEDICAL
MICROBIOLOGY

REINHOLD BOOKS IN THE
BIOLOGICAL SCIENCES

CONSULTING EDITOR: PROFESSOR PETER GRAY
Department of Biological Sciences
University of Pittsburgh
Pittsburgh, Pennsylvania

The Encyclopedia of the Biological Sciences, edited by Peter Gray

Biophysics: Concepts and Mechanisms, by E. J. Casey
Cell Function, by L. L. Langley
Chordate Morphology, by Malcolm Jollie
Concepts of Forest Entomology, by Kenneth Graham
Cytology, by G. B. Wilson and John H. Morrison
Ecology of Inland Waters and Estuaries, by George K. Reid
Evolution: Process and Product, Revised Edition, by Edward O. Dodson
Management of Artificial Lakes and Ponds, by George W. Bennett
Manual of Insect Morphology, by E. Melville Du Porte
The Plant Community, by Herbert C. Hanson and Ethan D. Churchill
Principles in Mammalogy, by David E. Davis and Frank B. Golley

SERIES EDITOR'S STATEMENT

THE SCIENCE OF MICROBIOLOGY IS DAILY BECOMING MORE COM-
plicated. Professional microbiologists must of necessity learn the complex
details of often bizarre metabolic pathways if they are to continue in the
currently popular research fields of transduction and the like. All this,
valuable though it is in pushing back the frontiers of science, is not of
much use to the professional worker whose interest lies in the practical
application of microbiology in the service of the medical profession and
its beneficiaries. Professor Wedberg's admirable book is specifically aimed,
as the title indicates, toward those who will devote their lives to the service
functions ancillary to the practice of medicine and to the routine, but
very important, aspects of industrial microbiology.

This book, therefore, emphasizes techniques far more than it does
theory, although the latter is nowhere neglected. Indeed, one of the most
valuable features of Professor Wedberg's work is that he contrives to give
just so much theory as will make the learning of techniques interesting
without placing a burden on the busy student. I am personally convinced
that books of this type are not only scarce but are urgently required in a
contemporary civilization leaning more and more heavily on the intelligent and well-instructed technical worker. I am, therefore, very pleased to
welcome it as an addition to the REINHOLD BOOKS IN THE BIOLOGICAL
SCIENCES.

Pittsburgh, Pennsylvania   PETER GRAY
January, 1963

Antony van Leeuwenhoek (1632–1723)—The Father of Microbiology

PARAMEDICAL
MICROBIOLOGY

STANLEY E. WEDBERG

PROFESSOR AND HEAD, DEPARTMENT OF BACTERIOLOGY
THE UNIVERSITY OF CONNECTICUT
STORRS, CONNECTICUT

NEW YORK

REINHOLD PUBLISHING CORPORATION

CHAPMAN & HALL, LTD., LONDON

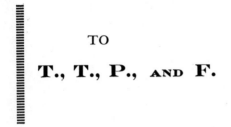

TO

T., T., P., AND **F.**

PREFACE

THIS BOOK IS BASED UPON GENERAL OULTLINES OF COURSES IN microbiology presented to students in pre-clinical nursing, physical therapy, medical technology, and pharmacy at the University of Connecticut. It has been written in a condensed, readable style to include basic fundamentals of microbiology with pointed applications for students in the paramedical sciences, and it provides core material around which a one-semester, or equivalent, course can be constructed.

In contrast to general, introductory texts employed in terminal courses designed to fulfill a biological science requirement, this book has been written for students who have indicated more than just a passing interest in science by their very choice of one of the paramedical sciences as a possible career.

Historical background material has been minimized to allow greater emphasis on the practical aspects of microbiology in the medically oriented sciences. However, some coverage of non-medical phases of the field has been included to call the reader's attention to relationships between the "good" and the "bad" microbes in health and in disease.

It is highly desirable that appropriate laboratory exercises be conducted concurrent with lectures in order that students may develop the dexterity and the mental skills that will be expected of them in their chosen field. Laboratory manuals with suitable experiments are available for this phase of directed study.

No attempt is made to create professional microbiologists of those who

participate in a course for which this book is employed as a text, but in-
quiring students who possess more than an introductory interest can expand their knowledge by employing the fundamental concepts presented
here as a base for collateral study of advanced texts.

A number of individuals, scientific societies, corporations, and pub-
lishers have kindly consented to inclusion in this book of certain illustra-
tions; the legends accompanying the figures acknowledge these permissions.
In addition, the trustees of *Bergey's Manual* have permitted free use of
material in the description of microorganisms throughout the text. Their
cooperation and encouragement are appreciated.

The writer expresses sincere thanks to all members of the Reinhold
organization for their complete understanding during preparation of this
book. A critical review of the original manuscript by Dr. Virginia B.
Braley, Associate Professor of Nursing at the University of Pittsburgh, resulted in a number of changes that improved both the content and the
makeup of the book. Particular gratitude is expressed to Mrs. Phyllis
Batten, copy editor, for valuable assistance rendered by suggestions for
improvements in arrangement and in wording of parts of the manuscript.

Appreciation is extended to Mrs. Gordon R. Hanks and to Mrs. Robert
E. Laramy who typed and retyped the manuscript.

STANLEY E. WEDBERG

Storrs, Connecticut

CONTENTS

Introduction   1

1. The Bacterial Cell   5
TAXONOMIC CLASSIFICATION OF BACTERIA   6
SIZES OF BACTERIA   7
SHAPES AND ARRANGEMENTS OF BACTERIA   8
PARTS OF A BACTERIAL CELL   10
THE GRAM STAIN   22
REVIEW QUESTIONS   24

2. Bacterial Metabolism   25
ENZYMES   25
LIGHT PRODUCTION   28
HEAT PRODUCTION   29
PIGMENT PRODUCTION   30
TOXIN PRODUCTION   32
CYCLES OF ELEMENTS IN NATURE   35
ANTAGONISM AND COOPERATION   36
REVIEW QUESTIONS   41

3. Cultivation of Microorganisms   42
REQUISITES FOR A SUITABLE MEDIUM   44
INOCULATION OF SUBCULTURES   54
STREAK PLATES   56

BLOOD AGAR PLATES   59

ASCITIC FLUID   60

BLOOD SERUM MEDIA   61

SELECTIVE MEDIA   61

ANAEROBIC TECHNIQUES   63

MICROAEROPHILIC TECHNIQUES   65

REVIEW QUESTIONS   66

4. Identification of Bacteria   67

TRANSFER OF CULTURES   67

STAINING PROCEDURES   70

MORPHOLOGY   72

CULTURAL CHARACTERISTICS   74

PHYSIOLOGY   75

REVIEW QUESTIONS   82

5. The Principles and Techniques of Sterilization   83

INTRODUCTION   83

DRY HEAT   87

MOIST HEAT   89

FILTRATION   99

STERILIZATION WITH GASES   102

STERILITY INDICATORS   103

REVIEW QUESTIONS   105

6. Control of Microorganisms by Chemical Methods   106

BACTERIOSTASIS   108

DISINFECTION   109

COMMON ANTIMICROBIAL AGENTS   118

TECHNIQUES FOR EVALUATION OF AGENTS   137

REVIEW QUESTIONS   142

7. Control of Microbes by Physical Forces   143

TEMPERATURE   143

DESICCATION   144

MECHANICAL PRESSURE   145

OSMOTIC PRESSURE   146

LIGHT AND RADIATION   147

ROENTGEN RAYS   149

CATHODE RAYS   150

SURFACE TENSION   151

SONIC AND ULTRASONIC VIBRATIONS   152

ELECTRICITY AND ELECTROPHORESIS   153

REVIEW QUESTIONS   154

8. **Microbiology of Water Supplies**   155

HISTORICAL BACKGROUND   155

NATURAL BODIES OF WATER   157

DUG WELLS   158

DRILLED OR DRIVEN WELLS   159

SPRINGS   159

CISTERNS   159

TREATMENT OF WATER   160

MICROBIOLOGICAL TESTING OF WATER   165

CHEMICAL ANALYSES   170

THE MICROBIOLOGY OF ICE   171

PUBLIC DRINKING CUPS AND FOUNTAINS   172

SWIMMING POOLS   173

REVIEW QUESTIONS   174

9. **Microbiology of Sewage**   175

COMPOSITION OF SEWAGE   176

DISPOSAL OF HUMAN WASTES   176

INDUSTRIAL WASTES   181

REVIEW QUESTIONS   182

10. **Microbiology of the Soil**   183

SOIL COMPOSITION: PHYSICAL, CHEMICAL, AND BIOLOGICAL   185

ROTATION OF ELEMENTS IN NATURE   187

SOIL AS A VEHICLE FOR PATHOGENS   191

ANTIBIOTICS IN THE SOIL   193

REVIEW QUESTIONS   195

11. **Microbiology of the Atmosphere**   196

COMPOSITION OF AIR   196

POLLUTION AND HUMAN HEALTH   198

CONTROL OF ORGANISMS IN THE AIR   199

AIR CONDITIONING AND HEALTH   201

SMOKING AND HEALTH   201

AIR-BORNE INFECTIONS   203

TREATMENT OF AIR   205

MICROBE-FREE ANIMALS   206

QUALITATIVE AND QUANTITATIVE ANALYSIS OF AIR   206

REVIEW QUESTIONS   208

12. **Microbiology of Food and Food Poisoning**   209

INTRODUCTION   209

MICROORGANISMS AND FOOD   210

SANITATION IN THE HOME AND IN PUBLIC EATING
    ESTABLISHMENTS 213
FOOD POISONING AND FOOD INFECTION 215
REVIEW QUESTIONS 228

13. **Chemotherapy**   230
HISTORY 230
RESISTANCE TO ANTIBIOTICS 237
REPRESENTATIVE ANTIBIOTICS 238
MISCELLANEOUS USES OF ANTIBIOTICS 239
CHEMOTHERAPY IN MALARIA 240
TESTS FOR ANTIBIOTIC ACTIVITY 241
REVIEW QUESTIONS 243

14. **Modes of Transmission of Microbial Diseases**   244
THE HUMAN BODY 244
ARTHROPODS AND OTHER VERMIN 256
FOMITES 258
FOOD AND WATER 264
REVIEW QUESTIONS 264

15. **Pathogenic Bacteria**   265
GRAM POSITIVE BACTERIA 266
GRAM NEGATIVE BACTERIA 302
REVIEW QUESTIONS 343

16. **The Fungi**   344
THE YEASTS 344
MOLDS 353
REVIEW QUESTIONS 358

17. **The Rickettsiae**   359
HISTORICAL BACKGROUND 359
CHARACTERISTICS 361
CULTIVATION TECHNIQUES 361
DISEASES 362
REVIEW QUESTIONS 371

18. **Viruses**   372
HISTORICAL REVIEW 372
PHYSICAL CHARACTERISTICS OF VIRUSES 374
CULTIVATION 375
DERMOTROPIC VIRUSES 380
PNEUMOTROPIC VIRUSES 387

NEUROTROPIC VIRUSES   391
VISCEROTROPIC VIRUSES   398
REVIEW QUESTIONS   401

19. **Resistance to Disease**   402
INTRODUCTION   402
THEORIES OF IMMUNITY   404
FACTORS INFLUENCING RESISTANCE   406
TISSUE FACTORS IN RESISTANCE   412
BODY FLUIDS AND THEIR RELATIONSHIP TO IMMUNITY   414
TYPES OF IMMUNITY   414
TYPES OF ANTIBODIES   415
COMMON SKIN TESTS   427
REVIEW QUESTIONS   429

Appendix   431

References   435

Glossary   439

Index   451

PARAMEDICAL MICROBIOLOGY

INTRODUCTION

There is in youth an unforgettable day that lights up all the rest of our lives. That day is the day when we meet those teachers to whom we owe our first enthusiasm. . . . Ah, what other moment, what fortune of our careers can ever be worth as much as that moment.

—Louis Pasteur

THE PARAMEDICAL SCIENCES PRESENT A REAL CHALLENGE TO SERIOUS, intelligent individuals who generally find their professional experiences to be most rewarding. But before a person can become an effective member of a medical team, he must apply himself diligently to academic preparation to insure that the knowledge gained may be put to effective use.

One of the vital links in this educational chain is an understanding of the basic principles of microbiology which includes the science of the life and actions of such microorganisms as viruses, rickettsiae, bacteria, yeasts, protozoa, and molds. A well-trained individual must have a sound background in this branch of medical science if he or she expects to deal intelligently with human suffering that stems from microbial activity.

The early history of this vibrant field makes fascinating reading. However, it is more pertinent for those who contemplate playing an active part in maintaining public health and in caring for the sick that they master modern techniques that have evolved from the fundamental discoveries and breakthroughs of the past. Paramedical scientists must be

1

practical individuals, and the application of medically proven concepts should be their primary concern.

In spite of the advent of chemotherapy, beginning with the "magic bullets" of Paul Ehrlich, then through the promise provided by sulfa drugs, and up to the antibiotics, the task of recognizing, isolating, identifying, and treating microbes and microbial diseases is still a major medical problem. Recent experiences encountered with the development of antibiotic-resistant strains of pathogenic organisms merely accentuate the critical need for a better understanding of microbes if man is to cope more effectively with these lethal agents.

An important member of the team is the nurse, and a dedicated individual is one who is endowed with more than just an average spirit of curiosity. Following the scientific cookbook to the letter without wondering why certain procedures are carried out or how microorganisms act is falling far short of the mark.

Microbiology, though only one discipline studied by the prospective nurse, is an important tool subject that assists her in understanding many medical procedures and practices commonly employed each working day. Such considerations as the sterilization of equipment to be used at the patient's bedside and in the operating room, the practice of asepsis (keeping microbes out) in modern hospitals, and the precautions required of those who are dealing with individuals suffering with communicable diseases, all are directly related to the fundamental principles of microbiology.

In addition to possessing broad knowledge in specific fields of biological science, a competent nurse must also understand human nature with all of its ramifications and peculiarities. The attitude of the nurse and her wise application of psychology can accomplish a great deal more in speeding the recovery of the sick than is sometimes appreciated. A patient who is optimistic about the future in general, and about his prognosis in particular, can assist the physician and the nurse greatly in the effective repair process required during convalescence. The nurse is in a unique position to do much to create the proper mental climate for getting the patient into a "therapeutic" frame of mind.

Some readers may question a discussion of this type in a textbook of microbiology, but the fact remains that a person who lacks the proper psychological approach to a patient might very well nullify or undo much of the painstaking medical therapy instituted by the physician. Psychology is an integral part of the over-all approach to treatment of those who are ill, and this branch of science should not be glossed over by those contemplating a career in nursing or in the allied professions which deal directly with patients.

The layman's idea of what a microbe looks like and how it goes about its task of trying to survive in a highly competitive environment is one that frequently requires drastic modification. Nurses and physicians provide a critical bond in the educational process as they instruct patients under their care in matters relating to accepted techniques for prevention of the spread of microbial diseases.

The nurse working in the delivery room and in the obstetrics ward not only has the privilege, she also has the solemn obligation to teach new mothers coming from all walks of life the modern practices recommended for maintaining the well-being of newborn babies. To leave the protection of the mother's body and to enter a world in which he is beset on every hand by microbial marauders is a radical adjustment for any infant to make. The transition for this new living being cannot successfully be bridged without the ever-present help of informed adults. The infant must be able to cope on at least equal terms with the powerful forces set in motion by microscopic organisms and by other biological and physical agents.

The success of health programs aimed at instituting sanitary practices throughout the world has been reflected in a graphic manner in recent decades by the dramatic drop in the infant mortality rate in countries where these advances have been practiced. The lack of similar health programs in certain other areas of the world presents a formidable challenge to those of us who enjoy the benefits of good health in sanitary surroundings during an ever-lengthening life span. A man's useful potential and productivity tend to be directly related to his state of health. Only when we become ill do many of us truly appreciate the blessings of good health, an asset so often taken for granted. In fact, it is probably only because we are well most of the time that we have a point of reference to help us realize when we are ill!

It was not too uncommon years ago to hear the statement that if a person wasn't suffering from a communicable disease when he entered a hospital, he could be reasonably certain of contracting whatever was "going around" that particular institution before he left. The hospital was referred to by many as "God's waiting room." The implications are crystal clear! Some individuals still refuse to live near a hospital for fear of contracting a disease that might mysteriously fly out the window and afflict folks in the neighborhood.

There is little justification for this "pest-house" concept in modern hospitals. The change in attitude, however, is not accidental. With the institution of sanitary practices has come a complete about-face and our confidence in hospitals and in the personnel who operate them has risen steadily. Through careful selection of workers, practical training programs, routine sanitary practices, and continuous self-evaluation, our hospitals today are attaining new peak standards.

Any effective teaching effort proceeds from the simple to the more complex and from the known to the unknown. In microbiology, therefore, we progress from the study of harmless microorganisms to a consideration of potentially dangerous microbes. It would be foolhardy to permit beginning students to toy with disease-producing (pathogenic) microorganisms without first providing a sound groundwork of instruction with the techniques for handling harmless organisms (saprophytes). Students must be allowed to develop confidence in their ability to manipulate cultures in a safe manner before they are confronted with the hazards of dealing with representative microscopic assassins. It would be folly to permit a person who has never set off anything more explosive than a firecracker to "pull the pin" on a grenade without first providing him with at least a minimum of instruction relative to the dangers involved! While handling microbes might not be considered equivalent to playing with a bomb, the potential outcome for the individual, or for those about him, could be just as final.

A course in microbiology should alert members of the medical team to the possible dangers that must be faced in dealing with the sick. They should come to recognize the ubiquitousness of microbes and what will be required to minimize their spread, especially with respect to the pathogenic species. This presentation of microbiology is primarily concerned with the disease-producing organisms, but the reader should constantly bear in mind that of the hundreds of species of microbes recognized and studied by man, relatively few are pathogenic.

Louis Pasteur (1822–1895), one of the giants of microbiology, once asserted that in time certain microbial diseases might be wiped from the face of the earth. Were he to emerge today from his ornate tomb in the Pasteur Institute in Paris, he would be amazed at the progress that science has achieved in the direction of fulfilling his prediction. But this is not the time to sit back and rest on our laurels. Much remains to be accomplished.

1 | THE BACTERIAL CELL

IN ORDER TO COMPREHEND WHAT TAKES PLACE IN HEALTH AND in disease, members of the medical family of scientists should be familiar with the structure and the function of cells. In simple terms a biologist might describe a cell as a minute, usually microscopic, structural unit of living matter enclosed within a membrane and consisting of a mass of **protoplasm,*** which envelops a controlling mechanism called a **nucleus.**

Cells arise from previously existing cells. Schleiden and Schwann in 1838 first reported that life was contained within sacs they called "cells," and these units may vary in size from microscopic to a foot or more in length in the case of certain nerve cells. Scientists who study cell structure and function are known as **cytologists** (Greek *kutos,* vessel; *logia,* study).

Protoplasm is an egg-white-like, grayish, semifluid material of varying viscosity and of complex composition consisting of carbohydrates, fats, proteins, salts, and water. Part of the protoplasm exists as a **colloid,** which might be described as finely divided particles, somewhat larger than molecules, too large to go into solution and yet too small and light to settle out; they are permanently dispersed in a liquid. The word "colloid" is derived from the Greek and means "gelatinous" or "glue-like." Attempts by man to synthesize living cells have met with failure since the finished products have always lacked that vital spark we call life.

---

* Boldface words and their definitions may be found in the Glossary (pp. 439–450).

Taxonomic Classification of Bacteria

Microbes, minute organisms including bacteria, protozoa, and fungi, are types of cells endowed with the usual characteristics ascribed to living things: growth, reproduction, and other metabolic processes. Contrary to popular belief, however, bacteria are not "bugs" in the zoological sense; they are members of the plant kingdom. Although it is true that a number of microbes exhibit the power of independent locomotion, this feature, in itself, is a poor criterion for classifying an organism as a plant or an animal. More scientific indices have been adopted for determining into which kingdom living things should be placed. When such functions as nutrition, respiration, and reproduction are considered, bacteria are found to be endowed with a greater number of significant characteristics ascribed to plants than those commonly associated with animals. True, some borderline traits do exist, but it is generally agreed by those who study classification, called **taxonomy** (Greek *taxis,* arrangement; *nemos,* law), that bacteria should be included in the plant kingdom.

The usual differences between plants and animals might be summarized as follows:

Plants	*Animals*
Cells have a definite shape and turgor, or rigidity	Cell shape may vary and have less turgor than plant cells
Contain cellulose	Lack cellulose
Require simple foods in solution	Prefer complex foods
Are chemosynthetic	Are chemoanalytic
Take in carbon dioxide and liberate oxygen	Take in oxygen and give off carbon dioxide
Cells divide by binary fission	Cells divide by longitudinal division

Upon further study, it becomes increasingly apparent that not all microorganisms possess the general characteristics outlined above for plants, and because of this it is not uncommon to hear the statement made that the line dividing plants from animals might be considered to run through the group of microorganisms called the bacteria. A number of colleges and universities offer microbiology in the department of botany—not an illogical choice; however in most of the larger schools where demand for a breadth of courses may be greater, particularly at the graduate level, it is customary to find microbiology standing on its own in an independent department.

Sizes of Bacteria

Before delving into a discussion of specific structures of bacteria it might be well to outline a few facts relative to size, shape, and arrangement of these microorganisms. It is customary to study bacteria under the oil immersion lens of a compound microscope, and this objective magnifies between 900 and 1000 times with the usual high-quality classroom

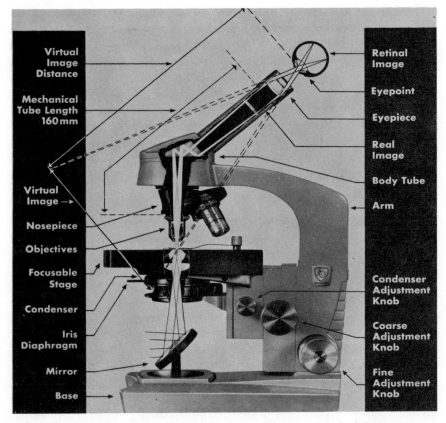

FIG. 1.1. Compound microscope. (Courtesy American Optical Company, Buffalo, N. Y.)

instruments. (A man magnified to the same degree would be over a mile high and 500 yards wide!) Because of the minuteness of microorganisms, it would be cumbersome to describe their sizes in terms of fractions of an inch. Instead we employ a unit of the metric system called a **micron** (abbreviated, μ, the Greek letter mu) which is approximately 0.001 millimeter. The usual microbes encountered in an introductory course of this nature generally fall within the range of 1.0 to 5.0 microns in length and about 1.0 micron or less in width. (The student is referred to the Appendix on pp. 431–433 for a condensed presentation of other units in the metric system.)

Shapes and Arrangements of Bacteria

A given species of organism can be expected to have a definite shape under a standard set of conditions, and this fact aids materially in the identification of pure cultures. Shape of a cell is one of the first clues that a bacteriologist employs when he commences his identification of microbes.

Three principal forms of bacterial cells are recognized: rods, spheres, and spirals. However under certain conditions, especially in older cultures containing an accumulation of metabolic wastes, so-called **involution** forms appear. They are rather bizarre, aberrant shapes or distortions of the three standard types. When such involution forms are transferred to a suitable medium, however, the offspring revert to the usual accepted shapes. Typical appearance, therefore, can best be observed in young (less than 24 hours) actively growing cultures. It is imperative for students in microbiology, if they hope to avoid pitfalls in their laboratory identification procedures, to remember that *only young cultures are reliable for studies of morphology* (size, shape, structure).

The terminology that is employed to describe the various shapes of microbes should be mastered by the student early in the course, and the following designations are basic to this understanding.

Rods

A rod-shaped organism is a **bacterium** or a **bacillus** (plural: *bacteria* and *bacilli*). The general term *bacterium* is applied to all bacteria regardless of their shape. Specifically, it means a small, rod-shaped organism that does not contain a spore and that stains in a prescribed manner (so-called gram negative, or pink) when subjected to a procedure known as the **gram stain.** This technique will be described later in the chapter. The word *bacillus* when written with a small letter usually refers to rod-shaped bacteria in general, but when capitalized Bacillus becomes a generic term meaning a rod-shaped, spore-forming, gram positive (purple) organism.

If, after dividing by **binary fission** (equal splitting at right angles to the long axis) rod-shaped organisms adhere to one another indefinitely, the pair of rods becomes a **diplobacillus,** or a **diplobacterium.** Should these two rods each divide in turn, the chain that forms becomes a **streptobacillus** or a **streptobacterium.** It should be pointed out that the accepted way to determine typical arrangement of a given species is to examine a young (less than 24 hours), actively growing culture in a fluid medium under the high dry objective (about $400 \times$) of a microscope. Scraping a bit of **colony** (a mass of growth on a solid medium, visible to the unaided eye), staining, and examining it under a microscope is not a satisfactory method for determining typical arrangements of organisms. It becomes apparent that the manner in which the growth is smeared on the slide will directly influence the arrangement of these organisms.

Spheres

Since spheres do not possess a long axis, division of bacteria of this type can result in more arrangements of the resulting progeny than is true for rods. For example, a pair of spheres might divide in the same plane and form a chain of four, eight, sixteen, etc. Or the original pair might divide in such a manner that a group of four (two under two) might develop. These four in turn might divide in a plane that would result in the formation of a cubical packet of eight (four behind four). Or the spheres could divide haphazardly into grapelike clusters. Each

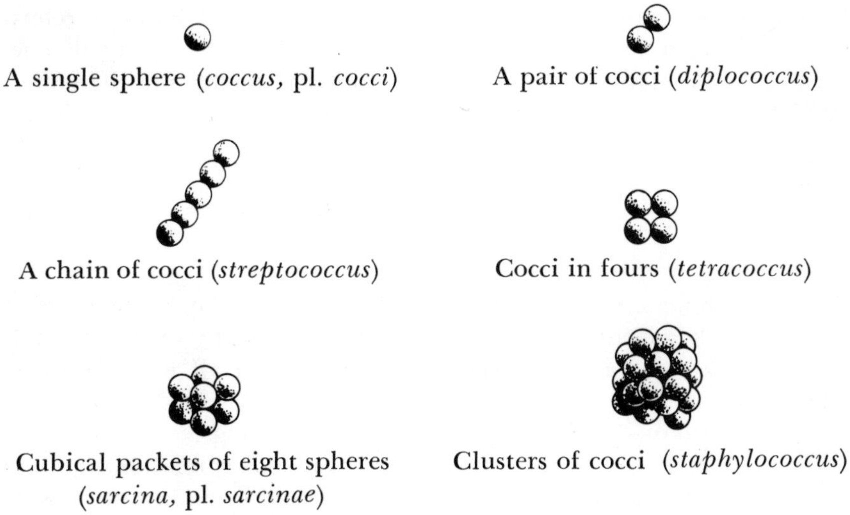

A single sphere (*coccus,* pl. *cocci*)   A pair of cocci (*diplococcus*)

A chain of cocci (*streptococcus*)   Cocci in fours (*tetracoccus*)

Cubical packets of eight spheres   Clusters of cocci (*staphylococcus*)
(*sarcina,* pl. *sarcinae*)

FIG. 1.2. Arrangements of cocci.

organism eventually reaches its particular ultimate arrangement, but at any given stage in development a microscopic examination would reveal all steps leading up to that final arrangement. This means, therefore, that a culture about eighteen hours old is best for determining the arrangement of most actively growing microbes.

A spherical-shaped microbe is a **coccus** (Greek *kokkos,* berry). The scientific designations for the various arrangements described above are given in Fig. 1.2.

At times it becomes difficult to determine whether a given organism is a true coccus or a short rod; such organisms are frequently tagged as **coccobacteria.** Some of the more common and severe microbial afflictions of man and of lower animals are caused by spherical-shaped bacteria, and a great deal will be said about them in later chapters.

Spirals

The spiral-shaped bacteria tend to resemble screws or springs under various degrees of tension, rather than mere wavy rods. Some writers refer to them as *helicoidal,* which means "coiled." Three principal types of spirals are recognized:

1. Vibrio, a curved rod with less than one spiral turn
2. Spirillum, a rigid spiral with one or more turns
3. Spirochete, a flexible curved rod with several complete spiral turns

When the word *spirillum* is written with a small letter it refers to curved rods in general, but when it is capitalized, Spirillum denotes a genus. These curved rods are typically found as singles and therefore the multiplicity of arrangements common to rods and to spheres does not apply.

Parts of a Bacterial Cell

Capsules

A curious material variously referred to as a slime layer, sheath, viscous coat, capsule, or envelope appears rather prominently on the outside of the cell wall of some bacteria and, probably, on all bacteria to some degree. In addition some microorganisms form a viscous material that is liberated into the medium in which they are growing.

Since the extent of this slime layer bears some relationship to the **virulence** (disease-producing power) of selected bacteria, the capsule is of medical importance. Inoculating·susceptible animals, including man, with graded doses of specific pathogenic organisms tends to encourage the production of capsular material on those organisms. This can be demonstrated by recovering some of the offspring of the injected microbes after a suitable incubation period and examining stained preparations under the oil immersion objective of a microscope. Growing bacteria in test tubes containing such dietary supplements as blood, blood serum, or other proteins may be employed to encourage capsule development.

Much speculation has taken place through the years (and the science of microbiology is only about 100 years old) concerning the exact role

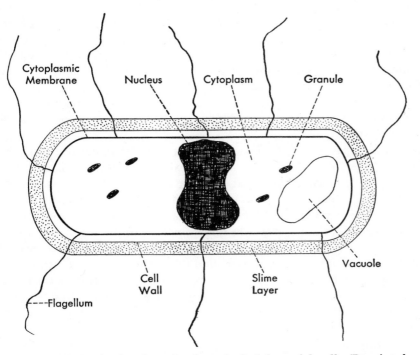

FIG. 1.3. Schematic drawing of a hypothetical bacterial cell. (Reprinted from S. E. Wedberg, *Microbes and You*, 1954, with permission of The Macmillan Company, New York, N. Y.)

played by this gummy product. Its composition appears to be principally polysaccharide in character, although other chemical substances have also been isolated from capsular material. Some investigators in the field view this layer as a protective armor whose principal function is to delay dehydration of the underlying vital structures when environmental conditions become adverse. Others consider the capsule as a bulwark against the natural defense mechanisms of the animal body being attacked. Perhaps its function is a combination of these two, plus others still not recognized.

Within the last decade a fermentable gum known as **dextran** has been isolated from the capsule of *Leuconostoc dextranicum,* an organism encountered in fermenting plant material and in prepared meat products. These bacteria have also been isolated from slimy sugar solutions. During the Korean conflict dextran appeared on the medical scene as a blood extender helping to ease the critical shortage of precious blood plasma. Although dextran is not a substitute for whole blood with its irreplaceable cellular elements, it does function in a manner similar to that of plasma through increasing blood volume and helping to ward off shock or keeping the victim from going into deeper shock. In cases of severe burns, for example, when blood fluids ooze from the damaged tissue, the loss of proteins and other blood constituents can seriously disrupt the chemical balance within the circulatory system and contribute to shock. Research continues in an attempt to develop other substances that will act more nearly like plasma and that may be used especially during catastrophes when enormous volumes of blood or plasma may be needed on short notice.

Capsules may also be found as the agent in such undesirable conditions as ropy milk or ropy bread. A rather small bacterium, *Alcaligenes viscolactis,* that is endowed with what might be considered a disproportionately large capsule, may find its way into a milk processing plant or into a bakery. The activity of this organism can cause serious economic loss unless the plant manager attacks the problem with intelligence and vigor. The capsule, because of its size and composition, increases the resistance of the underlying organism to heat and to the chemicals that are normally employed for food plant sanitation. Unless the condition is cleared up rather promptly, the dairy or bakery may lose customers who, strangely enough, object to purchasing stringy bread or milk that must be snipped with shears!

The linkage between pathogenicity of an organism and marked capsule development appears to be explained, at least in part, on the grounds that encapsulated microbes may remain viable for extended periods of time within the **leucocytes** (white blood cells) whose function is to combat foreign invaders through the ingestion process called **phagocytosis.** It has been demonstrated that some of these still-living bacteria can find their way out of the phagocytes; once released, the microorganisms may continue to multiply at a high rate. In time the numbers of invaders may be increasing at a speed faster than the white blood cells can pick them up—a fulminating infection. The defenses of the body break down, and ultimately the patient dies unless suitable medication is instituted to reverse the reaction. The capsule is not generally considered to be toxic in itself.

The usual dyes employed for staining bacteria are not commonly picked up and retained by capsular material, but if the underlying bacterial cells become stained, microscopic examination reveals a halo effect around the organism. Techniques for staining bacterial capsules directly will be discussed in a later chapter.

In the case of *Diplococcus pneumoniae,* an etiological agent in pneumonia, the so-called "types" of pneumonia are based upon differences in the composition of the capsular material; over seventy-five separate types have been reported to date.

Flagella

Some bacteria have the power of independent locomotion when they are growing or are suspended in suitable fluids. Motility is not a characteristic of all bacteria, however. Microbes are not able to move along dry surfaces, and this fact has considerable significance for nurses in controlling the growth and spread of pathogenic organisms.

The structures that enable bacteria to swim are called **flagella** ("little whips"). True motility should be distinguished from the trembling or jiggling oscillation termed **brownian movement** which was first described in 1827 by the botanist, Robert Brown. This latter motion is characteristic of all minute particles, whether they are alive or dead, when they are in fluid suspensions. Motility of bacteria means actual progress "against the tide," so to speak.

Since bacteria are single-celled, flagella cannot be considered separate structures in the sense that arms, legs, or wings of animals are. Flagella are extensions or extrusions of the cell. Pijper of South Africa has postulated that the capsular polysaccharide is twisted off in threads as a *result* of cell motion and that so-called flagella are more or less artifacts that are not the *cause* of motion. Although his theory can evoke considerable discussion, most bacteriologists still consider flagella to be the primary initiating force behind the motion of microbes.

Flagella are extremely delicate and can be removed by the mere shaking of a bacterial culture. The diameter of these whips is approximately 0.03 micron, while their length may extend up to many times that of the cell from which they arise. Electronographs published by Knaysi of Cornell University reveal that flagella extend through the slime layer and the cell wall, and that they originate in small spherical bodies, about 100 millimicrons in size, that lie between the cytoplasmic membrane and the cell wall.

Because they are so minute, flagella cannot be observed by the usual staining techniques employed for microscopic work, and hence a routine examination of a culture does not include observations for the presence of flagella. Motility found in a suitably prepared culture of bacteria implies the presence of flagella. In order to bring these minute cell projections within the range suitable for observation under a microscope, the careful application of a **mordant** will build up the thickness of flagella. Mordants serve to fix the dye by combining with it to form an

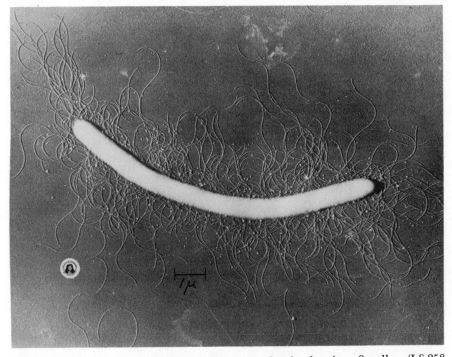

FIG. 1.4. Electron micrograph of *Proteus vulgaris* showing flagella. (LS-258 Courtesy American Society for Microbiology.)

insoluble compound. One such mordant consists of a mixture of tannic acid, ferrous sulfate, and gentian violet. After treatment with a mordant the flagella will possess a diameter great enough to make them visible under the oil immersion objective (about 950 ×) of the usual compound microscope. Electron microscope observations do not require build-up with a mordant, since the increased magnification possible with this instrument is sufficient to bring the flagella within view.

The activating or exciting mechanism of locomotion in bacteria is not clear. Careful observation of organisms growing in semisolid media, which slow down the action, reveals spiral-like waves along the flagella. In relation to the length of bacteria, the speed of some species is almost jet-like. Bacteria apparently do not have a fixed anterior or posterior, and the direction of movement appears to be changed at will. Speeds up to 100 microns per second have been observed—in relation to the length of the organism, a speed comparable to an automobile traveling at one hundred miles an hour or more. While the rate is not maintained at the maximum, brief bursts of speed are remarkable; microbial "high octane fuel" must be held in reserve for the times when the cells feel the need to get away fast from danger in the form of poisons, heat, and other unfavorable conditions that suddenly arise in the environment. Motility provides the mechanism which enables organisms to seek greener pastures when food supplies dwindle and to permit them to absent themselves from areas of unfavorable environment.

FIG. 1.5.   Schematic drawing of a hanging drop preparation.

One of the techniques devised to examine microbial motion is a **hanging drop** preparation. When a drop or two of a young (less than 24 hours) bouillon or infusion broth culture is placed on a thin cover slip and this preparation is inverted over a special concave slide, direct microscopic observations of living cultures can be accomplished. Since the preparation is unstained, it becomes necessary to reduce the amount of illumination reaching the slide; otherwise bright beams of light will pass directly through the organisms and nothing will be seen. It is customary to locate the drop on the slide under low power by focusing on the edge of the drop before switching to the high dry objective which yields magnifying powers in the range of from 400 × to 500 ×. Such relatively large organisms as protozoa, however, may be viewed conveniently under the low power (100 ×) objective.

The number and arrangement of flagella on a given organism are relatively constant, giving rise to the following general classification scheme:

Atrichate	without flagella
Monotrichate	one flagellum, usually at one end
Lophotrichate	a tuft of two or more flagella at one end
Amphitrichate	one or more flagella at each end
Peritrichate	flagella arranged around perimeter of the cell

Cell Wall

The cell wall of a microorganism is frequently considered to include both the outer wall proper and the underlying plasma or cytoplasmic membrane. Strictly speaking, however, these two parts of the cell should be discussed as separate entities since their composition and function are not identical.

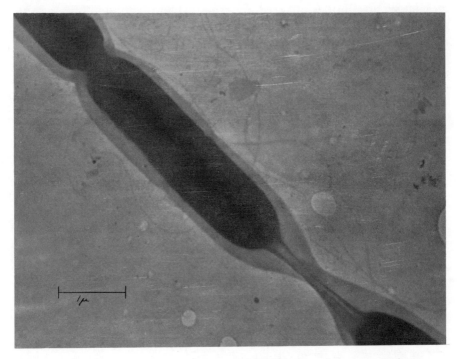

FIG. 1.6.   *Bacillus cereus* 34,000 ✕. (LS-58 Courtesy American Society for Microbiology.)

With the aid of electron microscopy the thickness of the outer wall of microbes has been measured and found to be in the neighborhood of 0.02 micron—well under one-millionth of an inch. This shell is a distinct, rather tough and yet flexible structure lying directly under the outer slime layer. Chemically speaking, the cell wall may be composed of such materials as cellulose, hemicellulose, mucin (nitrogen-containing compound), and such sugars as glucose, mannose, and galactose. Composition varies, as one might expect, with different species and with the medium on which an organism may be growing.

A number of vital functions are served by the cell wall of this unicellu-

lar organism which lacks defined mouth parts or any well-defined structures designed for the digestion of food and the excretion of metabolic
wastes. The minuteness of bacteria dictates, to some degree, the limits
of their existence, since microorganisms are compelled to rely upon the
presence of food that is in solution. This is termed **holophytic** feeding.

Any material must pass tests of suitability by the cell wall before it is
sent along for further consideration by the more fastidious underlying
cytoplasmic membrane. Any conditions which affect the permeability of
these two selective barriers will, therefore, have a direct and sometimes
profound effect upon the metabolism of the protoplasm encased within
the cell jacket. Understanding this "Achilles heel" of bacteria has helped
man to devise ways and means for destroying unwanted microbes.

The relatively rigid outer wall of bacteria enables them to maintain
their predetermined shape better than do the more flexible walls associated
with animal cells. It has been reported that bacterial cell walls are capable
of withstanding osmotic pressures up to twenty atmospheres, and on a
dry-weight basis the walls may constitute as much as 45 per cent of the
cell. The firm shell of bacteria is one of the reasons pointed out earlier for
their classification as plants. When such a cell is placed in a **hypertonic**
(strong) salt or sugar solution, moisture tends to leave the cell and the
protoplasm may be observed to draw away from the outer wall as the
cell volume decreases.

Being as small as they are, bacteria possess a high ratio of cell surface
to cell volume, and relatively large quantities of food can be ingested
and enormous amounts of work can be accomplished in a given time
period. Some might go so far as to say that bacteria are all surface.

Cytoplasmic Membrane

This selective membrane that lies just inside the cell wall should be
thought of in terms of a two-sided barrier rather than as a mere mechanical wall. Anything that goes into the cell must pass inspection, and
those substances desiring egress must also be approved by the cytoplasmic
membrane. In contrast to the cell wall, the underlying membrane is relatively elastic. When a cell is placed in a hypertonic salt solution and the
protoplasm draws away from the cell wall, the cytoplasmic membrane
also shrinks and forms an envelope-like cover around the protoplasm in
a process called **plasmolysis.**

The fact that certain substances are rejected and others are accepted
for passage through this "inner tube" makes it, like the cell wall, semipermeable in character, and the process by which substances soak through
the membrane is called **osmosis.** This built-in control mechanism is a
valuable structure for maintaining the well-being of the cell since it

permits entrance of simple or of partially digested foods, salts in solution, and gases, and allows the exit of wastes, including toxins or poisons, to the surrounding environment.

It is the build-up of these metabolic products that determines to a degree how long an organism can continue to reproduce itself at a maximum rate. When the wastes reach a toxic concentration, not only is reproduction stopped, but the cells may die from "stewing in their own juice." Some of this accumulation of by-products of metabolism, particularly acids, can be controlled within prescribed limits by incorporating into the media certain compounds called **buffers.** These buffers might be likened somewhat to sponges that sop up the poisons to the limit of their capacities, and the organisms are protected for a time from premature self-induced death.

The cytoplasmic membrane, which is about one half a millimicron in thickness—hardly more than a few molecules, therefore plays a vital function in the life of the cell.

Some writers refer to this membrane as a surface tension membrane holding the encased protoplasm together in an almost invisible skin that sets the outer limits of the cytoplasm. The molecules of protoplasm tend to be drawn in at the surface, and this snuggling up of molecules results in the formation of concentrated protoplasm containing various **lipoproteins,** according to these observers. Obviously much more remains to be learned about this curious structure.

Nucleus

The **nucleus** of a cell is, according to most definitions, a well-defined central controlling area within the protoplasm. In bacteria, however, the usual staining procedures fail to reveal such a circumscribed body. The application of usual nuclear dyes to bacterial preparations generally results in the staining of the entire cell, suggesting that nuclear material is diffused throughout the cell. It is possible, however, to treat bacteria by special staining techniques that will result in the appearance of darkly stained areas that act like "usual" nuclear material found in cells other than bacteria.

Through the developmental years of the relatively young science of microbiology there have been those who have proposed that bacteria are so primitive that they do not require a particulate nucleus. The opposing school contends that because all of the physiological actions of a living organism must be carried out within so tiny an organism, microbes must be extremely complex and must require an efficient controlling mechanism—whether you call it a nucleus or something else. Some of the common beliefs expressed about the bacterial nucleus include the following:

1. Bacteria possess no nucleus. The entire cell is composed of cytoplasmic material.
2. Bacteria are practically all nuclear material.
3. Enough chromatin (or portion of the protoplasm that takes up nuclear dyes) is present in bacteria to give the impression that the entire cell is composed of **nucleoprotein.**
4. The usual techniques employed for determining nuclei are not delicate enough to bring out the nucleus as a sharp body. Special growth conditions, as well as selected staining procedures, are required to differentiate nuclear material from other constituents of the cell.

If all cells possess a regulatory body, it is illogical to assume that bacteria are an exception. When cell function is considered, it is not of vital concern whether the nucleus is diffuse or a well-defined mass within the cytoplasm. That problem can be left in the hands of cytologists.

Granules

Young cells just a few hours old generally appear to have a homogeneous composition, but as the culture grows older, dark-staining bodies may become apparent when the cells are treated with selected dyes. Since these granules differ in color from the rest of the cytoplasm, the dark areas are termed **metachromatic granules.**

The fact that granules appear in the later stages of life of some microorganisms has led some investigators to conclude that these particles might represent accumulations of wastes that have not been disposed of, in the usual processes of osmosis, through the membranes to the surrounding environment. Some granules, on the other hand, may appear in relatively young cultures and tend to disappear as the organism becomes older. This latter observation suggests the possibility that certain granules might represent areas of reserve food materials that are metabolized as the need arises. Perhaps both theories have merit.

We do know that the chemical composition of these bodies varies from time to time even within a single species and from organism to organism. Such diverse materials as fat, glycogen, starch, sulfur, and iron have been identified. The etiological agent of tuberculosis, *Mycobacterium tuberculosis,* was reported by Much in 1907 to contain specialized granules, which have since been named **Much's granules** in honor of their discoverer. He observed that these bodies apparently are capable of giving rise to viable (living) rod-shaped organisms. When the tuberculosis bacteria are once stained (which requires more drastic procedures with concentrated dyes than is true for other organisms), the cells are difficult to de-stain except in the presence of acid–alcohol for prescribed periods of time. Hence the mycobacteria are called acid-fast. Color-fastness is one peculiarity of this genus of bacteria; other characteristics of this pathogen will be discussed in a later chapter.

A prominent substance found in many granules is a nucleoprotein called **volutin.** These inclusion bodies may appear as transverse bands, beads, or just irregular masses, and are sometimes referred to as Ernst-Babes granules in recognition of their co-discoverers. Granules are so typical in the diphtheria organisms (*Corynebacterium diphtheriae*), that preliminary identification of this species may be made by discovery of them. The presence of these granules, coupled with **pleomorphism** (many sizes and shapes), is characteristic of this organism.

When a swab culture is taken from a patient with a "red hot" throat and the smear is properly stained, an experienced technician can offer the physician in a matter of minutes a preliminary opinion as to whether the etiological agent is a possible streptococcus or a diphtheria-like organism. It should be made clear, however, that diphtheria is not diagnosed on the basis of a smear alone. In fact, it is not the function of a clinical laboratory to diagnose any disease. A physician should use the laboratory to confirm his own diagnosis or to offer possible clues that might aid in diagnosing disease. The only sure way to identify an organism that might be found in an infectious process is to isolate it, run it through tests to include **morphology** (size, shape, structure), **cultural characteristics** (how it grows on various media), **physiology** (what it does to various food substances), and in some instances **serology** (study of one aspect of its chemical structure) to separate closely related organisms. In the case of diphtheria, virulence tests should be conducted in susceptible animals to prove that the toxins are present. Such a series of tests may require the better part of a week; therefore if the physician should wait for the final laboratory report before commencing treatment, his patient may have left this vale of tears. Early clues as to the possible nature of the infection become extremely important, and early treatment with diphtheria antitoxin can have a profound effect upon the prognosis of the disease. Should the completed laboratory findings fail to confirm the presence of virulent diphtheria organisms, the antitoxin that has been administered probably will do no harm to the individual.

Another disease caused by an organism that produces rather prominent granules is plague. This malady is transmitted from rat to rat and from rat to man through the agency of infected rat fleas. The microbial cause of this affliction is *Pasteurella pestis* which, when suitably stained, reveals characteristic granules located at the poles of the rod-shaped bacteria. Again, a competent bacteriologist who has had practical experience with this organism may be in a position to furnish the physician with an early preliminary report that could warrant initiation of appropriate medication.

Spores

A structure found in selected rod-shaped bacteria is the **endospore,** a tough resistant body that aids the organism in its struggle for survival during periods when environmental conditions become unfavorable. Two principal genera of microorganisms produce spores, and most of the species in these genera are found in the soil where competition is extremely keen.

The first genus is *Bacillus* and consists primarily of nonpathogenic bacteria, although the etiological agent of anthrax, *Bacillus anthracis,* is an exception. The genus *Clostridium* represents those intriguing organisms which grow only in the absence of air. They were first described by Louis Pasteur in the late nineteenth century. These **anaerobes,** as they are called, will be discussed in some detail later since such diseases as tetanus (lockjaw), gas gangrene, and botulism are caused by members of the *Clostridium* genus.

While most "ordinary" protein, including non-spore-bearing bacteria, coagulates in the presence of a moist heat of about 60°C for about ten minutes, some bacterial spores can be boiled for as long as five hours without being inactivated. To a nurse this fact has great practical significance. Since bacteriologists define **sterilization** as the complete removal or the killing of every living cell, plant or animal, it is clear that the common notion held by laymen that boiling something for ten minutes sterilizes it is not based upon biological fact. In many situations this **sanitizing** procedure, which boiling accomplishes, may be sufficient, but in the operating room where bacteriological sterility is mandatory, boiling such objects as instruments to be used in an operation could be disastrous. Boiling is better than nothing and has been employed successfully under emergency conditions when sterilizers were not available, but this is not a practice that can be sanctioned in the surgery section of a well-run modern hospital.

One of the most difficult concepts that students in elementary microbiology must grasp is this idea of complete freedom from any living thing when true bacteriological sterility is to be practiced. This aspect of microbiology is of such vital importance in nursing and in medical practice that an entire subsequent chapter will be devoted to it.

Before a spore develops, the parent cell is said to be in its **vegetative stage** of growth, and such bacteria are relatively easy to kill by conventional methods. Once the spore is formed, however, temperatures above boiling for varying time periods, depending upon the bulk to be treated, must be employed to inactivate these resistant bodies.

Spores formed by molds or yeasts are more reproductive mechanisms than protective devices, since more than one spore is produced per organism; these spores are not much more resistant than vegetative cells. Bacteria, on the other hand, develop but one spore per cell, and this might be considered a form of reproduction without multiplication.

It is difficult to demonstrate these resistant bodies in most young cultures of bacteria since, like granules, spores appear more characteristically in the later stages of growth of a culture. The exact mechanism of spore formation is far from clear. The spore appears to represent a condensed form of protoplasm and its relative position within the cell is a rather constant feature of each spore-forming species. This furnishes one additional clue to the observer who is attempting to identify an organism. Some spores, particularly those found in the clostridia, are so large that the **sporangium** may swell to more than twice its usual size. When such swelling takes place in the center of the rod, a spindle-shaped organism results. If the spore is terminal in its location, racket-shaped organisms develop.

It is difficult to stain spores by the usual techniques, and hence they may stand out as refractile bodies with the remainder of the cell colored by the particular dye employed.

A completely satisfactory explanation for the marked increase in resistance of spores to heat and to chemicals that are destructive to vegetative cells has not been formulated, but a number of theories have been put forth. Some investigators feel that spores are a dry form of protoplasm with an increased calcium content, and hence are not as readily coagulated by heat and chemicals as is "normal" protein. Other workers submit that the water content of bacterial spores is almost as great as that found in vegetative cells, but the water is "bound" rather than "free." (An example is a hard-boiled egg. Even though the egg has a high concentration of water, it seems dry because its water is bound rather than free.)

With the accumulation of knowledge about cells in general, the recognition of additional structures within bacteria and increase in our understanding of units already recognized can be expected.

The Gram Stain

Unstained organisms are sometimes difficult to observe under the higher magnification lenses of a compound microscope, since light tends to pass directly through the cell. But by the application of stains the outlines of the organisms are more clearly defined, and some of the internal structures can be differentiated with the aid of selective dyes.

One of the most important staining techniques employed in microbiology is the **gram stain** which was developed by the Danish scientist Christian Gram in 1884. He discovered that when anthrax bacilli were treated with methyl-violet followed by contact with an iodine solution, the cell-dye complex was firm enough to resist decolorization when the smear was placed in alcohol. Some other bacteria, on the other hand, lost the violet color in the alcohol. Those cells which retain the violet color are termed **gram positive** and those organisms which lose the violet color in alcohol are known as **gram negative.** These latter organisms pick up a dilute dye solution, such as safranin or basic fuchsin, after treatment with the alcohol, whereas the gram positive cells reject this counterstain because the cells are already firmly stained with the violet dye. Since this initial discovery a number of modifications have been introduced in the gram staining procedure in an attempt to make the reaction more reliable, especially for borderline cells which are weakly gram positive and may vary in their reaction.

Preference for the various modifications of this fundamental stain will vary from one laboratory to another, but in recent years one technique that has met with particular favor is the **Kopeloff-Beerman** method. The steps involved in this procedure will be outlined.

After a suitable smear has been prepared on a clean slide and the preparation fixed in a flame, the slide is run through the following series:

1. Immerse in crystal violet for two minutes.
2. Wash gently in tap water to remove excess dye.
3. Dip in Kopeloff-Beerman iodine solution for two minutes. Shake off excess iodine.
4. Agitate the preparation in acetone for ten seconds.
5. Wave in the air to speed evaporation of the acetone.
6. Immerse in aqueous basic fuchsin for twenty seconds.
7. Carefully wash off excess dye in a jar of tap water.
8. Blot the preparation gently with bibulous paper, complete the drying high over a flame, and the slide is ready for examination under the microscope. It is customary to employ the oil immersion objective which magnifies almost one thousand times with most student microscopes.

For best results it is necessary to use young agar cultures of organisms, preferably less than twenty-four hours old, since known gram positive cultures older than this tend to stain atypically. Gram negative species do not change their staining reaction, but if an older culture upon staining is found to be gram negative, the observer cannot be certain whether it is truly gram negative or merely a gram positive species that has lost its affinity for the crystal violet stain.

Considerable research has been devoted to the nature of the gram reaction, and the answer appears to lie in the chemical composition of the cell surface. Gram positive cells contain **ribonucleic acid** which forms a complex with the protein, magnesium, crystal violet, and iodine which "fixes" the dye in the cell and makes it relatively resistant to the decolorizing power of acetone. Gram negative bacteria lack ribonucleic acid and the acetone readily removes the crystal violet dye. Being colorless after the contact with acetone, gram negative cells can pick up the color of the basic fuchsin which serves as a counterstain, and hence these gram negative cells emerge pink.

The gram reaction of microorganisms is also correlated with such characteristics of cells as their susceptibility to antibiotics and inhibition of their growth by chemicals. More will be said about these differences in later chapters which deal with pathogenic organisms, their cultivation, and their identification.

Review Questions

1. If a bacterium is a single cell, why must it be so complex in structure and composition?
2. What arguments can be put forth to support the belief that bacteria might be animals instead of plants?
3. Contrast a bacterium with a bacillus.
4. Defend the belief that flagella are the cause rather than the result of locomotion.
5. If a cell has no well-defined nucleus, can nuclear material still be considered a central controlling mechanism for the cell?
6. What limits the magnifying power of a compound microscope?
7. Contrast the mode of operation of an electron microscope with that of an ordinary light microscope.
8. How does the surface-to-weight ratio of man compare with that of bacteria? Of what importance is this to microbes?
9. What principal differences exist between members of the genus *Clostridium* and the genus *Bacillus?*
10. May other dyes be substituted for those presently employed in the gram stain? Why?
11. Is there any good reason why the word "germ" is rapidly being replaced by the newer designation "microbe"?
12. Of what advantage is the power of independent locomotion to a cell?

2 | BACTERIAL METABOLISM

ALTHOUGH SINGLE BACTERIA ARE TOO MINUTE TO BE VIEWED WITH the unaided eye, when such organisms multiply into millions and billions of cells, not only are we able to see them as a visible mass, but their presence is made known by both physical and chemical changes brought about in their environment. Microorganisms are beehives of chemical activity in a total living process called **metabolism.** The whole purpose or drive seems to be to stay alive and to create more of their own kind.

Enzymes

The very existence of microorganisms depends upon the complex action of digestive juices called *enzymes* (Greek *in yeast,* or *leavened*) which are produced within living cells, are not living themselves, and yet constitute a vital component of every living cell. Edward Buchner in 1897 firmly established the concept that physiological action of these intriguing juices can be carried out in the absence of the cells that created them.

The term "enzymes" was coined by Willy Kühne who considered them to be *soluble ferments composed of any number of complex organic substances capable of transforming substrates through a catalytic process.* A **catalyst** is a substance that cannot initiate but can alter a chemical reaction without itself being changed and without becoming a constituent of the end products formed. In fact when the reaction is completed, the catalyst can be found exactly as it was before the action was initiated.

Organic means pertaining to or derived from living matter. There are also inorganic catalysts employed in various chemical activities, especially in industry. Platinum, for example, can spark the union of gaseous hydrogen and oxygen. In general, inorganic catalysts are less specific in their action than are organic catalysts.

Each microscopic organism possesses its personal array of selected catalytic agents, and since biochemical reactions are an important basis for classification schemes, enzymic reactions are basic in any consideration of taxonomy. The nucleus of a cell is generally conceded to represent the heart or controlling mechanism of living matter, but if one considers that the very existence of life depends upon the ingestion and subsequent utilization of food, and these reactions in turn are dependent upon enzymes for their completion, it would appear difficult to say which constituents of the cell are more important. In reality, however, all components of a cell working in harmony are vital to survival. Without a controlling nucleus, enzymes could not be produced nor would they function; in the absence of enzymes, the nucleus would be ineffective.

Energy for cells is provided through the action of **respiration,** which, simply stated, means the oxidation of compounds to release stored energy. When something is oxidized, there must be a simultaneous reduction of another compound, and if this transformation takes place in the absence of gaseous oxygen, the process is **anaerobic** and this is **fermentation,** which provides energy much less efficiently than the aerobic process. Life without air was first reported by Pasteur in 1861, and more will be written about this type of microbial existence in the discussion dealing with anaerobes implicated in gas gangrene and in lockjaw.

Every living cell must exert itself if it is to survive, since the cell that does not work does not eat. If we believe that matter can neither be created nor destroyed, then it is up to the cells to rearrange the supply of elements at their disposal in such a manner as to make them available for metabolism. Whether this is carried out aerobically or anaerobically, it should be understood that no single enzyme is capable of transforming complex organic matter into useful material without the assistance of a battery of allied enzymes, each one of which has a specific and limited function.

The permeability of the cell wall and of the underlying cytoplasmic membrane will determine what passes into the cell and what is to be rejected. **Exocellular** enzymes can be liberated to attack complex food molecules and break them down into simpler products which are then able to diffuse into the cell. Within the cell still another series of chemical transformations will be set into motion by the **endocellular** enzymes whose activity is limited to the cell proper.

Some enzymes have been extracted, purified, and crystallized, and the first enzyme so purified was **urease** which was crystallized in 1926 by an American biochemist, James Sumner. Like all enzymes studied since then, urease was found to be a protein substance with high molecular weight. Because they are large molecules intermediate between a suspension and a true solution, enzymes are placed with the colloids which do not settle out spontaneously. One unit of enzyme is capable of transforming hundreds, or even thousands, of units of substrate. Since they are not used up in the reaction, only minute amounts of these ferments are required to accomplish enormous amounts of work. Enzymes are heat-labile with their point of inactivation correlating closely with the maximum growth temperature of the organism producing them. Hit the enzyme and you have struck a fatal blow at the life blood of a cell. In fact, this is the basis for using chemotherapeutic agents, such as antibiotics, which block enzyme systems of pathogenic organisms. The usual factors of temperature, light, pH, chemicals, concentration, etc., can be expected to affect enzymatic reactions.

Two major groups of enzymes produced by cells are called **constitutive** and **adaptive.** All cells have a storehouse of enzymes that can be called upon to produce relatively rapid and predictable results. These are the constitutive enzymes which help us to identify bacteria through accepted biochemical changes brought about in usual laboratory media. But when a culture is placed in an environment to which it is not accustomed, adaptive enzymes are called forth, and usually some delay is encountered before the cells adapt to their new surroundings and produce sufficient enzyme to permit the organisms to survive. Should the adaptive enzymes be produced "too little and too late," the cell perishes.

A group of bacteria called **autotrophs** demonstrate a highly developed synthesizing ability in that they can put inorganic constituents together and form cell substance with carbon dioxide as the source of carbon. These are in contrast to the **heterotrophs** which derive their carbon from degradation of organic matter.

With certain exceptions, enzymes are named by adding "ase" to the substrate acted upon or to the chemical reaction involved. A few examples are the following:

Substrate	*Enzyme*
Carbohydrate	Carbohydrase
Lipid (fat)	Lipase
Protein	Protease
Gelatin	Gelatinase
Lactose	Lactase

Reaction	*Enzyme*
Oxidation	Oxidase
Reduction	Reductase
Removal of CO_2	Decarboxylase
Removal of H_2	Dehydrogenase

While urease can hydrolyze only urea with the liberation of ammonia, a lipase may attack several types of lipids. A protease, however, cannot transform carbohydrates or fats, and vice versa. In other words, an enzyme is usually highly specific both for the reaction it catalyzes and for the substrate attacked.

It is difficult for a writer of an elementary text in microbiology to know how deeply he should delve into the complexities of a field as wide and involved as enzymology, but with this much of a presentation of fundamentals, interested students may expand their knowledge in the area by referring to advanced texts in biochemistry or in microbiology.

Light Production

The ability of living organisms to produce light is termed **bioluminescence, photogenesis,** or **phosphorescence.** Light from a single cell is not visible; it is only when masses of these tiny lamps get together that we can detect the light being emitted.

This unusual characteristic is limited to a few species of molds, bacteria, and flagellated protozoa that can oxidize restricted substrates and yield a cold light similar to, if not identical with, that produced by fireflies. The enzyme luciferase acting upon the substrate luciferin appears to be the mechanism involved in the process.

Many a camper has undoubtedly wondered why certain decaying tree stumps glowed like huge watchful eyes in the darkness of the forest as the wind activated the reaction. For the youngster on his first camping trip the mysterious glow probably adds a bit more excitement to his experience and brings into sharper focus some of the ghost stories he has heard!

Light-yielding organisms are called photogenic, a term commonly employed to describe people who photograph well. When our skin emits favorable light patterns into a camera lens, we are not producing light in the same manner as the microorganisms are doing in their metabolism, but the term is descriptive, nevertheless. When sufficient light is produced by a microbial culture, it may be bright enough to permit the cells to be photographed by their own illumination. If a few liters of sea water broth inoculated with bioluminescent bacteria and allowed to grow at an optimum temperature are aerated in a dark room, enough light can be produced to permit a person to read newsprint in the eerie glow.

As far as is known, light production is merely an interesting side reaction in metabolism and is of no vital importance to the well-being of a cell. In fact, organisms may continue to glow for some time after their death. There is evidence that bioluminescent species exhibit somewhat more resistance to the lethal effects of ultraviolet light than is true of the non-phosphorescent species. Could these bacteria have been used to any advantage in research as tracers before the era of radioactive isotopes?

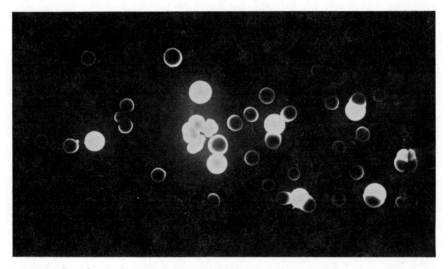

FIG. 2.1. Luminous bacteria photographed by their own light. (Courtesy A. C. Giese, Stanford University.)

Heat Production

Every living cell generates some heat in its metabolism, but a few species of microorganisms produce what would appear to be a disproportionate amount of extra heat; these organisms are called **thermogenic.**

Such **thermophiles** (heat lovers) do not just endure high temperatures, they actually thrive in an environment of 80°C in such places as piles of moist organic matter or in hot springs. This is a most unusual type of protoplasm that can withstand temperatures well above the point where most protein is coagulated. Although optimum and minimum growth temperatures vary with the species and are somewhat dependent upon whether spores are present, it is fair to state that from 55-65°C is ideal for the greater number of them, with 40-50°C as a minimum range for their metabolism.

Improperly dried hay or grain can develop temperatures that have been measured as high as 70°C, due directly to microbial action, and while this in itself is insufficient to cause spontaneous combustion, which requires a much higher kindling temperature, the initial microbial thermogenesis provides a good booster system on the way toward combustion. At this point chemical reactions are set into motion, perhaps by a sudden gust of wind coming through a barn door, for instance, and the hay goes up in flames. Hundreds of such fires are reported annually in the United States, and they are all preventable by proper curing of the hay before storage. Remove the moisture, which is an important prerequisite for microbial growth, to a level below the point at which active metabolism can take place, and spontaneous combustion from such biological sources can be eliminated.

A **pyrogenic** organism also produces heat but in an indirect way. It stimulates man or other animals to develop a fever which is not heat produced directly by the invading organisms. Even dead cells or cell fragments found in fluids to be used for intravenous injections may be pyrogenic, and such foreign material must be eliminated from biologicals such as saline or saline-glucose solutions to be used for restoring body fluid levels.

Pigment Production

Bacteria capable of manufacturing pigments are called **chromogenic** organisms, and just about every color of the solar spectrum can be produced by one or more species of microbes. Oxygen tension, pH, temperature, light, and nutrients in the medium will influence pigment production. Sometimes even moderate deviations in these factors can have pronounced effects on the amount and the intensity of colors produced. In general, infusion media are superior to beef extract as a means of enhancing chromogenesis, and since oxygen is essential in the process, surface colonies growing on a suitable solid medium will exhibit more color than either subsurface colonies or growth in a fluid where available oxygen supplies are limited. With the exception of green and purple pigment producers which prefer light in their metabolism, most chromogenic species find darkness more suitable.

Through the years, there has been some limited basis for the belief that a correlation exists between pigment production and pathogenicity, especially with respect to the staphylococci. *Staphylococcus aureus* (golden color) is probably found in more cases of serious infections than the variety *Staphylococcus albus* (white), but the distinction is not always clear-cut. Many people have died from infections caused by the white staphylococci. On the other hand, one of the brightest reds obtainable from bacteria is formed by *Serratia marcescens* which, as far as we know, is a strict saprophyte. Because so many color variants are produced by this species, it has been the subject of rather intensive studies in recent years from the standpoint of genetics. It holds a place in microbiology somewhat similar to that of fruit flies in zoology, insofar as investigations of genetic characteristics are concerned.

A colony of a pigmented organism growing on a solid medium, especially an infusion agar, where the color does not diffuse into the adjacent medium is called **water-insoluble;** pigments which impart color, not only to the colony but to the medium as well, are **water-soluble.** Another scheme for classifying pigments is based upon their solubility in alcohol or in water, as indicated in these examples:

Soluble in alcohol but not in water—*Serratia* species
Soluble in water—*Pseudomonas* species
Insoluble in either water or alcohol—*Micrococcus citreus*

Some pigments do not develop until after they have been excreted (or secreted?) and are then oxidized. This is characteristic of *Pseudomonas* species. Green and purple sulfur bacteria can assimilate carbon dioxide in the presence of light, owing to the presence of bacteriochlorophyll—a substance similar to, but not identical with, the chlorophyll found in higher plants. These sulfur bacteria are somewhat unusual in that we consider bacteria to be non-chlorophyll-containing organisms under the heading of Thallophytes. The physiological function or significance of pigments in microbes is poorly understood, but as far as is known, loss of chromogenetic power has little or no measurable effect on the metabolism of the cells.

In 332 B.C., when Alexander the Great was directing the siege of Tyre by the Macedonians, the men in his army became alarmed when they discovered red spots throughout the inside of the loaves of their bread. We know today that these spots were nothing more than pigmented bacteria that had found a favorable medium. Since many of his men took this to be an unfavorable omen, Alexander had a soothsayer interpret the phenomenon. The soothsayer explained that since the spots occurred inside the bread and did not exist on the outer crust, it meant that the men inside the wall were in for a bloody destruction. Whether this was sufficient to raise the morale of his troops to new heights or whether the poor souls inside the walls had had enough, is difficult to say, but Tyre fell shortly thereafter. Who can doubt the power of a bacterium? Or was it the persuasiveness of the soothsayer?

The close resemblance to blood that spots of *Serratia* produce on foods has created other interesting incidents throughout history. Spots developing on communion wafers made from unleavened bread have been taken to have some religious significance by the uninformed. In 1819, when the city of Padua, Italy, was plagued with spotted corn mush, town officials, under the pressure of public clamor for an explanation, were forced to undertake a study of the cause, and from this investigation eventually emerged the "miracle organism," *Serratia marcescens*. The generic name was given in honor of Serafino Serrati, the Italian physicist who invented a steamboat at Florence sometime before 1787. Just what the connection is between this gentleman and red spots on corn mush is far from clear to the writer! The species name, *marcescens,* is derived from the Latin and means "dissolving into a fluid or viscous matter." Since this organism is **proteolytic,** the specific name appears to be a bit more scientific.

Toxin Production

A toxin may be broadly defined as a class of poisonous substances formed as secretion products of cells. They are normal waste products or actual components of cells that have power to damage plant or animal cells. Any consideration of microbial diseases must examine the relationship between the nature of microbial infections and the mechanisms by which the damaging results are carried out *in vivo.* Some species produce several types of poisons which react in diverse ways in the test tube and in the body. Certain micrococci produce a *leucocytic toxin* which acts against white cells; a *hemotoxin* that has an affinity for red blood cells; an *enterotoxin* which sets up reactions in the intestines; a *lethal* toxin that might kill mice or rabbits; and a skin-killing poison, called a *dermonecrotizing* toxin.

A characteristic of toxins is their affinity for particular types of cells: nerve cells, erythrocytes, leucocytes, muscle tissue, etc. An incubation period is required before the toxic effects become manifest, and this delay is generally of longer duration than with common poisons. A fuller discussion of the mechanism involved in a number of pathogenic processes will be undertaken in a later chapter dealing with specific diseases.

Toxins might be liberated as a countermeasure to the defenses thrown up by body tissues in response to invasion by microbes; or they may provide a device for increasing the invasiveness of pathogens as they attack susceptible areas of plants or animals. Tissue damage may occur at the point of infection or the poisons may be absorbed into the blood stream and lymph channels and spread throughout the body to appropriate cells for which the toxins have a predilection.

One of the points in favor of the attacked host in such a battle with microbes is the relatively restricted portals of entry available to the toxins. Some must get deep into tissues that have been badly damaged and are "dirty wounds" (gas gangrene); others must find their mark via the digestive tract (food poisoning); and still others prefer to lodge in the dark, wet recesses of the tonsils and lower throat (diphtheria).

When a living cell excretes its poison during active metabolism and the toxin is liberated free into the medium, such an excretion is called an **exotoxin.** It is also known as a true or soluble poison, and many of these are considerably more potent than cobra venom, molecule for molecule. If the lethal agent is not liberated by the cell during its life because the toxin is intimately bound with the protoplasm and is not released except by physical or biological (autolysis) forces after the death of the cell, such a waste product is an **endotoxin,** a name given to it by R. Pfeiffer. These are relatively insoluble poisons.

A nurse cannot be expected to become an expert in toxicology, but an understanding of the fundamental principles involved in microbial pathogenicity will certainly place her in an advantageous position to cope more effectively with the wide variety of human infections she is likely to encounter in the daily practice of her profession. An organism endowed with the ability to manufacture and put forth a powerful poison has a built-in ally when it comes to tackling a living host that may outweigh the microbe a million- or a trillion-fold. It seems strange with such unfavorable odds that the microscopic aggressor has emerged the victor in so many battles.

The following comparison will outline some of the major characteristics of the two principal groupings of toxins:

Exotoxins	*Endotoxins*
1. Essentially proteins	1. Complex mixture of proteins, polysaccharides, and phospholipids
2. Relatively unstable	2. Relatively stable
3. Specific in their action and can stimulate production of specific antitoxins	3. Not particularly specific; poor **antigens**
4. Lethal dose generally found in minute amounts; as little as 1 mg might kill millions of mice	4. 1 mg generally contains less than 10 lethal doses for mice

Exotoxins	*Endotoxins*
5. Generally labile in presence of heat and chemicals	5. Heat stable and not as readily affected by chemicals
6. Produced mainly by gram positive cells	6. Origin mainly in gram negative cells
7. May be inactivated by proteolytic enzymes	7. Relatively unaffected by proteolytic enzymes
8. Organisms manufacturing toxin tend to remain localized while toxin spreads	8. Tend to invade body and spread

A few examples of diseases involving exotoxins include: diphtheria, scarlet fever, lockjaw, botulism, gas gangrene, and certain infections caused by streptococci. Diseases of endotoxin etiology include typhoid fever, paratyphoid fever, and dysentery. A later chapter will concern itself with immunity and techniques available for inducing artificial protection against microbial invasions; however, it should be mentioned here for the sake of completeness that **antitoxins** are employed to combat exotoxins, as a therapeutic as well as a prophylactic measure. **Vaccines** (suspensions of killed, weakened, or in some cases living cells) are generally employed as prophylactic techniques for preventing future infections with endotoxin-producing microbes.

Diphtheria toxin was first described by Roux and Yersin in 1889, and the following year Von Behring, Frankel, and Kitasato reported that if this toxin produced by *Corynebacterium diphtheriae* was heated to 70°C for one hour, the toxicity factor was inactivated without any measurable impairment of the ability of the heated material to incite production of specific antitoxin when suitable doses were injected into appropriate animals. Such an altered toxin is called a **toxoid.** Adding of chemicals, such as formalin, to true toxins will accomplish the same change.

In 1892 Pfeiffer demonstrated that the lethal portion of the cholera microbe (*Vibrio comma*) was so intimately bound to the protoplasm within the cell that it could not be found in the cultivating medium until the cell had died and autolyzed. These were years of exciting discoveries, and the dynamic science of microbiology began to attract the attention and efforts of leading investigators of the era. It was not until 1924, however, that Ramon advocated the addition of formalin to exotoxins as a means of converting them into toxoids; the next step was the addition of alum to the mixture to precipitate the toxoid in a more concentrated form with fewer nonspecific fractions that contributed little or nothing to the immunological reaction upon injection of toxoids.

Cycles of Elements in Nature

The point was made earlier in this chapter that there is a limit to the available supply of elements in nature. This quantity is sufficient for the foreseeable future only if the elements are put to proper use and are circulated. Most microbial transformation occurs in the soil which has been described as the region where geology and biology meet. If the restricted supply of foodstuffs in the soil became bound up in living matter and could not at some future time be released for future generations, life would eventually grind to a screeching halt when the well of elements ran dry. It is only through never-ending cyclical changes from organic to inorganic, from reduced to oxidized, and from soluble to insoluble, and then the reverse of these reactions, that organic refuse is prevented from gathering and cluttering up the "lebensraum" of man and other forms of life, and the limited supply of elements is kept in constant use. Continuity of life is dependent upon release and utilization of all elements that make up a living organism.

Every living cell requires carbon, hydrogen, oxygen, and nitrogen, as well as a host of other substances varying in quality and in quantity with individual plant and animal cells. Remarkable and complicated reactions ensure efficient utilization of the world's supply of elements, and this section will present the highlights of a few biological systems that are involved with representative vital elements. More detailed descriptions of cycles in nature and the roles played by specific organisms will be presented in Chapter 10 which deals specifically with the soil and its over-all function in the economy of nature.

Living organisms are constantly struggling to maintain their basic nitrogen needs. Man, for example, after he has metabolized his ingested food, excretes nitrogen in his urine in the form of urea. The urea eventually finds its way into the soil where it is attacked by such gram negative bacteria as those belonging to the *Proteus* genus. These microorganisms eventually convert this nitrogen compound into ammonia (NH_3) which is toxic for most plants and animals. But through another series of microbial oxidations, the ammonia is changed into nitrites (NO_2) and finally into the more oxidized nitrates (NO_3) which are utilizable by plants in their metabolism. After being absorbed as soluble foods through the root hairs of the plants, the nitrates are converted into plant tissues which may then be ingested by animals, and we are back where the cycle began. This presents the nitrogen cycle in its simplest form; it is much more involved and complicated by side reactions than the brief review indicates. You and I have a rendezvous with the nitrogen cycle not only as living creatures, but also when our life terminates and we become a part of future generations upon the release of elements bound in our cells.

Carbon is another primary constituent of all protoplasm. The air we breathe contains approximately three parts of carbon dioxide (CO_2) in ten thousand (.03%). This concentration naturally varies from the relatively clean air of the country and mountains to that found in great industrial areas where smokestacks and combustion engines belch forth their wastes to pollute the atmosphere and influence the carbon content of the air.

Plants, through the process of **photosynthesis,** utilize the carbon dioxide of the air by combining it with water in the presence of light by means of the catalyst chlorophyll, and this complex is converted into plant material. During plant metabolism, oxygen is released and is used for respiration by animals who in turn liberate carbon dioxide as a waste product. A useful balance is thus created between plants and animals, with members of each kingdom being dependent upon other forms of life for their very existence.

Cycles for hydrogen and oxygen, the remaining two basic elements in carbohydrates, fats, and protein, are tied up rather closely with nitrogen and carbon utilization in nature. Their main form outside of cells is as water. Although a few species of bacteria can act directly on hydrogen gas to convert it to water in the presence of carbon dioxide, this is not a common reaction. Atmospheric oxygen is employed in energy transformations by plants and animals except for the group of anaerobic bacteria that utilize organic sources of oxygen.

Every element has its specific cycle, some better understood than others, but space will not be taken here to elaborate further on this phase of bacterial metabolism.

Antagonism and Cooperation

It is doubtful that complete harmony prevails in any form of living matter, whether it be a thinking human being or a microbe. Life is a constant series of adjustments, and some of these relationships existing between microbes will be considered—some philosophically and others with respect to conditions we recognize to be in existence.

Antagonism

Toxins, it was concluded earlier in this chapter, serve a definite function in preparing the way for pathogens to carry out their unhealthful work. The poisons liberated may exert lethal effects not only on the tissue cells of the host being attacked, but other microbes may feel the sting of aggressiveness as the poisons push them aside or actually become involved in consuming the weaker members. This explains, at least in part, why a "dirty" wound into which many species of organisms have been driven frequently terminates with a single pure culture of the most aggressive microbial invader. It is true that the natural defenses of the body assist in this weeding out process through the action of the "clean up squad" of **leucocytes** as they ingest and destroy invading foreign cells. But the biological struggle involves intermicrobial forces as well as the usual resistance thrown up by the invaded host tissues.

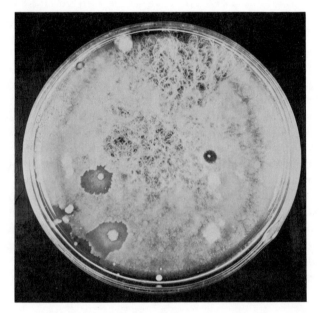

FIG. 2.2. Microbial antagonism. (LS-143 Courtesy American Society for Microbiology.)

The term **antibiotic** has been given to the antagonistic action exhibited by products released from living organisms acting against other living cells. This phase of microbiology is a complicated science in itself, and no attempt will be made here to do more than introduce the topic for consideration as one more factor in microbial metabolism.

Alexander Fleming, the British bacteriologist who discovered **penicillin** in 1929, was not the first person who had noticed the inhibitory effects produced by living organisms growing in mixed cultures on nutrient agar platings. But he was a leading scientist who tried to put his observations of this unique natural phenomenon to practical use in medicine. (In a *Pepion Adventure* we read of a peasant sorceress who cured wounds with moldy bread! Was this a strain of *Penicillium?*)

Students enrolled in bacteriology courses are constantly being reminded by their laboratory instructors to avoid the unforgivable sin of allowing extraneous organisms (contaminants) to gain entrance to their pure cultures. But the era of antibiotics would have been delayed indefinitely, if not permanently, if Fleming's faulty technique had not permitted the mold *Penicillium notatum* to find its way onto the surface of his plating of *Staphyloccus aureus,* a gram positive coccus with which he was working.

Again, quite by chance, this particular species of mold happens to produce a powerful antibiotic that is relatively nontoxic to human beings. Thousands of tests since Fleming's discovery have shown only too well how few antibiotics that exhibit promising effects *in vitro* can be employed for animal injections. They do more damage *in vivo* than the relatively small amount of good they provide by killing microbes. There is little point in having an operation a success if the patient succumbs from side effects. It was another good stroke of fortune that penicillin is active primarily against gram positive cells, and in Fleming's plate the gram positive staphylococci happened to be the effective target that day.

It was not until eight years later, however, that Florey and some of his co-workers developed techniques for purifying penicillin and began to evaluate its possible use as a therapeutic agent in medicine. Initial findings were heartening; many species of troublesome organisms were shown to be remarkably susceptible to the action of this new "miracle drug," as it soon came to be called. Man had harnessed another microbial waste for treatment of human disease, just as previous investigators had found that potent toxins could be attenuated and put to use in the production of antitoxins.

As more and more reports appeared in the scientific literature applauding the merits of penicillin, an undercurrent began to develop suggesting that the relatively brief era of the microbiologist was about to terminate. At last a panacea for microbial diseases had been discovered! It was not long, however, before more sober evaluations began to come in. We had won a battle but not the war. Not only were there a considerable number of gram negative organisms that were refractory to the action of penicillin, but suggestions began to be made that strains of bacteria which had responded to the new drug were beginning to display resistance to even greater doses than those originally found to be effective. After about fifteen years the problem of resistance took on serious proportions. The mighty staphylococci that had fallen so readily under the lethal action of penicillin were now rearing their ugly infections with greater frequency, and no matter how overwhelming the dose of antibiotic administered, the infections continued to flourish. Serious outbreaks in our hospitals, especially in nurseries and children's wards, reached epidemic proportions. The "fading" bacteriologists of a few years earlier now became the fair-haired boys, and their services were in great demand for solutions to the growing menace. The best recommendation that emerged from these studies all over the country seemed to be: Return to the principles of **asepsis** and **antisepsis** set forth by Lister and Semmelweiss. Clean up in the old-fashioned way and stop depending upon antibiotics to cover a creeping carelessness which had developed with the successes made possible by prophylactic as well as therapeutic doses of miracle drugs.

As we look back over the last two decades, we must conclude that penicillin and the antibiotics that have followed it have made notable inroads against microbial diseases. Years have undoubtedly been added to life expectancy in areas of the world fortunate enough to have had the benefits of the wonder drugs. But pausing too long to look back may delay discoveries that can make our lives even healthier and more enjoyable. The search for new and better antimicrobial agents continues, and each contribution provides one more link in the ever-strengthening chain that will eventually strangle these microscopic marauders.

Cooperation

Not all organisms are out to get their fellows. It is interesting to note a number of metabolic reactions in the microbial world where two or more species work together for mutual good. Such a relationship is called **symbiosis.** On the roots of legumes we find swellings, or nodules, that are packed with bacteria known as *Rhizobium leguminosarum.* These microbes can "fix" atmospheric nitrogen, a gas that is found in concentration of about 78 per cent in the atmosphere, and yet in that form it is unavailable to most bacteria and higher plants. The legumes, in turn, supply the bacteria with their nutritional needs, and the association between these two quite diverse forms of plant life is mutually beneficial.

Synergism is another interesting relationship which involves the interaction of two or more species producing an end result that the organisms could not produce as individuals. As we shall see in a later discussion of water analysis (Chapter 8), the preliminary screening reaction for separating potable water from polluted water is based upon the fermentation of lactose broth resulting in the manufacture of both acid and gas as end products. Frequently a raw water sample may contain a mixture of bacteria the sum total of whose enzymatic actions might yield a positive presumptive reaction in lactose. Yet when the sample is purified and the individual species recovered from the sample are tested, no single pure culture has the enzyme system capable of breaking down the disaccharide, lactose.

Commensalism describes a condition where an organism may live as a parasite but does no harm to the host. Such a relationship exists in our intestines, for example. A parasite generally not only lives at the expense of a host but actually does harm to the invaded tissues. In **metabiosis** an organism produces substances or creates conditions that are favorable to other species. An aerobe might, for instance, reduce the oxygen tension sufficiently to permit an anaerobe to become established in a given area. As in other areas of life, the world of microorganisms is one of constant adjustment, involving both conflict and cooperation for its continuance.

FIG. 2.3. *Rhizobium leguminosarum* in root
nodules of a cow pea plant.

Review Questions

1. What chemical processes should be included under the heading of metabolism?
2. How do respiration and fermentation differ? How are they alike?
3. Name some inorganic catalysts that might be used in industry.
4. What requirements must be met before an adaptive enzyme can operate effectively?
5. Name some enzymes not ending in -*ase*.
6. Do you believe it might be practical to harness and utilize the light produced by some microorganisms? Defend your answer.
7. If bacteria produce so much heat, why don't we burn our hands when we handle tubes containing billions of actively metabolizing cells?
8. Are bacterial pigments of any commercial value? Why?
9. How might toxins benefit bacterial cells which produced them?
10. How have scientists in recent years tapped the antagonistic potential of microbes?

3 | CULTIVATION OF MICROORGANISMS

NATURE PROVIDES MANY MICROORGANISMS WITH SUITABLE FOOD and adequate living conditions but, like humans, each species has its own particular and sometimes peculiar likes and requirements for optimum growth. Some microbes, especially **pathogens,** may be extremely fastidious in their needs, whereas most **saprophytes** are generally content to accept almost any food that is offered to them. The more specialized the food requirements, the fewer the possibilities for survival in nature where competition is so keen.

A number of species of microorganisms under ideal growth conditions are capable of doubling their numbers once in about every twenty minutes. Thus the demands for food become increasingly urgent if the offspring are to be supported. If this geometric progression continued unchecked for twenty-four hours, the progeny of a single cell would number 2,361,183,241,434,822,606,848. And if this fantastic rate of multiplication were allowed to go unchecked for about one week, the volume of cells produced would occupy a space greater than that of the earth.

Fortunately for mankind certain checks and balances are set into motion and microbes are prevented from overwhelming our planet. Such factors as food supply, accumulated metabolic wastes, temperature, moisture, activities of competing forms of life, etc., control the reproductive rate of bacteria. Otherwise you and I would not be here.

Not all microbes are capable of such rapid multiplication, however. The fission time for some species may be hours rather than minutes.

The etiological agent of tuberculosis, *Mycobacterium tuberculosis,* for example, has a relatively long generation time, and this helps to explain in part why it takes so long for an individual to develop the clinical symptoms of this dreaded disease after living organisms have gained access to the body. This disease has, in other words, a relatively long **incubation period.**

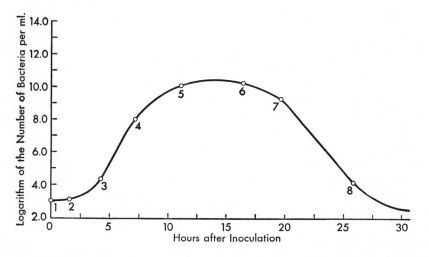

FIG. 3.1. Bacterial growth curve. (Reprinted from S. E. Wedberg, *Microbes and You,* 1954, with permission of The Macmillan Company, New York, N. Y.)

Clinical microbiology, which is of particular interest to members of the nursing profession, involves the isolation and the identification of organisms from patients, and any such study to be successful involves a thorough understanding on the part of the technician of the specific growth requirements of pathogens. An improperly collected specimen that is not truly representative or one that has been stored too long before being delivered to the laboratory can nullify all of the painstaking work of the microbiologist. It therefore behooves nurses to comprehend the great importance of acceptable sampling and prompt delivery of specimens. Because so many pathogenic organisms tend to die relatively quickly upon drying, holding a throat swab for several hours after collection, for example, may yield negative or misleading findings that will delay effective treatment and prolong the period needed for recovery of the patient. When a physician decides that a laboratory examination of a specimen is warranted, he is entitled to get the best possible information in the shortest time. This calls for close cooperation on the part of the nurse and the laboratory personnel who conduct the tests.

It should always be remembered that a hospital exists exclusively for the welfare of the patient. Every procedure, from the initial administrative admission through the final disposition of the patient, must be directed toward efficient and intelligent handling of the afflicted individual. When a person is ill enough to require hospitalization, he is frequently oversensitive and hypercritical about the treatment he receives at what many consider to be an exorbitant cost. The nurse can do much to make the patient feel that he is a human being whose welfare is paramount, and that he is not just a number on the books in the front office.

Too often individuals enrolled in a basic course in microbiology are not permitted to prepare diets for the cultivation of bacteria, and for this reason they do not fully appreciate the exactness with which the ingredients are blended. Although some people may not feel flattered at the prospect of being chefs to microscopic gourmets, this phase of microbiology is fundamental to the success of clinical laboratory work.

The diet that is prepared is called a **medium** (pl. *media*), and it must be tailor-made for the particular organisms to be cultivated. In putting a medium together specific requirements must be fulfilled if the end product is to serve as a suitable substitute for the natural environment of microbes. These prerequisites include:

1. An adequate amount of moisture
2. Food materials in suitable form
3. Correct acidity or alkalinity, known technically as pH
4. Sterility in a strict microbiological sense
5. Appropriate physical properties (solid, liquid, clarity, etc.).

Each of these requirements is so important that a brief discussion is necessary.

Requisites for a Suitable Medium

Moisture

It was stated previously that bacteria obtain their nourishment through holophytic feeding, and that the permeability of the cell wall and the underlying cytoplasmic membrane is the deciding factor as to what enters and what leaves the cell.

Although water is not itself a food, it is vital in varying amounts to all life since it serves as a carrying agent both for food and for metabolic wastes in solution. Bacteria are more like aquatic than terrestrial plants and therefore their moisture content may range up to 90 per cent or even higher. This furnishes us with a clue that any medium designed to grow bacteria should be relatively high in water content, and a perusal of the composition of commonly employed media will substantiate this fact.

It is highly desirable that media used in the hundreds of laboratories scattered throughout the country and in other countries be standardized insofar as possible to insure uniform results. Since many media these days are made from dehydrated ingredients prepared in large central laboratories, the principal variable in the finished product is the water added to reconstitute the medium. Because some of the ingredients of water vary from one area to another, distilled water must be employed if all batches of finished product are to be uniform in their composition.

In preparing substrates for the cultivation of organisms it should be borne in mind that proper concentration of food materials is just as important as supplying all of the required elements. Careful weighing of ingredients becomes imperative.

The cells of our bodies are bathed in solutions whose salt concentration is slightly less than 0.9 per cent. This is known as a **physiological solution.** It is **isotonic** (has equal osmotic pressure) for the cells. Any major deviation from this concentration, higher or lower, will adversely affect the speed of cell multiplication and the metabolism of the organism, whereas a well-balanced diet will encourage rapid multiplication over a prolonged growth period.

The rather high moisture requirement of bacteria is of practical significance in nursing practice. The remarkable resistance to drying exhibited by some of the spore-forming pathogens implicated in such diseases as lockjaw (*Clostridium tetani*) and gas gangrene (*Clostridium perfringens*), and the threat of these microbes under set conditions should not be minimized. More will be said about these bacteria later. Some of the more delicate microbes, including those associated with such diseases as gonorrhea (*Neisseria gonorrheae*) and syphilis (*Treponema pallidum*), cannot long survive in the absence of moisture. Although there are authenticated cases of the transmission of these venereal diseases through the agency of **fomites** (inanimate objects) where prompt contact has taken place with infectious material, blaming an inanimate object like a toilet seat for a case of venereal disease does not stand up under bacteriological scrutiny in many cases.

The drinking cup on the village green in a bygone era was responsible for the dissemination of selected pathogens including streptococci, since the moisture on the lip of the cup is sufficient to keep organisms alive for varying time periods: The common drinking cup is a health hazard, and its passing has been a step forward for public health. The common communion cup is rapidly becoming a thing of the past in many of our churches for the same reason. While a shiny silver chalice does exert a certain amount of antibacterial action, the time factor between communicants precludes any effective germicidal power.

Food Materials in Suitable Form

The presentation of food is not enough for sustaining microbial life. The elements must be in solution and in a form that can pass across the semipermeable membranes that exist as hurdles around the cytoplasm of the cell. A bacterial cell can hardly be expected to get excited about an iron pipe tossed to it for a meal, but when that same iron pipe is properly broken down and united with other elements in suitable combinations, the iron could help to support prompt and sustained growth of iron-requiring bacteria.

The air we breathe is composed of about 78 per cent nitrogen gas. Every living cell, plant or animal, must have nitrogen, an essential constituent of protein. However, very few species of organisms have the ability to metabolize gaseous nitrogen as such, and hence this gas is of relatively little use to microbes. Farmers spend millions, perhaps billions, of dollars annually for fertilizers designed to supply, among other things, precious nitrogen, but this element is provided in commercial fertilizers principally in the available oxidized form of nitrates (NO_3). Similarly, each substance found in living cells can only be taken in by those cells if it is in suitable form.

For years students have been taught in biology courses that a convenient way to remember the names of the elements required by cells is in the sentence "See **(C) Hopkins Cafe** where the food is **mighty good**" (carbon (C), hydrogen (H), oxygen (O), phosphorus (P), potassium (K), iodine (I), nitrogen (N), sulfur (S), calcium (Ca), iron (Fe), and magnesium (Mg)). Although requirements vary for different microorganisms, the above-mentioned chemical elements do represent the basic substances required by cells. The important fact, however, is their *availability for use by the cell.*

Correct pH

A medium composed of an adequate amount of water and suitable food is still of limited value to microorganisms if the acidity or the alkalinity deviates too greatly from the optimum required for growth. Here again we must recognize and cater to the peculiarities and specific demands of organisms if we expect to encourage their growth under controlled conditions.

Since a course in chemistry generally precedes an initial exposure to microbiology, the meaning of the term pH should not be completely foreign to users of this textbook. It seems appropriate, nevertheless, to devote a few paragraphs to a brief discussion of specific applications of acid–base control in the field of microbiology.

The pH scale runs from 0 to 14 with the neutral point at 7.0. At this midpoint there exists a balance between hydrogen (H) ions and hydroxyl (OH) ions. Most of the commonly encountered bacteria prefer neutral or slightly alkaline conditions for optimum growth, at least at the outset. If pure water were analyzed, one liter would be found to contain a total of $0.000,000,000,000,01$ (10^{-14}) gram of hydrogen and hydroxyl ions. Since pure water is neutral in reaction, there would be an exact balance between hydrogen ions and hydroxyl ions, or $0.000,000,1$ gram of each type of ions per liter. The negative logarithm of this decimal is minus 7.0, and for convenience this is converted to a positive number on the pH scale. Thus a perfectly neutral solution is said to possess a pH of 7.0. As the number of hydrogen ions decreases, the relative number of hydroxyl ions increases, and the pH rises, that is, its number becomes greater than 7.0. Conversely, when the hydrogen ions increase, the number on the pH scale decreases. A drop from a pH of 7.0 to 6.0 represents a tenfold increase in hydrogen ions. (See Table 1.)

TABLE 1

Hydrogen Ion Concentration and pH

Grams of hydrogen ions per liter		pH	Number of times acidity or alkalinity exceeds that of pure water	
1.0	(10^{0})	0.0	10,000,000	↑
0.1	(10^{-1})	1.0	1,000,000	
0.01	(10^{-2})	2.0	100,000	Acid
0.001	(10^{-3})	3.0	10,000	
0.000,1	(10^{-4})	4.0	1,000	
0.000,01	(10^{-5})	5.0	100	
0.000,001	(10^{-6})	6.0	10	↓
0.000,000,1	(10^{-7})	7.0	0	Neutral (pure H_2O)
0.000,000,01	(10^{-8})	8.0	10	↑
0.000,000,001	(10^{-9})	9.0	100	
0.000,000,000,1	(10^{-10})	10.0	1,000	
0.000,000,000,01	(10^{-11})	11.0	10,000	
0.000,000,000,001	(10^{-12})	12.0	100,000	Alkaline
0.000,000,000,000,1	(10^{-13})	13.0	1,000,000	
0.000,000,000,000,01	(10^{-14})	14.0	10,000,000	↓

For the preparation of most common laboratory media employed in the cultivation of the usual microorganisms encountered in nursing practice, a relatively simple method is available for determining pH levels. This technique, employing indicator dye solutions, is satisfactory within the accuracy required, namely about one-tenth of a point on the pH scale. In research projects where extremely accurate determinations are required, an electrometric device called the **potentiometer** is brought into use. This same piece of equipment is needed for determining the hydrogen ion concentration of colored or turbid solutions which would mask the colors of indicators and make them ineffective.

Dyes employed for pH determination are usually weak organic acids or bases and they possess the characteristic of changing color as the pH deviates. Each such indicator has an effective range of about 1.6 points on the pH scale, for example, from 6.0 to 7.6 in the case of the commonly employed dye **brom thymol blue.** Below or above these limits the color changes are either nil or so imperceptible that our eyes are unable to detect them with any degree of accuracy. When choosing one of the many available indicators, it is customary to select one whose midpoint is close to the final pH desired in the medium. This improves accuracy of the reading since a slight change in hydrogen ion concentration at the midpoint of an indicator results in a relatively greater color change than is true when you approach either the lower or the upper effective limits of the indicator dye.

Since so many of our media are poised at about the neutral point on the pH scale, brom thymol blue with its midpoint of 6.8 is frequently the indicator chosen. The following table lists representative indicators that may be used for visual determination at various pH levels.

TABLE 2

Indicators and Their pH Ranges

Name of indicator	Effective pH range	Color on lower side	Color on upper side
Thymol blue	1.2–2.8	Red	Yellow
Bromphenol blue	3.0–4.6	Yellow	Blue
Congo red	3.0–5.0	Blue	Red
Methyl orange	3.1–4.4	Orange red	Yellow
Brom cresol green	3.8–5.4	Yellow	Blue
Methyl red	4.4–6.0	Red	Yellow
Chlorophenol red	4.8–6.4	Yellow	Red
Litmus	4.5–8.3	Red	Blue
Brom cresol purple	5.2–6.8	Yellow	Purple
Brom thymol blue	6.0–7.6	Yellow	Blue
Phenol red	6.8–8.4	Yellow	Red
Cresol red	7.2–8.8	Yellow	Red
Thymol blue	8.0–9.6	Yellow	Blue
Cresolphthalein	8.2–9.8	Colorless	Red
Phenolphthalein	8.3–10.0	Colorless	Red
Alizarine yellow	10.0–12.0	Colorless	Yellow
LaMotte sulfo orange	11.0–12.6	Pale yellow	Deep orange

While the procedures being practiced may vary in detail from one laboratory to another, a description of the preparation of a common nutrient medium, including the adjustment of pH, should prove useful.

PREPARATION OF STANDARD NUTRIENT AGAR

The formula for one liter of this widely used medium is as follows:

Peptone (0.5%)	5.0 grams
Meat extract (0.3%)	3.0 grams
Agar (1.5%)	15.0 grams
Distilled water	1000 milliliters

Adjust pH to 7.0

Peptone, which is a standardized digest of protein (usually lean meat), supplies an available source of nitrogenous food and carbon. Peptone also serves as a buffer.

Meat extract is a protein-free and carbohydrate-free residue after extraction of lean meat (beef) with water, and it supplies many essential minerals and growth-activating substances to the cells.

Agar is a complex carbohydrate (polysaccharide) extracted as a rule from a certain Pacific Ocean seaweed. It belongs to the galactans and is quite stable to the actions of microbial enzymes. This makes agar more desirable than gelatin as a solidifying agent in the preparation of a liquefiable solid medium to be employed for the cultivation of microbial colonies.

Distilled water, while not a food in itself, serves as a carrying agent for foods and for wastes. The turgor of the cells depends upon the presence of an adequate supply of water.

Weigh out the peptone and the meat extract and place them in a saucepan containing the distilled water. Heat gently to dissolve the ingredients. (*Note:* the agar is not added until after the pH adjustment.) When they are in solution, place a few drops of the broth in one of the depressions in a white porcelain dish called a **spot plate.** To this sample add one drop of brom thymol blue indicator and mix well with the aid of a clean glass stirring rod. Compare the resulting color with a series of known pH color standards set up in test tubes and previously checked electrometrically.

If the color on the spot plate does not match the color of the known desired pH standard (and it probably will not, since meat extract is acid in reaction), adjustments can be made by adding appropriate chemicals to bring the ions into proper balance. In this case the broth might have an initial pH of 6.4 or 6.5. By addition of a few drops of 10 per cent sodium hydroxide (NaOH) to the entire batch of medium in the sauce-pan and thorough stirring, the excess acid can be neutralized. Recheck on the spot plate and, by trial and error, adjust the pH to as near 7.0 as possible at this stage in the preparation. Should too much alkali be added the error can be rectified by the addition of a drop or so of 10 per cent hydrochloric acid (HCl). With experience a student learns the appropriate quantity of acid or alkali required for a given volume of medium pre-pared from standard dehydrated ingredients.

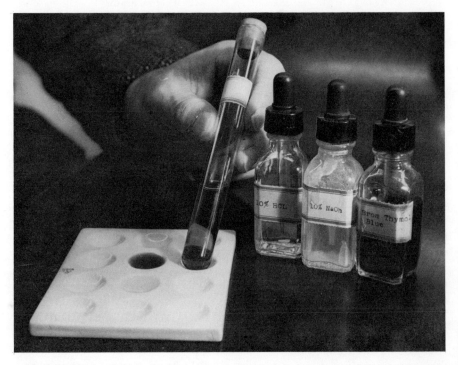

FIG. 3.2. Determining pH using a spot plate and brom thymol blue indicator.

A very important factor in the success of accurate pH adjustment is the presence in the medium of buffers which have been mentioned in an earlier chapter. The buffer prevents rapid changes in pH of solutions upon the addition of small amounts of acid or alkali. Without the aid of buffers even minute amounts of these chemicals would result in marked changes in pH of the medium. Microbes, unless prevented from doing so by buffers, may generate enough acid or other metabolic waste to digest themselves.

Having adjusted the pH to the desired point as accurately as the spot plate technique will allow, make a final and more precise determination in a **color comparator block.** This is usually a block of wood that has been painted black and into which holes have been drilled to accommodate test tubes. Peep holes are cut through the bottom of the block as shown in the diagram. This allows the observer to look through the tubes placed in a selected arrangement within the block.

FIG. 3.3. Equipment employed for determining pH colorimetrically.

The principal reason for a second pH determination is to compensate for the natural color of the medium which affects the color of the pH indicator, and to compare like volumes of fluids dispensed in tubes of equal diameter. You may wonder why the original determination is not carried out directly in the color block without resorting to the preliminary spot plate test. It can be. But it takes only a few drops of medium to check the pH in a spot plate, whereas the block requires at least five milliliters of broth for each determination. Repeated testing (not uncommon for students carrying out this procedure for the first time) can rapidly use up the relatively small batches of medium generally prepared per student before the desired pH level has been attained, unless preliminary tests and adjustments are conducted with a spot plate.

If, when viewed through the peepholes in the color block, the two sides (AB and CD) match in color, the pH can be assumed to be near enough to the desired standard for all practical purposes.

When the broth (peptone, meat extract, and distilled water) has been adjusted to the neutral point, the carefully weighed agar is added. Agar is neutral in reaction and hence will not alter the pH of the medium.

Before the application of heat to dissolve the agar (melting point about 90°C), the pan and its contents should be weighed and the results expressed in grams. It is amazing how much water is lost through this heating process which involves active boiling for several minutes to insure that the agar is thoroughly dissolved. Constant stirring is required to prevent scorching, and once the medium begins to bubble, the heat must be controlled to prevent boiling over of the agar medium. When the agar is in solution, reweigh the pan and its contents. The difference in weight between the original medium prior to heating and the post-heated medium indicates the number of milliliters of distilled water required to bring the contents back to its original weight. For all practical purposes one milliliter of water weighs one gram. Details of tubing, plugging with nonabsorbent cotton, sterilizing, and storage of the medium vary considerably from one laboratory to another, and therefore any detailed discussion of these aspects of media making will be left to individual instructors.

Sterility

The topic of sterility is so basic to an intelligent understanding of proper handling of patients from the standpoint of microbiology that a separate chapter will be devoted to it. However, a few paragraphs are needed to explain the general technique of sterilizing a batch of standard nutrient agar.

A relatively simple thing like the introduction by Schroeder and Dusch of cotton plugs in tubes and flasks of media was a boon to microbiology. Fluid media dispensed in test tubes and stoppered with cotton plugs are usually exposed to live steam under pressure in a closed chamber known as an **autoclave.** This device is based upon the same principles as those employed in home pressure cookers used for canning purposes. When the steam pressure is raised to fifteen pounds per square inch above that of the atmosphere, a temperature of 121°C is attained, and if small batches of media are held at this moist temperature for a minimum of fifteen minutes, microbiological sterility can be achieved. The larger the bulk

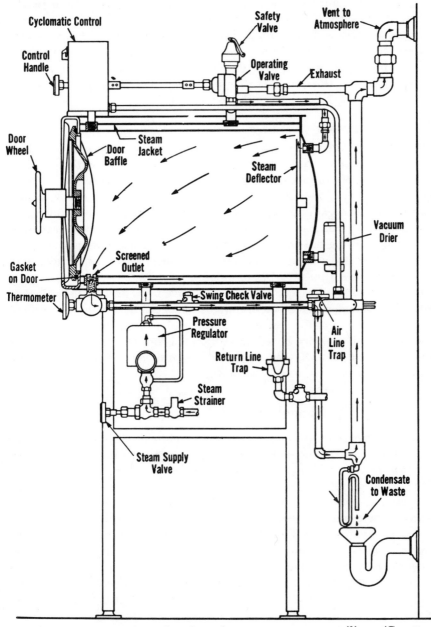

FIG. 3.4. Diagrammatic section through a steam pressure sterilizer. (Courtesy American Sterilizer Company, Erie, Pa.)

being processed, however, the longer must be the exposure time in the autoclave to assure sterility. The exact details for effective operation of an autoclave will not be covered here, nor will the discussion of filters that are employed for sterilizing fluids adversely affected by heat. Chapter 4 will discuss these topics in some detail. One thought that should be made perfectly clear at this point is that *bacteriological sterility is an all or none proposition. There are no degrees of sterility!*

Physical Properties

A medium is generally prepared with a specific purpose in mind. Should you desire to study motility of bacteria, for instance, this particular observation is conducted in a liquid medium. If, however, the cultural characteristics of a bacterial colony are to be determined, the substrate upon which the organisms are cultivated must contain a solidifying agent such as agar or gelatin to give the medium body and to keep the growing mass from diffusing too far into the medium. Certain studies may require a medium that is sparkling clear; other observations may not be adversely affected if the medium is turbid or colored.

Because so many different types of tests have been devised for studying particular characteristics of the hundreds of species of microbes described to date, countless numbers of media, some differing in their composition from others only slightly, have been concocted through the years. Laboratory work in an introductory course in microbiology might involve two or three dozen of these media, at most.

Inoculation of Subcultures

Having prepared appropriate media to conduct a study of organisms, let us now consider how such substrates are employed in the isolation of an organism.

There are so few places in nature where bacteria are found as pure cultures that one of the primary steps in the study of a culture is to obtain a single species free from all other microorganisms. Going back to the early days in microbiology when fundamental ground rules were being established, it is interesting to review the clever approaches to the problem. You, as beginners, are in a unique position in this regard, and if you were asked to devise techniques for separating microbes from their fellow organisms, how would you do it? With the equipment available today and with our expanded knowledge in allied sciences, some students might arrive at the answer a good deal more quickly than did Robert Koch, Louis Pasteur, Paul Ehrlich, Joseph Lister, Antony van Leeuwenhoek, and some of the other outstanding pioneers in bacteriology. More likely, they would flounder about before arriving at a useful solution to the problem.

Bear in mind that people as recently as one hundred years ago harbored very strange ideas about the biological world. Belief in such things as spontaneous generation (**abiogenesis**), that is, life arising from dead matter, was commonplace. It took the brilliance of a Pasteur to demonstrate not only to laymen, but to his fellow "learned" scientists that even mi-

FIG. 3.5. Counting colonies by use of a Quebec colony counter.

crobes must come from other microbes. Life begets life. What a mess the biological world would be were life to arise willy-nilly from just anything. The limits of knowledge at that time were responsible for some of the ill-devised experiments that "proved" beyond a shadow of a doubt to most persons at the time that life arose spontaneously.

Thanks to pioneer experiments, with their mistakes and their successes, modern techniques make it possible to separate even closely related species of organisms from each other with a high degree of success and a minimum of instruction. One of Koch's pioneer experiments for isolating the predominating organism in a bacterial mixture from its neighbors was the basis for modifications which led to today's methods. Progress is usually the result of minor modifications of known methods. Startlingly new ideas are less frequent than most people realize. Those who do achieve breakthroughs in science will usually be the first to admit that without discoveries of the past, present accomplishment would largely be impossible.

When a number of tubes of sterile broth are lined up and transfers prepared by carrying over material from one tube to another in a series, sufficient dilution is eventually reached to permit the predominating organism to be carried over in pure culture, theoretically, into one of the tubes. Incubation of these cultures should, therefore, reveal a pure culture of the predominating bacteria in the highest dilution that shows growth. It should be apparent that sometimes this technique will work and frequently the effort will meet with failure.

The simple expedient of adding a solidifying agent like agar to the series of broth tubes greatly enhanced the usefulness of the procedure. When the agar medium is melted and then cooled to between 45° and 50°C, the serial transfers made, and the contents of the tubes poured into individual petri dishes and allowed to solidify, the trapped organisms, upon suitable incubation, develop into visible masses of growth called *colonies*. When the serial dilutions have been carried out sufficiently, the colonies will be far enough apart to permit "fishing" them out as pure cultures into tubes of suitable media.

As bacterial colonies develop in agar media, the size, shape, and color (if pigment is produced) of the colonies will vary with the different levels of oxygen tension existing within the medium. Submerged or embedded colonies will tend to be smaller and will lack pigment, whereas surface growths will have free access to atmospheric concentrations of oxygen and will be larger and show **chromogenesis** if color is one of the characteristics of the species being investigated.

Since the size, shape, and color of a pure culture of bacteria may vary greatly in a plate prepared from a serial dilution in which the colonies are growing at different levels of oxygen tension, visual inspection of such a plate will fail to reveal whether a single culture or a mixture of organisms is involved.

Streak Plates

A natural outgrowth of the above findings was the development of plates in which all colonies grow on the surface of the solid medium. Such a technique is known as a **streak plate**.

By drawing the surface of a wire loop containing test organisms across the surface of a hardened nutrient agar medium, it is possible to obtain isolations of pure cultures of microbes from mixtures of organisms. Different laboratories have their own techniques for preparing streak plates, but two of the more commonly employed methods will be outlined in order to explain the general theory involved in such a procedure. It should be pointed out that the decision as to whether one technique is superior to another insofar as preparation of streak plates is concerned rests, in the final analysis, on the degree of success obtained by inexperienced technicians. The pattern of streaking suggested by some instructors may differ markedly from the recommended procedure of another individual, but if both methods result in a high percentage of successful isolations, the exact pattern of streaking turns out to be a matter of preference.

A petri dish has a surface area of approximately 65 square centimeters. A loopful of a bacterial suspension may contain millions, or even billions, of organisms. Yet by merely streaking the loop containing these organisms over the surface of an agar medium in a scientific manner, it is possible to obtain single, well-isolated colonies of organisms that will arise where single cells or groups of cells are deposited on the medium. Precautions must be taken to minimize contamination of the medium from outside sources. The instructor can demonstrate this procedure to you.

Method 1

This technique consists of starting the streaking at one edge of the plate and progressing away from that point in such a manner that every square centimeter of agar surface is touched by the loop.

If the loop contains enormous numbers of organisms, however, the technician may run out of agar surface before sufficient dilution of culture has been effected. It is suggested, therefore, that if Method 1 is to be employed, a *film* of fluid culture rather than a biconvex loopful be employed. Perhaps fifty or more strokes of the loop across the agar surface may be required to insure adequate separation of microbes. The loop should be kept moving away from the point of original inoculation since retracing the streaking may pick up too many organisms and fail to yield isolations in the space available.

Method 2

A higher percentage of successful isolations can probably be obtained by Method 2 than by many other procedures, and a number of laboratories prefer it, or some modification of the method, over the straight streaking technique.

The procedure is as follows:

1. With a glass marking pencil draw a "T" on the outside bottom of a petri dish containing the solidified medium. The relative proportion of the three sections should be about as indicated in Figure 3.6.

2. Bend a wire loop to form a flat surface when the handle is held at about a 45° angle. Aseptically transfer a loopful of the test organisms to the surface of the agar plate marked "1" in the diagram. At least fifteen strokes of the loop should be made across the entire surface of section 1, using extreme care to avoid plowing under the seedlings. When this is done properly, no visible breaks in the agar surface should be apparent.

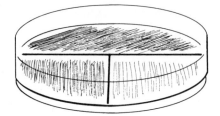

FIG. 3.6. Diagram of how to prepare
a streak plate.

Practice is required before the neophyte learns just how much pressure can be applied without penetrating the agar surface. Most agar media contain between 1.5 and 2.0 per cent of solidifying agent; this concentration yields a consistency that might be compared with the "skin" that forms on top of a gelatin dessert that has been allowed to stand for several days. Although this does provide a relatively firm surface on which to glide a metal loop, great care must be exercised to prevent tearing of the agar.

3. At this point burn off the remaining culture on the loop. After allowing the wire to cool for a few seconds, draw the loop across section 1 in a zigzag pattern to pick up some of the organisms previously deposited on the agar.

4. Without flaming the loop streak these organisms over section 2, employing *at least* 30 strokes.

5. Sterilize the loop once again, allow it to cool, and then draw it over section 2 in a zigzag motion.

6. Without sterilizing the loop streak area 3 with the material picked up from section 2. Once again use at least 30 strokes.

7. Flame the wire loop before setting it aside. This is a wise precaution whether the test microbes are considered to be pathogenic or saprophytic.

The above procedure generally will yield plates on which, following suitable incubation, can be found isolated colonies. These individual pure cultures may appear on any of the three sections of the streak plate, depending upon the initial concentration of suspensions being plated. A typical distribution of colonies is shown in Figure 3.7.

Since all colonies develop on the surface of the agar when this procedure is followed, it is possible to ascertain with some degree of accuracy whether the growth represents a mixed culture or a pure culture of a single species of organisms. Such characteristics as size, shape, and color of the surface colonies are employed as criteria for this determination of

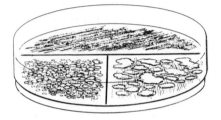

FIG. 3.7. Characteristic distribution
of colonies on a streak plate.

purity. Well-isolated growths can be picked from streak plates to suitable media, usually agar slants, and when visible growth appears, suitable stains can be prepared for examination under a microscope. A number of the more common tests employed in the identification of organisms will be described in some detail in Chapter 4.

Blood Agar Plates

While standard nutrient agar permits the cultivation of most common bacteria, pathogenic species, especially upon primary isolation from the body, frequently will grow poorly or not at all unless dietary supplements are furnished. In clinical microbiology a most useful medium for the isolation of pathogens is blood agar which contains from 3 to 10 per cent of fresh uncoagulated blood that has been added aseptically to an isotonic sterile medium.

Blood requirements vary from the less fastidious species that merely grow better in an enriched medium to such organisms as *Hemophilus pertussis*, the etiological agent in whooping cough, which fails to grow unless it is supplied with a relatively high (40 to 50 per cent) concentration of blood. The generic name, *Hemophilus*, means "blood-loving," and several significant pathogenic species belong to this genus.

Streptococci, the cause of a number of man's afflictions, may be classified on the basis of visible changes produced by a colony growing on blood agar. This alteration or breakdown of blood is known as **hemolysis.** Some cocci, including *Diplococcus pneumoniae* which is most commonly implicated in lobar pneumonia, produce a hazy zone with a slight greenish tinge adjacent to the colony on a blood agar plate. This reaction is called **alpha hemolysis.** When bacteria secrete or excrete substances which cause a complete dissolving (lysis) of the red blood cells as shown by a clear halo around a colony, this is indicative of **beta hemolysis.** Organisms which do not cause any visible change in the blood medium are referred to as **gamma colonies.** More will be said about these reactions and their significance in particular diseases in subsequent chapters.

Hemolytic reactions on blood agar may be enhanced when **sandwich plates** are prepared. Organisms are streaked on a suitable agar surface, and on top of this is poured a thin cap layer of blood-containing agar which is allowed to solidify. The metabolic products responsible for hemolysis diffuse into the surrounding medium in which the colony is embedded, and hemolytic reactions may be read after an incubation period.

The causative organism in the venereal disease gonorrhea (*Neisseria gonorrheae*) grows well on a blood-containing medium known as **chocolate agar.** When blood agar is heated to 80°C until the blood turns brown (avoid overheating), changes occur in the chemical composition of the medium and gonococci flourish.

Ascitic Fluid

Various animal fluids other than blood serve as excellent media or as additives to basic media for enhancing microbial growth. Ascitic fluid, which is primarily diluted lymph, collects in abnormal quantities in the peritoneal cavity in a condition known as "dropsy." This nutritive fluid is usually clear, slightly yellow, and may coagulate upon standing. Hospital laboratories engaged in clinical microbiology generally collect this lymph from cadavers during autopsies. Since the body's resistance mechanisms break down at the time of death, bacterial invasion of tissues and fluids occurs in a relatively short time following death. But by passing of ascitic fluid through suitable sterile filters, it may be freed of contaminating microorganisms prior to being added aseptically to a sterile basic medium to be employed in clinical laboratory studies.

Blood Serum Media

Corynebacterium diphtheriae, the causative agent in diphtheria, is noted for two rather characteristic features. Upon suitable cultivation the organisms appear pleomorphic (different sizes and shapes) and their interior contains dark granules when the smear is stained. One of the substrates that has been employed successfully for growing these pathogens is Loeffler's medium which is prepared from blood serum and veal infusion glucose broth that is generally coagulated in a slanting position in a test tube. In addition to rapid growth on this medium, the diphtheria cells readily develop the characteristic granules. A number of modifications of the original formula have been suggested for this medium since its introduction, and for this reason textbooks and laboratory manuals may not appear to agree on the composition of Loeffler's serum medium.

Selective Media

One of the major problems encountered in the isolation of pathogenic organisms is the interference, and in some instances an actual overgrowth, by contaminating bacteria not associated with the specific disease under investigation. The incorporation into media of inhibitory substances, such as dyes and other chemicals, serves to retard the growth of unwanted bacteria. In general this inhibitory chemical, which is termed a **bacteriostat,** parallels the gram staining reaction. It might be said at this point that gram positive bacteria appear to be more sensitive to inhibitory agents in media than are the gram negative species.

A few representative selective media that are of importance in clinical microbiology will be mentioned briefly, but the list is by no means complete.

Endo Agar

This solid medium is useful for the cultivation and detection of so-called **enteric organisms,** those whose natural habitat is the digestive tract. Such bacterial diseases as typhoid, paratyphoid, and dysentery are typical of this group in man. Endo agar is designed to inhibit the multitude of gram positive cells that also normally inhabit the enteric tract. Among other constituents this formula incorporates sodium sulfite and basic fuchsin to inhibit the gram positive cells, while the other constituents in the medium encourage gram negative bacteria to flourish.

In bacteriological water analysis it is not customary to try to isolate the enteric pathogens (such as *Salmonella typhosa* or *Shigella dysenteriae* which cause typhoid fever and dysentery, respectively), since the procedure would involve too long a time with success being questionable unless relatively high concentrations of the disease-producing bacteria were present in the water. Instead the bacteriologist looks for the presence of *Escherichia coli,* a normal inhabitant of the intestines of all warm-blooded animals. This gram negative organism is found in enormous numbers in fecal material and its survival in water is relatively long. A full discussion of water bacteriology will be presented in Chapter 8, but for the present it can be said that *Escherichia coli* when grown on endo agar produces a characteristic reddening of the otherwise flesh-colored medium. In addition, coli will precipitate the basic fuchsin dye on the top of the colony, producing a metallic-like sheen or lustre which is very characteristic of the species. Species closely related to this organism are called *coliform* bacteria.

Eosine Methylene Blue Agar (E.M.B.)

This selective medium acts in a manner similar to that of endo agar, but in E.M.B. the inhibitors of gram positive bacteria are the two dyes eosin Y and methylene blue. Characteristic growth of significant bacteria assists the technician in the selection of gram negative colonies that may be the cause of the enteric upset.

Tellurite Agar

Diphtheria cultures are usually made from swabbings of the nose and throat, and the complexity of the microbial flora in these areas complicates the isolation of the diphtheria cells unless the nonpathogenic organisms can be inhibited. Tellurite incorporated into a blood-containing medium serves to retard the growth of many bacteria, both gram positive and gram negative, at the same time that it allows *Corynebacterium diphtheriae* to grow in a characteristic manner. A number of modifications of this medium are available, but the underlying mechanism of bacteriostasis is essentially the same in all cases.

S.S. Agar

This medium is highly selective for the cultivation from stools of species of *Salmonella,* the cause of typhoid and paratyphoid fevers, and of *Shigella,* the genus to which the dysentery organisms belong. Ten ingredients comprise S.S. agar, consisting of inorganic salts with brilliant green serving as the inhibitor of gram positive bacteria as well as of the saprophyte *Escherichia coli.* Space will not be taken here to go into the various types of culture reactions that are of significance to a clinical bacteriologist. Laboratory manuals and other textbooks may be used as reference for this type of information.

Bismuth Sulfite Agar

This is another highly selective medium designed especially for the isolation of *Salmonella typhosa* from body discharges. When public health authorities conduct examinations of food handlers, one important purpose is to detect typhoid carriers—persons who may be healthy to all outward appearance but who harbor pathogens. Bismuth sulfite agar is frequently employed along with other selective media in laboratory studies on stools submitted by food handlers. The typhoid cells produce characteristic black colonies on this medium, while gram positive cells and the coliform group of bacteria are inhibited. Brilliant green is the dye that serves as the bacteriostat, while other ingredients assist in the development of characteristic colonies which form on the medium.

Azide Agar

Sodium azide is one of the bacteriostatic agents employed to inhibit growth of the relatively resistant gram negative species of bacteria. This medium serves a useful function in the isolation of gram positive organisms such as streptococci and staphylococci from mixtures of organisms.

Brilliant Green Bile Media

This dye is inhibitory for most bacteria, but in suitable concentration members of the coliform group do grow, and therefore tests being conducted on water or milk for the presence of coliforms may employ a medium containing brilliant green and bile as inhibitors.

All of the media described so far are designed to aid in the isolation of specific organisms from mixtures. Once these cells have been obtained as pure cultures, their identification can proceed according to organized schemes. Chapter 4 will enumerate some of the considerations employed by the microbiologist in his ultimate quest for the name of the genus and the species of the organism under investigation.

Anaerobic Techniques

Not all microbes that are provided with a balanced diet and optimum temperatures will grow unless in addition the gaseous atmosphere is of the proper composition. Organisms must secure energy for growth through a chemical process called **oxidation,** but the mechanism by which this is accomplished will vary with the species. Most cellular oxidations involve the removal of hydrogen from compounds rather than the addition of oxygen. In other words, biological oxidations are generally dehydrogenations.

Anaerobes are those organisms which employ some hydrogen acceptor other than oxygen. In contrast to **aerobes** in which oxygen enters a cell by diffusion and may be used for respiration, anaerobes carry out their metabolism in the absence of free oxygen. In fact they may be killed by the presence of uncombined oxygen.

Ingenious devices and complex media have been perfected for creating conditions favorable for the cultivation of anaerobes. Oxygen may be removed physically, chemically, or biologically. The underlying principles of these techniques will be presented and representative methods will be mentioned, but no extensive treatment of exact details required for creating anaerobiosis will be reviewed since they vary widely from one laboratory to another.

Physical Methods

Boiling liquid media for about ten minutes will drive off dissolved oxygen. After freshly-boiled and cooled media are inoculated, the medium is covered with a layer of sterile petrolatum to maintain anaerobic conditions.

Plates and tubes containing test organisms may be stored in a special pressure-resistant jar which can be evacuated with the aid of a vacuum pump. The jars are then filled with nitrogen, evacuated, the atmosphere replaced with carbon dioxide, evacuated once more, and the jars are finally filled with hydrogen. A small dish containing platinized asbestos is placed in the container to catalyze the union of any free oxygen with the hydrogen to form water. This is one of the better techniques for creating and maintaining anaerobic conditions, especially for streak plates on which isolations of pure cultures are being attempted.

Chemical Methods

When pyrogallic acid is mixed with sodium hydroxide, the resulting reaction involves the prompt uptake of any free oxygen. It is possible, therefore, to employ this principle in specially constructed dishes or in tubes, and the method works well.

Burning phosphorus is another means of creating anaerobic conditions, but there are dangers in handling this material and it is not recommended for general class use, particularly at the elementary level.

Sodium thioglycollate is a strong reducing agent. When it is incorporated into media, anaerobes can be cultivated in open tubes of broth. Thio broth is the medium of choice for checking sterility of biologicals since aerobes, anaerobes, and those organisms in between are capable of growing at different levels of oxygen tension existing within the test medium.

Biological Methods

Fresh plant and animal tissue provides sufficient reducing power to permit anaerobes to grow. Egg–meat medium in spécial broth is an excellent food for the cultivation of anaerobes, and even the more fastidious species will grow well when the inoculum is heavy and deep in the tube of egg–meat.

When large surface areas are inoculated with aerobic bacteria, the cells can utilize sufficient oxygen within closed containers to permit anaerobes to flourish. While this technique is not used as widely as some of the others, it does, nevertheless, provide an interesting biological method for creating suitable atmospheric conditions to permit proper respiration and growth of anaerobes.

The problem of cultivation of anaerobes has direct significance in nursing practice when one considers that gas gangrene, lockjaw (tetanus), and botulism are diseases caused by organisms that carry out their respiration in this interesting manner.

Microaerophilic Techniques

Microaerophiles are those organisms that require an atmosphere containing a reduced oxygen content. They prefer neither atmospheric concentrations nor anaerobic conditions; rather, their requirements lie someplace in between. When grown in a tube of thioglycollate broth, microaerophiles will grow as a ring at a level in the tube where conditions are optimum for their particular type of respiration. Most of these organisms prefer an increase in carbon dioxide content in addition to a reduction in free oxygen.

One of the simpler techniques for creating these conditions is to light a candle in a screw-top jar and then close the container. By the time the oxygen level has dropped to the point where it can no longer support the flame, the carbon dioxide liberated during combustion has risen and the oxygen tension is almost ideal for cultivation of such representative species as *Neisseria gonorrheae* (the cause of a venereal disease) and *Neisseria meningitidis* (the etiological agent of epidemic meningitis).

Review Questions

1. What would constitute a balanced diet for a nonpathogenic bacillus? How might this differ from a strict parasite?
2. Why do taxonomists change the scientific names of bacteria from time to time? Do they ever return to previous names after a change?
3. What fomites must be considered particularly important in the spread of contagious diseases?
4. How does titratable acidity differ from pH?
5. What significant advantages are offered by commercial media?
6. Make a list of common sterile materials employed in routine hospital practice and indicate the precise method used to sterilize each substance.
7. What streaking patterns in addition to the ones described in the text might be employed to prepare satisfactory plates for isolation of pure cultures of bacteria from mixtures?
8. Why are blood derivatives so favorable for the cultivation of pathogenic organisms?
9. Why are bacteriostatic media generally ineffective in retarding growth of some microbes after the first 24 hours of incubation?
10. How can anaerobes breathe in the absence of free oxygen?

4 IDENTIFICATION OF BACTERIA

HAVING CULTIVATED THE COLONIES OF BACTERIA ON SUITABLE media, the investigator's next step in the game of determining the genus and species of the organism is to ascertain the purity of the isolation. Then a series of subcultures can be inoculated.

Transfer of Cultures

It is customary to transfer microbes from one tube to another by means of a straight needle or a wire fashioned into a loop that is securely attached to a metal handle. Nichrome wire may be used, since it heats and cools relatively quickly. Although techniques for aseptically manipulating microbial cultures will vary with individual instructors, the following general principles apply.

Air contains dust in amounts that vary with the location and with the degree of air movement. Microbes are transported on these particles which serve as "magic carpets" for organisms that are unable to move under their own power unless they are suspended in suitable fluids. Since dust tends to fall perpendicular to the floor in a quiet atmosphere, any tube or flask that is left open, even for brief periods, is subject to outside contamination. To minimize this possibility it is best to hold such containers at an angle of about 45 degrees while they are open. This will make the opening relatively smaller as far as dust dropping from above is concerned. It is best to hold only one tube in the hand at one time while making transfers, although some instructors may permit two or

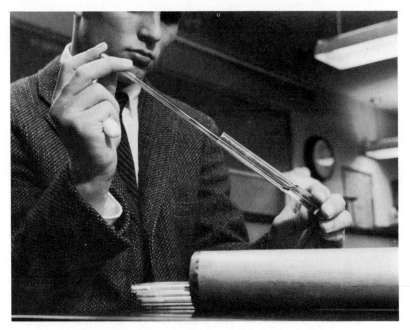

FIG. 4.1. Accepted technique for pipetting.

FIG. 4.2. Method of holding a test tube and cotton plug.

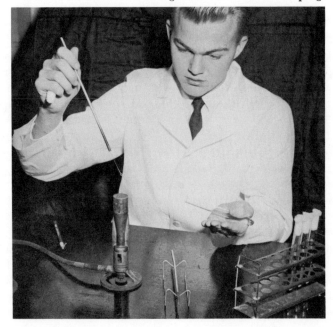

FIG. 4.3.   Pouring medium into a petri dish.

FIG. 4.4.   Method of streaking an agar surface.

more tubes to be opened at one time if special precautions for protecting the cotton plugs are observed. A petri dish lid should be held directly above the agar surface in the plate to protect the medium from contamination.

Colonies are generally transferred to a tube containing a solid medium that has been allowed to harden in a slanting position. Such an **agar slant,** or **agar slope,** furnishes a greater surface of the medium within the tube than would be possible were the agar allowed to harden while the tube was held in an upright position. After the wire is sterilized in an open flame and allowed to cool for several seconds, the lid of the petri dish is lifted just high enough to permit the technician to insert the needle and to remove a representative portion of the colony for transfer to the surface of the slant.

When agar slant tubes are opened it is essential that the cotton stopper be held in such a manner that the part of the plug to be reinserted after the transfer has been effected touches nothing. Never lay a cotton plug down on a table or on any other surface. Consider everything about you to be contaminated. This is one of the most difficult concepts of microbiology for beginning students, and in the field of nursing a thorough realization of this fact is essential if asepsis and sterile techniques are to be practiced.

The lip of the tube should be held in a flame for a second or two to kill any organisms present. Run the wire containing the organisms across the surface of the agar slant to subculture some of the microbes, but avoid breaking through the surface of the agar medium. After the transfer has been accomplished, flame the lip of the tube once again to burn off any cells that might inadvertently have been deposited during the transfer process. This heating also serves to protect the cotton plug from contamination by the test organisms. Replace the cotton as promptly as possible and sterilize the transfer needle before putting it into a suitable holder. Strict attention must be paid to every detail in the manipulation procedure if purity of cultures is to be maintained.

Incubate the inoculated slants at a temperature appropriate for the organisms being cultivated. That is, if the microbes are derived from the human body, a temperature close to 37°C is usually optimum; cultures from air, water, or soil do better at from 25–30°C.

Staining Procedures

To confirm the purity of the isolate on the slant a representative sample of stained cells should be examined under the oil immersion objective of a microscope. It is recommended that a sizable area, at least equivalent to that of a five-cent piece, be marked off on a clean glass slide with a wax marking pencil. This will serve to limit the area over which the cells are to be spread, and it also aids the technician in locating the organisms on the slide.

Microbes will not adhere to dirty glass. It is essential, therefore, to remove dirt and grease with a suitable cleansing agent. Pumice (volcanic ash) is a particularly reliable substance, but no matter what agent is employed, the slides must subsequently be rinsed thoroughly in water to remove all traces of the cleaning powder. If a slide has been properly scoured, water should spread on it evenly with no tendency to gather in small droplets.

Only young cultures in the prime of youth—less than twenty-four hours old—can be expected to yield reliable staining characteristics. Older cultures contain metabolic wastes that interfere with retention of dye by microbial cells and tend to distort their morphology.

After the bacteria have been suspended in a loopful of tap water on a clean slide and have been spread over the prescribed area, the smear should be dried carefully. Avoid excessive heat, particularly while the preparation is moist. Overheating may also affect both the morphology and the staining characteristics of cells. While drying the film without the aid of heat is probably best, evaporation of the moisture on the slide can be hastened with little or no damage if the slide is kept moving high above a flame where the temperature is comfortable for the fingers holding the slide. If the temperature is too hot for the fingers, it is probably too hot for the cells on the slide. After the film is visibly dry, it is customary to **fix** the organisms by passing the slide quickly through an open flame two or three times. Since the moisture content of the preparation is relatively low at this point, the dry heat of the flame does not adversely affect the visible characteristics of stained cells.

If one is interested only in the general size and shape of microorganisms, flooding the slide with a dye such as methylene blue or crystal violet for a minute or two will be sufficient to stain bacteria and to facilitate their being examined under the higher power lenses of the microscope.

However, when the staining technique is designed to show differences between species or to bring out specific structures within the cells, the procedure is called **differential staining.** This may involve the use of several steps and more than one dye, as in the gram staining technique described in an earlier chapter. The gram stain is one of the first steps that must be carried out if we are to identify an organism as to genus and species.

Should the stain reveal what appears to be a pure culture from the standpoint of morphology, growth from the agar slant can then be used to inoculate a number of subcultures for study of physiological reactions that can aid in identification.

In an introductory course of this nature it is not necessary to go into an elaborate discussion of the dozens of reactions that would be studied in advanced microbiology, but a certain number of representative tests should be understood even by those entering the field for the first time. Individual instructors may wish to supplement this list or even to delete some of the tests to be discussed here, and the student should understand that this science is presented in different ways by different instructors.

The identification of bacteria is based upon three principal considerations: **morphology, cultural characteristics,** and **physiology.** Each of these will be discussed and the descriptive chart on page 80 may be used as a guide. Brief definitions of terms used on the chart may be found on page 81.

Morphology

Stains

GRAM REACTION

Of the usual tests employed to determine size, shape, and structure of bacteria the gram stain is by far the most important. As indicated previously only young, actively growing cultures can be relied upon for determination of the gram reaction, and standard nutrient agar is the medium of choice for cultivating most organisms to be stained by this differential technique. Species requiring blood agar or other dietary supplements naturally must be grown on the medium which will support their growth. Although twenty-four hours has been set as the maximum age for a culture to be subjected to the gram stain, cultures nearer to fifteen or eighteen hours old are usually optimum, especially for the borderline or gram variable species which tend to be weakly gram positive. Such cells often give a gram negative reaction when metabolic wastes begin to accumulate.

Examination of a gram stained smear under the oil immersion objective can supply information as to the size and shape of the organisms being studied, in addition to their gram reaction. If the bacteria are found to be gram positive, this immediately eliminates from further consideration hundreds of gram negative species. It should be apparent that an improperly prepared gram stain could lead a student off on a tangent trying to identify a species that may not exist.

Since there are only three basic shapes of organisms, finding a rod, for example, eliminates all spheres and spirals. Each step in the process continues to narrow the possibilities, until finally the correct identification has been accomplished. There are occasions, particularly in an advanced course in microbiology, when even after all of the prescribed tests have been completed, the reactions fail to match any organism listed in *Bergey's Manual of Determinative Bacteriology*. Since not all microbes have been discovered and described, the possibility of having an "unknown unknown" does exist. But in an elementary course failure on the part of the student to identify a pure culture may be due to any number of improperly prepared tests, and the student is advised to go back and recheck all reactions, beginning with the gram stain.

SPORES

Spores usually develop in older cultures when wastes begin to build up to levels that are toxic for bacteria. Since spores appear to represent primarily a device to protect cells during adverse environmental conditions, it is rather uncommon to find these structures during the active logarithmic phase of growth of a culture. Spores are not found in gram negative rods, spheres, or spirals. There is little point, therefore, in conducting spore tests on organisms other than gram positive rods, and not all of them contain spores. The usual staining techniques are not satisfactory for demonstrating spores. Dyes must be driven into these spores with heat. A number of acceptable techniques are available, and only one will be described here.

1. Prepare the film on a clean slide in the usual manner.
2. Flood the slide with 5 per cent malachite green and apply heat directly from a flame either from above or from below the slide which may be supported on the flat surface of a tripod. Steam for about one minute to drive the stain into the thickened spore case, but boiling the dye or allowing the stain to dry during the heating process should be avoided.
3. Wash off excess dye by carefully rinsing the slide in a jar of tap water. A direct stream from the faucet should be avoided or the preparation might be washed from the slide.
4. Apply a weak counterstain such as safranin for about two minutes. The parts of the cell other than the spore will pick up the pink dye, whereas the spores will appear as deeply stained green bodies. Some spores may be extracellular, whereas others will be within the cell wall. The older the culture the more spores can be expected to be found outside of the cell.

Not only is the presence of spores an important consideration in the identification process, but their size, shape, and location within the **sporangium** (cell wall) is particularly significant.

CAPSULE

It is probably correct to state that all bacteria have some kind of a capsule. The size of this sheath and its significance may vary between cells, and except in the case of a few pathogenic organisms and a few "troublemakers" in food industries, students in the paramedical sciences will not be particularly concerned with capsules or methods employed for their staining. This is not a routine laboratory procedure nor is it generally carried out in the usual identification process.

Motility

Not all bacteria possess the power of independent locomotion in liquids, and sometimes a key difference between closely related species may lie in the presence or absence of motility. Except for a few unusual species, cocci may be said to be nonmotile. As is true with the gram reactions, only young cultures should be employed for motility determinations. Broth cultures less than 24 hours old are used for preparing hanging drops for this purpose. Special thick depression slides are used, rather than the usual flat type of microscope slide. A loopful or two of the liquid culture is transferred to a thin **coverslip** which is then inverted over the concavity and sealed with water or with grease to retard evaporation of the drop during examination under the high dry objective which magnifies approximately 450 ×. Brownian movement, described in Chapter 1, should be distinguished from true motility in which the organisms make independent progress across the field of the microscope.

Cultural Characteristics

There are at least three principal means by which the cultural characteristics of bacteria may be studied: colonies developing on a streak plate, growth on an agar slant, and appearance of the growth in a suitable broth medium.

Colony Appearance

A surface colony on a solid medium furnishes information as to the size, shape, color, and consistency of the visible mass of organisms. The speed of growth is considered to be rapid when well-developed colonies appear in less than twenty-four hours. If two days are required for visible growth, this is considered to be moderate, and any cultures that take three days or more to grow are said to be slow. Although these time periods are arbitrary, they do serve a useful function.

Slant Growth

Information similar to that obtained from an isolated colony is furnished from an agar slant culture; in addition, if the stroke on the surface of the slant is made with a straight needle, the tendency for the growth to spread or to remain along the line of inoculation may help to characterize some species and to aid in their identification.

When pigment is formed by an organism (chromogenesis), the color may be said to be water-soluble if the pigment diffuses from the growth into the surrounding agar medium which is usually composed of about 90 per cent water. Most bacterial pigments are of the water-insoluble type, that is, the colony or the growth along a slant may exhibit color, but the pigment remains within the cells and does not spread into the adjacent medium. Pigment formation requires free access to atmospheric concentrations of oxygen. Hence only surface colonies should be examined to gain information relative to chromogenic activity of organisms.

Broth Cultures

In examining a broth culture of an organism three main features should be observed: surface growth, clouding of the medium, and the amount and type of sediment at the bottom of the tube. The descriptive chart on page 80 lists a few of the possible reactions that might be encountered. When none of these descriptions apply, the student should write in appropriate information to describe growth of the particular organism as he sees it.

Physiology

While much information can be gleaned from a study of the morphology and the cultural characteristics of an organism, the real heart of identification of microbes lies in the study of their physiology—the science that treats of the functions of living cells. It is a study of the effects produced through the activity of complex enzyme systems of organisms. A few representative physiological tests will be discussed briefly.

Nutrient Gelatin

This incomplete protein, which is normally a solid below 23°C and a liquid above 25°C, is capable of being attacked by the enzymes of some organisms, and such altered gelatin fails to solidify when it is chilled to below 23°C. This is one of the drawbacks of gelatin as a solidifying agent in media. Agar is not attacked by bacteria, with the exception of some marine forms of organisms. When the enzyme gelatinase is liberated by bacteria being cultivated in a nutrient gelatin medium, the gelatin fails to gel. Since some organisms produce gelatinase, and others fail to do so, this test provides one means of separating certain organisms from others.

When pathogenic species derived from the human body are to be identified, cultures being tested in tubes of nutrient gelatin should be incubated at or near the body temperature of 37°C which will liquefy the medium without enzyme activity. Before it is possible to determine whether or not gelatinase has been produced by the test organism, it is necessary to cool the tubes to below 23°C for several minutes. If the medium remains fluid after chilling, the bacteria are gelatinase positive. The speed and completeness of liquefaction will vary with species of organisms.

Brom Cresol Purple (B.C.P.) Milk

When the pH indicator brom cresol purple is added to tubes of fresh milk which are then autoclaved, organisms inoculated into such a medium are capable of eliciting a number of significant reactions based upon their ability to attack the carbohydrate (lactose, or milk sugar) or the protein (casein) in the milk.

B.C.P. milk normally has a color that can be described as a dirty gray. When acids are formed through the breakdown of milk sugar, the pH of the medium drops and the milk turns yellow. Any attack on the protein, with its attendant alkaline end products, will cause the indicator to turn purple.

Milk reactions, in general, are somewhat slower than many other physiological reactions, and for this reason tubes of B.C.P. milk should not be called negative before five days of incubation at the optimum temperature. Since some of the color changes are not very marked, it is well to hold the tube next to an uninoculated tube of milk which serves as a control.

The ability of some bacteria to produce more acid than other organisms may result in the pH of B.C.P. milk being depressed to the point where the casein coagulates, or forms a curd. This reaction occurs at a pH of about 4.6. Such an acid curd is firm enough to allow the tube to be inverted without disturbing the milk in the bottom of the tube. Eventually a fluid called **whey** will be expressed, and this fluid generally collects on top.

Milk may also exhibit a soft-curd without an accompanying drop in pH of the medium. Such a reaction is a **rennet** or **sweet curd** caused as the result of the liberation by organisms of the enzyme rennet or rennin which transforms the soluble casein in milk into insoluble paracasein.

This enzyme is the active ingredient found in some soft curd desserts commonly consumed in many households. Commercial rennin is obtained from extracts of the stomach of calves.

Microbes may attack a rennet curd in a process called **proteolysis.** This reaction is evident when a tube of B.C.P. milk is approximately neutral, exhibits a rennet curd, and has a watery layer on top of the soft curdled milk. Proteolysis may be distinguished from the formation of whey on the basis of pH and the hardness of the curd.

Methylene Blue Milk

Methylene blue when added to fresh milk serves to indicate changes in **oxidation–reduction.** This dye is not a pH indicator. When oxygen is removed either mechanically by a vacuum pump or biologically by the enzyme **reductase** produced by some bacteria, methylene blue will turn from a robin's egg blue to its white **(leuco)** form. To demonstrate that this is a reversible reaction, a tube of methylene blue milk that has turned white can be made to revert to its original blue color by simply shaking the milk and reincorporating atmospheric oxygen.

Methylene blue indicator serves a useful function when **anaerobes** (those microbes that grow only in the absence of free oxygen) are being cultivated in sealed containers. When air is removed from the jar by means of a vacuum pump and inert gases are added to replace the natural atmosphere, a tube of methylene blue milk can indicate whether anaerobic conditions have been attained within the vessel prior to incubation at the optimum temperature for the anaerobes being cultivated.

Fermentation

A very helpful physiological reaction in diagnostic microbiology is the study of the ability of microbes to ferment carbohydrates. Organisms differ in their ability to attack monosaccharides, disaccharides, polysaccharides, and higher alcohols. In some cases none of these substances can be fermented; in other instances, only acids may be formed from the breakdown of one or more sugars; and still other organisms are capable of liberating enzymes that can form both acids and gases from one or more of the carbohydrates.

A convenient technique for studying fermentation reactions is the use of **Durham fermentation tubes** in which a small vial is inverted within a larger tube containing the nutrient broth and the fermentable substance. During sterilization of the sugar broth in an autoclave the inner vial becomes filled with the fluid as the temperature of the medium cools down at the end of the heating period. The filled inner vial will then come to rest on the bottom of the parent tube containing the broth.

If gas is liberated during fermentation, these gas bubbles will rise to the surface of the medium and some gas will become trapped within the inner vial and will displace some of the broth. By incorporation of a pH indicator in the medium, color changes will denote whether acids have been formed. Brom thymol blue is frequently employed as such an indicator in Durham fermentation tubes, or a special reduced basic fuchsin called **Andrade's indicator** may be employed. Andrade's is colorless at neutrality and on the alkaline side of pH 7.0, but the indicator turns pink when the pH drops to the acid side.

Generally the fermentation reactions of only two or three sugars are studied in an elementary course in bacteriology, but advanced students may employ many more than this number in attempting to identify unknown cultures.

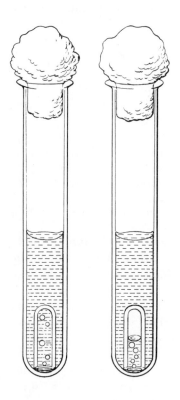

FIG. 4.5. Durham fermentation tube showing trapped gas.

Indole Test

Another biochemical test that is employed in the separation of microbial species is a measure of an organism's ability to attack the amino acid tryptophane, splitting off the fraction of the molecule known as **indole**. Bacteria are inoculated into tryptone broth, a medium rich in tryptophane, and allowed to incubate for at least two days; if the test species liberates the required enzyme, indole will be set free into the medium. This fraction of the tryptophane molecule can be detected by carefully floating on the surface of the tryptone broth culture a small quantity of Ehrlich's aldehyde (paradimethylaminobenzaldehyde) which turns a cherry red color in the presence of free indole in the medium. Heating the tube slightly will tend to intensify the reaction. The indole test helps to separate closely related species of organisms, and the reaction is an important one employed in bacteriological analysis of water (see Chapter 8).

Urease Test

An organism frequently encountered in medical practice is a gram negative rod belonging to the *Proteus* genus. It may be implicated in such conditions as bladder infections (**cystitis**), kidney infections (**pyelitis**), severe burns, and flesh wounds. Morphologically, members of the *Proteus* group resemble other gram negative rods, some of which may be harmless, others of which may cause enteric disturbances. One of the distinguishing physiological tests for *Proteus* is its ability through the enzyme protease to decompose urea in a highly buffered nutrient medium with the production of sufficient ammonia to push the pH up to at least 8.1 where the phenol red indicator in the medium turns red or cerise. This reaction is evident usually in less than 24 hours. This test when coupled with the usual cultural and physiological reactions materially aids in the positive identification of bacteria of the *Proteus* genus.

Endo or Eosine Methylene Blue Agar

These two selective media are employed in the preparation of streak plates to inhibit the growth of gram positive species and to provide distinguishing colonies of certain gram negative bacteria. (The student is referred to Chapter 3 for additional information relative to these differential and selective media.)

Oxygen Requirements

Microorganisms differ widely in their oxygen requirements for growth. Molds, for example, are strict **aerobes.** In order to grow they must have uncombined oxygen as it is found in the atmosphere. Some of the pathogenic members of the genus *Neisseria,* including the gonococcus and the etiological agent in epidemic meningitis (*Neisseria meningitidis*), find the usual concentration of atmospheric oxygen unsuited for their growth. These organisms prefer a reduced oxygen tension but an increased carbon dioxide level of approximately 10 to 15 per cent. Such organisms are classed as **microaerophiles.**

At the other end of the scale we find those microbes that can metabolize only combined oxygen which the organisms release through their enzyme systems from complex foods as required. Such bacteria are called **anaerobes.** A fourth category includes those cells which can live either aerobically or anaerobically, and they are **facultative.** They may display a preference for free or for combined oxygen, and some investigators designate them as **facultative aerobes** or as **facultative anaerobes** depending upon their specific preference. The techniques for creating these various types of environment for microbes will not be discussed here.

DESCRIPTIVE CHART FOR BACTERIA

Morphology

VEGETATIVE CELLS:

Forms: spheres, short rods, long rods, spirals.

Arrangement: singles, pairs, chains, fours, cubical packets, clusters.

Size: _____ *Sketch:* _____

Capsules: absent, present.

Staining reaction: Gram: _____

Motility: absent, present.

SPORES: absent, present.

Location: central, subterminal, terminal.

Sporangium: not swollen, swollen.

Cultural Characteristics

COLONY: Medium: _____ Age: ___ days.

Growth: slow, rapid, moderate.

Form: punctiform, circular, rhizoid, irregular.

Surface: smooth, rough; dry, moist; dull, glistening.

Elevation: flat, raised.

Edge: entire, wavy, filamentous, curled.

Sketch: _____

SLANT: Medium: _____ Age: _____ days.

Growth: scanty, moderate, abundant.

Form: threadlike, beaded, rhizoid, spreading, filiform.

Elevation: flat, raised.

Optical characters: opaque, translucent, iridescent.

Pigment: _____ water soluble, water-insoluble.

Consistency: butyrous, viscid, brittle.

Medium: grayed, browned, greened, unchanged.

NUTRIENT BROTH: Age: _____ days.

Surface growth: ring, pellicle, none.

Clouding: none, slight, moderate, heavy.

Sediment: none, scanty, abundant; flocculent, granular, viscid on agitation.

Physiology

NUTRIENT GELATIN: Age: _____ days.

Liquefaction: none, slow, rapid; slight, moderate, complete.

BROM CRESOL PURPLE MILK:

Reaction: acid, neutral, alkaline.

Curds: none, acid, rennet.

Proteolysis: none, slight, moderate, complete. Age: _____ days.

METHYLENE BLUE MILK:

Reduction: none, slight, moderate, complete. Age: _____ days.

FERMENTATIONS:

Glucose: negative, acid, gas, _____ days.

Lactose: negative, acid, gas, _____ days.

INDOLE TEST:

Negative, positive.

UREASE TEST:

Negative, positive.

ENDO OR EOSINE METHYLENE BLUE AGAR:

Growth: absent, present.

Color: absent, present.

Metallic sheen: absent, present.

RELATION TO OXYGEN:

Aerobic, microaerophilic, facultative, anaerobic.

ADDITIONAL TESTS:

Name of organism: _____ Habitat: _____

BRIEF DEFINITIONS OF TERMS FOUND ON DESCRIPTIVE CHART FOR THE IDENTIFICATION OF BACTERIA

1. **Brittle:** Growth which breaks easily into large component parts.
2. **Butyrous:** Having the physical properties of butter.
3. **Capsule:** An envelope around the bacterial cell wall.
4. **Cubical Packets:** Arrangement of *Sarcina* in groups of eights.
5. **Entire:** Refers to the regular, unbroken edge of a colony.
6. **Filamentous:** Threadlike growth.
7. **Filiform:** Uniform growth following line of inoculation.
8. **Flocculent:** Flaky.
9. **Habitat:** Where a species is found naturally.
10. **Iridescent:** Multiple coloration.
11. **Metallic Sheen:** Metal-like appearance when examined by reflected light.
12. **Opaque:** Will not permit passage of light.
13. **Pellicle:** A surface filmlike growth.
14. **Punctiform:** Small pinhead or pinpoint colonies.
15. **Rhizoid:** Branching, rootlike type of growth.
16. **Sporangium:** The spore case or cell wall surrounding the spore.
17. **Subterminal:** Located just inside the end of the cell.
18. **Terminal:** Located at the end of the cell.
19. **Translucent:** Permits passage of light but is not transparent.
20. **Vegetative:** Actively growing cells.
21. **Viscid:** Sticky, gelatinous type of growth.
22. **Water-soluble Pigment:** Color diffuses from the colony into the surrounding medium.

Review Questions

1. Why are cotton stoppers so effective for plugging tubes containing microbial cultures?
2. If a tube containing a microbial culture is flamed after the cotton stopper is removed, why should it be necessary to flame the lip again before the stopper is returned to the tube?
3. What determines the temperature at which cultures should be incubated?
4. What is the basis for selecting 24 hours as the dividing line between a young and an old culture?
5. What is a differential stain?
6. In the identification of bacteria, which is more important, morphology or physiology? Defend your answer.
7. If spores are composed of protein, why does boiling fail to inactivate so many spores even after prolonged heating?
8. When bacteria are chromogenic, does the pigment of most species tend to be water-soluble or water-insoluble?

9. May indicator dyes other than brom cresol purple be added to milk in the study of physiology of the species?

10. Differentiate between the formation of whey and the fluid that forms in brom cresol milk tubes that exhibit peptonization.

11. A great deal of the gas liberated during fermentation within a Durham fermentation tube is lost to the atmosphere. Can you design a set-up in which more gas might be trapped?

12. What are the limits of Andrade's indicator as a measure of pH changes?

THE PRINCIPLES
AND TECHNIQUES
OF STERILIZATION

Introduction

THE PRINCIPLES AND APPLICATIONS OF **asepsis** (KEEPING ORGAN-
isms out), **disinfection** (destroying organisms already present), and **steri-**
lization (killing or removing every living cell) have more practical
everyday bearing on nursing and medical practice than any other aspect
of microbiology. A thorough comprehension of the techniques employed
is mandatory if physicians and paramedical personnel who come in direct
or indirect contact with patients are to perform their role effectively as
informed members of a medical team. People go to hospitals and to other
medical installations in search of relief from **disease** (which literally
means "being uncomfortable"), and patients have a right to expect that
those with whom they deal will do all in their power to minimize opportunity for the spread of microbial infections. Although all nurses must
understand the general techniques used in sterilization, it would not be
a wise expenditure of time for each nurse to do the sterilizing of her
equipment and materials on her individual ward. Better control of material with fewer inventory losses results when a hospital has a central
sterile supply area run by a specially trained person, frequently under
the direct supervision of the chief nurse. Substantial savings can be realized in the purchase of fewer pieces of expensive sterilization equipment
with subsequent reduced upkeep.

All nurses, and especially the surgical nurse, should understand the use of heat as a sterilizing technique. When blended in the correct ratio heat and moisture are extremely destructive to microbial life. Killing by heat is primarily the result of coagulation of protein, the substance of which bacteria are composed. As the moisture level decreases, the temperature must be increased to provide an equivalent lethal action. This can be demonstrated quite readily in your own kitchen. Take a frying pan and heat it to 60°C. In another pan place some water at the same temperature. Drop an egg (protein) into each pan. The egg will congeal faster in the

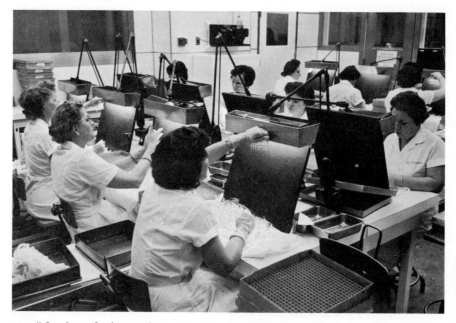

FIG. 5.1. Ampule inspection. (Courtesy Smith, Kline and French Laboratories, Philadelphia, Pa.)

water than it will on the relatively dry surface of the frying pan. This simple experiment should help you to understand why it is necessary to use a higher temperature for a longer time to sterilize materials in a dry oven than is required in a steam sterilizer.

A nurse will eventually find herself in contact with a patient who has a contagious disease. Unless she knows not only the nature of the pathogenic organisms involved and their mode of transmission, but also the accepted techniques designed for handling such contaminated objects as dressings, clothing, and equipment, the nurse might contract the infection herself and possibly spread the disease to others whose resistance may be relatively low. The invisibility of bacteria to the naked eye makes their handling unique, and a great respect must be cultivated for these microscopic enemies.

As was pointed out in the earlier discussion of media making, there is no such thing as partial sterility. Something either *is* or *is not* sterile. Only when every living cell—plant or animal, microscopic or macroscopic —is killed or physically removed can a substance be said to be sterile. One of the most difficult concepts for an instructor to get across to a beginning class in microbiology is that practically everything around us is contaminated. It is a wise teacher who bears down immediately in the very first laboratory period and insists that only accepted techniques for handling cultures will be tolerated. If microbiology courses do nothing more than to make students painfully conscious of aseptic technique, the long-range benefits for nursing and medical practice will be great.

Much of the difficulty encountered in recent years with resistant staphylococcus infections in our hospitals undoubtedly stemmed from the fact that some of the basic tenets of asepsis and disinfection, originally set forth in the latter half of the nineteenth century by the Scottish physician Joseph Lister, have been ignored, forgotten, or glossed over. The advent of such "miracle drugs" as **penicillin** and other antimicrobial agents led to a lowering of sanitary standards in many quarters. Some persons even ventured to predict that the bacteriologist, by his own discoveries, would soon work himself out of a job! This tune changed when the staphylococcus problem reared its ugly head. The cry for more and better trained microbiologists was heard from coast to coast.

Indiscriminate use of prophylactic "shots" of antibiotics tended to become a substitute for basic cleanliness and bacteriologic common sense. The unsuspecting patients were the victims of this folly, and frequently the shadow of death crept over the bassinets in some of our hospital nurseries where particularly susceptible newborn infants paid with their lives. This period of relative letdown in the practice of strict aseptic technique represents one of the gray periods in the history of medicine. Although it was a bitter lesson to learn, the shock has had a salutary effect in that it has prompted a dramatic revival of microbe-consciousness among all hospital personnel.

The classical picture of an operating room (O.R.) populated with gowned, hooded, and masked individuals is the zenith of asepsis and disinfection. Few laymen fully appreciate the long chain of preparatory events leading up to that moment when the patient is rolled into the inner sanctum of the O.R.

Medicine has made great strides forward in the last hundred years in its attempt to prevent microorganisms from gaining access to the exposed vital organs once the outer protective barrier of relatively resistant skin and body wall has been breached by the surgeon's scalpel. Prior to the discoveries of Lister it was not uncommon for a physician garbed in his long black frock coat to carry the tools of his profession in his dirty pocket. Operations bordered on the gruesome. A person unfortunate enough to require an amputation before the era of anesthetics might be tied down or physically restrained by individuals with powerful muscles and with stomachs strong enough to hold out against the gory sight amidst the piercing screams as the surgeon hacked away at the afflicted limb with a dirty, perhaps even rusty, saw! Man has come a long way since those primitive days in medicine, and some of the procedures that have evolved for insuring asepsis and sterility will be discussed in this chapter.

There are many techniques for freeing materials of living organisms. Some procedures, as will be pointed out, fall far short of the objective of bacteriological sterility. These procedures are known as **sanitizing,** or making objects safe for selected use in which the presence of low numbers of non-disease-producing organisms is permissible. Each method in the following outline will be considered from the standpoint of applicability to nursing practice.

1. Dry heat
   a. Incineration
   b. Hot air

2. Moist heat
   a. Pasteurization
   b. Boiling
   c. Live steam
      i. Flowing
      ii. Intermittent
      iii. Under pressure

3. Filtration
   a. Seitz filter
   b. Chamberland filter
   c. Berkefeld filter
   d. Sintered glass filter
   e. Collodion membrane

4. Gases

Before discussing each of the above techniques a few words about the two principal scales employed for expressing temperatures seems in order.

Whenever a temperature is given, it is important to indicate whether the figure is in terms of Fahrenheit or centigrade. Gabriel Fahrenheit invented the first accurate thermometer in 1714, and in the United States temperatures are expressed in terms of this scale. In many other countries and throughout the scientific world, however, it is customary to use the centigrade scale.

The freezing point on the centigrade scale is 0 degrees, whereas on the Fahrenheit scale it is 32 degrees; the boiling points are 100° and 212°, respectively. Anyone engaged in scientific work should be able to convert temperature from one scale to the other, and there are a number of suggested methods for such calculations, one of which will be found in the Appendix (p. 433). Your instructor may introduce you to other equally reliable schemes.

Dry Heat

Incineration

Bacteriologists generally employ straight needles or wires fashioned into loops for transferring microorganisms from one tube or culture dish to another. The wire may be platinum, but more frequently less expensive material such as nichrome wire is used. These metals stand up well under repeated flaming and cooling and they possess the added attribute that they heat and cool rather quickly. A few seconds of exposure in a flame will incinerate all material on the wire.

A number of materials with which a nurse deals in her daily practice can best be disposed of by burning. Although used cotton swabs, applicator sticks, tongue depressors, soiled dressings, sputum cups, sanitary tissues, etc., can be treated by other techniques, these items are expendable and burning is certainly one of the easiest, cleanest, and most reliable means for sterilizing and disposing of them with utmost safety.

Hot Air

When heat is applied to cells coagulation and eventual death of the cells will occur. However the speed of this reaction bears a relationship not only to temperature, but also to the amount of moisture present, as is shown in Table 3.

Certain substances do not lend themselves well to sterilization by moist heat either because they change their physical or chemical characteristics, or because the moisture is unable to mix with the materials being treated. Oils and greases fall into the latter category. Glassware, including pipettes and petri dishes, should not be wet after sterilization, and hence dry heat in an oven is advocated for their treatment.

TABLE 3
Coagulation of Egg Albumin

Per Cent Water Present	Coagulation Point, Degrees Centigrade
50	56
25	74–80
18	80–90
6	145
0	160–170

Dry heat has less penetrating power than moist heat, and oven temperatures may be somewhat more difficult to control throughout the sterilizer. This combination of poor penetrating power and lack of moisture demands that dry sterilization be carried out for a longer period and at a higher temperature than is true for steam heat. In general it takes at least one hour and a minimum temperature of 160°C to accomplish sterilization in a hot air oven. The bulk being treated and the nature of the material being sterilized will determine exposure periods. Table 4 lists a few representative materials used in nursing and in medical practice that should be treated with dry heat.

TABLE 4
Hot Air Sterilization

Material	Exposure Time in Minutes at 160°C (320°F)
Glassware	60
Glycerine–1 oz.	120
Instruments (cutting edge)	60
Needles (hypodermic)	120
Oils, mineral	120
Petrolatum	120
Petroleum jelly–1 oz.	120
Powders	150
Syringes (wrapped)	60
Vaseline gauze–4 oz.	150

An improper understanding of the stringent requirements of dry heat sterilization for certain types of material has, unfortunately, been the cause of some needless infections in patients. Vaseline gauze, for example, is probably still being "sterilized" in an autoclave in some hospitals. Since petroleum jelly is very low in its moisture content, there is little opportunity for coagulation of bacterial protein to occur in the core of such material, with the result that the product is virtually being subjected to dry heat at 121°C for about fifteen minutes. This type of treatment is practically worthless and gives the unwary user a false sense of security.

Another fact not always appreciated is the length of time required for dry heat to penetrate a substance like petroleum jelly or mineral oil. If vaseline is spread out in a one-fourth-inch layer, it will require about 65 minutes for the entire mass to reach 160°C, the minimum temperature necessary for hot air sterilization. A one-ounce jar will take 110 minutes and a four-ounce quantity, 165 minutes to attain minimum sterilizing temperature. The exposure period of at least one hour must be added to these time periods to insure sterility.

Vaseline gauze, unless adequately treated with heat, could conceivably do the patient more harm than good. Some physicians prefer this type of covering for burn cases, whereas others deplore the use of any greasy type of bandage. Since severe burns are susceptible to infections even when aseptic techniques are practiced, the use of contaminated vaseline could initiate inexcusable microbial complications during the period when normal convalescence should be under way.

The amount of vaseline gauze packed in trays to be sterilized should not be over twenty layers thick, according to experimental findings, and it should be covered with about four ounces of previously liquefied vaseline. Such a preparation in the usual type of tray employed for the purpose will not exceed one-half inch in depth, and the oven treatment should extend for about 150 minutes *after the material has attained a sterilizing temperature of 160°C*. About 80 minutes are required for such a volume to reach this temperature.

Moist Heat

Pasteurization

When Louis Pasteur originally applied his technique of selective heating, he did it to destroy undesirable organisms that were causing spoilage of French wines. Pasteurization today, however, is designed primarily for making milk, dairy products, and other foods *safe* for human consumption. Improved keeping quality, although a valuable adjunct, is a purely secondary consideration. Foods are pasteurized at temperatures considerably below that of boiling, and since the object of this treatment is not to sterilize the food, the time and temperature relationships are based upon extensive studies aimed at determining the minimum time and heat combination required for a reasonable margin of safety for each material.

Each microbe has its own **thermal death point** (T.D.P.) which may be defined as the lowest temperature that will kill a 24-hour-old broth culture of the organism in ten minutes. Since bacteria do not all die at the same time, owing to differences in heat resistance, there is also a **thermal death time** (T.D.T.) which is the number of minutes required for a given temperature to inactivate every living cell in a given volume of medium. Such factors as moisture, pH, composition of the medium, and the bulk being tested all influence this thermal action, and it becomes necessary to indicate all of these points when expressing T.D.T. for a given organism.

Until relatively recently pasteurization of milk was generally carried out by a **holding method.** The milk was heated to 145°F (62.7°C) for 30 minutes, and then rapidly cooled to below 50°F (10°C). In a plant engaged in the processing of large volumes of milk this procedure requires a tremendous amount of valuable floor space, to say nothing of the expensive holding tanks needed to maintain the product at the pasteurizing temperature for the stated time interval.

To overcome these disadvantages the **short-time high-temperature** technique was developed. In this process the fluid is held at 160°F (71°C) for from 15 to 17 seconds, and rapidly cooled to below 50°F. The heating can be accomplished by passing the milk through a series of coils having a diameter such that a pump of known speed and capacity can keep the fluid moving through the pipes at the proper rate of flow to insure the correct time exposure at the prescribed temperature.

The basis of pasteurization time and temperature employed in a dairy plant is the resistance of *Mycobacterium tuberculosis*. This organism is the most resistant pathogen one might conceivably find in milk. When properly carried out, modern pasteurization methods make foods safe for human consumption. It should be borne in mind, however, that this selective heating does not *sterilize* the food; resistant spores in some species of organisms and even some non-spore-forming bacteria can withstand heating at temperatures up to boiling.

Much has been written concerning the decrease in food value of milk as the result of pasteurization. Without delving into all of the classical arguments about this assertion, we can say that vitamin C is destroyed by this heating process. However, since even raw milk is naturally low in this particular vitamin (one reason why milk is called nature's *most nearly* perfect food), the majority of bacteriologists seem to be of the opinion that it is better to inactivate what little vitamin C exists in raw milk and to supply children with extra citrous juice or vitamin C in their diet, than it is to feed raw milk that *might* contain virulent organisms. The unfortunate fact remains that just looking at a glass of milk is not going to tell you whether pathogens are present. A spoiled apple is readily detected on top of a barrel of fresh fruit and can be discarded, but a microscopic organism which may be packing a lethal punch eludes such macroscopic detection.

The advantages of pasteurized or of raw milk can be debated at length; it makes an excellent topic for classroom discussion. But to a bacteriologist engaged in endeavors that relate to the health of the public, the presence of even one case of a preventable disease is important. That little number in the table of statistics, while perhaps not significant to a mathematician, takes on tremendous importance if the case happens to be *you!*

It is of historical interest to mention at this point that passing electricity through milk to pasteurize it has been tried, but the technique is rarely, if ever, used today. It is not the electrocution of the microbes that causes the lowered bacterial count, but rather the heat generated in the medium that is responsible for the lethal effect.

Boiling

The bubbling action that occurs when fluids are heated takes place at different temperatures depending upon the altitude above sea level. The higher the altitude the less atmospheric pressure is being exerted upon the surface of the fluid, and "boiling" occurs at a lower temperature. It becomes important, therefore, to stipulate the actual temperature at which this bubbling takes place if the word "boiling" is to have scientific meaning. Table 5 lists the boiling point of water at a few representative locations throughout the United States. When people move from an area near sea level to one that is a mile or more above sea level they soon discover that potatoes, for example, will not cook in twenty minutes but may require up to double that time because boiling occurs at such a relatively low temperature.

TABLE 5

Relationship of Altitude to Boiling Point of Water

		Boiling Point of Water	
	Elevation	Degrees C	Degrees F
Sea level	0	100.0	212.0
Denver, Colorado	5280	94.3	201.7
Tahoe, Nevada	10,000	89.1	192.4
Pikes Peak	14,109	87.0	187.0

It is not the bubbling action associated with boiling that is important; it is the temperature created before the water "blows its top" that determines microbe-killing potential. It is possible to lower the boiling point of water under controlled conditions by subjecting the contents of a container to partial vacuum. This technique has practical industrial applications, for example, in the concentration of fruit juices where moisture removal is desired without employing a high temperature that might alter or inactivate the substance being concentrated.

To most laymen boiling is practically synonymous with sterilization. We know that some heat-resistant spores can withstand boiling at 100°C for periods up to five hours. Hence, boiling a baby's bottle to "sterilize" it may sanitize the article and make it safe for use, but in the bacteriological sense the bottle is not necessarily free of living organisms and is therefore not sterile. In many instances this type of heat treatment may suffice, but in surgery something next to the best is not good enough.

In the absence of a hot air oven or an autoclave, the killing action of boiling water may be increased by the addition of 2 per cent sodium carbonate. This technique is advocated for sanitizing instruments, in a dentist's office, for example. Some of the so-called "antiseptic solutions" employed by some dentists leave much to be desired. Bacteriological tests have revealed the relative ineffectiveness of some of these compounds, and dentists should be alerted to the possible spread of oral organisms, many of which may be potential pathogens, from one individual to another when instruments have been inadequately treated. This problem, as it applies to dental practice, needs more study; in the meantime, controlled heat is the best means for treating dental instruments.

Educated people are supposed to think for themselves. More of us should be asking ourselves, our physicians, and our dentists if some of the techniques being practiced in medicine and allied fields are not outmoded in the light of present-day knowledge. The hocus-pocus, for example, of wiping off the skin with that "magic" 70 per cent alcohol prior to injections is more *show* than *effect*—but more about this in a later chapter.

In short, boiling should be employed for sanitizing only when more effective methods for reliable sterilization are not feasible. Because there is no easy short-cut method available for detecting the presence of thermostable spores, it must always be assumed that these resistant bodies are present, and materials must be treated accordingly.

Live Steam

Live steam has a temperature of 100°C and its ability to sterilize must be examined in the same light as boiling, since flowing steam possesses the same limitations with respect to the killing of spores.

FLOWING AND INTERMITTENT

It is possible to sterilize some thermolabile fluids that cannot withstand the relatively high temperature of autoclaving by a process known as **Tyndallization** if the heat is applied intermittently with periods of incubation between heat treatments. Many spores will germinate into vegetative cells during these alternate incubation periods, and such vegetative cells are relatively susceptible to the temperatures of flowing steam. In general this intermittent heat treatment extended over a three-day period will result in sterilization, but there are definite limitations to its use. In addition to the prolonged time factor, changes in the medium being treated may occur during the intervening incubation periods when the residual spores are being permitted to germinate.

STEAM UNDER PRESSURE

When steam is allowed to enter a container, the temperature will increase at a predictable rate as pressure (expressed as pounds per square inch) is increased.

Moist heat under pressure is particularly destructive to bacteria and other microorganisms. An **autoclave** is generally used in this form of sterilization. Small volumes of material can be sterilized by being subjected to 15 pounds of steam pressure for a minimum of 15 minutes. As can be seen in Table 6, such a pressure raises the temperature of moist heat to approximately 121.5°C. The exposure time required for sterilizing items is directly related to the bulk and the physical makeup of the material. Considerable research has been conducted on sterilization by steam under pressure, and Table 7 summarizes the recommended exposure times for representative substances encountered in nursing practice.

TABLE 6

Relationship Between Steam Pressure and Temperature

Steam Pressure Lb per Sq In.	Approximate Temperature	
	Degrees C	Degrees F
0	100.0	212.0
5	109.0	228.0
10	115.5	240.0
15	121.5	250.5
20	126.5	259.5
30	134.5	275.0
40	141.5	287.0

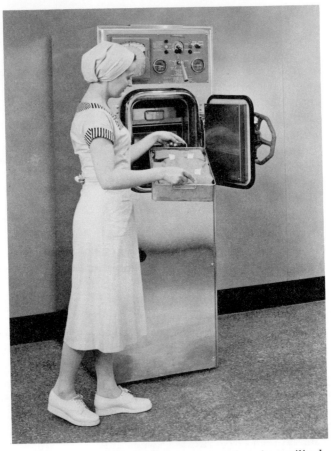

FIG. 5.2.   Tray of wrapped instruments ready to be sterilized.
(Courtesy American Sterilizer Company, Erie, Pa.)

In installations where autoclaving is carried out at 20 pounds of steam pressure, exposure times may be less than those listed in Table 7.

Each hospital sets up its own standard operating procedures for preparing various packs and materials to be used in surgery. The individual in charge of surgical supply is charged with the responsibility for having sufficient quantities of sterile materials on hand for all emergencies as well as for routine uses. It is unwise to build up large stockpiles too far in advance, however, because resterilizing is necessary when the agreed storage time period has expired. The length of storage before resterilization is recommended varies from hospital to hospital, but muslin-wrapped packs are generally resterilized once every two weeks. Dating

TABLE 7

Recommended Exposure Time for Materials to Be Sterilized in an Autoclave

Article	Exposure Time in Minutes at 15 Pounds Steam Pressure (121.5°C)
Catheters (latex, woven base)	15
Cystoscopes (Kirwin type)	15
Diapers	30
Drains (rubber tubing)	20
Rubber gloves	15
Instruments (routine)	15
Intravenous sets	30
Jars, dressing (loosely packed)	30
Maternity packs	30
Mattresses (hair) and foam rubber	30
Rubber tubing	20
Scalpel blades	30
Solutions (aqueous) in pyrex flasks	
125 ml	15
200 ml	15
500 ml	20
1000 ml	25
2000 ml	35
Serum bottle–9000 ml	55
Milk dilution bottle	15
Surgical packs	30
Sutures (boilable tubes)	15
Syringes (unassembled)	30
Tongue depressors	30
Transfusion sets	30
Trays (all kinds)	30
Utensils	15

of each pack, usually in pencil on each covering, is very important. Storage of sterilized materials in relatively dust-free and dry cabinets is imperative.

Proper preparation of packs to be autoclaved cannot be overemphasized. It is a science in itself. Tie cords are preferable to safety pins which may tear the fabric and present a potential hazard for contamination. Not only must the items be arranged in a logical order for efficient removal when used in the O.R., but the technique of spacing is vital if proper circulation of steam is to be assured within the pack. Basins and utensils should not be placed in the same bundle with textiles, since the metals may trap air and result in insufficient heating throughout the pack. Effective drying after sterilization may also be impeded by basins within a pack. It is not improper to sterilize these solid metal objects in the same autoclave load as fabrics, but they should be wrapped in separate bundles. Lighter materials should be placed in the core of the pack where steam penetrates last.

There are accepted steps in the operation of an autoclave which should be followed if the apparatus is to perform efficiently and effectively.

1. Don't pack objects too close together in the autoclave. Arrange items in such a manner that they will afford the least possible resistance to the incoming steam.

2. Don't make packs too large or too tight; otherwise, uniform penetration of steam will not take place.

3. Choose a covering for the packs that possesses a porosity that will serve the specific needs of the material being sterilized. A covering that is too tight may not allow adequate penetration of the steam, whereas fabrics that are too loosely woven may not retain sterility of the contents when the pack is removed from the autoclave and stored for future use.

4. Remove as much trapped air from the autoclave as possible before closing the outlet valve to build up the required pressure. Bear in mind that it is the *temperature,* not the *pressure,* that does the sterilizing. Fifteen pounds of cold air trapped in an autoclave will sterilize nothing.

5. Before setting the clock to time the exposure period, check the thermometers, both at the inlet and at the outlet of the autoclave, to insure that the required sterilizing temperature zone has been reached. Refer to appropriate tables provided by the manufacturer to determine how long the pressure should be maintained for a given type of material to be sterilized.

When a cross-sectional diagram of an autoclave is examined (see Fig. 3.4), it will be seen that the steam passes through a pressure regulator which is, as a rule, automatically set to deliver between 15 and 20 pounds of pressure per square inch. Cracking the main inlet valve to control the flow of steam becomes unnecessary, and the operator can turn the valve until it is wide open. As the steam leaves the reducing valve it enters the outer jacket of the sterilizer at the top rear of the chamber. Since steam density is only about one-half that of air, the steam tends to gravitate toward the top. As the volume builds up, it forces the colder air out of the chamber at the discharge point located in the lower front bottom of the autoclave.

The screen that covers this discharge vent must be cleaned regularly, preferably daily in a hospital where the equipment gets constant use.

This cleaning will insure free flow of the steam. Failure to keep the plug screen clean could result in cold air being trapped in the chamber, and the required temperature might never be attained. With one-third of the air trapped in the autoclave, for example, the temperature would reach only 240°F (115.5°C), which is insufficient to accomplish sterilization in the usual exposure period.

An understanding of the enormous pressure that can build up behind a locked autoclave door will help the operator to respect the construction that goes into the manufacture of a steam sterilizer. With 15 pounds per square inch on an autoclave door having a diameter of 20 inches, the total pressure within the machine amounts to several tons! Safety mechanisms are, therefore, incorporated into the doors to prevent their being opened so long as there is pressure within the sterilizer. This safety feature is designed to protect absent-minded operators or uninformed individuals from their own errors.

Although various types of paper and plastic materials are being tested as wrappers for surgical packs, a double thickness of muslin probably is still the most popular material in use today. Muslin is easy to work with, is an efficient dust filter, and yet is sufficiently porous to allow ready access to steam during autoclaving. Bear in mind that microbes cannot walk on dry surfaces; they can only swim or be carried by the tide. The wrapping, therefore, must be made of a material that will dry quickly after the pack is removed from the sterilizer. As the trapped steam condenses within the pack, it creates a vacuum, and the suction thus created may be sufficiently great to draw in contaminating organisms unless efficient covers are used on the packs.

When the sterilizing period is completed, drying of the packs can be carried out in at least two accepted ways. If the door is "cracked" after the pressure has dropped, the moisture will gradually leave the material as it sits in the warm chamber. Removing the pack immediately after sterilization and placing it on a relatively cool metal surface will cause condensation of water under the wrapping, and this could eventually lead to contamination of the contents. Loss of about 65 per cent of the moisture in a 12-pound pack has been found to take place in about 30 minutes by the "cracked door" technique, but one disadvantage is that the moisture is released into the room.

A better technique, and one more commonly employed with modern machines, is to apply negative pressure (a vacuum) to the sterilizer at the conclusion of the heating period. This draws off the steam from the chamber and from the pack without having it expelled into the room. Operating instructions are supplied by the manufacturer for autoclaves equipped for this type of suction, and directions should be followed to the letter for best results.

Rubber gloves come in such intimate contact with the patient that it is of paramount importance that extra attention be devoted to their cleaning, wrapping, and sterilizing. Since blood, both moist and dried, will be found on gloves after an operation, it is necessary that the gloves first be rinsed thoroughly with *cold* water, followed by a good washing in *warm* water. A mild detergent applied gently with a brush will help to remove dried organic matter. Leaks, even minute ones, cannot be tolerated in surgical gloves; hence every glove should be subjected to close

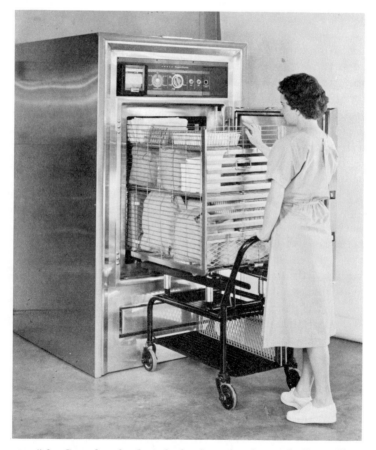

FIG. 5.3. Complete load ready for insertion into a bulk sterilizer. (Courtesy American Sterilizer Company, Erie, Pa.)

scrutiny by being blown up and tested for leaks under water before it is dried in preparation for future use. Any gloves showing leaks of any kind must be discarded from surgery, but they might find use in other departments of the hospital—as protection for the hands of dishwashers during the washing of laboratory glassware, for example.

Talcum is gradually being abandoned in favor of starch-containing compounds for powdering gloves. The powders are used primarily to make it easier for the surgeon to slip on the gloves. Talcum may prove irritating to tissues, whereas the starch compounds have less of a tendency to irritate; in addition, they are somewhat moisture-absorbing, according to some surgeons.

The dead ends in the fingers of gloves may trap air and interfere with proper sterilization unless great care is exercised in preparing them for autoclaving. The wrist part should be folded over the palm with a piece of gauze or muslin inserted to separate the two surfaces. Another piece of gauze should be placed inside of the glove deep enough to reach the opening to the fingers and the thumb. This will tend to keep the gloves open during the sterilizing process and will minimize the possibility of dead air spaces in the fingers. A tray containing about a dozen of these setups can be sterilized as shown in Fig. 5.3. The gloves can then be stored in billfold-type covers.

Filtration

Some fluids are materially altered in their physical or chemical composition when subjected to heat. Proteins, such as egg albumin, blood serum, and plasma, congeal as the temperature approaches 60°C. Certain disaccharides and polysaccharides break down into their simpler components when they are heated at the usual sterilizing temperatures. Freeing such fluids of organisms requires, therefore, some technique other than heat, and various types of filters have been developed for this purpose. Some of these filters are purely mechanical sieves designed to physically remove all organisms from fluids.

Since bacteria carry a negative electrical charge, it is possible to manufacture filters composed of positively charged materials which tend to attract the organisms to the walls of the pores as fluid is drawn through the filter. Even though the pore size of the filter is larger than some microorganisms, the attraction caused by differences in electrical charges results in the removal of the microbes. Filters also are employed for the separation of toxins and other metabolic products from the bacterial cultures which produced them.

Seitz Filter

When shredded asbestos is tightly compressed under great pressure, a Seitz filter pad is produced. These pads are clamped into special metal devices and the entire unit is autoclaved after the metal holder has been inserted into the neck of a flask equipped with a side arm. If suction is applied to the flask or positive pressure to a special valve on top of the filter, fluids can be drawn through the asbestos pad and collected in the sterile flask. Electrical charge differences are not operative in a Seitz filter; it effects a purely mechanical removal of the microorganisms. A differential of not over 150–200 mm of mercury is advocated for encouraging filtration without sacrificing dependability. Pressure, if too extreme, may draw the bacteria through the filter and nullify the action of the pads.

Chamberland Filter

Chamberland filters are also known as Pasteur-Chamberland candles. They are composed of unglazed porcelain varying in porosity and fashioned into the shape of a candle or a hollow porous cylinder closed at one end. These candles are fitted through metal and rubber connections into the neck of a suction flask to which vacuum can be applied to draw fluids through the honeycombed porcelain. Care must be used to ensure that these filters are not handled in a manner that will allow them to become cracked; if they are, bacteria and other organisms may find their way into the filtrate. Since bacteria normally carry a negative electrical charge and the Chamberland filter carries a positive charge, filtration action is enhanced.

Berkefeld Filter

When **infusorial (diatomaceous)** earth, obtained from the ground silica-like bodies of algae, is mixed with graded sizes of carbon, fashioned into the shape of candles similar to the Chamberland filter, and fired at a high temperature in a furnace, the carbon particles are burned out, leaving pores of a known diameter. Three usual grades of porosity may be obtained. These are known as V (German *viel,* coarse), N (normal), and W (German *wenig,* fine). Keeping Berkefeld filters clean requires special care, but when they are clean the mean pore sizes are about 3 or 4 microns in diameter. Heating the filters before they are properly cleaned can plug the pores and reduce their filtering power to uneconomical levels. If clear water is run through them immediately after use, followed by a 0.5 per cent solution of potassium permanganate, then a 5 per cent sodium bisulfite solution, and a final rinse with cold water for a few minutes, Berkefeld filters can be maintained in reliable working order.

Sintered (Frittered) Glass Filters

Until relatively recently reliable sintered glass filters were made almost exclusively in Germany from Jena glass, but American manufacturers are now producing excellent filters of this type.

FIG. 5.4. Sintered glass filter. (Courtesy Corning Glass Works, Corning, N. Y.)

Special glass is finely powdered, placed into molds, and heated in an oven just hot enough to permit the glass particles to adhere to each other without flowing together into a solid mass. The technique of accomplishing this is highly specialized. The final porosity of the filter discs so prepared is directly related to the size of the glass particles employed in manufacture coupled with the degree of heating employed. A well-made sintered glass filter is very reliable for filtering organisms out of solution or for the separation of metabolic products, such as toxins, from the organisms that produced them. By drawing sulfuric acid containing 1 per cent sodium nitrate through the filter, effective cleaning can be accomplished. Since dichromate cleaning fluid tends to become adsorbed on the glass, it is not wise to use this material on sintered glass filters, even though copious quantities of water are run through after the cleaning operation.

Collodion Membrane Filters

Filters with pore sizes as small as 0.005 micron can be made from such materials as collodion or cellulose acetate, the pore size being controlled by the combinations of solvents used in their manufacture. Such filters are generally prepared as discs that will fit on a perforated base that slips into an apparatus to which suction or pressure can be applied. Highly technical research projects may employ such filters for studying the diameter of particles in a given medium. These pads must be sterilized prior to use by modified heating techniques or by the application of some of the newer germicidal gases.

Sterilization with Gases

One of the most promising recent developments in the field of sterilization has been the introduction of powerful germicidal gases for the treatment of materials that otherwise are adversely affected, either chemically or physically, by dry or by moist heat. The use of such gases is essentially the application of chemical warfare techniques against microbes.

A relatively simple organic compound, **ethylene oxide** (C_2H_4O), that vaporizes rapidly above 10.8°C (51.4°F), freezes at minus 111.3°C, and displays considerable sterilizing power at room temperature in a relative humidity of about 35 per cent, has opened a new approach to the problem of sterilizing heat-labile substances. Because ethylene oxide is extremely flammable in a concentration as low as 3 per cent in air, it is generally blended with up to 90 per cent carbon dioxide which yields a commercial product marketed as **carboxide.** Freons (fluorinated hydrocarbons) may be used to produce nonflammable mixtures with ethylene oxide. The cost of sterilization by this germicidal gas is still higher per unit volume of material than that for conventional steam or hot air, but the absence of damage to the treated material tends to offset the economic disadvantage.

Germicidal gases will undoubtedly gain favor as means of sterilizing heat-sensitive materials in our hospitals. Some of the advantages of ethylene oxide are that it is

1. bactericidal and not merely bacteriostatic;
2. lethal for all microorganisms;
3. able to penetrate packing material of relatively low permeability;
4. readily removed by aeration and hence leaves little residual (one exception is thick rubber tubing that has been found to retain the gas for several hours);
5. effective at room temperature (about 70°F);
6. active at relatively low humidity levels of about 35 per cent;
7. not damaging to more than a few materials;
8. commercially available in quantity.

As is true with all known germicides, ethylene oxide has certain disadvantages which should be enumerated:

1. it is costly in comparison to steam and hot air;
2. it is flammable unless diluted with carbon dioxide or freon;
3. the killing action is slower than with other techniques;
4. the special equipment required for its use under controlled conditions adds to the initial cost of the gas.

Sterilization of sutures, catheters, and various instruments employed in the medical, nursing, and dental professions is commonly carried out with liquid germicides. However, as we mentioned with respect to dental instruments, this type of treatment is all too often ineffective, since sterilization means the *absence of life*. There can be no compromise with this meaning in medical practice.

Sanitizing of bedding, including pillows, mattresses, and blankets, has received increased attention by our hospitals and institutions in recent years as a direct result of the serious problems created by the development of increasing numbers of antibiotic-resistant microorganisms. The spectre of staphylococcus infections, particularly in hospital nurseries, is ever-present. An intensive study and re-evaluation of common hospital practices presently under way may result in the formulation of specific recommendations for gas sterilization of bedding on a practical scale.

Sterility Indicators

Although the only true measure of sterility is a bacteriological test, ingenious indicators have been developed to indicate whether the proper temperature–time exposure has been carried out. If these techniques are used wisely and their limitations appreciated, they have a definite use in the intelligent operation of a central sterile supply department of a hospital. The underlying principles of these indicators vary somewhat, but one common procedure is to place a chemical having a known melting point into an ampoule that can be inserted in the core of a batch of material to be autoclaved. If the chemical has melted (or changed color, as may be the case with some test substances), it can be assumed that a prescribed minimum temperature had been attained for at least a known minimum time period.

Pure sulfur, for example, melts at 248°F (120°C) in from nine to eleven minutes. Since fifteen pounds of steam pressure will yield a temperature very close to this figure, the operator has evidence that the live steam had penetrated to the core of the pack for at least nine minutes. With an increase in temperature the time required for melting sulfur decreases, but as the temperature drops below 248°F a materially longer exposure time period is required to melt this pure element. These temperature and time relationships are indicated in Table 8.

TABLE 8

Melting Time and Temperature of Pure Sulfur

Temperature		Melting Time
Degrees F.	Degrees C.	Minutes
244	118	70–85
246	119	27–35
248	120	9–11
250	121	2.8–3.2
253	123	1.5–1.7

As has been pointed out, the coolest point in the autoclave is near the front bottom of the chamber. An indicator placed within a bundle located at this point in the sterilizer should certainly supply useful information to the individual operating the autoclave. However, regular exhaustive bacteriological sterility checks must be conducted as part of the routine efficiency check on the operation of any system.

Another commonly used technique for testing the efficiency of a sterilizer is to place selected heat-resistant spore-forming cultures of bacilli in strategic locations within different bundles of materials being treated with steam. By subculturing adequate samples of these test cultures into a suitable medium, such as thioglycollate broth which supports growth of aerobes as well as anaerobes, absence of growth in the medium after a minimum incubation period of 72 hours indicates that the autoclave is functioning properly.

Review Questions

1. Differentiate between asepsis, disinfection, and sterilization.
2. If an antibiotic retards or interferes with the growth of an organism, why isn't an antiseptic an antibiotic?
3. What determines whether a substance or material should be sterilized by moist heat or by dry heat?
4. Convert 121°C into Fahrenheit.
5. What determines the minimum time and temperature for pasteurization of a food product?
6. Review the underlying principles of preparing surgical packs for sterilization.
7. Is there any material advantage in using a filter that is positively charged for sterilizing small volumes of fluid?
8. What applications to hospital practice might ethylene oxide eventually have?

6 CONTROL OF MICROORGANISMS BY CHEMICAL METHODS

HEALTH MAY BE DEFINED AS THE COMPLETE HARMONY BETWEEN an individual and his environment. From this definition it becomes clear that workers engaged in fields dealing with the mind and the body have a direct interest in trying to create or to maintain this harmonious relationship. The control of microorganisms is an important part of this group effort.

If the medium of television has done nothing else, it has through animation and other forms of advertising made millions of people more conscious of the activities of their vital organs and more aware of the microbial populations harbored on the skin, in the mouth, and on the teeth. Radio, newspapers, and magazines have added their voices to this campaign. Whether this is a good thing is debatable. It is difficult to believe that our nation is inhabited by many individuals whose well-being will be jeopardized unless they drink, rub on, or inhale the hundreds of liquids, creams, ointments, and "goos" that flood the market today.

Advertising has mushroomed into a multibillion dollar industry, and its impact on the buying habits of the public cannot be minimized. In her contacts with people a nurse is likely to be asked her opinion as to the merits of a patent medicine or other health product being given the current play in the various advertising media. Self-medication should be discouraged since it can under certain circumstances be a dangerous practice. In cases of doubt on the part of the nurse, patients should be referred to their State Food and Drug Commission or equivalent agency, since this body is delegated the power to deal with advertising claims being made for prescribed groups of products on the market. Like many enforcement agencies, however, consumer protection departments tend to be understaffed, and it becomes difficult for them to keep up in their evaluation of the hundreds of new products flooding our stores each year.

Some of the claims being made today for medicines, cosmetics, etc., are only a steppingstone from those of the medicine man of yesteryear. Today it is on a grand scale, but the "pitch" hasn't changed much. The huckster now reaches millions of potential customers at one time, whereas the medicine man had to be content to stand on the tailgate of his wagon as he extolled the virtues of his questionable nostrums to relatively small groups of people who even in those days flocked to purchase the panacea of the moment. When P. T. Barnum, or Mark Twain, or whoever it was, said that a sucker is born every minute, he wasn't far wrong! In defense of the advertising profession, however, it should be pointed out that not all advertising is objectionable or false. From the chaff a few kernels of truth can be winnowed.

The State of Connecticut has established an Advisory Committee on Foods and Drugs made up of scientists representing the disciplines of medicine, dentistry, veterinary medicine, pharmacy, chemistry, and microbiology. The Committee meets regularly with representatives of state enforcement agencies to discuss suspected false or misleading claims being made for various products. In a general sort of way this volunteer committee serves on a local scale the same function as that served by the American Medical Association Council and similar national groups. The purpose of the Connecticut Committee is to supply state agencies and other groups with a disinterested opinion as to the therapeutic status of various remedies or other preparations that might influence health. Other states have given thought to organizing similar advisory committees patterned after the Connecticut plan. Having served as a member of the pioneer committee since its inception in 1948, the writer highly endorses this approach as one means of attacking the ever-present problem of dealing with questionable claims being made by some manufacturers.

After these introductory remarks, let us consider a few specific chemicals and their modes of action as they relate to the control of microbial populations.

Any force which alters the optimum environment of microbes—whether it be temperature, osmotic pressure, pH, accumulation of wastes, dehydration, or other factors—will probably inhibit the growth of or kill selected microorganisms. Species exhibit a tremendous variation in this respect, and what may be a severe shock to one cell may only make another organism "slightly uncomfortable."

There are a number of instances in nursing practice where the removal or the killing of every living organism (sterilization) may not be required, but inactivation of pathogenic species may be of paramount importance. Techniques employed for control of microbial populations will vary, depending upon the ultimate goal of the treatment.

Bacteriostasis

Dyes

As was pointed out in Chapter 3, it is possible to retard the growth of selected organisms by incorporating into media specific dyes or other chemicals in relatively low concentrations. The addition of too much of the chemical may inhibit the growth of the types of bacteria you are attempting to cultivate, or even cause their death. Since this phase of microbial control was covered earlier, there is no need to repeat the information here.

Osmotic Pressure

Another bacteriostatic effect is produced when organisms are surrounded by high concentrations of sugars or salts, and osmotic pressure forces come into play. Home canning puts this principle to practical use; the process is reliable for the preservation of a number of foods over extended periods of time, if the containers are properly sealed at the conclusion of the heating process. Salting of foods has been practiced for ages, and this bacteriostatic action is particularly important in those areas of the world where refrigeration is limited or nonexistent. Many of those who employ sugar and salt as preservatives may not understand the scientific principles behind the procedure, but experience has taught them that it is a reliable method.

Antibiotics

The introduction of antibiotics has wrought tremendous changes in food technology by lengthening the shelf-life of many foods, e.g., poultry. In the concentrations employed, these antimicrobial agents serve as bacteriostats and thus retard food spoilage. Antibiotics are also incorporated into feeds to speed up growth of the birds and to reduce the time required before they are shipped to market. Some individuals have become concerned about the indiscriminate use of antibiotics in foods to be used for human consumption, and perhaps some of their fears are grounded in fact. Time will tell.

Disinfection

People's definitions, even those of microbiologists, do not agree fully as to the exact meaning of the word **disinfectant.** To some it implies the killing of pathogenic organisms on objects other than the body of man or of lower animals. To other workers in the field the action may apply to any object, animate or inanimate. Most bacteriologists agree in general, however, that disinfectants are aimed primarily at killing disease-producing microbes. Under certain circumstances where all of the micro-organisms in the area are non-spore-bearing and are particularly suscep-tible to the chemical being employed, a disinfectant could conceivably sterilize the area, but such complete destruction of living cells should be considered as the exception rather than the rule.

Antiseptics are frequently weaker in their concentration and in their activity than are disinfectants, and antiseptics are usually considered to prevent an infection by killing the pathogens before their numbers reach the point where visible infection has become established. In other words, an antiseptic might be thought of as an agent which prevents an infection from gaining a foothold, whereas a disinfectant is aimed at destroying the microbes that have already established an infectious process. To some individuals, the two words are synonymous.

Any attempt to control microbial populations by the use of chemicals depends upon a number of variable factors. A substance that might work well in a test tube (*in vitro*) may be completely ineffective or inappropri-ate in the body (*in vivo*) of man or of lower animals. Each object to be treated presents an individual problem, and only by understanding the limitations of specific chemicals can individuals concerned with health put these substances to intelligent use.

The human skin is endowed with a powerful resistance to microbial invasion. However when breaks occur in this protective barrier, no matter how minor they may appear to be, prompt treatment should be given to the cut. This extra care can nip in the bud what could otherwise develop into a serious infection. How often we hear of individuals who develop **septicemia** (blood poisoning) following a minor prick of a finger with a thorn. Prevention takes a bit of extra effort, but not enough people are willing to take this trouble at the moment such action can do the most good.

In the case of deep, dirty wounds, on the other hand, the usual first aid precautions, although helpful, may not be sufficient, and more extensive treatment by a physician is warranted. Depending upon the nature of the wound and the source of the contamination, an injection of tetanus antitoxin may be required to prevent the development of lockjaw (**tetanus**) which is caused by the action of a powerful toxin liberated by the anaerobe *Clostridium tetani*.

There is at present no substance or compound that can be classified as a perfect disinfectant, since all known products possess one or more disadvantages.

Criteria for an Ideal Disinfectant

HIGH GERMICIDAL (MICROBICIDAL) POWER

All conceivable combinations of microorganisms might be encountered in a given situation. Wounds are not contaminated with a pure culture of a microbe except in very unusual circumstances. Therefore the germicide should possess a wide spectrum of activity. "Germ" is used here in its broadest sense to include all types of microbes, not just bacteria. The compound should be strong enough in the concentration recommended for its use to allow for some dilution without marked reduction in the killing power of the solution.

SOLUBLE IN A NUMBER OF FLUIDS

If the compound is to be effective in the destruction of microorganisms, it must be able to dissolve with ease not only in the universal solvent, water, but also in body fluids. When a disinfectant is applied to a wound, the blood and tissue fluids found in the area should be able to accept the chemical and allow it to be diffused throughout the entire wound.

PENETRATING POWER

This characteristic is related to both solubility and surface tension. Since microorganisms can penetrate deep into damaged tissues, the disinfectant should be able to follow them. Once the chemical comes in contact with the organisms, penetration into the cell proper is essential if killing is to be accomplished.

Much of the lethal potential of disinfectants lies in their ability to disrupt the colloidal balance existing within the protoplasm of the cell. By having a low surface tension, a chemical is better able to penetrate materials and it is for this reason that many effective compounds are dissolved in alcohol (a tincture) which has a relatively low surface tension. When the chemical is dissolved in water, this is known as an *aqueous solution*.

HOMOGENEITY

Any product bearing the caution: "Shake well before using" is of limited value as a disinfectant for use by the general public whose concept of "shaking well" varies considerably. The label indicates that the active ingredient of the product is not evenly dispersed. It may be in the supernatant or it may have a relatively high specific gravity and fall to the bottom of the liquid. Improper or insufficient agitation of the bottle before use could result in the disinfectant's being much weaker or much stronger than is required to do the job effectively. If the chemical is too powerful when applied to an open wound, it could cause severe damage to healthy tissue, and healing of the wound might be impaired. Or scar tissues could be built up beyond the amount normally expected for a wound of that type and could cause unnecessary disfigurement. Gangrene could even develop in severe cases.

Shaking can be scientifically controlled within limits, and this becomes of the utmost importance when technicians are preparing dilutions for making standard bacterial counts of milk, water, or other fluids. The prescribed technique is to shake the bottle twenty-five times, over a space of one foot, through an arc of ninety degrees, in seven seconds. If all bottles of nonhomogeneous disinfectants were shaken in accordance with these specific directions and the material used immediately, the lack of homogeneity could be minimized. Can you picture thousands of untrained laymen taking the time and the trouble to read such instructions and then carrying them out? Notice the wide variations in your own classes when a group of students are instructed to shake a sample in the specified manner. Compounds can be made homogeneous by being subjected to high frequency sound waves, but this adds one more step in the manufacturing process and some manufacturers are reluctant to do it.

EFFECTIVE AT ROOM TEMPERATURE

It is an established fact that as the temperature is increased, the speed of chemical reactions, including that of disinfectants, can be increased up to a point. Beyond that point the effect of the heat itself brings about a reaction over and beyond that of the chemical being employed as the disinfectant. Under most circumstances it is not practical to heat disinfectants for ordinary use. Compounds designed to kill microorganisms should, therefore, have sufficient activity at ordinary room temperatures to be effective on both inanimate and animate objects.

NO EXCESSIVE AFFINITY FOR EXTRANEOUS ORGANIC MATTER

Microbes are organic and disinfectants naturally should react with them, but some chemicals have such a marked affinity for organic matter that unless large volumes of the disinfectant are applied to an area, the active ingredient may be used up by extraneous organic debris before all of the microbes have been reached.

Chlorine is one such disinfectant that has a strong tie with organic substances, and this point will receive further attention later in this chapter as well as in the discussion of the bacteriology of drinking water. Ideally, a disinfectant should destroy all of the pathogens in a wound; otherwise, the infection might flare up anew and prolong the recovery and repair processes.

NONTOXIC TO MAN OR TO LOWER ANIMALS UNDER THE CONDITIONS OF USE

Many chemicals that are effective in destroying microbes unfortunately may cause severe reactions or even death when taken internally by man. The powerful disinfectant tincture of iodine, for example, is extremely poisonous to humans, and is sometimes swallowed by people with suicidal intent. They may not realize that the suffering that accompanies ingestion of that agent is intense. There are less painful ways to go! A few compounds, including those of cyanide, if applied to an open wound may be absorbed in quantities sufficient to cause highly undesirable systemic reactions. The ideal situation would be for the agent to be toxic to a wide variety of organisms and, at the same time, nonpoisonous when ingested by man and other animals. Such compounds are relatively rare, but chlorine is one agent that can be ingested in the concentration in which it is effective against pathogens in water without producing adverse reactions in man. Most disinfectants, however, are labeled with the symbolic skull and crossbones, and pointed warnings emphasize that the content of the bottle is for external use only.

NONCORROSIVE AND NONSTAINING

The matter of corrosion should be considered from several standpoints. Storage is one. Most corrosive substances can be stored in glass or in lead-lined containers if need be, so this is not a major objection. But the importance of its being noncorrosive lies in the use to which the disinfectant is to be put. For example, the walls, ceiling, floor, equipment, and furniture in an operating room must be washed thoroughly after each operation, and this cleaning process should be followed by treatment of the area with a suitable germicide. Since many items in the O.R. are made of metal, it is highly desirable that corrosion be avoided. As soon as a smooth metal surface has become etched with chemicals, microorganisms are provided with just that many more lodging spots. In addition, the effect on patients of such unsightly metal surfaces should not be minimized.

Deeply colored disinfectants have both advantages and disadvantages. Stains may ruin the appearance of fabrics and pieces of equipment; on the other hand, a colored chemical when applied to a skin surface prior to surgery provides visible evidence that the entire area has been treated with the germicide. Manufacturers will frequently cite this argument in support of their product, and there is some logic in their favor.

DEODORIZING POWER

Although it is probably best to have an odorless compound for use in most situations, offensive odors such as those one might encounter in gangrenous wounds, severe burns, or in excreta, may be masked by the application of a suitable compound. If a disinfectant is to have an odor, it is better that it be pleasant. That "hospital smell" is unnecessary these days, at least in the concentration found in some institutions. A bit more scrubbing will obviate the need for the use of strong-smelling chemicals.

DETERGENT POWER

Cleaning power is a desirable adjunct for a disinfectant if the detergent action can be incorporated without impairing germicidal activity or causing damage to healthy tissues surrounding an open wound.

REASONABLE COST

The price of the disinfecting compound should be within the reach of most individuals if the disinfectant is to be commonly employed for first aid use in homes. When it is packaged in convenient-sized bottles with a capacity of about one ounce and furnished with a convenient applicator, generally a glass rod attached to the screw top, widespread use of an effective germicide can be fostered.

Factors Influencing Disinfection

TEMPERATURE

Disinfection is a chemical reaction and, as such, it is affected by the same forces that influence any chemical activity. In chemistry we learn that by raising the temperature 10°C we may roughly double the speed of a chemical reaction up to a certain point; beyond that point the rate of increased activity diminishes. Eventually the point is reached where the heat itself is sufficient to coagulate protoplasm and kill the organisms independent of the germicide. It is at room temperature that germicidal action should be strong, since applying warm or hot chemicals to an area may not always be feasible.

TIME

Even the most rapid chemical reaction requires time, and the process of disinfection is no exception. Too often the layman has the mistaken notion that the moment an antiseptic or a germicide is applied, all microbes are killed instantly. Although there are many factors controlling the speed of inactivation of organisms, it is safe to state that under most circumstances an instant is not long enough to accomplish effective disinfection.

Students working in a bacteriology laboratory are cautioned to wash their hands and the table tops with a germicide at the conclusion of each exercise. The added advice to leave the chemical in contact with the skin for a minute or two before washing it off is certainly in order. Unfortunately the quick "lick and a promise" characteristic of small children has a habit of carrying over to college-age youth in numbers that are disturbing to a conscientious microbiology instructor who is giving laboratory instruction with pathogenic organisms. A keen awareness of potential hazards at this stage in the educational career of a prospective nurse can return rich dividends in later clinical experience.

MOISTURE

Water plays a significant function in the killing of microbes. Just as moisture is directly related to the time and the temperature required for heat to kill organisms in an autoclave or in an oven, it is closely correlated with a number of reactions responsible for the destruction of microbes by chemicals. Ethyl alcohol, for example, has been found to be optimum for coagulating protoplasm of organisms when the proportion of alcohol to water is about 70 to 30 by weight. Absolute alcohol (100 per cent) does very little good as far as microbial destruction is concerned if it is employed as a germicide. In fact it is probably fair to say that even the bottle of overworked 70 per cent alcohol used so commonly in medical practice exerts relatively little bactericidal power when it is employed in the usual manner on a skin surface prior to injections. The time factor is generally much too short to be of any material value.

If alcohol is being used merely as an agent to cleanse the skin mechanically, it should be pointed out that there are more efficient agents, including acetone and ether, that can cut the dirt and soil more effectively with the subsequent physical removal of trapped organisms. Although the curve of germicidal activity for ethyl alcohol does reach a peak at a concentration of about 70 per cent, this time-honored compound is overrated from a bacteriological point of view in the opinion of the writer.

HYDROGEN ION CONCENTRATION

Most bacteria thrive best when the pH of their environment is close to neutrality. Any marked deviation from pH 7.0, either on the acid side or on the alkaline side, will tend to work adversely toward microbes. This is one reason why acid foods like tomatoes are relatively easy to preserve. The heat of boiling plus the high acidity provide a very effective combi-

nation for destroying organisms. Marked deviation in pH for disinfectants must be measured in terms of disadvantages (e.g., tissue damage)
that might accrue before manufacturers shift the pH of their products in
anticipation of increasing effectiveness.

CONCENTRATION

It does not necessarily follow that the higher the concentration of a
germicide the more effective will be its killing power. Each agent has its
optimum strength, above and below which some drop-off in activity must
be expected. Bichloride of mercury appears to be most effective when it is
diluted about 1:1000. Tincture of iodine has a useful range for most skin
applications when it is a 2 or 3 per cent solution. Although somewhat
stronger concentrations of selected chemicals may be more destructive to
microbes, similar increase in damage could result in the surrounding
healthy tissue so vitally needed to stimulate repair and healing of a
wound. An examination of a list of commonly used germicides will reveal
the wide range of diversity with respect to recommended concentrations,
and a number of considerations have influenced the judgment of those
who recommend stated strengths for specific uses.

SURFACE TENSION

The matter of surface tension is closely related to penetrating power
which has already been discussed under the characteristics of an ideal
disinfectant; the points need not be repeated here. Suffice it to say that
our more efficient disinfectants are prepared as **tinctures,** and their lower
surface tension directly affects the activity of the compound.

EXTRANEOUS MATTER

Whenever a disinfectant displays an attraction for organic matter, the
degree of this affinity must be considered when deciding which germicide
should be used under a given set of conditions. Chlorine, for example,
is very effective in treating drinking water, but the dirtier the water, the
more chlorine must be added to satisfy the relatively high demands of
organic matter other than the bacteria. A false sense of security can be
created unless the individual realizes that sufficient chlorine must be
added to compensate for this factor. It is for this reason that water passed
through a sand filter is easier to chlorinate, with less deviation in the
final chlorine concentration (expressed as so many PPM, or parts per
million).

The difference between the chlorine concentration that is effective in
destroying pathogenic organisms in drinking water and the amount that
can be detected **organoleptically** is rather small. Pinpoint accuracy with

daily uniformity in chlorine content will result in fewer complaints to the water company by irate citizens. There is always a small minority who have extra sensitive taste buds (the tea taster types), and these individuals can detect even minor variations in chlorine content.

Since the home remedy type of first aid disinfectant is usually applied to minor cuts in which blood and tissue fluids will be present, the compound recommended for use should not be overly active with extraneous matter in the area being treated.

Chemical Reactions Involved in Disinfection

There is much that is not understood about the action of chemicals on microorganisms. It is probably a safe assumption, however, that when a germicide comes in contact with microbes, the actual chemical change responsible for the death of the organisms is not a single reaction but rather a series of changes, the combination of which may eventually result in the death of the cells. Although this discussion will treat these reactions as separate entities, it is well to bear in mind the complexity of chemical disinfection.

The speed and the nature of the final destruction of cells will depend upon whether an organism is an aerobe or an anaerobe, whether it is a spore-former or a vegetative cell, whether it is a pathogen or a saprophyte, plus a host of other variables many of which are not understood. Minor changes in moisture content or in temperature may be sufficient to kill such fastidious pathogens as *Neisseria meningitidis,* the organism responsible for epidemic meningitis. Therefore the action brought about by chemicals cannot be separated from these physical forces on the cells.

COAGULATION

Any agent or process that tends to disrupt the colloidal balance existing within a cell has the potential for killing organisms. If disruption is mild, the affected cells might recover and go on to reproduce themselves. Survival of an organism is correlated with the magnitude of the imbalance imposed upon the cell's protoplasm.

In Chapter 5 it was pointed out that the principal mechanism by which the autoclave and the hot air oven work to destroy organisms is coagulation of the cellular protoplasm. The presence of moisture materially enhances the speed of heat coagulation. Hence the steam sterilizer can accomplish the task at a lower temperature (121°C), and in a shorter time (about 15 minutes for small batches) than is possible for the dry air oven which requires 160–170°C for a minimum of one hour to accomplish the same objective.

Chemical coagulation may also throw microbial protoplasm out of balance when the negatively charged colloidal particles are neutralized by certain metallic ions. The degree of chemical action bears a relationship to the valence and to the atomic weight of the metal. Heavy metals such as copper, silver, iron, and mercury induce considerable activity.

Such organic substances as alcohol, phenol, and formaldehyde are also active in coagulating protein, and whatever destructive effect they may have on microorganisms can be attributed in large measure to this type of a reaction.

OXIDATION

Oxidation is the addition of oxygen or the removal of hydrogen or electrons, and this is harmful to microbes. When hydrogen peroxide (H_2O_2) breaks down into water (H_2O) and nascent oxygen (O), the released oxygen causes oxidation of the cells. Not too many years ago hydrogen peroxide was one of the more common agents found in the family medicine chest, but since its penetrating power is rather limited and its germicidal action is relatively weak, this antiseptic probably is useful only for topical application in skin abrasions where it has ready access to the contaminating microbes. Another oxidizing agent sometimes employed on skin infections is potassium permanganate $(KMnO_4)$.

HYDROLYSIS

An important biological reaction is one brought about when water is added to a molecule, followed by splitting of the molecule at the point of linkage where the water is introduced. This is called **hydrolysis** and is the opposite of condensation. When cells come in contact with hot water or steam, hydrolysis as well as coagulation of the protein takes place.

FORMATION OF SALTS WITH PROTEINS

One of the commonly employed disinfectants in microbiology laboratories is mercuric chloride (bichloride of mercury) in a dilution of 1:1000. The mercury in this case combines with the protoplasm of the organisms and forms a mercury proteinate which interferes with the normal functioning of the cell. When someone swallows mercury, either accidentally or with suicidal intent, one of the first-aid antidotes is to have the victim swallow raw eggs since mercury has a strong affinity for protein. After waiting for a suitable period of time, the patient is induced to vomit by one means or another, and the mercury attached to the egg white is thus removed. The attending physician may want to pump out the patient's stomach as an additional precaution to get rid of any residual mercury, if possible.

This affinity for protein of mercury and certain other substances such as silver nitrate and phenol compounds results in the formation of proteinates which disrupt the metabolic activity of cells. Organisms treated with sublethal doses of mercuric chloride may be "revived" by subculturing the microbes in a suitable medium such as thioglycollate broth which neutralizes the inhibitory effect of the mercury and allows the reprieved organisms to multiply.

LOWERED SURFACE TENSION

Organisms differ markedly in their reactions to changes in surface tension. Resistant cells may display no visible alteration in their structure, whereas sensitive cells like the pneumococcus (*Diplococcus pneumoniae*) actually dissolve in the presence of the bile salts, hexylresorcinol, synthetic detergents, and wetting agents. The tuberculosis organism (*Mycobacterium tuberculosis*) grows as a heavy wrinkled pellicle on the surface of broth media because of the **hydrophobic** (literally, "fear of water") nature of the cells. By the addition of surface tension depressants to the medium it is possible to grow these pathogenic bacteria in the depths of the liquid medium rather than on the surface.

Common Antimicrobial Agents

The market is flooded with all types of chemical agents designed to cure man's ills, prevent disease, or to make him more socially acceptable as he moves about in an aura of sweet-smelling odors concocted to stimulate the senses and to counteract unpleasant odors. The scientific value of many of these nostrums is highly questionable; however, some antimicrobial compounds have withstood the test of time. A discussion of a few of them should provide the student with some basis for individual thought about this important aspect of nursing practice. Simple laboratory experiments are available for evaluating the germicidal power of chemicals, and a few of these accepted techniques will be outlined later.

Alcohol

More faith has been placed in alcohol as an antiseptic or disinfectant than is warranted when we consider the ways in which the medical profession and allied sciences employ it. Alcohols vary in their action on microbes, but alcohol in any concentration cannot be relied upon to sterilize a skin surface even in the absence of spores. (There are those who support the opposite view that alcohol is highly underrated as a disinfectant.)

When a physician is preparing to make an **intradermal** (into the skin), a **subcutaneous** (under the skin), or an **intramuscular** (into the muscle) injection, it is the usual practice to saturate a pledget of cotton with alcohol, take a few rapid swipes at the area to be injected, and then within seconds to introduce the needle. Unfortunately antisepsis and disinfection do not take place in such a short space of time. Some of the dirt and trapped organisms are removed by the sheer mechanical action of the low surface tension alcohol, thus reducing the number of potential microbes available for introduction through the broken skin. Good old soap and water is almost as effective, and acetone and ether are superior as cleansing agents. The tremendous capacity of our bodies to combat microbes is one of the main reasons why relatively few infections develop following hypodermic injections.

Ethyl alcohol is probably the most common form of alcohol used by physicians. Studies reveal that a concentration of about 70 per cent alcohol *by weight* (77% by volume) is the most effective against microbes, but even at this optimum strength the disinfecting power of alcohol is not outstanding. After clinical thermometers are wiped free of organic matter, hospital personnel sometimes soak them in 70 per cent isopropyl alcohol for several hours between uses. The reaction can be enhanced considerably by the addition of 0.5 per cent iodine to the alcohol. Long contact is better than short exposure, but better agents are available for disinfecting thermometers.

Methyl alcohol not only has a lower degree of activity against microbes, but in addition its fumes are especially harmful to the eyes. The use of this chemical as a disinfectant should be discouraged.

Propyl, butyl, and amyl alcohols exhibit more germicidal activity than does ethyl alcohol, with the antimicrobial power correlated with an increase in molecular weight.

Halogens

CHLORINE (Cl)

Chlorine has had an interesting history in the development of microbiology, and it is still one of our better disinfectants when used under specified conditions. It may be employed either as a gas, which is difficult to handle by an inexperienced operator, or it may be used in a number of combinations of both wet and dry compounds.

One of the great advances in public health was the introduction of chlorine for the purification of drinking water. Large water treatment plants prefer to use liquid chlorine rather than compounds of this chemical, since pure chlorine adds no inert matter to the drinking water. Statistics are overwhelming in support of this health measure. Like many other progressive movements in medicine, however, the addition of chlorine to drinking water met with pockets of public resistance, just as fluoridation does today and pasteurization did years ago when it was advocated.

One needs but to study the history of warfare to be impressed by the correlation between a safe supply of drinking water and the improved health of the military. Interestingly enough, World War II was the first American conflict in which more men died from enemy action than from disease. We have made real progress in civilization!

Millions of people today can turn on their faucets and drink the water with complete assurance that the supply is safe. When chlorine is added in sufficient quantity to yield a residual of approximately 0.3 parts per million (PPM) at the tap, the water is rendered free of harmful bacteria and yet is not objectionable to the taste (except, perhaps, to a relatively few individuals who have hypersensitive taste buds). A slight over-chlorination, however, can be detected by almost anyone, and for this reason the sanitary engineer is compelled to control the introduction of the chemical within rather narrow limits.

While it is true that many persons are blessed with supplies of treated water from towns or municipalities, millions of others must rely upon dug wells or drilled wells for their drinking water. Unless these wells are carefully constructed according to specifications developed through experience by sanitary engineers, private water supplies can be a source of disease and misery. When a dug well becomes contaminated by one means or another, and if the cause is corrected, the introduction of chlorine into the well in definite proportions can convert an unfit water supply into one that is potable. Chapter 8 will consider in greater detail water supplies and their chemical treatment.

Swimming pools need not be a source of skin infections or enteric upsets when the water is properly treated with chlorine. The concentration of the chemical must be maintained at a higher level than is true for drinking water. With chlorination, circulating pumps, and efficient sand filters, swimming pools can provide healthful recreation to many whose homes are not near natural bodies of water, and to those who like to swim indoors during the colder months of the year.

When chlorine is added to water, the killing power of the chemical is attributed to the action of hypochlorous acid (HClO) which in turn decomposes into hydrochloric acid (HCl) and nascent oxygen (O). This form of oxygen is very active and cells are killed through oxidation of their protoplasm. Some chlorine may also combine directly with parts of the cell and act as a poison.

The firmness with which the chlorine is bound in combination with other substances will determine in part its effectiveness in destroying microbes. Common table salt, sodium chloride (NaCl), is composed of two powerful poisons, but the chlorine is tightly bound to the sodium and is thus not able to break away and bring about the oxidation necessary for microbial destruction. (Parenthetically it might be stated that sodium chloride in the proportion of one teaspoonful to a cup of warm water is highly recommended by many physicians as a gargle for relief of the symptoms of sore throat. It is as good as many commercial "soothing agents" and is probably better than most of them—to say nothing of its relatively low cost.)

Chloramines are chlorine compounds in which one or more of the hydrogen atoms in an amino group are replaced with chlorine. They have the advantage of being more stable than calcium hypochlorite, which is chlorinated lime, and their relatively slow release of the agent over a period of time is an advantage. Sodium hypochlorite has found extensive use in the dairy industry for the treatment of pipelines, pails, milk cans, and bottles. Restaurants sometimes employ this form of chlorine for rinsing drinking glasses after they have been washed free of organic matter. Chloramines may be used effectively in hospitals for the disinfection of body wastes.

IODINE (I)

One of the old reliable standbys in the household medicine chest is a bottle of tincture of iodine with its traditional poison symbol. It is one of the more effective disinfectants in use today. An occasional individual may display an allergic reaction to iodine—but then, every disinfectant will undoubtedly be found to work adversely on some hypersensitive person.

Iodine possesses a wide spectrum of activity against many types of microorganisms, including certain fungi and viruses. Pure iodine is a bluish-black substance that does not dissolve too readily in water, but is quite soluble in alcohol which also enhances its penetrating power. Two per cent sodium iodide may be combined with 2 per cent iodine in alcohol to increase the germicidal activity.

When initially introduced as a disinfectant, iodine was prepared as a 7 per cent tincture, but this strength was found to be irritating and destructive to healthy tissues around the treated wounds; in some cases more harm than good was accomplished by its use. Today most tinctures of iodine sold across the counter for household use are about 2 or 3 per cent strength.

Iodine appears to combine with protoplasm, and it blocks normal enzymatic activity with the eventual result of death of the cell. Organic mercurials, including merthiolate and metaphen, have replaced iodine in the surgical section of a number of hospitals, and a similar trend appears to be developing in home medicine cabinets.

Iodine is extremely toxic when taken internally, and it should be kept well out of the reach of small children. More than 500 under the age of five die each year in the United States from ingestion of common household poisons ranging from shampoo to shoe polish. These deaths are in addition to the estimated 600,000 annual nonfatal poisonings of youngsters whose digestive tracts are not sufficiently damaged to cause death. Some of these unfortunates might be better off if they were afforded the relief that death would give them.

Proper labeling of poisonous substances with the names of the active ingredients and proper first aid measures could provide physicians with vital information that could save lives and prevent permanent damage to body tissues through the administration of prompt countermeasures. It is impossible for physicians to know the contents of the more than 250,000 different drugs and household products which are potential killers when misused. Even the Poison Information Centers set up in some of our states are kept busy trying to maintain their card files up to date. Parents have a real obligation to stay one jump ahead of their offspring who find attractively shaped bottles and metal containers particularly intriguing.

FLUORINE (Fɪ)

Of the four **halogens** fluorine is chemically the most active, but its use as a disinfectant is definitely limited. Fluorine does have public health significance, however, in the reduction of dental caries. Decayed teeth that are not properly taken care of can serve as foci of infection that could subsequently lead to serious long-range conditions, including rheumatic heart disease.

It was observed some years ago that in areas where fluorides were found as a natural constituent of drinking water, growing children in particular exhibited a decidedly lower incidence of tooth decay than the population of the country as a whole. There are limits within which fluoride concentrations are beneficial, with about 1 PPM being considered optimum by most authorities in the field. Above this level teeth tend to become mottled (stained) but their hardness is noticeably greater than that found in the teeth of persons who consume nonfluoridated water.

It has been shown by controlled experiments that topical application of a 2 per cent sodium fluoride solution to the teeth of young children markedly reduced the amount of decay. Recommendations for the spacing of these applications may vary from one community to another; one series that has been advocated calls for painting the teeth with sodium fluoride at four weekly intervals at the approximate ages of three, seven, ten, and fourteen. When stannous fluoride is used, a single application is recommended for the same age groups, with additional treatments if a child has exceptionally poor teeth. Some physicians prescribe sodium fluoride drops for very young children. These may be put into the child's milk or orange juice for several years.

Although the outer application of chemical may not deter dental caries quite as effectively as ingestion of fluorides in drinking water, the topical application is one means by which the known benefits of this modern public health measure can be made available to persons living in areas where fluorides, either natural or as additives, are not available in drinking water. Each year the number of cities adopting fluoridation of municipal water supplies is increasing as the result of vigorous backing by progressive health agencies.

The exact mechanism by which fluorides inhibit tooth decay is far from understood. Some investigators feel there is a direct linkage between the bacterial flora, mouth acidity, and dental caries. The presence of large numbers of high acid-producing species of the genus *Lactobacillus* is reported to bear some relationship to tooth decay, but many bacteriologists question this belief.

In recent years manufacturers of toothpastes have incorporated fluorides into their product in the form of stannous fluoride. Ammoniated dentifrices are designed to help reduce mouth acidity; this action is temporary, however, and unless the underlying cause of the acidity is removed, the value of ammoniated toothpastes must be accepted with reservations. Chlorophyll is another additive found in certain dentifrices, but the amounts added (along with vegetable dyes) can hardly be expected to serve as an efficient deodorant. When all of the advocated additives are removed from dentifrices, one can't help but wonder how much room is left for the toothpaste!

It appears to be the consensus among dentists that one of the best means for controlling decay is to brush the teeth as soon as possible after eating in order to remove food particles upon which bacteria can feed and from which acids can be produced. No toothbrush, regardless of scientific design, can be expected to remove all food particles from between the teeth, especially in individuals whose teeth are very close together. Dental floss has real value in oral hygiene, and more people should avail themselves of this technique for removing lodged organic matter not flushed away by the action of saliva. Increased consumption of sugar appears to bear a close relationship to dental caries, especially in children. More attention needs to be paid to prevention of tooth decay and fewer means will then be required to repair the damage to these important structures of our body.

A brief comment on the sanitation of toothbrushes might stimulate the student to give more thought to oral hygiene. The toothbrush possesses potential for being a fomite of considerable importance in the dissemination of respiratory organisms. It would come as a great shock to many were they to discover how filthy, bacteriologically speaking, is the usual toothbrush. Students permitted to do so by their instructors might conduct an interesting research project on the types and the numbers of organisms harbored on toothbrushes.

The old porcelain toothbrush rack in the family bathroom still exists in some homes today. While it might be somewhat difficult to prove the point, it appears logical to assume that some respiratory ailments might be spread in a family through the agency of such a rack. Holders are sometimes designed to store the brushes upright in such a manner that moisture from one brush might contaminate the bristles in nearby brushes when pools of water collect and allow microbial migration. It should be obvious that any contact between toothbrushes should be avoided, and drying of the bristles should be encouraged by proper storage of the brushes between brushings of the teeth.

Within recent years one manufacturer has introduced a toothbrush into whose bristles has been incorporated a germicidal substance that has been found to be relatively effective in combatting microbial populations on the brush. As the bristles wear down, more of the active germicide is released. There is probably some merit in this type of toothbrush as one additional approach to improving oral hygiene. The recent introduction of electrically operated toothbrushes has received the plaudits of some dentists who feel that gum massage provided by the "scientific" action of the bristles might be beneficial to the gums.

BROMINE (Br)

Bromine is listed in some textbooks as a disinfectant, but it certainly has not received the attention devoted to the other three halogens from the standpoint of microbial destruction. Bromine is caustic and has a suffocating odor and any uses it might have as a disinfectant are probably limited.

Compounds of Heavy Metals

The salts of a number of heavy metals, when considered as a group, are found to exert varying degrees of germicidal activity. However the fact that a compound is a salt of a heavy metal does not assure that it will affect microorganisms adversely. A brief consideration of a few commonly employed compounds in the heavy metal series will point out some of their strengths and weaknesses insofar as antimicrobial activity is concerned.

SILVER (Ag)

An interesting phenomenon called **oligodynamic action** (Greek *oligos,* small; *dynamis,* powerful) is exhibited by silver. It can easily be demonstrated by seeding a tube of melted and cooled (45–50°C) nutrient agar with a test organism such as *Staphylococcus aureus* or *Escherichia coli,* and pouring the seeded medium into a petri dish containing a shiny coin (a dime works well). When the agar solidifies the medium is incubated at a temperature optimum for the test species of bacteria. Examination of the plate after growth of the organisms has occurred should reveal a clear zone or halo surrounding the coin. Apparently sufficient silver ions disperse into the medium to inhibit or to kill the bacteria. A suggestion has also been made that radiations emitted from the coins might account for at least part of the reaction.

This antagonistic effect of silver ions is one explanation put forth by microbiologists in support of the belief that coins are not of primary importance in the dissemination of common diseases, in spite of their constant handling by all types of microbe-laden hands during the course of a single day. Small children, who put practically anything into their mouths, could conceivably acquire certain infections through the medium of coins, but adults who use reasonable care in washing their hands before eating food probably need not be overly concerned about picking up pathogenic organisms from the "filthy lucre" they handle during the course of a day.

When the opinion is expressed that being a bank teller and handling quantities of money day after day predisposes the individual to more than a normal "dose" of bacteria, the fact may be overlooked that inhaling millions of droplets of saliva sprayed through a teller's window by untold numbers of people in varying degrees of health is far more important in relation to dissemination of microbes than is the handling of coins. In time a bank teller presumably could build up a hyperimmunity to a wide variety of saliva-borne organisms. A survey of the illness rates among persons engaged in occupations involving direct contact with the public might make an interesting project for someone who has more than a passing interest in microbiology.

Silver nitrate as a 1:1000 solution is quite toxic to a number of organisms, and even when diluted as much as 1:10,000 this chemical may serve as a bacteriostat.

A drop or two of 1 per cent solution of silver nitrate instilled in the eyes of newborn babies has proven to be an effective prophylactic measure against *ophthalmia neonatorum,* blindness caused by the destructive action of *Neisseria gonorrheae* picked up by infants as they pass through the birth canal of mothers infected with gonorrhea. This preventive technique is called the Credé process in honor of its first proponent. Most states require the attending physician at a birth to use silver nitrate or penicillin as a means of preventing needless loss of vision in innocent victims. It is important to remove excess silver nitrate from the eyes of the babies by flushing with sterile distilled water in order to prevent irritation of the delicate membranes of the eyes after the chemical solution has accomplished its intended purpose. A study of the cause of sight loss in pupils presently enrolled in our schools for the blind reveals a dramatic drop in blindness caused by gonococci since the introduction of the Credé technique.

Organic compounds of silver including Argyrol and Protargol act as local disinfectants without irritating delicate membranes. Gauze impregnated with various silver compounds has shown some promise as a germicide when applied to localized infections. Water may be made safe for human consumption by passing it through silver-coated sand. In fact, water containing as little as 40 micrograms (4/1000 of a milligram) of silver is markedly bactericidal.

MERCURY (Hg)

Some of the earliest antiseptics and disinfectants suggested for use were inorganic mercury compounds, and in the last few years a series of organic mercurials have appeared on the market. Some bacteriologists say that mercurials are poor germicides and there is no place for them in modern disinfection. Perhaps this is too strong a statement; the organic compounds like mercurochrome, merthiolate, and metaphen have gained wide acceptance and are less toxic than the inorganic compounds of silver.

Bichloride of mercury (mercuric chloride, $HgCl_2$) has enjoyed general use through the years as a disinfectant. In fact, Robert Koch used it against anthrax as far back as 1881. Because mercuric chloride is rather corrosive (in fact, it is popularly known as corrosive sublimate), its use has been somewhat restricted. Although some textbooks tend to minimize its usefulness as a disinfectant, when used in a concentration of 1:1000 this compound is very effective for cleaning table tops and laboratory benches before and after laboratory experiments in microbiology have been conducted. It has also been used for years as a hand rinse by students in many reputable teaching laboratories.

When diluted more than 1:1000 mercuric chloride becomes a bacteriostat and may even be worthless when the concentration is reduced to below 1:5000. The principal action of mercury compounds is their coagulative effect, but there is good evidence that mercury attacks enzymes containing sulfhydryl groupings.

Some hospitals may still be using mercuric chloride as a soak for clinical thermometers, but unless mucus, sputum, and other organic debris are removed first, this chemical has limited value in this phase of nursing practice. Naturally, thermometers treated in this manner have to be washed free of mercury prior to being placed in the mouth of a patient. Better compounds are available for soaking thermometers, and mercuric chloride probably should not be employed for this purpose unless nothing else suitable is available.

A number of insoluble compounds of mercury, including mercuric oxide and ammoniated mercury, are used in ointments as antiseptics.

Merthiolate in a dilution of about 1:10,000 serves a useful function as a preservative for sera, vaccines, and certain body fluids. Spinal fluid which is to be sent through the mail to a central laboratory for various tests provides an excellent medium for a number of bacteria, and during the warmer months of the year a sample of spinal fluid during transit could become heavily overgrown with microorganisms whose physiological effects could render the fluid useless for laboratory tests. But a small amount of merthiolate added to a collecting tube can serve as a bacteriostat without impairing the value of the sample as far as many laboratory tests are concerned.

COPPER (Cu)

The salts of copper are better algicides and fungicides than bactericides. Copper sulfate is commonly used to control algal growth in open bodies of water and **Bordeaux mixture** is employed to prevent fungus diseases in plants.

In rural areas it is not uncommon for people who do not have access to central water supplies for fire control to dig a "water hole" near their home for use in an emergency. During the warmer months of the year algae frequently build up an objectionable green scum on the surface of these ponds. If enough copper sulfate is added to yield a final concentration of 2 PPM, algal growth is inhibited. A somewhat stronger concentration of the chemical may be required to rid a body of water of a well-established mat of algae.

Having these water supplies near at hand has prompted many individuals to stock the holes with fish, both for control of larvae, especially those of mosquitoes, and as a source of food for human consumption.

Copper sulfate is a poison for fish when certain levels of the chemical are attained, and the following concentrations have been suggested as the upper limits of tolerance. (The figures in parentheses are the approximate number of pounds of the chemical per million gallons of water required to obtain the parts per million indicated.)

Trout	0.14 PPM	(1.2)
Pickerel	0.40 PPM	(3.5)
Goldfish	0.50 PPM	(4.0)
Perch	0.75 PPM	(6.0)
Black bass	2.1 PPM	(17.0)

Oxidizing Agents

The germicidal power of oxidizing agents can be attributed to the release of nascent oxygen (O) which combines with organic matter, including bacteria. Opinions vary, however, as to the effectiveness of this chemical reaction for the destruction of microorganisms.

OZONE (O_3)

Ozone is germicidal to vegetative cells and may be employed as a substitute for chlorine in the treatment of small bodies of water such as swimming pools. This relatively inexpensive agent has met with more favor in Europe than it has in the United States.

HYDROGEN PEROXIDE (H_2O_2)

For years hydrogen peroxide has been an old stand-by in the first aid kits and medicine cabinets of many homes, but its effectiveness as an antiseptic has probably been overrated by many who use it routinely. Hydrogen peroxide is generally prepared as an aqueous 3 per cent solution. When it comes in contact with exposed tissue, the enzyme **catalase** splits it into water and nascent oxygen. There is disagreement as to the degree of penetrating power exhibited by H_2O_2 in wounds, but its bubbling action undoubtedly helps to loosen some organic matter and entrapped microorganisms as it thus acts as a limited lavage for wounds.

Although it has a low degree of toxicity for tissues and is nonirritating, the compound is rather unstable and, in contrast to a number of other agents that persist after application, the effect of hydrogen peroxide is not prolonged once the bubbling action ceases. The general consensus appears to be that this chemical is a mild antiseptic at best, and its use should probably be limited to topical abrasions where it has an opportunity to come into intimate contact with the affected area.

POTASSIUM PERMANGANATE ($KMnO_4$)

Potassium permanganate is a strong oxidizing agent and a useful germicide under certain controlled conditions. However it readily combines with organic matter to form the brown manganese oxide (MnO_2) which reduces its effectiveness somewhat. Physicians have employed weak solutions of $KMnO_4$ for the treatment of genito-urinary tract infections, and since it can oxidize organic poisons, some success has been achieved when this agent was used to counteract the effects of snake bite poisoning.

HALOGENS

The halogens act as oxidizing agents and should be mentioned here, but since they have already been discussed (pp. 119–124) the facts need not be repeated.

Phenolic Compounds

PHENOL (C_6H_5OH)

Phenol, a coal tar product, is also known as carbolic acid. It is composed of colorless or slightly reddish crystals that are soluble in water. Its characteristic odor is responsible for that "hospital smell" which is so objectionable to many individuals.

This chemical gained its initial reputation in microbiology through the classical pioneer experiments conducted in the 1870's by Joseph Lister who employed carbolic acid in the treatment of wounds and as an antiseptic in surgery. Viruses and bacterial spores, however, tend to escape the lethal action of this chemical. Modern aseptic surgery is based upon Lister's significant findings, together with many other advances that have been proposed and adopted since then. Phenol is used as the standard against which other chemicals are compared in the **phenol coefficient test** to be described later in this chapter (see p. 140). It should not be inferred from this that phenol is an ideal germicide; far from it.

A large number of derivatives of phenol exhibit some disinfecting value, with cresols and certain proprietary derivatives being most useful. Weak phenol may be employed on open wounds for short periods, but since this chemical causes coagulation of tissue, prolonged contact or excessive concentration might cause sufficient tissue destruction to initiate gangrene.

The strength of phenol for use in microbiology and in allied fields usually varies within the limits of 1 and 5 per cent, depending upon the use to which it is to be put. Some laboratories employ phenolic compounds for washing down work areas and pieces of equipment, floors, walls, and ceilings. Pipettes are sometimes soaked in these chemical solutions after use and before being washed. Body wastes, including sputum, urine, and feces, may be treated with phenol, but contact must be long enough to insure penetration and effectiveness. A small amount of soap has been reported to increase the activity of phenol, but large amounts merely spread the phenol into the soap in such a manner that the power of phenol is nullified.

Theories to explain the action of phenol against organisms vary from the formation of proteinates or albuminates to the physical adsorption of the chemical on some internal part of the cell, thus interfering with normal cell metabolism. There is also evidence in support of the proposal that phenol and related compounds may exert surface action on the cells which favors cytolysis.

CRESOL $(CH_3C_6H_4OH)$

Cresol is another coal tar product, and it is an **emulsified** disinfectant. Its relatively weak affinity for protein accounts in part for its comparatively low germicidal power, although it does merit use as an antiseptic. Tricresol, which is a mixture of orthocresol, metacresol, and paracresol, can be emulsified in water to the extent of about 2.5 per cent, at which strength it is about twice as effective against organisms as is 5 per cent phenol. The soapy characteristics of cresol make it a good cleaning agent, but because alkalis diminish its activity, cresol should not be added to soapy water.

Lysol is a proprietary preparation that is about five times as germicidal as phenol against selected bacteria when evaluated by the phenol coefficient technique.

Tricresol in a concentration of 0.15 per cent is useful for the preservation of biologicals, including vaccines and therapeutic sera. According to some physicians, however, tricresol should not be incorporated into fluids to be used for **intrathecal** (spinal canal) injections because of the possible danger of chemical meningitis.

Soaps and Detergents

When oils and fats are boiled with potassium hydroxide, the end product becomes a soft soap. Sodium hydroxide is employed in the manufacture of hard soaps.

From the time that a child is old enough to understand, the word "soap" takes on a very definite meaning that goes hand in hand with "cleanliness." There is good bacteriological evidence in support of the parental admonition to Junior to wash his hands with soap and water before eating. Soaps have held the respect of microbiologists from the earliest days of our relatively young science, but these agents are probably better for the mechanical removal of dirt, oils, and lodged organisms than they are for disinfecting skin surfaces.

Experiments designed to increase the microbe-killing capacity of soaps by medicating them with such chemicals as phenol or cresol have yielded conflicting results. An actual lowering of effectiveness of the soap may occur with these germicides; in some cases no measurable change can be detected. Present-day medicated soaps frequently incorporate *hexachlorophene* as the active ingredient, and if the limitations of the vehicle are appreciated, it is probably accurate to state that such soaps are better than the nonmedicated varieties. The idea of fortifying the action of cleansing agents by incorporating germicides has spread to other items including shampoos and toothpastes, but the usefulness of hexachlorophene in the latter products is not nearly as spectacular as the "ad" men would have you believe.

Hexachlorophene does not appear to be active against gram negative organisms, but since most of the bacteria on the skin are gram positive, marked reduction in microbial numbers can be recorded through the combined mechanical and chemical action of fortified soaps.

When the newer medicated soaps appeared on the market some physicians began using them on their hands to the exclusion of other soaps with the idea of gradually building up on their skin a thin film of the chemical to minimize the viable microbial population. Some of the laboratory hand-washing tests yielded such encouraging results that support for adoption of medicated soaps probably shifted to an extreme. Some surgeons developed the notion that this approach to hand-washing might permit a reduction in the time of the pre-operative scrub that has been a standard technique in well-run hospitals for years. Although it is difficult to assert with authority that reliance upon medicated soaps tended to result in a lowering of sanitary standards in some hospitals, this possibility must be considered along with so many other factors that pulled our hospitals into the situation leading to the problem of resistant staphylococci. Nothing must be overlooked in the reestablishment of pre-antibiotic techniques of asepsis in our hospitals.

Many physicians will come out in strong opposition to those who criticize medical sanitation practices, but to microbiologists who for years have decried the indiscriminate use of antibiotics as substitutes for asepsis, it has been rather interesting to note in the articles written by doctors in scientific journals, as well as in popular magazines, statements to the effect that our hospitals must return to former standards of sanitation if the staphylococcus problem is to be conquered. The standards never should have been lowered in the first place!

Detergents (Latin *detere,* to rub away or clean) are usually more effective as cleansing agents than are soaps. There are three general categories of detergents: **anionic** (negatively charged), **cationic** (positively charged), and non-ionic. Although they are all relatively good as cleansing agents, their antimicrobial ability varies widely. *Sodium lauryl sulfate,* which is anionic, is generally less effective in inhibiting or in killing bacteria than are the cationic compounds, whereas the non-ionic agents are not significantly active against microbes.

The cationic detergents include quaternary ammonium compounds that possess relatively complex nitrogen structures and exhibit germicidal power in high dilution. Some "quats" remain bacteriostatic even when diluted as much as 1:200,000. They are fungicidal and kill protozoa, but viruses enjoy somewhat more resistance to these agents than do bacteria. Zephiran (alkyl dimethyl benzyl ammonium chloride) is one of the quaternary ammonium compounds that has been adopted as a disinfectant in a number of hospitals. Because these compounds are noncorrosive, stable, germicidal, and possess cleansing action, they have found general acceptance for sanitizing equipment and utensils in dairies, restaurants, and food processing plants. The destructive action of "quats" appears to be a combination of inactivation of enzymes, denaturation of proteins, and alteration of the cell surfaces which permits lysis of selected organisms.

A useful word, **sanitize,** has crept into our vocabulary in recent years. It expresses the type of action that one might expect from most soaps and detergents when they are properly employed in conjunction with hot water. When dishes are rinsed free of gross particles and are washed in hot soapy water containing a detergent, some harmless microorganisms may remain, but for all practical purposes the dishes have been cleaned, or sanitized, sufficiently from a bacteriological point of view, and they are esthetically acceptable.

One more link in the chain required for the spread of pathogens has been broken with the introduction of properly functioning mechanical dishwashers in public eating establishments and in our homes. Powerful detergents and temperatures well above the tolerance for human hands combine their action to remove and to kill potentially dangerous bacteria which might be spread from one infected person to susceptible individuals using the same eating utensils. The problem of adequate sanitation in restaurants has always been a knotty one, but if the final rinse water in a dishwasher is maintained at 180°F for at least twenty seconds, no one need be concerned about survival of potentially harmful organisms. Those with even elementary training in microbiology should become more conscious of sanitation not only in restaurants, but in their own homes as well. Much food poisoning could be avoided were more attention given to some of the simple sanitation practices. One shudders at the lack of cleanliness at soda fountains and beer taverns where glasses are sometimes fortunate to receive a cursory cold water rinse between customers. Town and state inspectors cannot be everywhere at all times to check up on these matters, and it should come as no surprise, therefore, that such diseases as trenchmouth (*Vincent's angina*) are disseminated through these fomites. Trenchmouth is an extremely contagious disease that has a habit of spreading like wildfire, especially on college campuses which frequently find themselves ringed with "hash joints" or "ptomaine palaces."

Dyes

In addition to serving as stains, indicators of pH and oxidation–reduction, many dyes exhibit a bacteriostatic or a bactericidal action on selected microorganisms. Whether the dyes merely inhibit or actually kill the microbes depends in part upon the concentration being employed. Clinical bacteriologists rely heavily upon dye-containing selective media for the isolation of bacteria from complex organic matter such as sputum and feces.

Gram positive cells generally exhibit greater sensitivity to the action of dyes than do gram negative species. Dyes presumably combine with the cell protein and disrupt the normal metabolism of the organisms. When the disruption is slight, the dye may serve as a bacteriostat, whereas major interference with metabolism may cause death of the cell.

Aniline dyes are useful in selective bacteriostasis. Eosine, methylene blue, and basic fuchsin serve as inhibitors in a number of selective media, and many organic dyes, including gentian violet, crystal violet, malachite green, brilliant green, and selected flavine dyes are commonly employed as **static** or **cidal** agents. Time is a factor when considering the action of dyes, and it is difficult to know where to draw the line separating inhibitory action and killing effect. When growth of an organism is inhibited long enough, the organism dies. Should a dye in this case be considered a bacteriostat or a bactericide?

The principle of dye action on microorganisms is employed by the medical profession through the use of gentian violet, for example, in the treatment of persistent bacterial or fungal infections of the skin.

There is evidence that dyes are adsorbed by the cells and thus disrupt the permeability of the cell wall and the underlying cytoplasmic membrane. Whether this is merely a physical blocking which interferes with cell metabolism or a more complex physical–chemical reaction is not clear.

Acid dyes are more active in a low pH, whereas the action of basic dyes is increased by increasing the alkalinity. By shifting the pH it is possible, unless the reaction has proceeded too far, to reverse the effects of the dye and to "revive" the still-living organisms.

An interesting phenomenon called **photodynamic action** can be demonstrated with some dyes when they are added in relatively low concentrations to fluid suspensions of bacteria. This dye–bacteria mixture when exposed to light will result in death of the microbes within a matter of minutes, whereas the same combination when stored in the dark at the same temperature may exhibit no reduction in the number of viable cells.

Fumigants

Today's college-age youth were not alive during the era when health officers tacked colored placards on the front door of homes in which someone was suffering from scarlet fever, diphtheria, whooping cough, smallpox, or other contagious diseases. Uninformed persons afraid of contracting these maladies would frequently walk on the other side of the street whenever they spotted such a warning indicating that the residence was under quarantine.

Fumigation in those days was a common practice in homes following recovery or death of the afflicted individual. Modern sanitation techniques call for thoroughly ventilating, cleaning, and disinfecting the sick room. However should the area be infested with bedbugs or other vermin, some of the newer pressurized cylinders of **aerosols** containing pyrethrum, DDT, glycol vapors, or other active ingredients have been found to be effective as an adjunct to the standard sanitary practices. A number of fumigants have been employed through the years for treating the atmosphere in confined areas, and a few of these chemicals will be discussed briefly.

FORMALDEHYDE (HCHO)

This gas, which is extremely irritating to the eyes, nose, and throat, has been used extensively in the past because of its toxicity to microbes when the humidity is high and the temperature is above 70°F. Prolonged contact of objects with formaldehyde will result in their sterilization, but only comparatively exposed surfaces are rendered free of living things, and the chemical persists for long periods, which can be annoying.

Formaldehyde is soluble in water to the extent of about 37 to 40 per cent, in which form it is known as **formalin**. From 5 to 10 per cent methanol is sometimes added to make the formalin more effective. Since the action of this compound is reduced little or not at all by organic matter, it has value for the disinfection of body wastes, including sputum, urine, and feces. The drawbacks of this chemical, however, limit its use, and it is not employed as a skin disinfectant.

Formalin is a common ingredient found in embalming fluid since it is capable of hardening or "fixing" tissues. The manufacture of toxoids depends upon the use of formalin to destroy the toxic portion of poisons without impairing their immunizing power.

SULFUR DIOXIDE (SO_2)

The pungent fumes of sulfur dioxide liberated when a match is struck appear to be irritating to microorganisms as well as to humans. The gas is prepared commercially by burning flowers of sulfur. It is sufficient to dismiss this noxious agent as a useful fumigant by stating that even though it is lethal for microbes, the problems involved in handling and using the material outweigh the good that can be accomplished in most instances.

HYDROGEN CYANIDE (HCN)

This product has little or no direct effect on bacteria, but disinfestation by hydrocyanic acid gas is widely practiced because of its acute toxicity for insects and for higher forms of life. When the "cootie" population in military barracks reached an annoying level during World War II, it was customary to evacuate the inmates, seal the windows and doors with tape, and fumigate the premises with cyanide gas. This is the same agent employed in execution chambers in the prisons of some of our states. It is an extremely lethal material, and those who are appointed to handle it must be thoroughly acquainted with the consequences of its use and misuse.

Only a few inhalations of cyanide gas render an individual unconscious, and the killing dose is not much greater. Gas masks may be equipped with special canisters containing appropriate chemicals designed to filter out cyanide gas fumes. This protective equipment allows an operator to set off the cyanide "bomb" in a room and to re-enter the building to ventilate it prior to its reoccupancy. In addition to the posting of large warning signs, special guards should be assigned to patrol an area being treated with cyanide gas to insure that no unauthorized person enters the area before it is safe.

GLYCOL VAPORS

To be effective in the destruction of organisms, glycol mists require a relative humidity varying from 45 to 70 per cent with a temperature below 80°F. Some of the other aerosols do not possess such critical moisture and temperature levels. Triethylene glycol appears to be superior to propylene glycol in the treatment of air in closed places, and these vapors are effective in minute concentrations. They are tasteless, odorless, nonirritating, and relatively nontoxic for humans even after prolonged periods of exposure. Yet they serve as antimicrobial agents.

A number of ingenious devices have been manufactured to inject these germicidal vapors into air conditioning systems, but there is little evidence to support their use in classrooms, theaters, or other gathering places where control of humidity is difficult if not impossible. A portable machine that draws over a hot roller a strip of paper impregnated with glycol compounds has been devised to vaporize the glycol and expel it into the air of a small room, and this treatment appears to reduce materially microbial populations in the air.

People talking, coughing, and sneezing can add enormous numbers of organisms to the atmosphere. Even the meow of a cat or the bark of a dog increases the number of droplets in which bacteria can be spread. In large offices where many persons work in a single room, the employer is confronted with the unpleasant fact that a common cold can spread quickly throughout his staff and materially influence absenteeism. It might pay such companies to treat the air of the office not only with the usual air conditioning to control temperature and humidity, but with glycol vapors as well.

Winter peaks of respiratory infections can be attributed in part to the fact that people remain indoors more during colder weather, thus increasing the number of close contacts with individuals who might be suffering from the "common cold." Overheated rooms with their relatively low humidity tend to accentuate the condition by drying out the normally moist mucous membranes of the nose and throat. Much has been written and much more will be said about the causes and possible cures of one of man's most annoying afflictions—the common cold. If you support the contention that sitting in a draft will result in your contracting a cold, there are those who will take the opposite view. The subject is too broad and controversial to take up here.

ETHYLENE OXIDE (C_2H_4O)

This compound was discussed in Chapter 5 with reference to sterilization techniques employed in microbiology. Ethylene oxide should be included here as one more agent that is available for the fumigation of such materials as mattresses and bedding, both of which present real problems in the constant struggle to maintain high standards of sanitation in our hospitals. The fact that this germicidal agent is most effective within certain limits of humidity and temperature means that special chambers must be employed in which these factors, along with pressure of the gas, can be controlled.

The relatively high penetrating power of ethylene oxide allows the sterilization of sutures and needles directly through special sealed packages in which they are stored. Leather goods, rubber, plastics, and similar items can be treated with this gas with complete assurance that the sterilizing process will alter neither their physical nor chemical makeup.

The exact mechanism by which ethylene oxide effects sterilization is not understood, but it would appear that the gas combines with the cellular protein in some way and alters its normal function.

BETA-PROPIOLACTONE

This material is probably better as a fumigant than as a germicide when the relative humidity can be maintained at about 70 per cent, which appears to be optimum for beta-propiolactone. The vapors are somewhat less irritating than those of formaldehyde. Beta-propiolactone has a low vapor pressure at room temperature, but because of its high degree of activity it requires only a low concentration to be effective.

This agent acts on the complex enzyme of cells and interferes with the vital process of cell metabolism.

One chemical explanation of the activity of beta-propiolactone is that alkylation takes place. This involves the replacement of an active hydrogen atom in an organic compound with an alkyl group. Spores are attacked by this type of reaction with little more difficulty than are vegetative cells. With other types of disinfectants it is probably the sulfhydryl group that is attacked, and in spores these are relatively protected or inaccessible, according to some theories.

Inorganic Acids and Alkalies

Even though these strong chemicals are able to act as powerful antimicrobial agents through the processes of hydrolysis and coagulation, the over-all destructiveness of inorganic acids and alkalies precludes their use as germicides except in unusual circumstances when no other agents are available.

Techniques for Evaluation of Agents

No attempt will be made to list all of the techniques and their various modifications that have been proposed through the years for evaluating the effectiveness of antimicrobial chemical agents. All of the present methods possess certain disadvantages, and because of the diverse nature of the compounds being employed as antiseptics and disinfectants, no one test is applicable to all compounds.

Labels on substances do not always reflect the true value of the product. Manufacturers' conflict with the Federal Food and Drug Administration, coupled with a need for "speaking the same scientific language," eventually gave rise to the development of standardized tests for the rising tide of new products. Circular 198 of the United States Department of Agriculture (December 1931) outlines accepted techniques for testing antiseptics and disinfectants. This publication represents a milestone in the history of standardizing these products. Both qualitative and quantitative methods are included in this publication, but the period since 1931 has seen the introduction of numerous modifications and improvements in testing techniques.

The results of any testing program must be considered in the light of eventual application in clinical situations, and it is frequently unwarranted to draw sweeping conclusions about a compound that stands up well when tested *in vitro;* application *in vivo* may prove the substance to be more harmful than helpful to a patient. Physiological and pharmacological data must be considered along with the bacteriological findings before a product can be said to be an effective antiseptic or disinfectant.

Filter Paper Disc Method

When the substance to be tested is not soluble or completely miscible in water, or when soaps, toothpastes, powders, salves, and ointments are under study, the filter paper disc technique has some value as an indicator of the effectiveness of the compound. The sterile paper is dipped into a young broth culture of *Staphylococcus aureus,* and the disc is then completely covered with the test chemical for a standardized time period (usually ten minutes), followed by subculturing of the paper in a suitable nutrient medium. The material must be teased from the disc in such a manner as to expose the paper before transferring it to a fresh tube of broth. This will minimize the amount of chemical being carried over into the final broth tube and tend to avert any bacteriostatic action in the medium. Following incubation of the broth at 37°C for 48 hours, the tubes are observed for evidence of growth. The disadvantages of this technique are obvious.

A modification of this method is to swab a nutrient agar surface with an even seeding of a fresh culture of the test organism. A sterile filter paper disc moistened with the chemical under investigation is then placed in intimate contact with the inoculated agar surface for 48 hours at a suitable temperature for the organism used. Any clear zone, or halo, around the disc indicates inhibition or killing of the bacteria. By cutting out a small segment of the agar in the clear zone with a sterile wire loop and subculturing the agar in a suitable volume of liquid medium, such as thioglycollate broth, it is possible to detect mere inhibition on the plate should the agar sample yield growth in the thioglycollate broth. If the subculture fails to grow, it indicates that the halo on the plate is the result of a bactericidal action and not just an inhibitory effect. The width of the clear zone may give some indication of penetrating power of the chemical being tested.

Agar Plate Method

A tube of nutrient agar melted and cooled to within 45–50°C is inoculated with 0.1 ml of a broth culture of bacteria to be tested and is poured into a petri dish. After the medium has solidified, the liquid, cream, salve, ointment, or powder is smeared over a prescribed area of the agar surface. Following a standard incubation period, zones of clearing in the agar adjacent to the test material can be subcultured into thioglycollate broth to determine whether the action is bacteriostatic or bactericidal.

Some chemicals lose much of their antimicrobial power in the presence of organic matter, and since open cuts and wounds are going to provide organic matter in the form of serous fluids, it is a logical approach in testing techniques to add about 10 per cent blood serum to agar plates before conducting the tests described above. As controls, similarly inoculated plates without serum should be run in a parallel series to note any marked differences in the size of the clear zones.

Penicylinder Cup Technique

In order to circumvent some of the disadvantages inherent in the filter paper disc techniques, the penicylinder cup method may be employed. It probably possesses a higher degree of reliability insofar as duplication of findings is concerned. Interpretation of the results as they relate to clinical application may be another story.

Two tubes of nutrient agar are melted and cooled in a water bath to between 45° and 50°C. One tube of the medium is poured into a sterile petri dish and is allowed to solidify. The second agar tube is inoculated with 0.1 ml of the test bacteria, and after the tube is rolled between the palms of the hands to distribute the test organisms, the inoculated medium is poured on top of the solidified agar in the plate. Before this cap of agar solidifies, a sterile penicylinder (usually made of porcelain or glass) is placed in the top layer of agar with an open end of the cylinder pointed up. After the medium has hardened, two drops of the test chemical are introduced into the embedded cylinder and the plate is incubated in an upright position at a suitable temperature. Clear zones adjacent to the cups are interpreted in the usual manner after wedges of agar have been subcultured in thioglycollate broth (see Fig. 6.1).

Two main advantages of this method are that the test material can be measured accurately, and the chemical must penetrate the agar at the bottom of the penicylinder and work its way back up through the area next to the cup if it is to produce a zone of clearing.

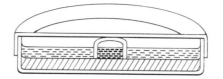

FIG. 6.1. Diagrammatic representation of penicylinder technique for testing disinfectants.

Phenol Coefficient Method

In 1903 Rideal and Walker proposed a method for quantitatively evaluating compounds intended for use as germicides, and this technique is known as the **phenol coefficient test.** A number of modifications have been proposed and adopted through the years, and in 1931 Ruehle and Brewer of the Federal Food and Drug Administration published the standard procedures still used today for evaluating disinfectants. United States Department of Agriculture Circular No. 198 outlines the exact details for conducting such tests.

The phenol coefficient (P.C.) is a number that represents the relative killing power of a germicide as compared with that of phenol under a set of highly specific *in vitro* conditions. Phenol is assigned number "1," and chemicals whose numbers are greater than 1 are able to kill the specified strain of test organism (either *Staphylococcus aureus* or *Salmonella typhosa*) at a higher dilution than the standard phenol.

The P.C. is calculated by dividing the highest dilution of the unknown chemical that kills all of the test organisms in ten minutes but not in five minutes by the dilution of phenol that has the same killing capacity. For example, if substance "X" when diluted 500 times can accomplish the specified killing and phenol can be diluted only 100 times to do the same thing, the P.C. is 500/100, or 5.0. This means that substance "X" is five times as effective as phenol *under the conditions of the test.* This last stipulation is important to remember because *in vivo* results do not necessarily parallel *in vitro* findings.

Before making any sweeping claims based upon phenol coefficient test findings, one should recognize the limitations of the method. As originally designed, this method was meant to compare phenol with phenol-like compounds. Other chemicals whose mode of action differs from phenol are not strictly comparable. Nor does the P.C. necessarily find value in clinical use of compounds.

The phenol coefficient for some representative compounds when tested against *Salmonella typhosa* and *Staphylococcus aureus* are approximately as follows.

TABLE 9

The Phenol Coefficient of Common Compounds

| | Phenol Coefficient | |
Compound	*Salmonella typhosa*	*Staphylococcus aureus*
Chloramine	100.0	133.0
Hexyl resorcinol	72.0	150.0
Hydrogen peroxide	0.01	
Iodine (tincture), 3%	5.8	6.3
Lysol	5.0	3.2
Menthol	5.1	5.0–8.0
Mercuric chloride 1:1000	100.0	143.0
Mercurochrome		1.7
Metaphen		1500.0
Merthiolate 1:1000	40–50	40–50
Tricresol	2.6	

Tissue Toxicity Method

As was pointed out in earlier discussions of disinfection, one of the major drawbacks of a number of chemicals as potential germicides is their damage to healthy tissues, and when tissue destruction is great enough, serious sequelae can develop. Ideally, the evaluation of the antimicrobial capacity of a disinfectant should be closely correlated with results anticipated when the agent is employed on or in the body. A number of techniques designed to measure tissue damage have been devised. Much of the pioneer work in this area has been conducted by Salle and his co-workers, beginning about 1935. These investigators studied the effect of germicides on the viability of chick heart tissue grown *in vitro*. From these tests a **toxicity index** was calculated. It is defined as the ratio of the highest dilution of a germicide required to kill chick heart tissue in ten minutes to the highest dilution of the agent needed to kill the test microbes in the same time period and under identical conditions.

Whenever the toxicity index number is greater than "1," the chemical is more lethal to the tissues than to the microorganisms; numbers less than 1 indicate that less damage is done to the tissues than to the bacteria. A few representative findings using chick heart tissue and tinctures of germicides indicate readings of 0.2 for iodine, 0.5 for mercresin, 3.3 for merthiolate, and 10.0 for metaphen. This approach to the problem of evaluating disinfectants appears to be a sound one and should be given more attention.

Review Questions

1. Which antiseptics and disinfectants commonly employed in your home fulfill most of the prerequisites for an ideal compound under conditions of use?
2. Which requirements of an ideal disinfectant are most commonly lacking in household compounds usually found in a first aid cabinet?
3. List five disinfectants or antiseptics and indicate their individual limitations.
4. What precautions can you suggest to keep poisonous compounds in the home away from young children?
5. Are there any advantages to giving a child a fluoride compound in his morning orange juice over those proposed for adding the compound to supplies of public drinking water?
6. Is oligodynamic action restricted to silver and silver-containing compounds?
7. What are the requirements for a good disinfectant to be used for treating clinical thermometers?
8. Is there virtue in medicating soaps? If so, with what types of compounds? Why?
9. Defend the statement that air conditioning may improve health.
10. Compare disinfectant testing techniques employing discs and penicylinders. Which method yields the most information?

7 CONTROL OF MICROBES BY PHYSICAL FORCES

Temperature

ALTHOUGH IN NURSING PRACTICE MANY TECHNIQUES DESIGNED TO control and to destroy microorganisms employ the use of chemicals, there are also a number of lethal physical procedures with which nurses need to become acquainted if they hope to deal with selected phases of their daily professional routine.

Chapter 5 outlined the effects of temperature, especially high temperature, on microbes, and these facts need not be reiterated here. But there is another aspect of temperature that must be understood, since this physical force has a direct bearing on the cultivation and growth of microorganisms. Most pathogens (and these are of primary concern in medicine and in the allied field of nursing) are somewhat restricted in their temperature requirements for growth and survival. Deviations from the optimum can exert profound effects on these more fastidious species.

Psychrophilic or **cryophilic** (both meaning "cold-loving") bacteria are of importance in medicine probably only from the standpoint of food spoilage. But this type of deterioration in a refrigerator generally is not of direct concern in too many cases of food poisoning. The thermostat on many home refrigerators is probably adjusted to cut on and off nearer 50°F than the desired optimum of 40°F. At the higher temperature food naturally will tend to undergo spoilage more quickly, but the types of products involved will determine to a great extent whether or not food poisoning might be a problem.

A public health nurse is in a unique situation as a potential educator as she visits the homes of people living at various economic levels. She can become a positive force in the instruction of individuals in all phases of human health. Not every home she visits will be equipped with a de luxe, super-duper, self-defrosting mechanical refrigerator, and sometimes the nurse will be forced to tax her ingenuity to come up with useful and practical recommendations for preservation of food, which is only one aspect bearing directly on maintaining human health.

On the upper end of the temperature scale are the **thermophilic** (heat-loving) organisms whose optimum growth takes place at about 55°C, but these unusual microbes can also be dismissed by the nurse and public health worker as etiological agents in disease. Food-processing plants, however, are constantly on the alert to prevent a build-up of thermophiles if the finished product is to have acceptable bacterial counts day after day. The pasteurizing equipment of a dairy, for example, may be an ideal location for the multiplication of heat-loving bacteria unless intelligent steps are taken to nip the potential problem in the bud.

The middle group (**mesophiles**) includes just about all of the microbes of direct medical significance, and it is in this temperature group that the pathogens fall. The farther away one gets from the ideal heat requirements for the propagation of organisms—whether it be higher or lower on the temperature scale—the less likely are undesirable organisms to gain a foothold and increase in numbers to the point where a health problem is created.

Desiccation

Most organisms thrive in a high moisture content. That is why most media are prepared with 90 per cent or more of water. When moisture evaporates under the influence of increased temperature, osmotic forces come into play, and the survival rate of bacteria under these conditions will depend, among other things, upon whether they possess spores which can tide the cells through unfavorable changes in their environment. Size and composition of capsules also have a bearing on the ability of the microbes to withstand periods of desiccation. Members of the venereal-disease group of organisms cannot long endure the lethal effects of drying. The syphilis spirochete, *Treponema pallidum,* and the gonococcus, *Neisseria gonorrheae,* are examples of pathogens that are particularly susceptible to drying, and this becomes a factor in any consideration of spread of these so-called "social diseases."

When cells are endowed with endospores, however, the length of time the organisms can remain viable is greatly increased, even after environmental conditions become relatively unfavorable. Spores of the anthrax bacillus (*Bacillus anthracis*) have been reported to have remained dormant in soil for periods up to fifty years. This is the principal reason why carcasses of animals that have been afflicted with anthrax should not be buried without some previous antimicrobial treatment. Incineration appears to be best for disposing of such animals. Some of the pioneer work of Pasteur and his co-workers brought this to light in their classical studies concerned with the grazing of sheep on land that had not been used for many years. Anthrax spores from animals buried decades previously eventually found their way to the surface of the ground through the agency of worms and weather, and sheep grazing on the grass contaminated by these long-dormant spores contracted anthrax and died.

Operating room personnel must constantly be alert to the potential hazards not only of the non-sporing but nevertheless resistant staphylococci which have wreaked more than their share of havoc in recent years, but also to the spores of pathogens that might be lurking in cracks, crevices, ventilators, or equipment. Whenever operations are conducted on patients who have had gas gangrene, for example, even greater care than usual must be directed toward thoroughly disinfecting all surfaces to minimize the opportunity for these pathogenic bacteria (*Clostridium perfringens*) to find their way into the wounds of future patients who will be occupying the same rooms.

It is not uncommon for hospitals to call on their bacteriologists and laboratory teams to conduct periodic and complete microbiological surveys of such sensitive areas as the operating room, wards, and kitchens to determine the types and relative numbers of prevalent organisms. This practice should be encouraged and expanded.

An interesting technique called **lyophilization** (freeze-drying) is available for the preservation of both vegetative cells and spore-producing organisms over long periods of time. Hospital laboratories may for long-range research studies take advantage of stock culture collections built up and preserved over a number of years. By rapid freezing of small quantities of organisms suspended in blood serum or in milk at $-60°C$, followed by dehydration from the frozen state through use of a vacuum pump, cultures can be stored in this dry condition and held in a vacuum in sealed tubes for almost unlimited periods with no appreciable alteration in the physical, biochemical, or serological reactions of the microbes.

Mechanical Pressure

Exerting physical pressure on microbes does not materially affect them, unless the force is extreme and the exposure prolonged. The size of the cells and their surface-to-weight ratio explain at least in part their relatively high resistance to mechanical pressure. Another consideration must be that the force is probably being exerted equally on the entire surface of the minute cells. In one series of reported tests pressures as high as 3000 atmospheres (one atmosphere is about 14.7 pounds per square inch) failed to kill selected bacilli and cocci, but when this pressure was doubled, the non-sporing cells were dead after fourteen hours. *Bacillus subtilis,* a sporing rod found in the soil, resisted pressures as high as 12,000 atmospheres for hours with no appreciable diminution in viability.

Sudden release of high pressure may be detrimental to cells especially when gases, even in minute amounts, are present within the organisms. Actual rupture of the cells may occur. When deep-sea divers ascend too quickly from considerable depths where the pressure is great, nitrogen gas expands in their systems and results in the formation of "bubbles in their blood" causing a painful condition popularly known as "the bends." In emergencies when individuals must be surfaced quickly, it is possible to place them in a decompression chamber where the pressure is gradually brought back to that of the atmosphere with a minimum of injury to the victim. Presumably the same type of reaction might be expected with microbes, within limits.

Osmotic Pressure

Osmotic pressure refers to the imbalance that exists when different concentrations of miscible fluids on either side of a semipermeable membrane attempt to equalize by diffusion through the separating membrane. A relationship exists between the number and the size of the molecules in a given volume of a solution and the osmotic pressure capable of being exerted. When microbes attack a complex material and break it down into simpler substances (for example, starch to dextrin to maltose to glucose), the end product can be expected to possess a higher osmotic pressure than the more complex parent material owing to the increased number of molecules released through the degradation process. On the other hand, synthesis of a complex substance from simpler materials should result in a finished product with a lower osmotic pressure than that of the materials from which it was formed.

It follows, therefore, that when living tissue is damaged either mechanically or through biological action, the simpler substances formed through the breakdown will have a higher osmotic pressure than the original healthy tissue. Swelling, called **edema,** results as fluids are drawn to the area from the blood vessels and the adjoining tissues. As tissue repair sets in, edema tends to diminish.

A solution is said to be **isotonic** when its osmotic pressure is the same as that existing on the other side of a semipermeable membrane, such as a cell wall. Any fluids, such as glucose solution, physiological saline (slightly less than 0.9 per cent sodium chloride), or combinations of the two, administered to patients via the intravenous route must be isotonic; otherwise, blood cells could be so severely damaged, owing to osmotic pressure differences, that injection would result in more harm than good to the recipient.

An organism placed in a solution having a higher osmotic pressure than the suspended cell will tend to lose water and shrink. Plants possess more rigid cell walls than do animal cells, with the result that little or no visible change in the size or the shape of the plant cells may be evident under these conditions, although the cytoplasmic membrane may draw away from the cell wall as the protoplasm contracts. The loss of water when cells are placed in strong (**hypertonic**) solutions causes **plasmolysis**—a shrinking of the cell or of the cytoplasm within the cell wall. This action is the basis of one technique designed to preserve foods where sugar or salt are added in relatively high concentrations. Such a hypertonic condition interferes with, or actually stops, normal metabolism of bacteria, including the spoilage-type species.

A cell placed in a solution of lesser concentration (**hypotonic**) than itself will result in fluids entering the cell and causing **plasmoptysis,** or swelling of the organism. If the cell wall is rigid, as is true of bacteria, and actual enlargement of the cell is prevented, then osmotic pressure builds up within the organism. As a group, young cells are generally more susceptible to many environmental changes than are older well-established cells.

Light and Radiation

Light is energy, and radiation represents energy traveling through space. Higher plants utilize chlorophyll, a green-pigmented material that catalyzes the combination of carbon dioxide and water to form plant substance in the presence of appropriate light sources. Most bacteria lack such a photosynthetic pigment, however, and are unable to utilize light in their metabolism. In fact, sunlight is decidedly germicidal under proper conditions of exposure except in selected microorganisms containing bacteriochlorophyll which serves in a manner analogous to the catalyst found in higher plants.

The visible rays of the spectrum, insofar as man is concerned, extend from about 3970 to 7900 Ångstrom units (one Å is $1/10,000$ of a micron), but it is the band around 2650 Å that is most lethal to microbes. Ultraviolet rays are beyond the violet band of the visible spectrum and infrared lies outside the visible red range. Except for the heat generated by infrared, no other demonstrable changes appear to be induced in bacteria exposed to these forces.

Radiations may effect both physical and chemical changes in cells. Time of exposure as well as distance from the energy source will determine whether ultraviolet light will kill cells, trigger genetic changes, or merely inhibit growth. Lack of penetrating power is one of the limiting factors insofar as ultraviolet light is concerned. Even thin layers of glass, water, or other fluids can serve as effective barriers for this type of radiation. Dust, clouds, and smoke blot out ultraviolet light, which means that few rays under 3000 Å have much of an opportunity to reach the streets of our cities where we have failed miserably in the control of smoke and other forms of pollution, a major threat to human health in our sprawling industrial centers.

We are told that darkness breeds sin, and if multiplication of bacteria is sinful, then this saying is true. Bacteriologists purposely maintain their incubators in the absence of light as much of the time as possible to avoid stray radiations that might slow down microbial propagation. Gram negative bacteria as a group are relatively susceptible to light, especially ultraviolet radiation; their gram positive counterparts may exhibit up to ten times the resistance displayed by the gram negative cells. Spores in general are less affected than are vegetative cells.

An intriguing observation was mady by Kelner who found that bacteria inactivated by ultraviolet rays could be revived by exposure to ordinary daylight if the original contact with the lethal light had not been prolonged. This is not in conflict with Pasteur's findings that life cannot arise from dead material. Kelner was not working with Lazarus-like cells that suddenly arose from the dead upon command. Rather, his exposed cells appeared lifeless as we commonly think of that term, but the spark of life lay dormant within the cells, waiting to be fanned by **photoreactivation** induced by daylight. Microbiological media exposed to ultraviolet lose some of their growth-promoting properties. One explanation proposes that hydrogen peroxide may be built up in the media and it may act as a bacteriostat or even a bactericide with selected organisms.

Controlled radiations emitted from germicidal lamps are playing an increasing role in the treatment of such areas as meat storage compartments, cubicles employed for aseptic filling of vials and ampoules with biologicals, stock culture transfer rooms, hospital wards, operating rooms, bakeries, schools, and banks. A number of restaurants have installed machinery for the radiation of drinking glasses as a part of their sanitizing programs. Toilet seats in public rest rooms are frequently equipped with ultraviolet light devices as a sanitary measure. The sugar industry has experimented with ultraviolet light as a means of controlling thermophilic bacteria that are a troublesome source of spoilage. Undoubtedly other industries will be finding new uses for germicidal lamps in still other ways in the never-ending search for ways and means to improve the quality of their products. In no instance should the use of radiation serve as a substitute for good old-fashioned cleanliness. Instead of a cover-up for unsanitary conditions, radiations should be employed as adjuncts to accepted techniques in sanitation.

Roentgen Rays

This type of radiation bears the name of a German physicist, Wilhelm Konrad Roentgen, who called them X rays. Peculiar powers of penetration are characteristic of these rays which can traverse living tissues. In fact, shadowgrams can be taken of such objects as bones embedded in tissues. Roentgen reported no appreciable effect could be noticed on the vitality of bacteria, presumably also embedded in tissues, but recent studies have indicated that X rays can be quite destructive to microorganisms, at least *in vitro*.

One effect of roentgen rays on cells is their ability to induce **mutation,** which means a permanent change in characteristics of the offspring of the cells. In bacteria these characteristics are transmitted through a genetic system similar to that found in higher forms of life. It is nature's way of assuring an orderly transmission through genes of morphology, cultural characteristics, and biochemical reactions of microorganisms. Sudden, spontaneous changes do occur in microbes, perhaps as frequently as one in ten thousand cells or as few as one in ten million. Most of these mutants are never seen because they are masked by the overwhelming numbers of unaltered cells. Were it not for the masking effect of the non-mutants in a culture, reliable descriptions of typical reactions to be expected with a given species of organism would be virtually impossible, and any orderly scheme worked out by taxonomists would be thrown into chaos. Through controlled radiation, however, the production of mutants can be stepped up many-fold in a given culture, and this increases the mathematical possibilities for isolation of such altered cells.

Not only is this type of research a scientific curiosity, but it has practical uses as well. For example, an organism that is capable of producing a given type of antibiotic might be bombarded with controlled doses of radiation to yield offspring whose antibiotic-producing capacity might be enhanced or even altered to modify its spectrum of usefulness in medicine. Mustard gas and ultraviolet light can also be employed as **mutagenic agents.**

The effects of radiation are of importance to human health in other ways than as possible antimicrobial agents. If we assume a future world population of five billion persons, the annual natural occurrence of major genetic defects is calculated to be within the range of from 700,000 to 3,000,000 cases. Natural background radiation may account for from 25,000 to 1,000,000 of this total. The balance can be traced to man-made exposures. Before anyone willingly allows himself to be exposed to man-controlled radiations, X rays or others, a careful evaluation should be made of the benefits to be gained weighed against possible harmful effects in the immediate or the long-range future.

I do not believe it is out of place in a textbook of this type to devote a few sentences to issue an additional warning to readers about potential radiation hazards. In this day when our diplomats and politicians devote such a great deal of time discussing control of atomic energy and we are constantly being reminded through all media of communications of the hazards of strontium-90 in the atmosphere, it behooves those of us who have anything to do with matters pertaining to human health to become even more conscious of the added dangers being imposed upon an un-informed public through unnecessary exposure to radiation in medical and in dental practice. There is, in addition, no conceivable justification for clerks to employ any type of radiation device in the fitting of shoes, whether it be on children or on adults. Too many of these machines lack proper safeguards against stray radiation, to say nothing of the jolt being imposed on the foot itself. Individuals under the age of thirty, according to experts in radiology, should take particular care to avoid man-made radiation except in extreme emergencies.

A recent study revealed that one third of all physicians and 95 per cent of dentists in New York State used roentgen machines in their practice. There is always room for tightening up protective techniques even among well-educated professional men, some of whom know only the barest de-tails of the potential hazards to themselves and to their patients. If per-manent damage to reproductive glands is to be avoided, leaded aprons and other available protective devices must be employed routinely to shield individuals from direct and scattered radiations. Cumulative rec-ords should be maintained by physicians and dentists to insure that their patients are not receiving dangerous levels of exposure, especially now when background radiation could climb to dangerous levels in a short time by accident or by design.

Cathode Rays

The type of force employed in electron microscopy, cathode rays, is also known as electron beam radiation, and its intensity is sufficient to kill microbes. In fact, a device called an Electron Accelerator can be used for sterilizing packaged materials in plastic bags at room temperature. Such items as frankfurters, hamburgers, bandaids, surgical supplies, and drugs can be successfully treated by this method, if the limits of penetrating powers are understood and practiced.

Surface Tension

Surface tension results from the attraction or cohesive force between molecules on the surface of liquids, and this brings molecules closer together at the surface to form an invisible film. This "togetherness" at the surface is known as surface tension. The supporting "film" of water can be demonstrated by floating a relatively heavy needle flat on the surface of a glass of water. The needle will remain afloat so long as the film of "condensed" water is not penetrated or the tension of the liquid lowered by the addition of surface tension depressants such as soaps, detergents, lauryl sulfate, alcohol, bile, or other similar agents.

It is this curious invisible membrane pulling the water inward that permits a glass to be filled fuller than full without running over. Surface tension and wetness are related. A low surface tension solution can come into more intimate contact with objects, and it is by this means that the active ingredient in a disinfectant, for example, can get at bacteria and bring about their destruction more readily.

Alcohol, because of its lower surface tension, is really wetter than water. A **tincture** (alcoholic solution) is better than an **aqueous** solution because of its greater wetting power. Our skin contains natural oils to keep the cells lubricated, and oil, as you know, repels water. To demonstrate the effectiveness of a tincture, place a drop of water on the back of your hand and notice how the water tends to retain its shape. Now next to it place a drop of alcohol, and notice how this lower surface tension liquid spreads more than the water. This spreading allows more intimate contact with the cells of the hand; when a wound, especially one with some depth, is treated, the high penetrating power of alcohol will permit better action on a greater surface than would be true if water were the carrying agent for a germicide.

The inward pull of the surface of a fluid is measured in a unit called a dyne (Greek *power*), which can be defined as the force which, acting on a gram for a second, imparts to it a velocity of a centimeter per second. This is approximately the force exerted by a milligram weight under the influence of gravity. Pure water gives a reading of 73.0 dynes, whereas ethyl alcohol has only 21.7 dynes. A higher tension fluid will draw itself together like a drop of mercury that lacks intimate contact with the supporting surface.

When bacteria grow in nutrient broth, each species of organism tends to grow in a typical manner: with a surface pellicle, or uniform clouding of the broth, or in the form of sediment. By alteration of the surface tension of this broth, pellicle formation can be prevented, since the surface film will be lacking and can no longer support the mat of microbial growth. *Mycobacterium tuberculosis,* the etiological agent in tuberculosis, is a **hydrophobic** (water-repelling) organism, and it grows typically as a wrinkled pellicle on suitable nutrient media. But if even minute amounts of a surface tension depressant are added to the broth, compact surface growth is absent and the pathogenic bacteria grow dispersed throughout the tube.

Sonic and Ultrasonic Vibrations

Sound waves are longitudinal mechanical vibrations. The human ear has the capacity to hear sound waves with frequencies extending from about 20 to 32 to 20,000 cycles per second. The higher figure tends to be lower as people become older. Supersonic is designated from about 8900 to 200,000 cycles per second. Vibrations above 200,000 are called ultrasonic.

Cells are adversely affected by high-frequency sound waves, and the damage appears to be attributable to an imbalance that develops within the cell, leading eventually to its rupture. As is true with all physical forces exerted upon microbes, differences in resistance exist between species. Spore-formers are considerably more resistant than such "delicate" cells as *Neisseria gonorrheae,* which are unable to cope with much of anything in the way of physical or chemical treatment. The organism responsible for diphtheria, *Corynebacterium diphtheriae,* a granule-laden cell, also exhibits considerably more resistance to vibrations than other non-spore-forming cells. Amplitude rather than frequency appears to determine killing power.

Gentle vibrations, or even rocking and rolling, will actually stimulate microbial growth in fluids. This positive action can be explained at least in part as being due to removal of concentrated waste products from the immediate area of the developing cells. This permits greater volumes of food to be carried to the cells and results in a prolonged logarithmic growth phase.

When organisms are exposed to lethal vibrations, death of all cells does not take place simultaneously. In fact, the viable count diminishes at a logarithmic rate. When gas bubbles, or foam, within the cells bombard the cell walls under the powerful influence of vibrations set at critical levels, the cells are broken up. This process is termed **cavitation.**

Through the years as investigators have literally torn cells to shreds, one of their problems has been to devise reliable means for releasing enzymes, endotoxins, antigens, cell walls, and other cell components in the never-ending search for truth—the ultimate goal of biological research. The earlier techniques of chemical extraction with or without heat always left something to be desired, because the method employed invariably altered the chemical or physical makeup of the test cells.

In recent years sonic oscillators have been perfected whereby discs of nickel or quartz crystals have been set into vibration at supersonic levels through the influence of alternating electric current. The adverse effects on the treated cells are now minimized and more useful information is being gained about the structure and the function of cell components.

One more approach to reduction in air pollution through control of smoke and soot in industrial centers may be through the use of sonic precipitators in smokestacks. Not only will this permit a reduction in these undesirable pollutants, but it will also remove the number of "magic carpets" on which bacteria can ride through the atmosphere. The use of electrostatic precipitators has already been proved feasible for the control of dust or mist. When these particles are ionized in an electrostatic field, they become charged and are attracted to collecting surfaces having an opposite charge. Every feasible avenue of approach should be pursued vigorously in this latest frontier of research to clear our atmosphere of unattractive particles that constitute a real threat to human health.

Electricity and Electrophoresis

While at first thought it might be assumed that bacterial cells suspended in water or milk could be electrocuted when a current is passed through the fluid, it doesn't in reality work that way. Resistances set up may result in the elevation of temperature to a point where organisms are coagulated, or the electricity might cause release of minute amounts of such toxic substances as ozone or perhaps even nascent oxygen, and these end products could bring about increased microbial mortality. Or if the current is intense and prolonged, electrolysis of some of the constituents of a medium might occur, causing deleterious effects on cells. It has been recommended by some workers that the passage of 2.5 volts of electricity through sewage effluent holds some promise in treatment of these wastes, since chlorine can be released in the process. But because of the strong affinity of chlorine for organic matter, it would appear that considerable amounts of chlorine gas would have to be made available before any material change in microbial content of the effluent could be effected.

Microbes possess a negative electrical charge in neutral solutions. This can be shown by passing an electrical current through a liquid in which organisms are suspended, and watching the microbes migrate toward the positive electrode (anode). Such movement in an electrical field is called **electrophoresis.** Differences in the speed of migration of cells and of components of cells serve as a basis for separating and identifying materials of different compositions. This phase of science is receiving increasing attention and results obtained from research currently under way should open still wider horizons for those interested in pushing back the boundaries of ignorance.

Review Questions

1. Why does refrigeration retard spoilage of food?
2. How does a thermogenic organism differ from a thermophilic one?
3. What is the action desiccation that makes it effective in controlling spoilage by microorganisms?
4. How can bacteria survive lyophilization when ordinary desiccation kills many of them?
5. Why should changes in osmotic pressure be more destructive to cells than mechanical pressure?
6. Gentle rocking of a bacterial broth culture stimulates cell growth. Why wouldn't more violent agitation be even better for maintaining active multiplication of organisms?
7. What is the relationship of generation time of bacteria to incubation period of a disease?

8 MICROBIOLOGY OF WATER SUPPLIES

Historical Background

TAKE A LOOK AT ANY MAP OF ANY COUNTRY. WHERE ARE THE large centers of population? Of necessity they are located near water supplies that can support large numbers of individuals, and when a city outgrows its water resources, it literally withers.

Although the annual rainfall in a given region is at the present time beyond man's control, he does exert influence over collecting, treating, and distributing water once it becomes available. Some of the considerations and problems involved in these steps will be discussed in this chapter.

Of all the beverages concocted by man probably none is more refreshing than a drink of nature's cool, clear water. Water is not a food for man, and yet he cannot survive long without it. But unless care is exercised in handling water supplies, disease, misery, and death will take their toll.

Except for the initial few minutes of a rainstorm when the moisture is washing out suspended particles to which microorganisms cling in the atmosphere, rainwater is clean and potable. What happens after it comes in contact with the earth's surface complicates the picture, and when it comes to making water an unclean thing, man is his own worst enemy.

Forward-looking public officials must be able to project their thinking, planning, and actual construction of water-storing facilities to take into account predictions for population bulges that have a habit of cropping up from time to time in our history. Conservative estimates based upon thoughtful studies call for supplying a minimum of 150 gallons of water per person per day through periods of protracted drought as well as during the months of normal precipitation. It becomes apparent from this figure that a community of any size is faced with problems of considerable magnitude as far as storage space for such volumes is concerned. In these days of mounting costs for public services, with increasing taxes being levied to finance these projects, leaders in our government must intelligently resist public pressure to economize foolishly in the area of supplying an adequate and potable reserve of water for the future growth and development of the municipality. An abundant supply of good water is a blue-chip investment that pays handsome dividends over the long term as well as in the years immediately ahead. The future belongs to those who are prudent enough to prepare for it, and truer words could not be written with regard to water.

There is in nature an unending cycle of precipitation, runoff, infiltration, storage, evaporation, and reprecipitation. The challenge of the sanitary engineer is to catch, hold, treat, and distribute as high a percentage of this water as possible at the lowest cost per unit volume. A quick examination of rainfall maps reveals how unbalanced the moisture supply is in a country such as the United States. It may vary from as little as less than two inches annually in Death Valley, California to as much as 135 inches a year in parts of the State of Washington. Problems of redistributing this uneven supply constantly occupy the attention of many groups of individuals engaged in a number of diverse occupations. Multimillion-dollar tunnels are being bored through mountains to re-channel or divert rivers to areas where nature has been miserly with its liquid wealth. Enormous dams have been constructed all over the world to capture billions of gallons of water to assure otherwise barren valleys of adequate supplies for cultivation of crops. Deserts can be made to bloom when they are furnished the proper combinations of moisture and organic matter.

Some of today's most critical problems responsible for international tensions stem from poor distribution of the world's water pool. Much of our fresh water from rivers and streams eventually finds its way into the ocean, and our job is to recapture some of this moisture from the almost limitless supply in oceans that cover approximately 72 per cent of the earth's surface. Millions, indeed billions, of dollars have been spent and will continue to be spent in attempts to make fresh water out of sea water at a unit cost that is not prohibitive. The day is probably not too far distant when atomic fuel will make this conversion economically possible.

Natural Bodies of Water

Lakes, rivers, and streams furnish fresh water to many communities, but such natural water is constantly subject to all types of contamination and should not be used for human consumption without some previous treatment: settling, filtration, chlorination, or a combination of these. Progressive states are adopting vigorous measures to compel municipalities to stop polluting their supplies of natural water, and it has been encouraging in recent years to see these efforts bearing fruit. Fish, once driven from our inland waterways, are beginning to find conditions more tolerable as man has reversed his unwise habits of contaminating his water supplies with chemical and biological wastes.

All natural surface water should be eyed with suspicion and should not be consumed without previous treatment. It is true that nature provides some degree of self-treatment of stored water, but the amount of improvement is controlled by a number of complex factors: physical, chemical, and biological. Erroneous statements are frequently made by uninformed persons that a stream will purify itself after flowing seven miles, or some other magical number pulled out of a hat. Distance has little to do with self-improvement of flowing water, but time, temperature, pH, and biological factors do influence the rate and completeness of breakdown of undesirable sediments in water. A sluggish flow for a few miles under favorable conditions might conceivably be more effective in water improvement than a rapid flow for fifty miles under different sets of conditions. Each situation must be judged on its own merits, and general statements are unjustified and unscientific. Aeration brought about through rapid flow of water or by spraying the water into the air through jet nozzles improves the taste largely through the release of undesirable gases, including hydrogen sulfide, but if pathogenic organisms are still viable, no positive sanitary gain has been made.

Aqueducts and old clay and wooden pipes of a bygone era were not constructed to withstand much, if any, pressure; hence they were located to follow the hydraulic grade line of the area. Points of origin wisely were located in uninhabited areas, and although in those days knowledge about bacteriology was practically nil, persons in authority did recognize that human wastes had to be disposed of at some distance from water which was to be used for drinking purposes. Even Moses, in biblical times, turned out to be quite a sanitarian! (See Deuteronomy 23:12, 13.) He had to lead his followers over great distances and must have faced sanitation problems of no small magnitude.

In seventeenth-century London the death rate at times exceeded the birth rate, owing primarily to consumption of grossly polluted water. A sand filter was installed in the water system of London in 1829, while the first filter in the United States was not put to practical use until 1872—some forty-three years later—in Poughkeepsie, New York. This system, with some modifications, is still in use today as it purifies water drawn from the Hudson River. The dramatic drop in the typhoid death rate dating from the installation of water filtration devices leaves little doubt as to the effectiveness of this sanitary measure on public health. Death rates of about twenty per hundred thousand population have plummeted to less than one typhoid death per hundred thousand at the present time in the United States.

Dug Wells

City folks frequently are not aware of the many means by which the water supply of their country cousins can become contaminated. Although an open dug well with its metal crossbar, rope, and appealing old oaken bucket may look charming in a New England setting, certain potential sanitary hazards exist that too frequently become realities.

When the top of the well is too close to the surface of the ground and the opening is poorly covered or not covered at all, small animals—cats, rabbits, chipmunks, field mice, moles, and even polecats—frequently fall into the shallow well and drown. If their presence is not discovered immediately, the end products of their decomposition some days later will most certainly arouse the suspicions of those who depend on this supply for their drinking water. Owners of dug wells frequently insist that the sanitary risks involved with an open well are relatively small, and they may choose not to install a tight-fitting cover to prevent access of small animals. Should such a well become contaminated, however, corrective measures can be instituted and the water can be restored to potability. For a time, until dilution factor takes over, there may be a bit more protein per unit volume of water than existed previously, but this is a relatively minor matter! The technique for such corrective treatment will be taken up later in this chapter.

Should you be setting out to dig your own well, or advising others in this matter, be sure to anticipate maximum water requirements, allowing for long dry spells when the ground water (water table) level drops, by digging a well deep enough and with sufficient diameter to yield the desired volume of water. Questioning others living in the area may provide valuable clues, especially in certain localities where "the wells run dry every summer." The following figures may be helpful for ready reference in determining water volumes in circular wells.

Diameter of the Well in Feet	Approximate Volume in Gallons per Foot of Water
3	50
4	95
5	150
6	200
7	290
8	375
9	475
10	590

Drilled or Driven Wells

There are locations and situations that call for deeper sources of water than can be supplied by dug wells. In such cases water is provided from drilled or driven wells. Sometimes such supplies are referred to as artesian, but strictly speaking, an artesian well is one which flows spontaneously as a result of internal pressure, and this is not true of the majority of drilled wells—at least not in New England.

Because of their depth, chances for contamination in these wells are markedly less than with surface water, but occasionally if the vein that is tapped happens to drain from a swampy area or from a polluted source that is not subjected to sufficient natural filtration, even driven wells can yield water that is unsatisfactory from a bacteriological standpoint. Nor is drawing water from deep in the ground any guarantee that the product will have a low mineral content. In some parts of the United States the mineral content becomes the major consideration when seeking water for human or for industrial uses.

Springs

We like to believe that clear, cool water gushing from a rock is bacteriologically pure, but unfortunately this is not always the case. The surroundings can ruin an otherwise good spring unless contamination from man or other animals is kept at a safe distance. When in doubt about the safety of spring water, the simple technique of boiling it for ten minutes will render the water safe and remove any question of potability.

Cisterns

If you lived on a small island surrounded by salt water, chances are good that if you dug or drilled a well, the water would contain sufficient salt to make it unpalatable in many instances. Here again local conditions vary and you might be fortunate enough to tap into a vein of "sweet" water. But in places where satisfactory water is not available from the usual sources, one solution to the problem is to install an artificial reservoir or tank to collect rainwater. Such a setup is called a cistern. Water is collected from roofs into tanks which may have capacities of hundreds of gallons. Filters are available for removing gross particles which might be flushed from the gathering surfaces, and still other filters can be installed to remove bacteria if chlorination is not employed. The housewife who has had to wash her hair or her clothes in "hard" water which reduces or even prevents formation of suds, appreciates the availability of soft rainwater which has not picked up the chemicals responsible for the "hardness" in many areas.

Treatment of Water

The problems connected with the treatment of water for industrial uses may not be the same as those attendant with water to be used primarily for drinking purposes and other household uses. Some of the undesirable minerals in water may constitute a real threat to the efficient operation of machinery in an industrial plant which may process enormous volumes of water in a single day. These same minerals may be of little or no consequence in water being piped in the relatively small volumes required for an average household.

Chlorination

A giant step forward in public health came when chlorine and chlorine compounds were added to public water systems. It should be emphasized here that chlorination is not a means for sterilizing water. This chemical treatment will sanitize the water, making it safe for human consumption —but sanitizing and sterilizing are not the same.

Apparently the first attempt to treat a public water supply with disinfectants dates to 1897 when bleaching powder was added to the water of Adrian, Michigan. Hypochlorite solution was first employed in Jersey City, New Jersey in 1908, and four years later commercial equipment became available for the application of gaseous chlorine through a device called a chlorinator.

An amazingly small amount of chlorine is required to check pathogenic bacteria in water. If the contact period is at least ten minutes and the pH of the water close to neutrality (7.0), a residual concentration of three tenths of a part of free chlorine per million parts of water (abbreviated 0.3 PPM) will kill the usual enteric pathogenic bacteria found in the

United States. Amoebic dysentery parasites (*Endamoeba histolytica*) can withstand this level and exposure of chlorine, and in areas of the world where this serious disease is endemic, filtration of drinking water through sand is recommended prior to chlorination. Because chlorine exhibits such a pronounced affinity for organic matter, enough excess chemical must be added to supply the initial demands and to insure proper residual levels.

When individuals with private wells run into difficulty with animals falling into their wells, a simple procedure can be put into operation to restore the water's potability. Scoop out the remains (cats are frequently found dead in pairs—one of each sex), or as much of the remnants as possible and chlorinate the well heavily. One accepted and time-tested technique is to mix about four ounces of chloride of lime in a pint of water. The lime will not dissolve too readily because of the insoluble calcium in it, but the active ingredient, chlorine, will go into solution if water is added to the lime slowly and first worked into a paste. For every estimated 100 gallons of water to be treated, add about 2 ounces of the concentrated lime solution directly into the well. Let it remain overnight before drawing water from the well to reduce the strong odor and taste of chlorine. Under normal circumstances such treated water should be fit for human use if the cause of the pollution was merely a dead animal. An ounce and a half of liquid bleach may be substituted for the chloride of lime should this material be more readily available in a given area. It is important to understand that unless the cause of pollution is removed, especially if the contamination is coming from raw sewage, chlorination is merely a temporary expedient and the harmful microbes will return to the well.

To calculate the number of gallons of water in a well resort to a little simple arithmetic learned in high school. Find the volume of a cylinder (pi times the radius squared times the depth of water in feet). This will be the number of cubic feet of water which must be multiplied by about 7.5 to convert the figure into gallons of water.

Filtration

Filtration involves passing water through layers of sand or other porous materials to trap gross particles, together with undesirable microorganisms, as a means of improving water for human consumption. Turbid water may need to be filtered since it may contain finely divided particles in the form of silt, plant and animal material, but a dirty appearance does not necessarily have a direct relationship to potability. Water may be undesirable to the eye, but it could be safer to drink than crystal clear water drawn from a questionable source. As someone once remarked, a clear sparkling water cascading from a spring may appear as such because of the sun's reflection off the backs of the typhoid cells! Actually, pathogenic bacteria suspended in water come out second best in competition with most saprophytes, and the latter can be expected to be in the majority in an unclean body of water, whereas in clear water where biological competition for survival is less keen, typhoid, paratyphoid, and dysentery organisms might survive for some time.

SLOW SAND FILTER

An efficient sand filter is capable of removing up to 98 per cent of the organisms present in water, in addition to reducing color by as much as 40 per cent when the filter bed is processing up to six million gallons of water per acre of filter surface per day. When the operation is initiated and the sand surfaces are relatively clean, bacterial removal is relatively inefficient. Only when a film of colloidal material (*Schmutzdecke*) builds up on the particles of sand is there a good mechanical as well as biological trap that can be relied upon to remove all pathogenic bacteria.

Filter beds vary from 2 to 4 feet in thickness with the top layer composed mostly of fine sand. This layer is supported by coarse sand, below which in turn are fine gravel, coarse gravel, and finally perforated drainage tiles to carry away the effluent. When clogging of the sand becomes such that the rate of water flow has been reduced to an uneconomical rate, cleaning is conducted by physical removal of the top inch or so of sand, and only when a considerable depth has been removed through repeated cleaning operations is the sand layer replaced.

RAPID SAND FILTER

When enormous volumes of water must be treated, it becomes impractical to tie up the increasing amounts of real estate required to operate a slow sand filter. A rapid filter is constructed on a similar principle, but a preliminary coagulation of suspended organic matter is carried out by the addition of chemicals, such as aluminum sulfate which in an alkaline state causes the formation of flocculent aluminum hydroxide. As this filmy precipitate settles in the water by gravity it brings down with it a great percentage of suspended organic debris. This reduces the load on the filters and allows up to forty times the volume of water to pass through the sand, which is more coarse than that employed with the slower system.

The same conditioning and build-up of a *Schmutzdecke* is not required, but in turn a higher percentage of bacteria may find their way into the effluent which should be chlorinated as an added safety measure. Filtered water has a more uniform concentration of organic matter, and this makes it easier for the engineer to control the chlorine residual within narrower limits. Raw untreated surface water varies in organic content from day to day, and this complicates the job of keeping the chlorine content even and at the prescribed level.

PRESSURE FILTERS

A compact water-treatment unit encased in steel serves a useful purpose in the filtering of small volumes of water in industry or for a swimming pool. Water is forced through the sand under pressure, but the efficiency

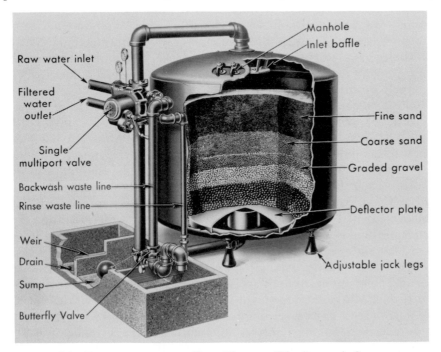

FIG. 8.1. Pressure type water filter. (Courtesy The Permutit Company, New York, N. Y.)

of this system is not as great as some of the others; hence, these devices have limited usefulness and are not recommended for municipalities even if the flow of water is sufficient to provide the required volume of water.

Diatomite filters have come into some prominence in recent years. They are based upon forcing water through diatomaceous earth. Some portable units recommended for camping trips also have the filter candles impregnated with silver to add its oligodynamic effect to the other principles of mechanical trapping of organisms through controlled pore sizes and differences in electrical charges. The filter material carries a positive charge, and the negatively-charged bacteria are attracted to the walls of the pores in the filter as water is drawn through the unit.

Fluoridation

Whenever public health authorities attempt to institute measures designed to improve human health, no matter how conscientiously their educational program is planned and executed a vociferous minority of indignant citizens can always be counted upon to speak against the advocated change. This pattern manifested itself when pasteurization of dairy products was advocated and when chlorination of water supplies came into being; today the target is fluoridation of water. Informed individuals and professional groups believe that fluoridation of public water supplies can materially reduce dental decay, especially in younger children where the teeth are still in their formative stages.

Fluoride ions are added to public water supplies in the form of sodium fluoride, sodium silicofluoride, or ammonium silicofluoride in carefully controlled quantities to yield a residual of one PPM which has been found to be optimum for reducing dental caries in children by as much as 60 per cent. Reports vary in different sections of the country as to the effectiveness of the procedure, but there is little doubt that fluoridation is a giant step forward in the direction of dental health improvement. The American Dental Association has given its backing to the procedure and public health departments on the local and state levels have joined forces to provide their support to this breakthrough in dental science.

Persons who reside in rural areas or in small communities where central water supplies are not available are advised to take their children to a dentist who can apply one of the fluoride compounds to the outside of the children's teeth according to a time schedule that has been found to be effective. Taking fluorides internally through drinking water is recommended in preference to topical-application of stronger solutions, but both programs should be pushed vigorously in order to reach as many persons as possible. Manufacturers of dentifrices have joined the ranks by adding fluorides, usually stannous fluoride, to their product in the rising tide of support for this progressive health program. The exact mechanism by which the chemical ion prevents dental decay is far from understood. It may be a direct combination with the tooth itself; it may be due to an interference with enzyme systems of acid-producing bacteria in the mouth; or, possibly, it is a combination of these and other as yet unrecognized mechanisms.

Microbiological Testing of Water

Most people take good drinking water for granted, and it is usually only when trouble is suspected that a second thought is given to the quality of what comes out of the faucet. When a rural family becomes ill with intestinal upsets, one of the first considerations of an alert physician is the possibility of an impure water supply which can transmit enteric disease. A properly conducted examination by a qualified bacteriologist can supply the physician with valuable information that might lead him to take appropriate corrective action. Newly dug wells probably should be tested for potability, especially if there is any question about proximity to sewage sources.

It is unwise to make a blanket statement as to what one should consider a safe distance separating a dug well from raw sewage. Drilled wells, in general, should not raise quite as many doubts, but even here the nominal charge for having a bacteriological analysis conducted would be well spent. Certain types of home loans (F.H.A. and V.A.) require proof that the water supply on the property to be purchased is safe for humans. Analysis of mineral content and pH may be added requirements for such loans. Adoption agencies will require proof of potability of water if the new parents do not obtain their water from an approved municipal supply. This is a sound precautionary measure for the protection of the child.

If polluted water is allowed to trickle straight down through 10 feet of moderately compact soil that is not honeycombed with gravel and other large particles that offer little filtering potential, pathogenic organisms have a difficult time getting through this type of a filter bed. However a distance of 10 feet laterally through ground is far from adequate. When a dug well is being prepared, therefore, soil should be packed around the top of the well for a depth of at least 10 feet. Better still, water-proof tile should line the well to the same depth.

An absolute minimum of 50 feet, and preferably 75 feet, should separate a dug well from the nearest sewage even when the sewage is at a level lower than the water in the well. Whenever sewage sources are at a higher elevation, the well must be placed considerably farther away than 75 feet. Each site must be examined before exact acceptable minimum distances can be stated. This evaluation is best conducted by a sanitary engineer who can draw on his experience and accepted practices in his profession.

Strange as it may seem to a novice in bacteriology, samples of water are not tested directly for the presence of typhoid, paratyphoid, dysentery, or any other enteric pathogen when the water is subjected to a bacteriological analysis. These organisms are relatively difficult to detect, especially if they are few in number. But it takes only a small number of typhoid cells (possibly only one) to infect a human host, and for this reason no chances can be taken that the rare cells might be overlooked in a test.

Sewage pollution from wastes of man and other animals can be detected with a high degree of accuracy by looking for the presence of a small gram negative rod, *Escherichia coli,* found in the intestines of all warm-blooded animals. This microbe serves as an index of pollution. The ability of *Escherichia coli* to ferment the disaccharide lactose with the production of both acid and gas is a unique physiological reaction for gram negative bacteria. This test serves as the initial step in water testing. If *E. coli* are found, then pathogenic bacteria *might* be present, and the water is polluted and *potentially* dangerous. It should be pointed out that *coli* taken by mouth are not in themselves considered to be pathogenic; it is the company they keep that makes them guilty by association.

A brief review of the steps involved in a bacteriological water analysis will point out the soundness of the technique that has been adopted by the American Public Health Association as a standard for laboratories to follow.

All samples to be tested must first be shaken in a standard prescribed manner; seven times, in the space of one foot, in an arc of 90 degrees in seven seconds. This will insure uniform distribution of organisms present in the water.

Presumptive Test

Tubes of lactose broth are inoculated with the water in a series as follows: five tubes with 10 ml, one tube with 1 ml, and the seventh tube with 0.1 ml. At the same time a standard plate count is conducted by plating 1 ml in tryptone-glucose agar. All tubes and the plate are incubated at 37°C for twenty-four hours.

At the conclusion of this incubation period the colonies that have developed on the agar plate are counted, and if the number exceeds one hundred colonies per ml, the water is not considered to be satisfactory, regardless of what shows up in the tubes of lactose broth. Should acid and gas fail to develop in any of the seven tubes inoculated, the lactose broth is reincubated for an additional twenty-four hours, or for a total of forty-eight hours before the tubes are judged to be negative.

Because acid and gas can be produced through synergism, a phenomenon described in Chapter 2, a positive reaction in lactose can be taken as only presumptive evidence that the sample *might* be polluted. In addition to *E. coli,* another harmless topsoil gram negative rod, *Aerobacter aerogenes* that closely resembles *coli* morphologically can also ferment lactose with the liberation of acid and gas. Its presence is considered undesirable since a properly protected well should not allow entrance of organisms from the bacteria-laden topsoil. If *Aerobacter* get into well water, any number of other bacteria, pathogenic as well as saprophytic, could also conceivably find their way in and create a real threat to health. There are so-called intermediate coliforms that also must be considered. They represent a group of fourteen species of gram negative rods that could come either from soil or from intestines, and they are able to produce physiological reactions somewhere between those of typical *coli* and *aerogenes*. More will be said about these intermediate forms later.

Confirmed Test

The second step in a bacteriological water analysis is to confirm any positive presumptive reactions by trying to determine whether they might be due to synergism or to the presence of coliforms—a term used to describe any one of the sixteen species including *coli, aerogenes,* and intermediates.

The confirmed test is an example of a bacteriostatic medium being employed to good advantage, and several time-tested media are available for the purpose. One of these is Endo agar, named in honor of its developer, a Japanese bacteriologist. In addition to the basic nutritional requirements incorporated in this medium, reduced basic fuchsin is added as a bacteriostat to retard the growth of gram positive organisms which do not concern us in this type of analysis. The inhibitory action is effective only for about twenty-four hours after the agar surface has been streaked. After that the gram positive bacteria can overcome the static action to varying degrees depending upon the species. Since the confirmed test is a search for gram negative microbes, Endo agar serves a useful purpose in this regard. Coliforms grow with characteristic colonies on this medium, and your laboratory experience will help you to recognize them.

A second useful solid medium for conducting the confirmed test is eosine-methylene blue agar, the name indicating the dyes employed to provide bacteriostasis. It works on the same principle as the Endo medium, but the colonial appearance of bacterial species differs.

To conduct the confirmed test a loopful of broth from a positive presumptive tube is streaked into the surface of either Endo or E.M.B. agar which is then allowed to incubate for not over twenty-four hours at 37°C.

Completed Test

Suspicious-looking colonies typical of coliforms are fished from the confirmed plate and are transferred to a standard agar slant and to a secondary lactose broth tube for incubation. In contrast to the presumptive lactose broth which is inoculated with raw water containing a mixture of organisms, the secondary lactose broth represents a pure culture of a suspected organism, and if acid and gas are formed in these tubes, synergism can be ruled out. Therefore, a positive secondary lactose broth tube, coupled with the appearance of gram negative rods as shown by a stain made from growth taken from the agar slant culture, completes the water test.

IMViC Reactions

A positive completed test is sufficient to condemn the water, but it may be wise when testing private water supplies to be able to tell the owner of the well whether the contamination is, in all likelihood, due to soil washings (as shown by the presence of *A. aerogenes*) or to the more significant sewage pollution (as shown by *E. coli*) with its potential danger of association with pathogens.

To determine more specifically the types of coliforms that yield a positive completed test, it is customary to run them through a series of four reactions called the IMViC tests: indole, methyl red, Voges-Proskauer, and citrate.

INDOLE TEST

This reaction is based upon the ability of an organism to produce free indole from the amino acid tryptophane. By cultivation in a suitable medium (tryptone or trypticase broth) for a minimum of forty-eight hours, certain species possess the necessary enzyme systems required to separate indole from the rest of the molecule as shown in the following reaction:

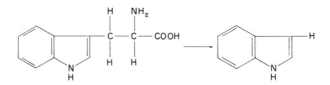

Since this chemical change is not visible to the eye, it becomes necessary to add an indicator to detect the free indole; Ehrlich's aldehyde (paradimethylaminobenzaldehyde) fulfills this requirement. After suitable cultivation of the pure culture, the indicator solution, which has a relatively low specific gravity, is carefully layered on top of the broth. If free indole is present, the aldehyde turns a cherry red color, which constitutes a positive test.

METHYL RED TEST

The amount of acid produced when coliforms attack glucose varies with the species; this is the basis of the methyl red test. A highly buffered (phosphate) glucose broth developed by Clark and Lubs is inoculated with the organisms and allowed to incubate at body temperature (37°C) for a minimum of forty-eight hours. If enough acid has been produced by the microbes, the buffering power of the broth is overcome and the pH drops to a level sufficiently low (about 4.6) to permit the indicator, methyl red, to turn red when a few drops are introduced into the broth culture. A negative test will yield a yellow color upon addition of the indicator. *E. coli* is positive, whereas *A. aerogenes* is negative.

VOGES-PROSKAUER TEST

Another differential chemical change, described by Voges and Proskauer, occurs when bacteria grow for from two to five days in Clark and Lubs broth. In the breakdown of the glucose a compound called acetyl methyl carbinol is formed. Its presence can be detected by making the broth strongly alkaline upon the addition of a few milliliters of 40 per cent potassium hydroxide (KOH). This alkali converts the acetyl methyl carbinol into diacetyl which appears as a pink color initially forming at the surface of the tube. The reaction may be enhanced by the catalyst alpha naphthol in an alcoholic solution. After shaking of the cultures to incorporate air, the tubes are stored at 37°C for from thirty to sixty minutes. *E. coli* is negative and *A. aerogenes* is positive for this reaction.

CITRATE TEST

Every living cell must have an available source of carbon to survive and metabolize. In the citrate test a synthetic medium (Koser's citrate) with sodium citrate as the sole source of carbon has been found capable of supporting the growth of *A. aerogenes* but not of *E. coli* which appears to lack the enzyme systems necessary to attack and release carbon bound in this particular molecular combination. Growth of the bacteria, as evidenced by turbidity in an otherwise water-clear citrate broth, constitutes a positive test.

Caution must be observed, however, in the manner by which the tubes are inoculated. Too heavy an inoculum or improper transfer can result in growth which is not a true measure of the metabolism of the culture being studied. It is conceivable that enough nutrients could be carried over from the standard agar slant from which the coliform is taken and could support the growth of a non-citrate-utilizing organism in the citrate broth. Or a large inoculum relatively free of medium could supply enough cells to be cannibalized by the carbon-hungry cells to yield a turbidity in the medium which would yield erroneous results in this particular type of nutrition test.

To avoid these pitfalls it is generally recommended that a light initial inoculation of organisms be made into a tube of sterile water, and a loopful of this water blank suspension be transferred into the Koser's citrate medium.

A typical *E. coli* is said to be IMViC $+ + - -$ and *A. aerogenes* is characteristically IMViC $- - + +$. With four different tests available in such a series varying from all-negative results to all-positive findings it becomes apparent that there are sixteen different combinations of these reactions. The fourteen types that do not match the two patterns described above are typical of the intermediate coliforms which can be found in either the soil or the intestines. Because their origin cannot be stated with certainty in every case, the presence of intermediates in a water supply must be looked upon as being undesirable, and such water should be condemned as being potentially dangerous.

Chemical Analyses

In the majority of cases private water supplies probably do not need to be subjected to chemical testing unless the owner finds that the water is having an adverse effect on the plumbing system. In addition, the Federal Housing Authority (F.H.A.) requires analysis of water for hardness, chlorides, iron, manganese, nitrates, and detergent before loans for certain property can be processed and approved. Experience, apparently, has convinced this agency that there is justification for this requirement.

Hardness tests determine the soap-consuming capacity, or the ability to produce lather, a consideration of some importance to a housewife. Chloride in the form of the chlorine ion is one of the major anions in sewage. While a particular bacteriological test may prove to be negative, a high chloride content must be looked upon with suspicion; either there are sewage byproducts in the area or the well is too close to salt water.

Iron is undesirable in excess because of the rusty appearance it gives to water and the nuisance it creates on clothes and fixtures. Iron can appear in many forms: a true solution, colloidal state, coarse suspended particles, or as ferrous or ferric compounds. Manganese, like iron, may cause objectionable and tenacious stains to plumbing fixtures. The pH of the water is another consideration in certain areas, and water that is too acid may do severe damage to pipes and equipment.

A relatively recent chemical problem that has presented itself, particularly in rural areas where inhabitants depend upon private wells for their water, is the presence of detergents in waters. This is probably the number one water problem to public health authorities at this writing. Detergents are man-made and are not altered or used up in the ground the way soaps are, and because of their staying power, they build up in the soil and make water foamy. We don't know as yet what level of detergents should be considered harmful to humans, but as is customary in matters dealing with public health, it is better to bend over backwards and condemn a water supply that contains these chemicals than to allow the consumer to go ahead and use the water for drinking, perhaps with long-range harmful effects. Many new homes in our mushrooming housing developments are equipped with automatic washing machines for clothes and for dishes, and if the waste water is disposed of in a dry well or a leaching bed, the surrounding ground can become saturated with detergents which eventually find their way deep into the ground. The writer has seen any number of drilled wells, one hundred feet or more in depth, which have become so saturated with detergents that when the faucet is turned on, little more than foam comes out. Foam may look appealing to some on a glass of cold beer, but it not only *looks* out of place, it *is* out of place in drinking water. Detergents present a real challenge to the ingenuity of sanitary engineers and chemists. The best advice to give someone who has the detergent problem is to have him return to the use of soap, dig or drill another well, and hope for the best!

The Microbiology of Ice

One should realize that freezing does not immediately kill bacteria in water. In fact it may take up to six months for enteric pathogens to die, and spore-forming bacteria may survive indefinitely. High standards of sanitation must be maintained in plants that manufacture ice and in those harvesting ice from open bodies of water. Authorities are not in complete agreement on the role that ice may play in the spread of disease, but to play safe, many communities require that natural ice harvested from bodies of water that might be contaminated must be stored for a minimum of six months, by the end of which time typhoid cells and other enteric pathogens appear to die.

Too often one hears people say that even though a cocktail glass may be dirty or has been used by someone else without being washed, it doesn't really matter because the alcohol in the drink will kill the "germs" anyway. Unfortunately, this is not so. Microbes from dirty glasses or from impure ice are not materially affected by the alcohol in a cocktail.

Manufactured or "artificial" ice which moves out into the market in relatively short time after being frozen, must be made from water of the highest purity. The control maintained in some ice plants can stand considerable improvement if the bacterial counts of water from melted ice is any criterion. There are those who feel that the potential danger from blocks of ice or from ice cubes is negligible, but this writer feels that this area of sanitation and public health should not be pushed under the carpet. Instances of intestinal upsets have been reported among students who have eaten in dining halls where the ice cubes were found to harbor large numbers of undesirable bacteria. Once the ice has been manufactured, it becomes equally important that it be stored and handled under sanitary conditions; otherwise, carriers of enteric diseases could very well set off an epidemic among those who use the ice in cold drinks.

Public Drinking Cups and Fountains

The health hazards that lurk in the old common drinking cup that used to hang on the village pump should be well known to most people today, but there are still some who either are not aware of the potential dangers or who will not be frightened by all this "scare talk." When one realizes the types and numbers of microorganisms in the human mouth—millions of them—the transfer of bacteria by means of a common cup should become more meaningful. We may be resistant to our own microbes, but to someone lacking these resistance factors these same cells can spell disease and death.

The syphilitic, the individual with a sore throat, one with active tuberculosis, and many others might have used that cup just a few minutes before you came along. Microbes require moisture and they can survive for considerable time on moist surfaces. You may think that your town doesn't have a common drinking cup; they went out of style years ago! Are you sure? What about that drinking fountain in your school or church where the water pressure is so low that hardly a trickle comes out when you turn the handle? You practically have to put your lips on the outlet to get any water. Isn't that the same as a common cup? Perhaps someone with a flair for design but with no background in microbiology designed an attractive guard on the drinking fountain to prevent contact of the lips with the outlet. And perhaps the water pressure is still too low to shoot out a reasonable stream that can be picked up without having the residue drop back on the faucet or bubbler. Any contact of the mouth with parts of the fountain makes it no better than the old rusty cup on the village green. All we have done in many of our modern buildings is to bring the common cup indoors!

Those of us engaged in public health have an obligation to call such unsanitary conditions to the attention of those who can and who should take corrective action.

Swimming Pools

A swimming pool, whether it be an expensive tiled area or a natural body of water, can provide healthful and refreshing bathing, or it can be a focus of infection that can cause misery and possibly death. When the call of the "ole swimmin' hole" in the spring lures youngsters to its banks, there are sanitary precautions that should be taken if the few minutes of fun are not to be followed by days or weeks of pain and misery in a hospital bed.

Stagnant bodies of water must always be looked upon with suspicion as possible swimming sites. Rats and other animals living on the shore like to take a cool dip too, but unfortunately a high percentage of wild rats harbor and excrete in their feces and urine a number of bacteria pathogenic for man. One of these is *Leptospira,* spiral-shaped organisms that are the cause of severe jaundice. Weil's disease, caused by *Leptospira icterohemorrhagiae,* has a fatality rate in humans as high as 25 per cent.

Another disease that can be contracted from swimming in contaminated water is middle ear infection with green pus caused by a gram negative rod, *Pseudomonas,* also excreted by small animals. Deafness will be the aftermath of this infection unless prompt attention is devoted to treatment, usually with antibiotics. Unfortunately, this organism exhibits a powerful resistance to the usual antibiotics employed against infections.

Sinus irritations and certain fungus infections must be added to the list of possible diseases contracted from contaminated water used for bathing. Outdoor ponds should have both an inlet and an outlet to insure a moving body of water with dilution factors helping to minimize any build-up of microbes to levels dangerous for human beings.

As our standard of living continues to reach new heights, one of the status symbols of success is the possession of an outdoor swimming pool. But the care of such pools may not be fully appreciated until the routine cleaning and disinfecting procedures are pointed out to the prospective owner.

Manufacturers of private pools generally recommend that the automatic machinery be adjusted to maintain a chlorine level about twice that recommended for drinking water, 0.3 PPM. If the level exceeds 0.6 PPM, eye irritation will increase; if it is much lower, the effectiveness of the chemical is lost. Only by the continuous introduction of chlorine into the circulating water can the safety of the pool be maintained.

The usual shower with soap preceding a dip in the pool is one means by which the chlorine concentration can be kept uniform. Perspiration and other organic matter on the body can use up chlorine very quickly and the residual will drop to an ineffective point. Even when no bathers are in the pool, chlorine is lost by mere exposure of the surface water to the air. Obviously, care should be exercised to keep out of the pool persons suffering from skin infections, whether they are severe athlete's foot, a body rash, or localized infections with pus. Staphylococci, which are the cause of many skin blemishes, can also cause severe eye inflammation (**conjunctivitis**) unless prescribed chlorine residuals are maintained.

Review Questions

1. What specific factors have tended to increase per capita water requirements in the United States?
2. Is it feasible to retard the rate of water evaporation from open reservoirs?
3. What percentage of the drinking water of the United States would you estimate must be purified to remove human and animal wastes before it is consumed?
4. What major advantages can you list for a drilled well over a dug well?
5. Are there chemicals other than chlorine that might be employed for making water safe for human consumption?
6. If a dug well has a diameter of 6 feet and there are 10 feet of water in the well, how many gallons of water are there in the well? How much chlorine would be required to treat this volume of water if the well were recently constructed?
7. Can you raise any valid objections to artificial fluoridation of a public water supply? What are they? Do they outweigh the positive benefits to human health?
8. Isn't it wasteful to condemn a water supply from which you have not isolated known enteric pathogens? Defend your answer.
9. Why might the presence in a water supply of intermediate coliforms have more sanitary significance than the presence of *Aerobacter aerogenes?*
10. What would you surmise might be the eventual answer to the detergent problem in our water supplies?

9 ‖ MICROBIOLOGY OF SEWAGE

SEWAGE MAY BE DEFINED AS THE DILUTE WATER-BORNE WASTES from households, industry, or municipal sources. This excludes solids such as garbage, ashes, and rubbish.

The point was made in the previous chapter that attempting to obtain sufficient water to provide over one hundred gallons per person per day presents a real challenge to any community where rainfall is limited and storage facilities are restricted. Having used the water, the town is now faced with what could be a still more troublesome problem: how to get rid of its liquid wastes. Proper disposal of sewage is of paramount importance in preventive medicine, and unless this operation is conducted scientifically, sewage will present a serious threat to human health. Should you believe that such a concern is of modern origin, open your Bible and read Deuteronomy xxiii:12, 13.

A conscientious public health nurse working in a rural area has to be an ingenious individual as she faces myriad unique problems with which an urban nurse need be concerned seldom, if at all. The "country" nurse must be equipped with a background in the paramedical sciences of sanitary engineering and bacteriology with a smattering of psychology and a lot of good common sense. All of these come in mighty handy in her day-to-day dealings with those families who must rely upon their own resources and ingenuity for the safe disposal of liquid and solid wastes.

175

Composition of Sewage

There is no such thing as a "typical" composition of sewage; it varies widely from day to day, even within small areas. However, the bulk of sewage is composed of about 99 per cent water with the remaining 1 per cent made up of urea, proteins, carbohydrates, fats, and soaps, some in the form of gross particles and others as colloidal suspensions. Much of this consists of unstable compounds capable of being broken down through microbial activity in a process called **biolysis.** In general, organic matter is more readily decomposed than are inorganic compounds, and degradation usually takes place in two stages: anaerobic followed by aerobic. The anaerobic microbes initiate the breakdown, producing foul-smelling unstable end products which are then further acted upon by aerobic organisms yielding relatively stable nonodorous compounds.

Kitchen wastes differ both chemically and biologically from toilet or laundry wastes, and the composition of industrial sewage varies widely with the industry. Packinghouse debris and liquid sewage from a brass or a rubber plant would have little in common. Chemicals expelled through water from a paper mill, oil refinery, or a tannery would support little or no microbial growth, whereas the sewage from a dairy plant, cannery, or brewery could consist of organic matter that would be ideal for the growth and action of a wide variety of microbes. The ultimate objective in sewage disposal systems is to remove or decompose solids, making them no longer objectionable. From the few examples cited above it becomes apparent that the techniques employed for accomplishing this feat must differ widely to fit the specific situation.

Disposal of Human Wastes

Private Homes

The average adult is said to excrete about 68 grams of urea, principally in urine, and approximately 20 grams of solids in feces per day. Since the pH of most household waste water varies between 6.0 and 8.5, the millions of bacteria excreted in fecal matter can survive and in certain instances actually multiply for extended periods with all of the dangers to health that this may entail. Excreted microbes include a wide range of organisms —bacteria, yeasts, and viruses—extending from aerobes through strict anaerobes, and saprophytes through parasites. The real danger of sewage lies in the unfortunate fact that a certain number (perhaps 5 per cent) of persons who contract enteric diseases including typhoid, paratyphoid, and bacillary and amoebic dysentery remain as healthy carriers and excrete viable pathogenic organisms for the remainder of their lives.

Some of these carriers realize the potential hazard they present to others as they wander about as mobile incubators generating cells packed with a lethal punch; others, through ignorance or indifference, take few if any precautions to keep their microbes from being transmitted to unsuspecting innocent victims. Typhoid Mary is an excellent example of one in the latter category. No one really knows how many cases of typhoid she caused, directly or indirectly, nor how many deaths could be traced to her carelessness.

As man moved indoors and brought his sanitary facilities with him, some health problems were modified or solved, but the basic challenge of safe disposal of human wastes remained. As greater numbers of individuals came to live in relatively close association with one another, first in villages, then in towns, and finally in cities, it became expedient for them to join forces to construct and operate some type of community disposal system. But before getting any deeper into a discussion of community problems, let's go back to the folks who still live in rural areas and are faced with the problem of getting rid of wastes coming from a single household.

One of the simplest techniques is to dig a hole and bury the excreta, but unless this is done with an understanding of potential hazards involved, diseases can be spread quite readily through the agency of flies and other vermin or through seepage into nearby water supplies. It is a recognized fact that filthy flies harbor and disseminate undesirable organisms, and if open wastes are within flying ranges of public eating establishments or kitchens in private homes, the potential danger exists that enteric pathogens will be carried to food eventually to be consumed by humans.

EARTH PIT PRIVY

The outhouse, also known as an earth pit privy, is one practical approach to the problem of waste disposal on a small scale, provided the system is so constructed that the access of flies and small animals is eliminated. Self-closing lids in these units should be standard equipment, together with tight construction to keep vermin out of fecal deposits. The privy must be of sufficient depth to allow adequate covering of organic matter with several feet of soil when the latrine is to be closed. Spreading oil over the wastes will prevent flies from using the organic deposits as a spot for laying their eggs should they get into the excreta.

An outhouse must be located in such a position that possible contamination of water supplies is avoided. Dug wells should be placed on higher ground than the average sewage sources if the topography of the land permits, and an *absolute minimum* of 50 feet should separate the two, with a distance of 75 feet or more strongly advocated. Sewage can travel relatively long distances through rocky, porous ground, which means that in some areas even one hundred feet may not be sufficient to insure elimination of sewage from surface water supplies or shallow wells.

CESSPOOLS

A cesspool is in effect a seepage pit that receives household wastes directly, but since sewage wastes can clog the openings and not all soils are porous and well adapted to receive the runoff, cesspools are not recommended. As bacteria decompose the solids, the partially digested material gradually finds its way into the surrounding ground where further breakdown by both anaerobes and aerobes proceeds. The exact details of construction of such systems will not be discussed, but needless to say, the covering on a cesspool must be tight enough to prevent creation of a nuisance.

SEPTIC TANKS

A septic tank is usually constructed of concrete or steel so that it is watertight. The capacity of the unit will vary with the number of individuals it must serve, but a suggested minimum volume is about 500 or 600 gallons of fluid. One should allow for any foreseeable expansion in family size (including in-laws!) before foolishly installing a tank that will have to be replaced a few years later by one of greater capacity. It does not pay to economize on this item if you contemplate building a home in a rural area where you are dependent upon such a system for trouble-free disposal of sewage.

Because of their specific gravity, some materials entering the digestion tank may float on the surface as scum, but the bulk of the solids drop to the bottom of the chamber as **sludge** which must be broken down into soluble or semisolid end products through biological action. Solids remain in the tank for approximately twenty-four hours before anaerobic microbial action permits the partially liquefied solids to move out as additional water is added to the unit. When solids are added at a rate in excess of decomposition, the tank will eventually become clogged and the solids will back up into the system, with unpleasant results.

If reasonable care is exercised in keeping out of the tank materials that cannot undergo active microbial decomposition, or substances that break down slowly, it should not be necessary to open and clean tanks as frequently as some folks do. If possible, fats and greases should be prevented from entering the system, since they are not readily attacked by bacteria and tend to build up in the tank. Grease traps should be installed between the kitchen sink and the septic tank, but having a grease trap that is not cleaned out periodically is like having no trap at all. Manufacturers claim that a cleaning once every three years should suffice for most properly installed systems, but the time factor naturally will be dependent upon individual situations. When cleaning does become necessary, tank trucks equipped with suction devices can remove excess sludge and dispose of it in areas approved for the purpose. Since pathogens might still be viable in sludge, great care must be exercised to prevent this harmful material from being used as fertilizer, especially on vegetables that are to be eaten raw. In addition, sludge disposal must be far enough away from water supplies to prevent their becoming contaminated.

Once the sludge has undergone the initial anaerobic decomposition in a septic tank, the next step involves disposal of the fluid, usually through a distribution system of pipes that are perforated to allow seepage of the effluent or pipes that are left open at the joints to accomplish the same ends. Such a system is usually prepared in a trench from 18 to 30 inches deep to get below the frost line, with gravel and sand as a receiving substance as the wastes leave the distribution pipes. To insure more or less even distribution of the partially digested sewage, it is customary to let the effluent flow from the septic tank into a box from which the tile pipes radiate into the surrounding prepared ground. The number of feet of drainage tile required to handle the liquid efficiently will depend upon such factors as tank capacity, slope of the land, porosity of the ground, and the temperature of the soil where the final aerobic microbial breakdown is scheduled to take place.

Community Treatment of Sewage

SEDIMENTATION TANKS

When sewage is introduced into a tank, sludge will settle out to varying degrees. In general, sedimentation is allowed to proceed for an hour or so before the liquid portion is pumped out, treated chemically (usually with chlorine), and discharged into a body of water where, if properly diluted, it will not prove to be objectionable. The remaining sludge may be transferred to drying beds from which it can be scraped and used for fill. Or the sludge may be further treated by one of the techniques to be described below, in order to decompose the organic matter into simpler and less objectionable products.

IMHOFF TANKS

A combination of sedimentation and digestion may be carried out in an **Imhoff tank** which may have a capacity up to several hundred thousand gallons of sewage. Such a device is divided into two compartments. Sewage flows into a V-shaped trough and gross particles settle into the lower compartment where anaerobic action takes place. Speed of biological action can be enhanced if the liquid sewage is first treated with alum or ferrous sulfate which acts as a coagulant. After two or three hours in the tank the sludge will have undergone sufficient digestion to permit removal of the organic matter through a sludge pipe or vent. Such partially treated solids are then allowed to undergo aerobic decomposition.

Stabilization of effluents from any type of digestion procedure must be accomplished if nuisances are to be eliminated, and this is done by passing the liquid over filtering beds composed of sand, gravel, pebbles, or other rough material that offers a hard surface area where aerobic activity can oxidize the organic content of sewage to simpler inoffensive end products.

INTERMITTENT FILTERS

This type of filter is composed of sand beds several feet in thickness. Liquid sewage is applied to a depth of 2 or 3 inches; the flow is then interrupted until the liquid trickles through the sand; before additional wastes are added, time is allowed for aerobic breakdown of the organic matter that has settled on the filter particles. The coating on the sand is made up of complex biological systems with bacteria, protozoa, and other microbes actively attacking the solids.

TRICKLING FILTER

A similar system which operates on the same fundamental principle is called a trickling filter. The liquid sewage is sprayed onto a bed of crushed rock, stones, gravel, or similar rough material to facilitate incorporation of air which speeds up microbial activity on the surface. This is a modification of an intermittent filter, since the revolving arm that deposits the sewage over the circular bed swings at a relatively slow pace and liquids have an opportunity to trickle through the bed, leaving solids on the surface, before another batch is deposited on the next rotation.

CONTACT BED

A technique formerly used quite extensively but which is gradually being replaced by other more efficient methods is called the **contact bed.** This consists of a water-tight tank filled with the usual type of crushed rock. Sewage is introduced into the unit and allowed to stand for a period; the tank is then drained and left undisturbed for another waiting period during which aerobic decomposition takes place.

ACTIVATED SLUDGE

Bubbling air through liquid sewage produces **activated sludge.** As the fluid is aerated a **floc** forms which traps colloidal matter in suspension, and biological decomposition proceeds at a rapid rate. The floc breaks up into smaller units which propel the reaction in a cyclical series extending over a period of from four to eight hours before the mixture is transferred either to a sedimentation tank or to the surface of a trickling filter, intermittent filter, or contact bed for final action. Such a system requires relatively little space and should it be desirable to discharge the effluent into bodies of water, less dilution is required than for raw sewage.

Industrial Wastes

In years past many industrial plants were located on the shores of rivers for at least two fundamental reasons: to secure water power for the creation of electricity with which to run the wheels of their machinery, and as an economical means of disposal of wastes. If the body of water was deep enough to accommodate boats, then cheap transportation for goods could be added to the other two reasons for choosing such an area.

The problem of discharging industrial wastes into rivers, streams, and lakes has undergone extensive investigation in recent years as our communities have come to realize, slowly but surely, the enormous damage being inflicted on one of nature's most valuable resources.

It costs money to pre-treat industrial wastes, especially when such substances as acids and toxic salts of metals are involved. These end products of industry must be modified or neutralized to cut down on their lethal action against bacteria, fish, and human beings. Industrialists who must answer to their stockholders naturally resist legislation designed to compel industry to install expensive facilities for treatment of plant sewage. Definite progress can be reported in our more progressive states where the problem has been faced head on and where the voters have been told the facts. The problem of river and stream pollution becomes even further magnified when the available supply of water is so limited that recirculation becomes necessary for drinking purposes and for other essential needs.

Unless the wastes are extremely toxic, a general rule of thumb states that one part of sewage can usually be safely taken care of in fifty parts of water where biological activity can break down the organic matter without the accompanying unpleasant odors associated with "overloading" a body of water. Adequate supplies of oxygen are required to cause normal sewage degradation. The more sewage present, the greater is the *Biochemical* (Biological) *Oxygen Demand*, abbreviated B.O.D. The technique of conducting a B.O.D. test is to place a known quantity of diluted sewage in a tightly-stoppered bottle containing a known amount of oxygen. At the conclusion of a five-day incubation period at 20°C the amount of oxygen consumed in the breakdown of the sewage is expressed in parts per million (PPM). Strong or medium sewage pollution will need several hundred PPM, whereas small amounts of sewage require less than one hundred PPM. These are arbitrary standards, but they have been accepted by public health laboratories conducting such tests as reliable criteria of the degree of pollution present in a given sample.

Through pre-treatment of industrial wastes and by controlling the quantity of sewage dumped into a body of water, overloading can be minimized or avoided. At the present time this, rather than an attempt to forbid any discharge of sewage into bodies of water, is the approach being taken by enforcement agencies.

Getting rid of radioactive wastes is an even more serious problem confronting health authorities, and various types of dumping grounds have been explored for their potential as safe areas in the immediate and the distant future. One approach by the Federal Government has been to suggest the use of special tight containers that can be dropped into deep ocean pits where decay of the radioactive material can take place. The length of such storage is directly related to the half-life of the "hot" wastes.

Old abandoned coal mine shafts have also been suggested as another discharge area, but there are many long-range drawbacks even here. Techniques might be discovered, for example, to make it economically feasible to rework mines which today have reached the point of diminishing returns. But mine shafts are probably safer than the ocean where fish and other forms of life could eventually become so contaminated with radioactive material that it would pose a real threat to people whose existence depends upon food they can harvest from a generous sea.

Review Questions

1. What is the difference between sewage and sewerage?
2. Is it easier to dispose of chemical wastes or biological wastes? Why?
3. If a distance of 75 feet is advised to separate sewage from a dug well when they are on level ground, how much would you increase the distance if the sewage is 25 feet higher than the water in a dug well?
4. What advantages are possessed by a septic tank that are lacking with a cesspool?
5. Does sludge have any commercial value? When should it not be used?
6. What information is supplied by a test for biological oxygen demand (B.O.D.)?
7. What type of ground is recommended for a leaching field adjacent to a septic tank outlet?

10 | MICROBIOLOGY OF THE SOIL

ASHES TO ASHES. DUST TO DUST. THIS IS THE ULTIMATE FATE OF us all if we are to play our predestined role in nature's plan. What happens to us and within our allotted plot of ground in one lifetime would fill volumes, but of necessity many pages would have to remain blank because of gaps in our knowledge as the search for truth continues.

Soil microbiology is an area of science that still holds many secrets waiting to be unlocked, but progress can be reported and definite inroads into the unknown are resulting in a better understanding of some of the complex biological actions and interrelationships existing in the "living" portion of the earth's crust we call **soil.** The principal habitat of microbes is soil and water, and this chapter will attempt to elucidate some of the highlights of living systems in the earth as they bear directly or indirectly on nursing and medical practices.

In general terms soil can be considered to be that relatively thin loose shell of the earth's surface where inorganic and organic matter support the growth of microscopic and macroscopic forms of life. Marine microbiology is a science in its own right, and therefore the ocean floor will not be included in this discussion, even though water does cover the major percentage of the earth's surface. Deserts at the other moisture extreme do not support plant growth except during those relatively brief periods when rainfall triggers the living potential in arid wastelands and it bursts into verdant life. Controlled irrigation can reclaim what is now useless land, and in the not-too-distant future man will undoubtedly be compelled to tap these vast resources to grow sufficient food and fiber for an ever-expanding world population.

The depth of soil varies enormously depending upon such factors as moisture, temperature, and the amount of organic matter present. In temperate climates soil depth may range from several inches to several feet, while in the tropics the depth may be ten feet or more. The deltas of some of the world's great rivers permit soil to be as much as several hundred feet in thickness.

Soil is created by gradual disintegration of rock through the shearing action of weather, especially freezing and thawing, coupled with chemical forces which aid in dissolving and precipitating materials in the loose surface layers of the ground. When mixed with organic matter and water these particles of rock, together with soluble salts, make up that active medium in which hordes of organisms find conditions suitable for their growth and multiplication. Topsoil tends to be dark because of its high content of organic matter, whereas subsoil, which is deficient in organic content and thus is lighter in color, extends to the underlying rock structure.

It is difficult to state with any degree of accuracy the average number of organisms one might expect to find in a given weight of soil, because there is no typical or representative sample. Chemical and physical compositions are undergoing constant and rapid change which naturally is reflected in altered microbial populations, sometimes favoring one group and at other times reversing environmental conditions to inhibit these same species.

It is probably accurate to say that the viable count of highly fertile soil might be expected to fall within the range of from a hundred thousand to hundreds of millions of bacteria per gram. A total microscopic count (living plus dead cells) could run into billions per gram, and such allied organisms as molds, algae, protozoa, etc., might range from hundreds to millions in a soil sample of the same weight. As a dwelling place for such a wide variety of species living in a highly competitive environment, the ground in reality is a complex biological clean-up system designed to insure that vital elements required by all living cells will periodically be released and returned to nature in an unending cycle which provides future generations with an opportunity to be created and sustained. Chemical elements are mere tenants in our bodies. What we do with them, and perhaps more important, what they do in us, profoundly affects our very existence.

Soil Composition: Physical, Chemical, and Biological

Soil is made up of solids, liquids, and gases, and the composition and ratio of each determines the makeup of the living matter whose growth can be supported. The mineral content reflects the parent rock from which the solids originated, with the following terminology employed to describe particle sizes:

Clay	0.005 mm and smaller
Silt	0.005 to 0.05 mm
Very fine sand	0.05 to 0.10 mm
Fine sand	0.10 to 0.25 mm
Medium sand	0.25 to 0.50 mm
Coarse sand	0.50 to 1.0 mm
Fine gravel	1.0 to 2.0 mm

In the pore spaces between the solid particles may be found carbon dioxide, nitrogen, and oxygen, together with the water that serves as a solvent for both food and wastes in the soil. In a given sample where special conditions prevail, gases other than those mentioned can be expected, sometimes in relatively high concentrations. Both mineral and organic solids impart structure, texture, and water-holding capacity to soil, and a sample of rich earth might be composed of from 60 to 70 per cent minerals, 3 to 10 per cent organic solids, and 10 to 20 per cent pore space. Air may constitute from 5 to 15 per cent of these open areas between solid particles, with the moisture content varying widely.

Cellulose is one of the more abundant organic substances originating from normal decay of vegetation. An artificially manured soil would naturally be rich in organic content. Other chemical ingredients of soil might include carbohydrates, from monosaccharides up through polysaccharides and higher alcohols, in addition to starch, gums, proteins and their derivatives, fats, waxes, organic acids, and growth-activating substances. All of these substances and many others comprise that edible portion of the soil called **humus** which may be especially abundant in forests or in bottomlands.

But soil is not just a collection of inanimate broken-down rocks mixed with humus and water; it is probably the most dynamic portion of our globe, changing second by second under the influence of the many forces which affect microbial growth in any medium. Microscopic organisms abound in the earth and they are endowed with considerable power to adjust to a changing environment through action on raw materials. Some species can adapt themselves better than others, as is true of any group of living organisms, including man.

The soil is well supplied with scavengers that assist in keeping the earth's surface relatively free of unpleasant dead material. Just visualize the mess we would be in if all of the plants and animals left over from past generations were piled in heaps cluttering the earth's surface. Man would long since have exhausted the available real estate for storage of such wastes on this planet.

Since this book is principally concerned with our microbial world, little detailed attention will be paid to macroscopic forms of life in the soil. Nonmicroscopic living things do contribute materially to the "health" of soil through the aeration they provide by root growth and physical burrowing of small animals. Earthworms, large and small, ingest considerable amounts of complex organic matter, digesting it and providing therefrom more readily available material for subsequent microbial metabolism. Protozoa, especially flagellates, ciliates, and amoeba, convert significant amounts of organic matter (particularly bacteria) into their own protoplasm.

A farmer might never have had a formal course in microbiology but by attending the practical school of experience contributed to by generations of successful tillers of the soil, he has come to learn that crops grow better when the ground is scientifically worked. If soil is too wet, supplies of air are cut off and conditions favor the development of relatively inefficient anaerobes. In such a case, draining of the area becomes necessary. Frequently a tight wet soil turns acid and must be treated with lime to neutralize this deterrent of bacterial growth. When the soil is too loose, moisture is lost quickly and the remedy is rolling to pack the particles closer together. All of these factors are not unlike the basic prerequisites for a good microbiological medium. What is favorable for microbes is generally conducive to soil fertility and efficient crop production. An increasing number of farmers today are benefiting from the educational programs offered by the Extension Services of our state universities in the constant quest for improved techniques for making man's efforts more productive through scientific utilization of God-given servants in the earth. It is estimated that up to four tons of bacteria are present in an acre of fertile soil, and when one considers the cell surface area and the work potential this figure represents, it staggers the imagination.

A special group of **autotrophic** bacteria are able to utilize inorganic materials and water with carbon dioxide as a carbon source as they build up compounds (chemosynthesis) in their metabolism. **Heterotrophic** bacteria thrive only in the presence of organic matter which they prefer to break down (chemoanalysis) in the preparation of a diet to their liking. Molds are found in relatively large numbers in soil where, among other things, they are responsible for the decomposition of such complex

material as cellulose which resists attack by most microbes. These filamentous molds also are important in helping to hold small soil particles
into aggregates which make for better soil texture and retard erosion.

Rotation of Elements in Nature

Because there is a limit to the supply of matter, nature has devised
ingenious schemes for assuring continued utilization of each element.
Death alternates with life, each state dependent upon the other for continuity. The essential elements (carbon, hydrogen, oxygen, nitrogen,
sulfur, phosphorus, etc.) are maintained in continuous rotation through
the ceaseless influence of specific organisms whose enzyme systems are
capable of tapping nature's storehouse of potential food. Although it is
not the intent in this text to take up each chemical and follow its predestined course, it does seem appropriate to discuss at least two of the
major elements required by all cells in order to give the reader some
conception of what keeps plants and animals rolling along generation
after generation.

Inorganic and organic matter are constantly being changed back and
forth, from one into the other. Chlorophyll-bearing plants serve as the
agency by which solar energy is transferred to living organisms, and
microbes are principally responsible for the degradation of organic
matter into inorganic end products.

The Nitrogen Cycle

Stated in its simplest terms, nitrogen undergoes the following major
changes in nature: *Animal life* to *ammonia* to *nitrites* to *nitrates* to *plant
life,* and finally back to *animal life.* These represent the main trunk line
over which nitrogen travels, but many specific local circumstances complicate the directness of the journey.

Every living cell has nitrogen as one of its basic constituents. During
metabolism of man and of other macroscopic animals, nitrogen leaves the
body through excretion of urine which contains a nitrogen compound,
urea, with the formula $CO(NH_2)_2$. When urea finds a way into the earth
bacteria, especially *Proteus* species, attack the compound and liberate
ammonia (NH_3). Ammonia might also be formed through decomposition
of the bodies of animals after their death. **Decay** is an aerobic breakdown;
putrefaction implies anaerobic decomposition.

Even in relatively minute quantities ammonia is toxic to most plants,
but some bacteria, namely the *Nitrosomonas* and the *Nitrobacter* genera,
are capable of oxidizing ammonia to nitrite (NO_2) which is further
oxidized by *Nitrobacter* into nitrate (NO_3), a form of nitrogen most

readily available for most growing plants. Once soluble nitrates gain entrance to the plants through root hairs, the nitrogen compound is quickly converted into plant protein which now becomes available for consumption by animals, and the cycle returns to its starting point.

With the atmosphere we breathe composed of approximately 78 per cent nitrogen gas, it seems an error on the part of nature that this form of the element is so useless except to a few genera of specialized bacteria.

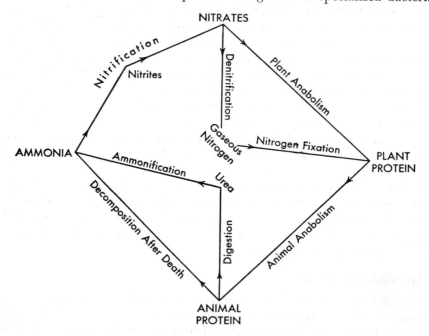

FIG. 10.1. The nitrogen cycle. (Reprinted from S. E. Wedberg, *Microbes and You*, 1954, with permission of The Macmillan Company, New York, N. Y.)

The tons of nitrogen suspended over every acre of ground throughout the world remain just out of reach of the plant life that depends so desperately on this element for survival. Each harvest depletes the soil of just that much nitrogen which must be replaced in one way or another if the ground is to support another crop. Farmers are faced with the need to spend considerable sums of money for the purchase of commercial fertilizers to accomplish this end.

When the pH of soil is above 6.0 a group of free-living bacteria known as *Azotobacter* can utilize atmospheric nitrogen gas in their metabolism in a process called **nitrogen fixation**. These microbes are gram negative in their staining characteristics and are relatively large rods, or even cocci. Some are almost yeast-like in their appearance. *Azotobacter* are reported to exhibit one of the highest rates of metabolism of any bacteria. Most microorganisms consume from 50 to 300 cubic milliliters of oxygen per milligram of dry weight of cells per hour, but *Azotobacter* may consume as many as 3000 cu ml. Under favorable conditions, from ten to forty pounds of useful nitrogen can be fixed by these bacteria per acre per year, but the exact mechanism by which this biological transformation takes place is far from understood.

A curious symbiotic relationship existing between the roots of legumes and a genus of bacteria known as *Rhizobium* accounts for the capturing of considerable amounts of nitrogen in the soil. When legumes are cultivated in a plot of ground they enrich the nitrogen content of the soil considerably beyond the normal amount one might expect from decay of plant material. This was recognized as early as 1837 when Boussingault first reported that the reaction was due to an actual fixation of atmospheric nitrogen. Further research revealed the intriguing symbiotic relationship existing between legumes and selected bacteria. Near the close of the nineteenth century an anaerobe, *Clostridium pasteurianum,* was isolated by Winogradsky who demonstrated that nitrogen could be fixed by these bacteria *in vitro* in the absence of plants. Rhizobia in association with legumes are estimated to add up to two hundred pounds of nitrogen per acre per year. This is part of the basis for rotation of crops in agricultural practice, and by turning under a cover crop of clover considerable "free" nitrogen is acquired by farmers. Certain blue-green algae, *Nostoc muscorum,* are also capable of fixing nitrogen, but this probably takes place more in water than in soil because of the specialized growth requirements of these plants.

The nodules formed on the roots of legumes by *Rhizobium* species are somewhat analogous to infections, but in this case both the host and the parasite benefit from the association. The plant gains nitrogen while the bacteria derive their energy requirements from the plant which they attack and invade. It is irritation to the roots that induces the formation of characteristic nodules, but in this case the plant apparently "enjoys being hurt."

An examination of the diagramatic representation of the nitrogen cycle reveals one highly undesirable side trip that is called **denitrification.** This represents the tearing down or undoing of the complex build-up of desirable nitrates from the original toxic ammonia. Since the primary aim of oxidation is to provide useful forms of nitrogen for plant use, it is gross waste to have denitrification step in and reduce readily available nitrates back into an already abundant supply of relatively unusable nitrogen gas.

When soils are poorly aerated or when they become acid, denitrification sets in under the influence of a wide variety of bacteria, both anaerobic and facultative. To prevent this reaction detrimental to soil fertility, an understanding farmer will loosen the soil through plowing to aerate it; he will add lime to neutralize the undesirable acids; and he may find it necessary to drain the land of excess moisture.

The Carbon Cycle

The reader should not gain the impression from the schematic representation that any cycle of elements in nature is a simple clear-cut process. Actions, interactions, and counteractions are constantly going on simultaneously.

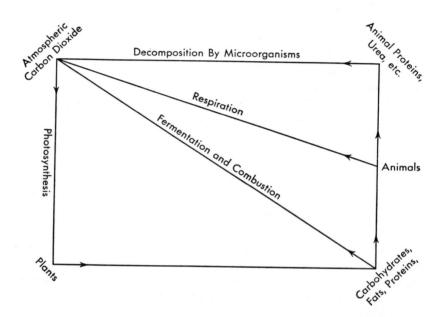

FIG. 10.2. The carbon cycle. (Reprinted from S. E. Wedberg, *Microbes and You*, 1954, with permission of The Macmillan Company, New York, N. Y.)

The carbon cycle is relatively more simple to outline than the nitrogen cycle, but this does not necessarily indicate that it is any less complex as a biological system. From the accompanying diagram the major steps in the cycle can be followed without elaborate explanation. One significant difference that should be pointed out between the two cycles is the relatively minute amount (0.03%) of carbon dioxide in the air. Even though this represents only three parts of CO_2 in ten thousand parts of atmosphere, the very survival of the plant and animal kingdoms depends upon it. In general it is stated that plants take in carbon dioxide and liberate oxygen, whereas animals do the reverse. This is an orderly equilibrium set up in nature, and although the concentration of carbon dioxide in a given locality may rise temporarily owing primarily to different types of combustion, the over-all concentration of this gas throughout the world is maintained at a remarkably steady level year in and century out.

The more one studies science and gains an insight into this astounding thing called *nature,* the more he should be impressed by the orderliness that emerges from what appears at first glance to be biological chaos. All life depends upon other living or dead organisms; how often we take them for granted. The creation of a human being from the union of two cells is such a complex process with thousands of crossroads that a single mistake any place along the line may result in an abnormal child. Isn't it a miracle that anyone turns out right? It was once believed that life could better be studied in minute single-celled organisms, since they did not possess the complex organs found in man or in other creatures. But when it is considered that all of life's processes must be carried out within the confines of a microscopic cell that is not equipped with ingenious cells to carry out specific functions, trying to understand the mechanics of a single microbe becomes even more difficult in many respects. Before it passes on, every living organism leaves some indelible mark as a result of its presence.

Soil as a Vehicle for Pathogens

More detailed consideration of pathogenic organisms found in the earth and elsewhere will be given in Chapter 15, but a few comments about the part played by soil in human disease should be mentioned as part of the present discussion.

When our protective barrier of relatively tough skin is breached and "dirt" gains entrance to a wound, the resulting infection is in most cases not directly caused by the soil that becomes embedded in the flesh, unless the wound is an extensive or a deep penetrating type. Instead the bacteria comprising the normal exterior flora of our bodies are more likely to be the culprits in the ensuing pathogenic process. Staphylococci once inside the skin find conditions favorable for their rapid development, with blood and flesh serving as the medium. Soil should not, therefore, be considered as the primary source of harmful organisms in most wounds, with the exception of the pathogenic anaerobes.

Lethal clostridia are characterized by their ability to produce potent poisons that fall into the group of exotoxins—those secretions or excretions liberated as a metabolic product during the active life of the microbes. Three principal categories of clostridia exist in the soil: those belonging to the gas gangrene group which depend upon damaged (traumatized) tissues for their establishment and development; *Cl. tetani*, a strict anaerobe which produces a nonextensive localized infection but a generalized toxemia when introduced *in vivo* under prescribed conditions; and the *Cl. botulinum* species which are not associated with invasion of tissues but rather produce extremely lethal poisons, especially in insufficiently heated neutral high-protein foods maintained under anaerobic conditions.

A number of anaerobic spore-forming rods are normal inhabitants of the intestines of animals, and this means that soils fertilized with excrement will have a considerably higher count of these pathogens per unit volume than unfertilized or virgin soils.

Nearly 80 per cent of gangrenous wounds examined during the two World Wars were infected with *Cl. perfringens,* and the experience in civilian hospitals has not been too different. A number of other clostridia are etiological agents in the remainder of the cases. Dirty wounds are characterized by their mixed bacterial flora, many species of which are instrumental in consuming available oxygen in the damaged area, thus creating favorable environmental conditions for the more fastidious anaerobes.

Clostridium tetani, the causative agent in tetanus (lockjaw), can be found in relative abundance in highly manured soils, especially when the fertilizer is derived from horses. This is one of the underlying reasons why so many wounds contracted during trench warfare in the fertile fields of France developed into tetanus. It seems unfortunate that progress in certain areas of science gains impetus only under the pressure and demands of armed conflict, but this without doubt holds true of our understanding of anaerobes, which came about during World War I. Information gained and techniques developed during this period and in the years that followed paid handsome dividends during the second world conflict when gas gangrene was not one of the leading problems confronting the medical profession in military hospitals. Cases that did develop were handled more scientifically and with marked success.

A deep dirty wound resulting from penetration by a rusty nail, a tin can, a pitchfork, or through an automobile accident must always be considered as a candidate for an anaerobic infection, and the wise physician takes routine precautions by injecting specific antitoxin as part of the prophylactic procedure. The specific inanimate object causing the wound is not directly responsible for lockjaw; rather, the circumstances and the type of wound into which living microbes were driven are the important factors. Anyone inclined to pound sterile rusty nails deep into his flesh would not contract either gas gangrene or tetanus unless viable pathogenic anaerobes were driven in along with the metal. (The reader is advised to accept this bit of dogma on faith without conducting a laboratory experiment to prove or disprove the theory!)

Clostridium botulinum is an interesting organism from a number of practical as well as theoretical standpoints. Since it produces the most powerful biological poison known to man (one ounce of purified toxin may contain as many as one million theoretical lethal doses for humans), this toxin has been accorded top priority as a potential agent for biological warfare. The etiological microbe is a normal inhabitant of the soil but the cell count per unit volume of earth varies in different regions of the world.

Spores of *Cl. botulinum* can withstand five hours of boiling. However, by employment of steam under pressure in an autoclave or a pressure cooker, these same spores can be killed in a fraction of this time, the exact exposure depending upon the volume of food being processed. Home canning of neutral high-protein foods (peas, beans, corn, etc.) without proper exposure to heat has been the main cause of botulism in the United States. Sausages and other types of processed foods appear to be implicated more frequently in other areas of the globe, especially in Europe. In defense of the food processing industry it should be stated that in the United States no cases of botulism have been traced to commercially canned foods since the early 1920's.

Antibiotics in the Soil

There is probably more keen competition for survival in the soil than anywhere else in the biological world, and because of this eternal struggle to emerge a living winner, man has tapped the microbial potential of soil in his quest for antibiotic materials useful in medicine. An antibiotic may be defined in a number of different ways. Selman Waksman, the discoverer of streptomycin, defines an antibiotic as a microbial product that inhibits or kills certain other living organisms.

Only a small fraction of microbes that exhibit antagonisms toward their own kind can be harnessed for combatting pathogens within the human body, since too often the damage inflicted is not restricted to microbes. Sacrificing healthy host cells is not a wise procedure in combatting bacterial infections. The old adage about a successful operation but the unfortunate demise of the patient must be remembered whenever chemical substances are to be employed *in vivo*. An ideal antibiotic aims at a bull's-eye located within a microbial target, without scattering damaging shots to healthy adjacent tissue. Before a new antibiotic can be marketed for human use, extensive microbiological, chemical, and pharmacological tests must be conducted to prove that the margin of safety will be sufficient to preclude any untoward damaging side-effects to the patient.

Almost any plating of soil samples will reveal microbial antagonisms to varying degrees, as evidenced by zones of microbial inhibition adjacent to selected colonies. Unfortunately, in most cases the reactions that occur *in vitro* may bear little or no relationship to what one hopes for when these same microbes are the target within the body. Sometimes the zones of microbial inhibition may represent mere lack of tolerance to excreted acids or other toxic wastes. When we examine the chemical structure of the accepted antibiotics presently being sold on the market, it becomes clear that there is no particular pattern of elements that can be associated with antibiosis.

The use of antibiotics is one form of **chemotherapy,** which may be defined as the treatment of disease by the injection of chemicals that retard the growth or actually kill a pathogenic agent without significant impairment to the host. Chemotherapy can also be conducted using synthetic drugs, but since these do not come from living cells, they are not, technically speaking, classed as antibiotics.

Many useful antibiotics have been derived from a group of saprophytic soil forms called Streptomycetes, which are described in *Bergey's Manual* as organisms growing in the form of branched threadlike elements (mycelium) with a typical aerial mycelium. When growing on laboratory media streptomycetes emit an odor resembling that of a newly plowed field or of decaying leaves. At least 150 species of this organism have been isolated, and an abbreviated list of a few species that have provided us with useful antibiotics includes the following:

Streptomyces erythraeus	Erythromycin
Streptomyces fradiae	Neomycin
Streptomyces griseus	Streptomycin
Streptomyces venezuelae	Chloramphenicol
Streptomyces niveus	Novobiocin

Penicillin, on the other hand, is a product of mold growth. Fleming's original penicillin, discovered in 1929, was derived from *Penicillum notatum*. Recent research has been aimed at algae as possible sources of chemotherapeutic agents. Chapter 13 will go into more details of antibiosis and chemotherapy.

Review Questions

1. What must be done to land in deserts to convert the upper layer into soil? How do soil and sand differ?
2. What effect would tightness of soil have on the microbial population?
3. If competition for microbial survival is keen in soil, where else might one look for similar antagonistic action?
4. Why are most bacteria heterotrophs rather than autotrophs?
5. Distinguish between putrefaction and decay.
6. Why, in general, are pathogens that are found in the soil spore-forming species?

MICROBIOLOGY OF
THE ATMOSPHERE

Composition of Air

CLEAN AIR CONSISTS OF A COMPARATIVELY UNIFORM MIXTURE OF gases including approximately 78 per cent nitrogen, 20 per cent oxygen, 1 per cent argon, 0.03 per cent carbon dioxide, and traces of a number of others. In addition the atmosphere contains moisture in the form of mist or vapor, suspended dust, pollen, and bacteria—all varying in amount from time to time in contrast to the relative stability in concentration of gases.

It should be pointed out that no microbes are indigenous to the atmosphere. Although air serves as a vehicle for the transport of microbes, the gaseous makeup of the atmosphere fails to provide the necessary requirements for the support and multiplication of such cells. Most organisms suspended in air are saprophytes, but their effect on man cannot be dismissed entirely because of the role they play in the spoilage of many foods.

Man inhales an average of 30 pounds of air every twenty-four hours, consumes about 2¾ pounds of food, and drinks approximately 4½ pounds of water daily. He can live for weeks without food, days without water, but only minutes without air. Such an indispensable factor in human health and survival requires more than just a passing comment.

Back in the time of Hippocrates (about 400 B.C.) it was accepted that bad air was a potential cause of pestilence, and even today a disease relatively common in vast areas of the world is still masquerading under the misnomer **malaria** ("bad air") in spite of the fact that we know this malady is transmitted by the bite of *Anopheles* mosquitoes and has no relation to the purity of the air. If an individual is bitten at the right time by an infected female *Anopheles* mosquito even in an air-conditioned atmosphere, the disease will develop.

For years the quality of food and drink has been subjected to the close scrutiny and supervision of public health authorities, but only relatively recently has air come under their watchful eye. Recent interest in the problem has been stimulated no doubt by mounting public determination to conquer troublesome smog (smoke plus fog) that has enveloped some of our centers of population. Air pollution is without question one of the current challenging public health frontiers that must be faced with courage and determination if man expects to provide healthful air for himself and his children. No longer can we afford to wink at the sight of belching smokestacks or at the odor of noxious fumes spewing from the exhaust pipes of increasing numbers of automobiles that are choking our highways as well as our lungs. There are those who believe that if cigarette smoking bears a direct relationship to the incidence of lung cancer, smog may be pushing this leader for a close second place. The odds against some folks who are exposed to a combination of the two factors seem rather formidable.

The World Health Organization defines health as "a state of complete physical, mental and social well-being, not merely the absence of disease or infirmity." Under this interpretation, anyone subjected to the irritation of toxic fumes in the atmosphere must be considered to be ill, at least to a degree, and unfortunately that includes millions of individuals throughout the world. Man has created these monsters; now he must learn to tame them.

A serious discussion of the atmosphere and the consequences of its pollution should be undertaken in a paramedical book of this type not only because the atmosphere we breathe is becoming an unclean thing in a mounting number of areas of population, but also because air must be considered one of the serious threats in the dissemination of microbes in our hospitals. Recent carefully conducted experiments have revealed the long-suspected fact that air in a hospital ward can harbor significant numbers of pathogenic organisms, especially staphylococci which someone has dubbed "the staph of death" as a counterpart to bread, the staff of life!

The presence of bacteria in air probably should be considered accidental, since air in itself cannot support microbial growth. It does, however, serve to support dust particles and moisture droplets being employed as "magic carpets" by microorganisms. Since bacteria cannot fly or walk, their independent motion is limited to liquids where flagella provide the power to propel the cells about. Transport from one point to another outside of liquids is wholly dependent upon a free ride on "things."

Pollution and Human Health

There are many different types of air pollutants, biological and chemical. Contrary to popular belief, the air is not usually loaded with microbes. The number of organisms found per unit volume of air naturally will vary with the history of the sample being tested. Dust-free and moisture-free air could be expected under. most circumstances to be bacteria-free, although an occasional free-floating cell might be present in the air at any given moment.

Dust can contain great numbers of microbes, especially bacteria, many of which are potentially pathogenic in their own right should they gain entrance through the required portal to appropriate locations within our body. Standard plate counts reveal millions of bacteria per gram of house dust, and in the immediate vicinity of a sneeze, especially one expelled by a person suffering with an acute respiratory infection, the air can contain enormous numbers of organisms, many of which could induce pathogenic effects in susceptible hosts. The air, walls, floor, and furniture in a room occupied by a person with an open *Staphylococcus* lesion can be shown to harbor hundreds of these viable organisms which settle on bedding and represent a potential threat not only to the patient from whom they arose, but probably more significantly, to the next occupant of that same bed and room.

The relationship between the count of dust particles and bacteria need not be a direct one, although it frequently is. *Types* of dust and their *origin* are more pertinent considerations. Nearly 50 million microbes per gram of street dust were reported in studies conducted in 1912 by Winslow and his colleagues. These findings have been modified somewhat with the passing of the horse and buggy, but even today samples taken from the same location will reveal high numbers of viable organisms of human and other animal origin.

Too much air pollution can materially reduce the penetration of sunlight in areas that could well use the benefits of solar radiation. In 1881 in Chicago the first smoke control ordinance was adopted, and in succeeding years a number of other large cities have followed suit. The visible evidence of what can be done about smoke abatement can be found in Pittsburgh which undertook a vigorous corrective program at the close of World War II. Visibility records published by the Weather Bureau showed a decrease in total number of hours of moderate to heavy smoke from 1005 hours in 1946 to 122 hours ten years later in 1956. The parallel reduction in dust and soot ranged up to 28 per cent during this same period. Such a substantial decrease can result in the saving of millions of dollars in cleaning bills for buildings, clothing, textiles, paints, etc.

Heavy air pollution can cause a marked increase in the death rate among that segment of the population already suffering from pulmonary and cardiac disorders. Those who survive may have their conditions decidedly aggravated by smog. This observation was well documented in the 1952 smog attack on London when some 4000 deaths in excess of the number normally expected in the time involved took place among individuals in these categories of disease. A particularly heavy build-up of smog in Donora, Pennsylvania in 1948 appeared to be the direct cause of twenty deaths and the illness of an additional 6000 persons in the area. Air pollution might be looked upon as that added straw that can break the camel's back in such cases. It has been estimated that air pollution in its various forms costs more than a billion and a half dollars annually in the United States. That amounts to over ten dollars for every man, woman, and child in our country, and it represents an unnecessary and preventable waste.

Control of Organisms in the Air

By the time the student has reached this point in a formal course in microbiology, it should be clear that the exacting techniques advocated for handling organisms in a laboratory are based in large measure upon attempts to exclude extraneous organisms found in the air from experimental pure cultures. Once man understood how microbes were disseminated, techniques were devised to minimize their spread, especially from one individual to another. Anyone engaged in nursing or in medical practice learns that covering a wound with a sterile dressing is designed to accomplish two ends: first, to refuse admittance of air-borne contaminants to the open lesion; and second, to prevent organisms already present in the wound from being dispersed into the atmosphere. It is at this point in medical practice that a nurse or other person working directly with the patient can assist or undo the effective work of the attending physician.

A high-speed photograph indicates that enormous numbers of microbes are sprayed through droplets during an uncontrolled sneeze unless proper precautions are taken to reduce the hazard by confining the expelled air within a handkerchief or a tissue placed over the mouth and nose. Persons suffering from upper respiratory infections are doing others a great disservice when they fail to remain at home, preferably in bed, particularly during the early stage of the illness. More man-hours are lost in industry because of the common cold (or whatever other fancy medical terminology you may wish to attach to this affliction) than any other single cause. Common sense and good judgment can do much to cut this staggering statistic.

FIG. 11.1. Inspecting an array of vials in a pharmaceutical packaging operation maintained under sterile conditions. (Courtesy Squibb, Division, of Olin Mathieson Chemical Corporation, New York, N. Y.)

Ideally, an operating room should be sterile in the strictest bacteriological sense of the word. Not only should this be true for the walls, ceiling, floor, and equipment, but the very air and all outer garments of those who work in the area should be microbe-free. We know this utopia cannot be attained at present, except in unusually controlled situations. It appears to the writer that one of the weakest links in the chain of asepsis in medical practice lies in the relative ineffectiveness of gauze face masks which are designed primarily to trap suspended organisms expelled from the nose and mouth of the wearer. Even a moderate expulsion of breath through normal talking may permit considerable saliva spray to be released into the surrounding area. It goes without saying that a cough or a sneeze can add proportionately greater numbers of microbe-laden particles to the air, and should the air in an operating room become contaminated by such droplets during surgery, the living cells cannot help presenting potential hazards to the patients.

A covering over the face that is tight enough to exclude the passage of microbes probably will suffocate the wearer, but it does appear feasible to improve on the efficiency of the relatively porous masks presently in use. Perhaps a mask containing one layer of Fiberglas, or some similar material, impregnated with a germicidal compound might help to reduce the number of viable cells that could escape through the fabric. Since moisture is a prerequisite for efficient chemical disinfection, the individual wearer could supply this ingredient through normal respiration. While such a filtering device might not offer 100 per cent protection, it would seem to be at least one step in the right direction. Progress of any kind is usually accomplished by taking baby steps prior to the giant strides that result in significant breakthroughs. It is the crystallization of many small contributions to science that periodically result in the announcement of great discoveries.

Air Conditioning and Health

The combination of humidity, temperature, and air circulation will determine the physical comfort of an individual at any given moment, but allowances must be made for relatively wide variations in human beings who do not dress alike or liberate heat and moisture to the same degree. The usual expressions of dislike for air-conditioned rooms in many instances are well founded. The sudden marked drop in humidity and temperature when we step into rooms that are overly air conditioned may actually lower our relative resistance, especially with respect to upper respiratory ailments. A chilly blast on the back of the neck does most folks no good and may be instrumental in causing stiff necks.

As much as 10 per cent of our population suffers from the irritations induced by pollens of various types. Efficiency of these persons may be improved by supplying washed air to their working areas, but the reduction in sneezes through such purification procedures may be nullified by too great a drop in the temperature and an overcirculation of the air. Air conditioning can be made to play a positive role in improvement of our environment, but like anything else it must be dealt with intelligently.

Smoking and Health

Since such a large number of our adult population apparently prefer not to breathe fresh air but rather the end products of tobacco combustion, it seems appropriate here to discuss briefly some of the hazards to health that smoking appears to precipitate. Smoking might be considered as the inhalation of air highly polluted with chemicals.

The "slaves of the weed" would rather brush aside the accusation that they are addicts, but in truth they must be considered as such. Friends of mine have told me they can stop smoking any time they want to do so; they have done it dozens of times! A few appalling statistics might strike home for a minority of readers, but the author's conclusion, based upon years of lecturing to young people relative to the potential dangers that lurk in the haze of smoking, is that few souls will be saved by the American Cancer Society's shocking statistics about to be presented. People have a natural aversion to being told what they should or should not do even though the evidence is overwhelming in support of the admonition.

What enormous long-range progress could be made all over the face of our globe if the annual expenditures for cigarettes and tobacco products were devoted to positive public health programs. In 1958 this waste amounted to $6,500,000,000 in the United States alone. The $125,000,000 spent on advertising rewarded the manufacturers with sales of over 450,000,000,000 cigarettes that year. It would be interesting for someone to calculate the estimated medical bills that probably resulted from diseases aggravated and precipitated by that quantity of tobacco.

The tobacco plant is American in origin. Columbus found the natives smoking these dried plants when he landed in 1492. When tobacco is burned the most familiar ingredient of the bitumen is nicotine, a poison so powerful that the intravenous injection of only a few drops can be lethal for a human being. Smoking one cigarette will add from 0.5 to 3.0 mg of nicotine to the blood stream, and 20 cigarettes smoked in ten hours will raise the level of nicotine to 0.14 mg per liter of blood. A single cigarette will elevate blood pressure about 10 mm in the diastolic phase and 15 mm in the cystolic phase, while your pulse rate is brought up an average of eight beats a minute. Smoking has been shown to decrease stomach motility and to impair appetite.

While all of the above changes in your body are going on, what effects might one expect to find as far as diseases are concerned? Regular cigarette smokers (a pack or more a day) have been shown to exhibit a mortality rate up to 68 per cent higher for their age group than that for nonsmokers. They have up to twenty times the prevalence of lung cancer, 63 per cent more coronary heart disease, and among smoking mothers the incidence of premature births is twice that for nonsmokers, according to several scientific studies.

The tragedy of these statistics as far as public health is concerned is the trend; the figures become more frightening with each passing year because children are beginning to smoke at a progressively younger age.

More than 30 per cent of youngsters in ninth grade are smokers and this figure leaps to over 50 per cent by the time the children become twelfth graders.

Anyone who thinks for himself must eventually ask himself a few searching questions about smoking and health. Are the so-called pleasures of smoking worth the gamble? The decision is an individual one to make, but if more people could see the brutal effects on lungs at autopsy in cases of persons who have died from lung cancer, or if they could witness the final tormenting days before death does the sufferer a favor, there is a faint hope that at least some of them would hesitate to light up in spite of the unrealistic claims made for filters and their tar- and nicotine-screening capacities. Those who smoke a pipe and do not inhale have a disproportionately high and unhappy prospect of developing lip or mouth cancer owing, in all probability, to the irritation that triggers susceptible tissues. The man who puffs on a big fat cigar is indulging in an adult version of thumb-sucking, according to some psychologists. You can't win.

Air-Borne Infections

Although dust, dirt, pollen, and other air contaminants are highly objectionable, the real threat to human health can be traced primarily to droplets originating within the nose and throat of individuals who expel them into the atmosphere in unbelievable numbers during talking, even in moderate tones, and particularly during coughing and sneezing when the explosive force magnifies the volume of the spray. Such moist particles remain suspended in the air for varying periods depending upon their size, prevalent air currents, and the relative humidity of the atmosphere at the time.

Those engaged in occupations that call for close contact with large numbers of other individuals in varying degrees of health cannot help but breathe in fantastic numbers of potentially harmful microbes. Give thought to the bank teller who is sprayed at close range by perhaps a hundred or more patrons each day, and the bus driver who goes through his rush hour routine breathing in the highly contaminated used and reused air of packed humanity. How about the school teacher who deals with a classroom of youngsters with running noses? Perhaps these public servants and many others should be awarded hazard pay for dangers beyond the call of duty.

It is not how many organisms you inhale each day that counts so much as the types of microbes taken into your system. A farmer working in a dusty, highly manured field might breathe in hundreds of thousands of saprophytic organisms during his daily toil, but nature has provided man with a relatively efficient filtering system to capture these particles and the bacteria they might be transporting. Our nose is lined with hairs to serve as a physical trap for gross particles, and moist mucous membranes catch additional organisms and inert microscopic particles. The tortuous passage through which inhaled matter must pass is another ingenious device for keeping foreign bodies out of our lungs. The system does break down on occasion when it becomes overloaded or when our resistance drops below a critical level, but in general we are spared the onslaught of any number of lethal agents because of nature's built-in protection.

The types of infectious respiratory ailments from which pathogenic microbes can arise include the common cold, pneumonia, diphtheria, influenza, tuberculosis, meningitis, whooping cough, various streptococcal infections, and a number of others. Each of these diseases will be dealt with in some detail in Chapter 15 which concerns itself with pathogens and their characteristics.

Adequate ventilation, especially during the colder months of the year when people spend more time indoors, should not be minimized in any over-all consideration of well-being. It is a simple yet effective counter-measure for air pollution and a blessing for the nonsmoker who does not wish to get his cancer second hand. Too many speakers, including even teachers of public health, drone on and on to half-conscious captive audiences confined within rooms that at times appear to be hermetically sealed, without giving a thought to allowing a bit of fresh air to creep into the conversation. Part of the job of trying to make a patient more comfortable must include supplying a reasonable change of air. This does not mean going to extremes and becoming a fresh air fiend who is content only when a minor gale is whipping through a room. Moderation is advised in all things and fresh air is no exception.

The use of a face mask has been discussed as one means by which the numbers of organisms sprayed into the air can be reduced, but this is a technique confined essentially to hospitals and to "sterile rooms" in industry. The average citizen on the street can hardly be expected to attire himself in such a face covering, although during epidemics of influenza in relatively recent times it was not uncommon to see home-made face masks being employed as a prophylactic measure. The effectiveness of such a covering under these conditions must be questionable. During heavy dust storms the use of handkerchiefs or light towels is advocated as one means for cutting down on the excessive amounts of fine dust that might otherwise be inhaled, with potential lung damage. But the viruses of influenza and other respiratory diseases cannot adequately be screened out by such a technique.

Treatment of Air

Chemical and physical treatment of air, particularly in confined areas, is not only feasible but desirable as well under prescribed conditions. Biological supply houses find ultraviolet lamps extremely beneficial in vial-filling rooms which generally are small cubicles accommodating one or two technicians who can work under highly aseptic conditions. Virology laboratories are constantly fighting bacterial contamination, and radiation of the air serves a very useful function. Some hospitals find ultraviolet lamps helpful in their operating rooms which are flooded with these germicidal rays between operations when the facilities are not in use. The ventilators must be kept scrupulously clean if they are not to serve as reservoirs for microbes, especially staphylococci, that escape the lethal action of germicidal lights or other treatments. Smooth surfaces, preferably ceramic tile, will make cleaning easier in operating rooms and organisms on these surfaces cannot escape from the ultraviolet light. The traps in floor drains should be kept filled with water to prevent contamination of the air from backwash of sewers.

Lord Lister (1827–1912) must be given the lion's share of the credit for developing aseptic techniques in our hospitals through his initial recommendations for "purifying" the air with a fine mist of carbolic acid, particularly in the environment of an operation. In recent years aerosols produced by release of low-surface-tension liquids confined under pressure have been used for air purification. The vapor phase of propylene glycol and triethylene glycol proves to be extremely germicidal. These same compounds when employed as aqueous solutions are comparatively ineffective against a number of organisms. A relative humidity of 40 per cent with the temperature about 76°F appears to be optimum for prompt lethal action of the vapor phase of such compounds against microbes. Glycols are odorless, tasteless, colorless, nonirritating, and nontoxic to humans apparently even after prolonged exposure.

While it is true that these glycol vapors are effective germicides, their usefulness in preventing disease is far from clear. It would seem, however, that it might be advantageous to incorporate these vapors into the air of spacious offices, for example, where large numbers of individuals work together. There might be sufficient reduction in upper respiratory disease under these conditions to warrant the expense of installing and maintaining a chemical purifier in the ventilation system. No doubt experiments have already been conducted to determine the advisability of this type of air treatment. Some might argue that once the workers have left the relatively pure air of the office and then are forced to mingle with the "contaminated" masses on subways, streetcars, and buses, the positive effects might be nullified.

Microbe-Free Animals

An interesting phase of microbiology is that concerned with the raising and studying of germ-free animals. Fundamental work in this area has been conducted for several decades at Notre Dame University. These unique animals might be considered to serve a similar function in science as a tube of sterile medium or a chemically pure compound. While many significant findings have already been reported in research employing these select animals, the full potential of this phase of biological science is just being tapped and the project is virtually still on the launching pad; the sky is the limit.

Qualitative and Quantitative Analysis of Air

One of the introductory experiments conducted in a number of elementary courses in microbiology is to expose the surface of petri dishes containing various media to the open air for varying lengths of time. Students are generally impressed with the interesting sizes, shapes, and colors of the bacterial and mold colonies that develop following appropriate incubation. A single cubic foot of air in a relatively quiet room would not be expected to contain many floating organisms, but in an area occupied by many individuals who are talking and moving about, both the types and the numbers of microbes in the air can be considerable. A bacteriologist with a handful of agar plates could have a real ball at a lively, talkative cocktail party!

No single medium will support the growth of all organisms one might expect to find in the air. Therefore any meaningful tests would of necessity have to be conducted with several types of media, each designed to support the growth of specific types of cells. For example, tomato agar favors the growth of yeasts, molds, and a number of bacteria; bacteriostatic media such as Endo agar or eosine methylene blue agar retard the development of gram positive cells at the same time that gram negative bacteria are allowed to flourish; blood agar is recommended for detecting bacteria that originate in saliva droplets and organisms that are blood-loving or hemolytic. Viruses and rickettsiae, highly parasitic entities, cannot grow on any of these media since they must be provided with selected living cells for their reproduction.

A number of clever air-sampling devices have been developed through the years. Some of these are inexpensive, whereas others may cost hun-

FIG. 11.2. Electrostatic bacterial air sampler. (Courtesy Gardner Associates, Inc., Scotia, N. Y.)

FIG. 11.3. Schematic diagram of electrostatic air sampler. (Courtesy Gardner Associates, Inc., Scotia, N. Y.)

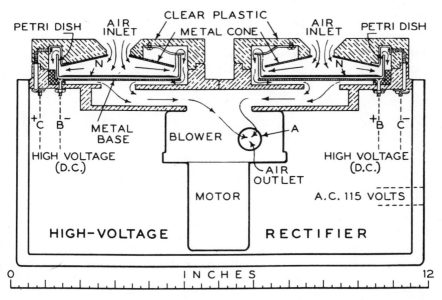

dreds of dollars. Should quantitative determinations of the microbiology of the atmosphere be desired, there are reliable machines that will sample measured volumes of air by drawing controlled amounts of the atmosphere across the surface of different media or through liquids which trap the suspended microbes. Another principle employed is the use of a high voltage electrostatic field to precipitate organisms from a given volume of air into special culture dishes.

If the estimated figures published in the literature are valid, there are in excess of 600,000,000 respiratory infections annually in the United States. Public health officials cannot sweep these figures under the rug and hope they will go away, and would not if they could. Improvement in human health requires constant endeavor in a never-ending task. If the air we breathe plays a role in the dissemination of the etiological agents in disease, increasing attention must be devoted to measures aimed at prevention of both biological and chemical pollution of the life-sustaining environment we call "air."

Review Questions

1. What types of microbial diseases are not usually spread through the agency of air?
2. Is there any reason apparent to you why bacteria are not normally found in the air unless they are being carried by dust particles or droplets of moisture?
3. Is there any correlation between the number of dust particles and the count of bacteria in air?
4. If microbes are put into the air by talking, coughing, and sneezing, shouldn't nurses and other paramedical personnel wear face masks whenever they are in close contact with patients?
5. If smoking is presumably so hazardous to human health, why do so many people who are engaged in the health sciences continue to smoke?
6. What types of investigations that could not be studied in ordinary laboratory animals might be conducted on microbe-free animals?

12 MICROBIOLOGY OF FOOD AND FOOD POISONING

Introduction

ANY MACHINE, WHETHER IT BE BIOLOGICAL OR PHYSICAL, IS wholly dependent upon suitable and adequate fuel for its operation. Prolonged burning of low-grade and unclean gasoline in an internal combustion engine inevitably results in breakdown, and the food humans ingest is not unlike gasoline in this respect. If man expects his intricate biological engine to run properly, every cell in his body must be given proper nutritional support and the wastes of metabolism must be eliminated before they build up to dangerous levels. At one of the critical developmental periods in life, namely adolescence, sensible eating habits that would fill the rigid demands of a rapidly developing body are too often sacrificed for the sake of being accepted by the crowd.

Hippocrates, centuries before Christ, recognized that not all foods may be equally suitable for every individual. Recall the number of persons of your acquaintance who are allergic to one or more foods commonly found in our everyday diets. Perhaps your own skin erupts with unattractive blemishes after you have eaten certain food. Many of these biological reactions are still poorly understood. Chemical alterations induced through microbial activity have made possible greater breadth in our dietary choices. By learning to control biological spoilage through the use of heat, refrigeration, drying, and the addition of chemical preservatives we can now preserve for year-round consumption many foods formerly

209

available only during their limited growing season in a relatively restricted area.

Autolytic enzymes which cause digestion of cells are important in modifying foods to make them more palatable, provided the degradation is not allowed to proceed too far. "Hanging" of meats, for example, makes them more tender than if they were eaten directly after the animal had been killed. Tenderizing is accomplished through enzymatic forces originating within the meat itself.

Probably few foods are universally accepted. Climate and other environmental factors influence the types of food that can be grown in any area, thus limiting the dietary habits of the inhabitants. Widely traveled people tend to become more tolerant of the variations in diet found around the world. And in many countries today, as transportation has improved through the addition of refrigeration facilities and the increase in speed, fresh foods can be made available within hours to residents of cities hundreds of miles away. This has had a somewhat leveling effect on the eating habits of entire populations.

As was pointed out in Chapter 10 on soil biology, the continuance of life on this planet depends upon the death of plants and animals for release of bound essential elements; at the same time, we believe that life must spring from previous life—unless one is an advocate of abiogenesis. If man's food comes from the soil, either directly in the form of edible plants growing in that dynamic medium, or indirectly through consumption of animals that have fed on these plants, then it is probably fair to state that life depends essentially upon microbes that make soil fertility a reality.

Microorganisms and Food

Should anyone doubt the significance of microorganisms in our daily existence, let him begin by listing the foods he consumes during the course of a single week. How many of these foods, begininng with our daily bread and butter, are available to enrich our diets because microbial activity made them possible? The findings of such a survey may prove to be a revelation to many who have given little or no thought to this aspect of their life.

A brief sampling of some of these foods might help to emphasize the point. Yeasts, through their ability to ferment carbohydrates, are responsible for the rising of bread and pastry dough, thus improving the texture. Samples of bread over 4400 years old have been found to contain remnants of yeasts and bacteria, indicating that these biological cells were employed accidentally or by design to cause leavening of the dough.

Fermentation may be employed to impart flavor to foods or to preserve them. In many cases it is difficult to draw a sharp line between these two processes. Vinegar, one of the oldest fermented products consumed by man, gets its name from the French *vin aigre*, meaning "sour wine." Pickles are prepared in brine which initiates a spontaneous fermentation through the natural microbial flora present on the cucumbers. Pure biological cultures may yield more uniform and reliable batches of pickles when the organisms are added to properly prepared basic ingredients. Olives may be treated with lye to make them less bitter before brine is employed to get the fermentation reaction underway.

Cocoa seeds are enclosed in a woody shell which is removed through spontaneous fermentation brought about by species of *Saccharomyces*, the true yeasts, which also improve the flavor of the seeds. During this process the temperature of the batch may rise to between 45 and 50°C, which undoubtedly aids in loosening the woody coating on the seeds. The plant *Coffea arabica* produces a ripe fruit which is a deep red color and these seeds are referred to as "sherries" before they are roasted to produce coffee as we know it. Extraneous matter can be removed from coffee beans either by exposing them to the sun or by soaking them in water. When cultures of true yeasts are added to the water bath, these seeds can be kept in the soaking troughs for a considerably shorter time than if natural fermentation were allowed to proceed. Fermentation of soy beans yields a commonly used sauce, and citron, prepared in Corsica, is made by employing a mixed fermentation in sea water. Sauerkraut, beer, wine, and hard liquors are other products that depend upon microbial activity for their manufacture.

Acid-producing bacteria, especially those species capable of attacking milk sugar (lactose), bring about desired changes in milk in the manufacture of a great number of dairy products. Selected bacterial cultures added to cream prior to churning it into butter determines to a large extent the final flavor, aroma, and general quality of the product. Pure cultures of *Lactobacillus acidophilus* were found by Rettger and his students at Yale University to produce a highly acceptable acid milk which was relatively popular as a drink during the 1920's and 1930's. It was believed at the time that acidophilus milk could be used for the treatment of constipation and other intestinal disorders, especially in older persons. These gram positive rod-shaped lactobacilli are found as part of the normal intestinal flora of infants, but are absent or greatly reduced in number as individuals become older. Part of the theory behind the drinking of acidophilus milk was the re-implantation of these organisms through daily consumption of the product which contained hundreds of millions of viable bacteria per milliliter. Bulgarian milk is still a widely used drink in a number of countries bordering the Mediterranean Sea, and many inhabitants of these areas attribute their long life to this item in their diet. *Lactobacillus bulgaricus* is the principal organism involved in the fermentation process.

Cottage cheese is prepared by adding selected pure cultures of lactic acid-producing cultures to pasteurized skim milk. After the proper acidity has been obtained, the curds are carefully cooked, drained, washed, salted, and creamed. Cheddar cheese is a product of bacterial attack on casein. Ripening proceeds through liquefying bacteria while casein degradation is largely due to naturally occurring enzymes found in milk. As many as 300 different species of bacteria have been isolated from cheddar cheeses. Some 900 individual cultures have been found in Swiss cheeses, with the microbial flora shifting during the ripening stages as conditions become more or less favorable for various groups of organisms. The so-called "eyes" and the flavor of Swiss cheese appear to be due to species of *Propionibacteria,* and if pure cultures of these bacteria are used as starters, fewer poor batches are likely to be encountered in the manufacturing process.

Molds, particularly members of the *Penicillium* genus, are instrumental in developing color and flavor in cheeses. Camembert is a soft cheese that is ripened from without by inoculation with *P. camemberti.* Roquefort cheese, on the other hand, is a hard cheese ripened by *P. roqueforti* that is distributed throughout the cheese to produce the characteristic flavor in addition to the blue-green streaks associated with this product.

These represent only a few of the many foods in our diet dependent upon microbial action for their manufacture; the list could be expanded considerably with little effort. A discussion of microbes and their role in food industries should not be dismissed without one general statement to the effect that untold millions of dollars worth of food are spoiled annually through undesirable microbial activity. A good percentage of this waste is attributable to lack of refrigeration, the use of which could materially retard the speed of metabolism of the implicated microorganisms.

Production of antibiotics is another microbial process, with soil serving as the source of the organisms. Chapter 13 will deal with these life-saving "miracle drugs."

Sanitation in the Home and in
Public Eating Establishments

Personal Hygiene of Food Handlers

Cleanliness and sanitation are words that have wide ranges of meaning and interpretation. What is acceptably clean to one individual may be revolting to another person who is extremely fastidious. Although it is possible to become overly microbe-conscious, there are intelligent approaches to this business of learning to live with your biological as well as your physical environment. By following basic principles one can avoid undue exposure to possible food poisoning attacks.

From the time you and I were old enough to understand what was being said to us, we were constantly being reminded to wash our hands before coming to meals, the idea being not only to create a somewhat more appealing sight as we faced our parents across the table, but also to remove microorganisms (usually referred to by laymen as "germs") clinging to hot little hands before bacteria could find their way into our digestive tracts. It is probably a wise idea to expose ourselves to a certain number of microbes if we expect to maintain a reasonable degree of natural resistance to pathogenic organisms, but there are limits for each individual beyond which it may be foolhardy to go. People differ as much in their tolerance to myriad diseases as they do in their fingerprints, no two persons being exactly alike in every respect. Because of these wide variations each person must be treated as an individual by his or her physician. What might be entirely suitable for one patient could be wholly undesirable for someone else.

When we consider that in the United States alone there are probably over 100,000 cases of food poisoning annually—a statistic that is a national disgrace—it would appear that many adults who prepare and handle food for consumption by others have either forgotten their lessons in sanitation taught during childhood or else they prefer to ignore established facts bearing on acceptable techniques for handling of foodstuffs. The soiled towel and the unpleasant dish cloth may harbor millions of bacteria.

Not only should the hands of food handlers be kept scrupulously clean, but fingernails must be short and free of gross dirt. Many foods we consume almost have to come in intimate contact with people's hands, but fingers too often are substituted as a matter of convenience in place of more acceptable spoons, forks, and knives. Unless a person has had some instruction in the science of microbiology, it must be difficult for him to comprehend the fact that millions of living organisms can occupy a space no larger than the head of a common pin. The fantastic speed of microbial multiplication under favorable conditions must be considered under any situation where moist food is to be kept unrefrigerated for any period of time.

How many food handlers "forget" to wash their hands after using a handkerchief or after visiting the toilet? How many of them cough and sneeze in close proximity to dishes of uncovered food? It takes real courage and faith to eat a meal in many public restaurants (especially in the popular so-called "ptomaine palaces" or "greasy spoons") where what goes on behind those swinging doors is hidden from the eyes of unsuspecting patrons. If you have never worked in a restaurant or visited the kitchen during a busy period, your education is far from complete. Food poisoning is a preventable disease and no stone should be left unturned by those in authority, especially the professional sanitarians, to improve standards of sanitation in public establishments in an effort to reduce food poisoning to its absolute minimum.

Some foods are much more likely to become contaminated with harmful microbes than are others because of the more direct and intimate contact they have with hands and because of the very nature of the food which makes them more suitable as microbiological media. We can ingest enormous numbers of common bacteria with little or no ill effects, but when these same organisms are permitted to multiply in unrefrigerated foods, bacteria can generate potent toxins which can trigger a series of unpleasant effects when consumed. All of these considerations have a direct bearing upon the personal habits and hygiene practiced by food handlers, and the problem of maintaining high standards of sanitation cannot be allowed to drift without constant attention to details. The writer remembers well a sign displayed in an Army mess hall during World War II in the European Theater of Operations. The message was: FOOD WILL WIN THE WAR, and underneath some wit had appended the notation: BUT HOW CAN WE GET THE ENEMY TO EAT HERE? While this was a gross exaggeration of the facts, in this instance, the thought expressed helped to focus attention on the problems involved in feeding large numbers of individuals without producing unpleasant aftereffects. Not only does an army march on its stomach (awkward as that may be), but the population as a whole requires an adequate, well-balanced diet consisting of wholesome food if it is to work and play with a feeling of well-being.

Flies and Other Vermin

The role of the filthy fly in the dissemination of microbes has been commonly accepted knowledge for a good many years, but only recently have carefully controlled experiments been conducted to determine both qualitatively and quantitatively the truth of this assumption. The very physical makeup of flies and roaches, with their hairy appendages, provides a suitable trap for collecting and harboring filth and accompanying microorganisms. Millions of bacteria can be found on the outer body surfaces of a single fly. A study of the species of microbes encountered leads one to the inevitable conclusion that human excrement as well as other types of wastes provide a suitable breeding ground for such vermin. Human fecal material might be discharged from carriers of enteric diseases, and if flies have unrestricted access to this material, the possibilities for contamination of foods are obvious. Typhoid, paratyphoid, dysentery, and other intestinal pathogens can survive for extended periods on the outer surfaces of flies and roaches, and, as has been demonstrated in the writer's laboratory, when some of these enteric bacteria are ingested in sufficient numbers by these insects, the host can serve as a mobile incubator with subsequent prolonged excretion of millions or billions of viable pathogenic bacteria over long periods. Often the pastry display cases in restaurants wisely are enclosed with glass or screening materials, but when flies find their way in, they can't get out! Their fecal deposits, especially on cream-filled pastry, can supply viable cultures of virulent organisms which multiply quickly at room temperature and build up potent toxins.

Rats and mice are a constant menace and threat wherever food is stored or served. Operators of food warehouses must be on constant alert to eliminate rodents in their establishments. Too often mice are carriers of *Salmonella* species, particularly mouse typhoid (*S. typhimurium*), and should mouse droppings come in contact with suitable food serving as a medium, real trouble can and does occur.

Disposal of Garbage

One moment we have before us a sumptuous spread, and in a few minutes a sweep of the hand converts the remains to garbage. In a land of plenty the amount of edible food that is scraped from plates and wasted is another national disgrace, especially when one considers the millions of human beings who must go to bed hungry night after night. But this is not the subject of this chapter, important as the topic may be in modern-day society.

Food Poisoning and Food Infection

Introduction

The expression *food poisoning* frequently is meant to include symptoms caused both by the ingestion of toxins performed by microorganisms and by the consumption of foods containing living pathogenic microbes which can multiply within the human digestive tract. Strictly speaking, the latter cases are more accurately described as *food infections.*

It should be made clear from the outset that the designation *ptomaine poisoning* is a misnomer in practically every instance of food-borne outbreaks. The word **ptomaine** is derived from Greek and means "dead body." Chemically, ptomaines are organic bases produced by splitting out the carbon dioxide from the acid group of specific amino acids, the so-called building blocks of proteins. Two such ptomaines, putrescine and cadaverine, are not even considered to be toxic when taken by mouth. Putrescine is derived from the amino acid ornithine, and lysine is the source of cadaverine. Perhaps some of the putrefactive end products of nitrogenous breakdown are poisonous for some sensitive individuals, but odor in itself is a poor criterion of toxicity. If there were a correlation between these two factors, limburger cheese would have dispatched an imposing number of gourmets long ago. The exact etiological agent in food poisoning and food infection can generally be pinpointed to the lethal action of specific bacteria or their metabolic products, and this chapter will attempt to highlight some of the accepted concepts relative to this aspect of human disease.

Characteristics of Food Poisonings

Although specific bacteria responsible for gastrointestinal upsets will naturally trigger particular reactions when ingested, the general syndrome of food poisoning in its broadest meaning will include some or all of the following symptoms: nausea, cramps, vomiting, diarrhea, sweats, fever, and other less well-defined reactions. In a severe food-borne outbreak acute illness will afflict a number of individuals who partook of a common meal, and the onset of the disease for susceptible persons can be expected to strike at about the same time for all individuals. However the total resistance of the host and the number and virulence of the ingested bacteria must be considered as leading determining factors in the length of time before unpleasant symptoms are triggered in the host. And it must always be borne in mind by those conducting epidemiological studies of this nature that it is not uncommon to find that some of the persons who eat the incriminating meal do not become ill, whereas others in the group who do not partake of the specific contaminated food will complicate the evidence by their psychic vomiting. They are the persons who vomit when they see others doing so!

Types of Food Poisoning by Biological Agents

Salmonella INFECTION

There are over 340 species of bacteria belonging to the genus *Salmonella,* a group of gram negative, non-sporing rods that are serologically related. These microbes may gain entrance to many foods and propagate under suitable environmental conditions, especially when temperature and moisture requirements are favorable.

Salmonellosis is a febrile disease with the body temperature commonly elevated as high as 102°F; temperature in excess of this figure may occur, however. Chills and abdominal cramps should be added to the usual triad of nausea, vomiting, and diarrhea. So severe is the loss of body fluids in acute cases that the salt balance of the patient may be markedly disturbed with the usual side-effects such a condition precipitates. Loss of consciousness may even occur under such circumstances.

The principal characteristics of this disease are associated with the release of bound endotoxins from the bacteria, and it is this feature of salmonellosis that accounts for the delayed clinical reactions after the food has been eaten. The bacterial cells must undergo breakdown, or autolysis, before the toxins fixed in the protoplasm are released within the **lumen** of the intestines where organisms lodge. Bacteremia or septicemia may be expected in acute cases of the disease, and this is one of the many reasons why recovery of the patient may be delayed.

It was Gaertner in 1888 who reported the first species of *Salmonella* to be recognized as the etiological agent in food infection, and the species he isolated was *S. enteritidis.* Examinations of the organisms implicated in reported outbreaks since his discovery reveal that *S. enteritidis* and *S. typhimurium* are the species most frequently found in human cases of salmonellosis.

Human carriers and infected vermin are the usual reservoirs of these microbes, and gastroenteritis of *Salmonella* etiology is usually traced to contaminated foods, especially meats, fish, fresh eggs (particularly duck eggs), and dried eggs. From a public health standpoint, the ingestion of raw eggs should, therefore, be discouraged. Lettuce, celery, and other vegetables eaten in the raw state may become contaminated by droppings of rodents, since wherever food is stored, rodents and other vermin are likely to be found. *Salmonella* organisms are non-sporing and hence are readily killed by exposure to a temperature of 162°F for as short a period as two minutes. (Cooked lettuce, however, leaves much to be desired!) Thorough washing of all vegetables to be consumed raw is our best defense against pathogens spread through this agency.

Foods may become contaminated in two general ways. The animal from which meat is derived may have tissues infected with live pathogens, or the eggs produced by some of the fowl may be highly contaminated. Human carriers with questionable habits of sanitation may transfer the bacteria through intimate contact with food that is not subsequently cooked sufficiently to inactivate such microbes.

Although paratyphoid fever is caused by members of the same genus as those described above, the clinical symptoms tend to be more severe in human cases. Three principal species of salmonellae are responsible for paratyphoid fevers: *S. paratyphi* (type A), *S. schottmuelleri* (type B), and *S. hirschfeldii* (type C). Typhoid fever, caused by *S. typhosa,* is more severe than all of the other members of this genus. The mode of spread for all of these bacteria is essentially the same. Chlorination of water and pasteurization of milk can be given the major credit for the dramatic drop in the incidence of enteric diseases, but the careless food handler is an ever-present threat to human health. Only constant vigilance and bold action on the part of the health authorities will minimize the damage these individuals can inflict on their fellow human beings.

BOTULISM

Clostridium botulinum, whose natural habitat is the soil, produces one of the most deadly biological poisons known to man, yet few laymen have ever heard of botulism, the disease that results from ingestion of their toxins. The causative agent is a large gram positive anaerobe whose spores are large and subterminal, giving the parent cells a snowshoe appearance when the organisms are examined under a microscope. The toxin liberated during metabolism of the cells is so powerful that one gram of relatively purified poison has been estimated to contain up to *one million human lethal doses.* Some workers have reported that as little as 0.01 mg of the botulinus toxin may be fatal for a human being.

Botulism is a food intoxication brought about principally through the ingestion of underprocessed preserved foods which are stored in sealed containers under air-tight conditions. The first reported cases of the disease were in Europe where sausages were responsible, and the name, *botulism,* literally means "sausage" (Latin, *botulus*). Spores of *C. botulinum* exhibit a remarkable resistance to heat, some having been able to withstand exposure to 100°C for up to five hours without being inactivated. This is a most unusual expectation for material that is protein in nature. Such a marked resistance to heat points up the importance of subjecting certain canned foods to steam under pressure which will allow the temperature to rise considerably above the boiling point.

Not since the 1920's has there been a case of botulism in the United States traceable to commercially canned foods. This speaks well for the food industry. It is the uninformed housewife who, unfortunately, has been responsible for the numerous cases that have occurred.

These anaerobes grow poorly, if at all, within the body of a warm-blooded animal. Hence the powerful neurotoxin produced by *C. botulinum* places this disease squarely in the category of a food intoxication rather than a food infection. Botulism is not an infectious process but rather a true toxemia, and at least five serologically distinct types of toxin, labeled A, B, C, D, and E, have been distinguished in addition to other less well-defined groups that have been reported in the literature. Antitoxin, to be effective, must be specific for the exact type of toxin which is responsible for its production, and in cases of emergency, when time is of the essence, a polyvalent antitoxin is generally administered until exact typing permits the administration of specific antitoxin.

Botulism involves a paralysis of that portion of the nervous system that acts on the involuntary muscles of the body. Death from this disease apparently is caused by failure of the skeletal musculature, leading to interference with breathing and eventual terminal asphyxia. Symptoms consisting of double vision and difficulty in swallowing generally appear in from 2 to 36 hours, but incubation periods as long as 4 days have been reported. Speed of death bears a direct relationship to the amount of toxin ingested, but histopathological changes in the victims are absent or slight.

The incidence of botulism is relatively so low that prophylactic injections are unwarranted except perhaps in situations where laboratory personnel are working with this lethal agent. A minute amount of treated botulinus poison acting as an injected antigen can stimulate production of significant quantities of antitoxin. The potential possibilities of such a powerful poison in biological warfare can only be surmised, but as long as any threat exists, government agencies must be prepared to manufacture on short notice huge quantities of specific antitoxins for prophylactic and therapeutic use in human populations.

During the fifty-year span covering the period from 1899 to 1949 there have been 483 *reported* outbreaks of botulism in the United States and Canada. These involved 1319 cases and 851 deaths—a mortality rate of almost 65 per cent. The therapeutic use of antitoxins has undoubtedly saved the lives of many who otherwise might have died from this disease, but delay in diagnosis and treatment may spell the difference between death and survival of those afflicted.

It is significant that when patients suffering from botulism were interviewed there seemed to be unanimous agreement that the suspected food either smelled or tasted "off." Even though the spores of *C. botulinum* are extremely resistant to the action of heat, the exotoxins produced by these anaerobes are relatively thermolabile. In fact, ten minutes of boiling will completely inactivate the toxic fraction of such biological poisons. The absence of signs of spoilage in home-canned foods that have not been subjected to steam pressure treatment should not be accepted as proof of edibility of the food. Perhaps spoilage has not progressed to the point where a change in appearance or odor is detectable. In any case, WHEN IN DOUBT, THROW IT OUT, but do not taste such foods before they have been boiled for ten minutes.

The question sometimes arises, Is one likely to contract botulism from frozen foods? Unless the frozen product was first stored under anaerobic conditions at a temperature suitable for the development of *C. botulinum,* the chances of this toxin being present in the frozen food are practically nonexistent. The temperature of food in the frozen state would preclude the production of toxin even if the anaerobic bacteria should chance to be present.

Through the commendable efforts of the Extension Services of our state universities, housewives, particularly in rural areas, are being taught the latest accepted techniques for preservation of home-grown food products, and you can be sure that the use of steam under pressure is the recommended procedure for canning neutral high-protein foods.

Staphylococcus FOOD POISONING OR INTOXICATION

Until a few years ago the word *Staphylococcus* was virtually unknown to the layman, but recently through widespread attention focused on medical facilities where staphylococcal infections have loomed as an increasing problem, this scientific term has become a household word. (Most folks may not be able to spell *Staphylococcus,* but neither can many students.)

The organism that has stirred up all the fuss, and justifiably so in the opinion of the writer, is one of the smaller bacteria. It is gram positive, spherical, arranged in grapelike clusters, and the cell measures about one micron or less in diameter. Nutritional requirements for the microbes are modest, and it is this fact coupled with their widespread distribution on our skin, in our noses, and in mouths of individuals suffering from infected tonsils or dental caries that make the staphylococci of urgent concern to public health groups. Chapter 15 will be devoted to some of the localized infections caused by these organisms; discussion here will be confined to the role played by staphylococci in the most common type of food poisoning or intoxication facing us every day.

It has been commonly accepted for decades that *Staphylococcus aureus,* which produces a golden-colored water-insoluble pigment when colonies grow on the surface of media, tends to be implicated more frequently in food-borne outbreaks than does the white, or *albus*, variety. Pigmentation and virulence were once believed to bear a direct relationship to each other, but today this belief is not universally accepted.

During metabolism the staphylococci liberate a soluble poison which has a particularly irritating effect on the walls of the intestines in human beings, but not all strains of even the *aureus* varieties are capable of generating enterotoxin of sufficient potency to trigger clinical symptoms when the poison is ingested. With the exception of humans and young kittens, animals appear to possess a degree of resistance to *Staphylococcus* poison even in relatively potent mixtures.

Staphylococci as a group are relatively tolerant of heat. Some cultures have been shown to withstand an exposure to 60°C for 30 minutes without being inactivated, and even 1 per cent phenol in 15 minutes has little or no effect on these cocci. This is somewhat unusual for a non-sporing organism. The enterotoxin produced by these bacteria also exhibits a remarkable resistance to heat. Boiling for 30 minutes may not be sufficient to destroy this thermostable poison. This means that the usual cooking techniques employed for most foods is insufficient to eliminate the hazard of food poisoning if the pre-formed toxin has built up to a critical level prior to cooking. Freezing has no effect on this poison.

The optimum growth temperature of staphylococci is between 28° and 37°C, and at this temperature range in a suitable medium the cells are capable of doubling their numbers in about thirty minutes. It is not difficult to comprehend that if such rapid multiplication occurs at least twice every hour under proper conditions, enormous populations of cells can build up with even a modest initial inoculum. Someone with unclean hands or an open draining lesion could easily contribute millions of potent staphylococci to a food being prepared. An unprotected sneeze could raise this number even higher. When one considers that each microbe may be likened to a poison generator consisting of a small cell volume but with a relatively high cell surface area through which the soluble toxin seeps, it is surprising that there are not more serious outbreaks than we already experience.

A few representative examples of the types of food most commonly implicated will point up the danger that thinking individuals should bear in mind the next time they find themselves invited to a picnic, wedding reception, church supper, or other large gathering where food is being prepared on a mass scale, often by inexperienced persons who are not well versed in the fundamentals of safe food preparation. The warmer months of the year are particularly dangerous as far as the incidence of outbreaks is concerned. Foods to arouse suspicion, and perhaps to be avoided completely in many instances, include salads of all kinds (especially potato salad), cream- or custard-filled pastry, creamed or precooked meats such as ham, pressed beef, or tongue, fish, meat pies, poultry and poultry dressing, sausages, and milk and its many by-products. This doesn't leave you much to eat, does it?

The food poisonings about which the public learns can usually be traced to gatherings of relatively large numbers of individuals where those who have prepared the meal are not equipped to provide adequate refrigeration during storage of the prepared foods. And in many cases these persons do not understand or prefer to ignore simple fundamental facts regarding bacteria and their capabilities.

Large bulk-type foods, especially those which come in intimate contact with human hands, are frequently involved since they are good insulators through which cold has difficulty penetrating in a reasonable period of time. Potato salad is one such food. The potatoes are cut by hand, made moist by the addition of salad dressing which in itself is a good bacteriological medium, and the finished product is then stored in the open for some hours before use. This is the classical story that is repeated so often, year in and year out. Even when refrigerators are available, if the salad is placed in a large container for chilling, it may take hours before the core of the salad is sufficiently cooled to retard active multiplication of bacteria lodged in the food. Those persons who are fortunate enough to be served portions of the salad that came from the outer surfaces which were cooled relatively promptly may be spared the unpleasant symptoms that will be the lot of the majority whose portions are scooped from the center of the container where metabolic waste products, especially enterotoxins, have had an opportunity to build up during storage.

Only by spreading such hard-to-cool foods in thin layers (2–3 inches in depth) prior to combining them into a large bulk can this type of food intoxication be avoided. Allowing large buckets of properly chilled potato salad to stand in a warm atmosphere, such as at picnics, may reverse the bacteriological picture. In such cases the outside layers of salad which warm quickly may contain the toxin, whereas the cooled center portions may now be safe to eat. The whole secret of prevention of such outbreaks involves clean hands during preparation of the food, good sanitary habits with scrupulously clean utensils, and the employment of sound refrigeration practices.

In recent years attention has been called to another serious type of "staph" intoxication spread through the agency of poultry dressing or "stuffing," especially in large turkeys. The reasons for the frequency of this type of poisoning are similar to those pointed out for potato salad. Hands come in close contact with the ingredients, and frequently the dressing is moderately warm before it is put into the bird. Even though the stuffed turkey is immediately placed into a refrigerator, the core of the dressing may not be cooled in sufficient time to prevent a substantial build-up within the dressing of staphylococci and their enterotoxins. Unfortunately, even though the turkey may be thoroughly cooked, the poisons produced by the bacteria will not be inactivated because of their thermostability. If it is necessary to stuff the bird the night before it is to be roasted, the dressing should be thoroughly cooled in shallow layers before being placed within the turkey.

Creamed poultry, chicken à la king, and sliced chicken and turkey are high on the list of foods responsible for frequent attacks of staphylococcus poisoning. As one examines the list of foods implicated in the majority of outbreaks of this nature, it becomes clear that unclean hands, mouth and nose droplets, and improper storage are the basis of the difficulty.

Eclairs and similar cream-filled pastry should be avoided during the warmer months of the year. In fact, many states forbid public sale of these items because of their frequency as villains in food-borne attacks. One fly trapped within a pastry display case can spread significant numbers of many species of undesirable bacteria to moist pastry which serves as an ideal medium for rapid multiplication of toxinogenic microbes when the environmental temperature is favorable. Although less difficulty, insofar as numbers of cases is concerned, is likely to be encountered during the other months of the year, it is, nevertheless, a wise precaution to store cream-filled foods under suitable refrigeration at all times, and out of the reach of flies and other vermin.

When staphylococcus poisoning strikes its victims, treatment may be considered to be supportive rather than being directed at the enterotoxin itself. Nature does its best to rid the body of these undesirable toxins through vomiting and bowel movements. The patient may require the injection of fluids, such as saline or saline plus glucose, to restore the balance of salt that is disturbed by continued vomiting and diarrhea. Any medication taken by mouth, especially during the acute stages of the attack, will be promptly rejected and eliminated from the stomach. An uneventful recovery can usually be anticipated in from 1 to 3 days, the time depending upon the severity of the specific attack and on the general resistance of the afflicted individual.

Anyone who has experienced a case of acute food poisoning will undoubtedly agree with the victim who summed up his experiences: "First I was afraid that I was going to die. But before I was through, I was afraid that I wasn't!" If one single individual can be spared the misery of an unnecessary attack after reading these last few pages, the effort will have been worth while. Elimination of food poisoning is probably not within the realm of possibility, but by being armed with a background of a few fundamental facts and by the application of common sense, we can certainly minimize the disease.

MISCELLANEOUS BACTERIAL FOOD POISONINGS

In addition to the three types of organisms already discussed—*Salmonella* species, *C. botulinum,* and *Staphylococcus* species—there are from time to time outbreaks initiated by other organisms, but the incidence is comparatively rare. It is conceivable, for example, that a sneeze or a cough can seed exposed food with streptococci and other microbes of mouth and nose origin. Metabolic wastes of these bacteria have been blamed for some food-borne disease. At times *Proteus* and *Escherichia* species have been reported in other cases of this type of illness. *Shigella* species may play an important role in food-borne outbreaks, particularly in warmer climates. This is discussed in some detail in Chapter 15.

Chemical Poisoning

The clinical symptoms of chemical poisoning frequently are difficult to distinguish from those of bacterial poisoning and the reader should realize that not all food poisoning is of microbial origin. A few examples will make this clear.

While major attention has been devoted to biological agents as causes of food poisonings, there are a number of gastric upsets that stem from toxic chemicals that find their way into foods. Many of these cases are probably not diagnosed as chemical poisonings because mass attacks are less likely to occur from this cause than from bacterial etiology. A few potential chemical troublemakers will be presented, but the order of presentation bears no relationship to toxicity.

ALUMINUM

Scare literature periodically appears on the scene attempting to call attention to the extreme hazards to human health when aluminum pots and pans are employed as cooking utensils. There is little doubt that most of the predicted dire consequences are exaggerated. Were this not so, the health statistics would certainly reflect astronomical morbidity rates when one considers the millions of people who daily cook their food in aluminum pots and pans. There is little concrete evidence that the use of aluminum is responsible for much, if any, human illness.

ANTIMONY

Enamelware may have an underlying base consisting, among other things, of antimony which can be toxic when taken internally. When the top layer of enamel chips away and the exposed antimony is allowed to come in contact with food, especially with acid foods under the influence of heat, enough antimony may be picked up in the food to cause gastro-intestinal disturbances within 30 minutes after ingestion.

ARSENIC

A number of plant sprays, including arsenate of lead, contain arsenic in one form or another. When you stop to buy those rosy apples at a roadside fruit stand on a crisp autumn day, the usual quick rub of the apple on your clothing to remove visible "dirt" and to bring out the shine may not be sufficient to reduce the arsenic or lead residues of the sprays. Abdominal cramps or other more serious symptoms may appear within minutes after ingestion of the unwashed skins.

CADMIUM

When acid foods come in contact with cadmium-coated utensils, enough cadmium may be dissolved to cause gastric symptoms within 30 minutes after the food is eaten. As little as 67 PPM of cadmium can induce an unpleasant reaction in humans. There is one reported outbreak in which acid fruit juices frozen in an ice tray containing cadmium as one of the elements caused severe illness of 29 children within a few minutes after the frozen "ice" was consumed.

CYANIDE

There aren't many instances where cyanide becomes a problem in human health, outside the gas chamber used by some of our states for dispatching criminals, but the few cases encountered on occasion are worth mentioning. Some silver polishes may have cyanide as one ingredient, and unless utensils are thoroughly washed in hot soapy water after the tarnish has been loosened by the polish, the residues on the silverware can cause distressing symptoms when ingested with food. Various types of cyanide gases are employed by exterminators who may be ridding a room or a building of vermin. It should be obvious that any food coming in contact with such lethal chemicals should not be eaten. Special gas masks are available for use by those who must enter the gas-treated area to ventilate the quarters after a cyanide gas treatment. One good inspiration of a cyanide-laden atmosphere can prove fatal.

LEAD

This toxic substance unfortunately produces a cumulative effect when it gains access to our body. One of the leading causes of lead poisoning in small children is toys, cribs, or other pieces of furniture covered with lead-containing paints that the youngsters chew on and swallow. Many states have legislation banning the use of leaded paints on any articles likely to be used by small children. Adults employed in factories that manufacture batteries must use special care to keep lead out of their food. In addition, the inhalation of lead-containing fumes in any industry can cause serious cases of poisoning. The Divisions of Industrial Hygiene of our State Health Departments are constantly on the alert to prevent unhealthy working conditions in industry, and the marked reduction in industrial hazards in recent years is evidence of the success of their efforts.

TIN

Great concern is voiced from time to time that Americans will eventually poison themselves by consuming the great quantities of food that are preserved in tin cans, but there is little evidence to support these fears. Brides-to-be should derive comfort from knowing that the can opener is still an accepted and useful item of inventory in the kitchen. Tens of millions of cans of food are annually packed away in containers made of tin and other metals, and the feared build-up of tin in our systems does not seem to be materializing. In reality the inner surface of most tin cans used today is coated with various protective layers which prevent foods from ever coming in direct contact with the underlying tin. The flavor that develops in foods stored in tins that have been opened is primarily caused by oxidation, and this is not cause for alarm from a health standpoint.

MISCELLANEOUS CHEMICALS

As we look back at some of the unsavory practices employed in food industries prior to passage of the Food and Drug Act on June 30, 1906, it becomes apparent that there were many alarming practices that could and did affect human health. Boric acid was used to preserve meats, milk, butter, oysters, clams, fish, and sausage. Milk was preserved with formaldehyde. Potassium permanganate covered up spoilage in meats, and hydrogen peroxide was employed rather extensively to improve keeping quality of milk, wine, beer, and fruit juices.

As scientific studies progressed in this area of human health, many time-honored practices became illegal, but a few chemicals were permitted within specified limits as acceptable preservatives. For example, 0.1 per cent sodium benzoate may be added to certain foods, but the label must so state. If such foods as catsup are made of high-quality raw materials (fresh, clean tomatoes), there should be little need for such additives. When shopping for catsup you may have to pay a few pennies premium for the better brands that do not contain sodium benzoate, but you can be sure that the extra expenditure represents some of the increased production costs necessary to market a high-quality product. In recent years there has been a trend by some bakeries to add approved chemicals to their baked goods in an effort to retard spoilage by molds during warm humid weather, and the practice appears to be gaining favor.

Poisonous Plants and Animals

In addition to food poisoning by microorganisms and chemical agents, some food poisoning or intoxication is the work of macroorganisms—plant and animal.

SHELLFISH

Certain types of shellfish can spread a paralyzing poison to human beings, probably through the agency of plankton called *Gonyaulax catenella*. Studies reveal that three thousand such plankton represent one lethal unit for a mouse, and the toxic compound appears to be an alkaloid. No effective treatment has been found for this disease which has caused some 250 reported cases with 38 recorded deaths.

FAVA BEANS

This bean is responsible for a condition found primarily among Italians who may consume such beans or who smell the blossoms of the plant for prolonged periods; the disease is known as *favism*. The symptoms include fever, anemia, jaundice, and malaise, but sensitivity of individuals varies widely within a given population.

SNAKEROOT

This is also known by the name **milk sickness.** When cattle eat snakeroot plants the animals develop trembles due to the compound *trematol* found in the plant, and if man drinks milk drawn from such cows, he may develop an illness generally involving weakness and severe vomiting.

MUSHROOMS

Unless you are an expert in recognizing edible and poisonous mushrooms, the best advice is to leave the task of identification to those who are experts in the field. Over seventy species of mushrooms are known to be toxic to man, and some of these are capable of causing death. Many cases of mushroom poisoning in the United States appear to be among immigrants from southern Europe who harvest mushrooms similar in appearance to the edible varieties in their native countries. Time and serious consequences frequently prove their judgment to be in error.

WATER HEMLOCK

This plant grows in swampy areas and is frequently mistaken for parsnips or carrots. The lethal fraction of the plant is a resin which when ingested causes convulsions. The mortality rate appears to be low, but the clinical symptoms of the poisoning are far from pleasant.

HONEY

Nectar gathered by bees from the blossoms of a number of plants (including azaleas, rhododendrons, and perhaps mountain laurel) may be toxic to humans when consumed in the form of honey produced by these bees. Mild to severe stomach upsets are not uncommon in such cases.

RHUBARB

During World War I when people were urged to plant victory gardens as one means for relieving the food shortage, some uninformed individuals recommended that the leaves of the rhubarb plant might make an excellent food supplement as salad greens. Unfortunately these leaves are rich in oxalic acid, and a number of deaths occurred before the health authorities could point out the great danger of eating such greens.

Many other toxic plants and animals are involved in contributing to human misery and mortality, but the above examples represent a fair cross-section of some of the possibilities to be avoided.

The more one studies and learns about the hazards of eating, the more he begins to wonder what is really safe and what might be potentially harmful. By avoiding consumption of foods that figure so prominently in food poisoning statistics, we can at least reduce our chances of falling victim to preventable gastric upsets. There is probably no asset more valuable to man than the gift of good health. We should do all in our power to maintain the highest peak of well-being, and we have an additional obligation to teach others less fortunate from the storehouse of available knowledge.

Review Questions

1. Since "eating out" is becoming a more common practice, what practical consideration, if any, should one give to minimizing chances for contracting food poisoning?
2. Distinguish between a food infection and a food poisoning.
3. How important is cleanliness of hands to human health? Consider individuals raised in various environments.

4. What is a simple test you can conduct to confirm a possible case of trench mouth?
5. What types of pathogenic microbes might be carried and transmitted by flies? by roaches? by mosquitoes?
6. How might the public be taught that ptomaine poisoning is a misnomer for the acute gastric upsets so common during the summer months?
7. Might one find staphylococci in a blood culture during a "staph" food poisoning outbreak? Would this make it a food infection if the blood culture turned out to be positive?
8. With all of the home canning that takes place in the United States, why don't we see more botulism than we do?
9. What advice would you give a family that feels the need to preserve their garden harvest of peas and beans for winter consumption and yet cannot afford to purchase a pressure cooker?

13 | CHEMOTHERAPY

History

THE SUM OF ADVANCES IN THE HISTORY OF RECORDED MEDICAL science has been completely overshadowed by the brilliant discoveries of the past hundred years, and microbiology has made significant contributions to recent progress. This paramedical science has made rapid and exciting discoveries in the relatively short time that it has existed as a recognized independent science, and one such wave of findings has been in the area of chemotherapy, the *in vivo* treatment of microbial diseases with chemicals.

An *antibiotic* is a chemical substance produced by living microorganisms capable of acting adversely against other microbes, and the competitive activity for survival that exists between living organisms is known as *antibiosis,* a term introduced in 1889 by Vuillemin. The vast science of antibiotics as we know it today, however, is hardly more than a few decades old.

Chemotherapeutic agents synthesized in a chemical laboratory have in the past been distinguished from the naturally occurring antibiotic substances obtained as by-products of microbial growth. Since some antibiotics in use today are being synthesized, the sharp distinction between these two groups of chemotherapeutic agents probably is no longer justified.

Nature's plan for insuring perpetuation of relatively strong animals is based upon keen competition, with the most fit individuals tending to push aside the weaker members of their group. It is the most powerful buffalo, for example, able to beat all comers who wins "the hand of the fair lady" and helps to produce strong offspring. Weaker males are provided with little or no opportunity to procreate. Man is probably one of the few animals where this interesting concept of survival of the more fit is not practiced to the same degree. As a result of this survival principle in the untamed living world of the soil, where competition for *Lebensraum* is extremely keen, nature has provided us with our richest source of chemotherapeutic agents.

The alarming build-up in resistance of microbes to once-effective antibiotics and other chemotherapeutic substances is one of the most challenging medical problems of our time. With this unfortunate turn in events, scientists are confronted with the necessity of producing more powerful and increasingly effective antibiotics. As long as pathogenic microbes are able to breach the relatively effective external and internal resistance factors with which we are endowed to varying degrees, man must continue to seek ways of staying one jump ahead of microorganisms if he expects to keep them in reasonable check.

The Magic Bullet

Paul Ehrlich (1854–1915) has been called the Father of Chemotherapy because of his pioneer efforts in 1910 in developing an effective arsenical (called the "magic bullet") to combat the spirochete of syphilis, *Treponema pallidum*. Anyone with an interest in scientific research is urged to read accounts of the laborious and classic experiments conducted by Ehrlich and his co-workers with six hundred and six different synthetic arsenic compounds in their zealous search for a cure to "cast out devils from the bodies of men." The tribulations of these investigators forcefully point up the fact that great discoveries do not always come about easily. Discouragements are usually more frequent than encouragements, and if anyone ever faced disappointments, Paul Ehrlich was such an individual. But through dogged determination in the face of many setbacks, the prize was finally his: an effective chemical agent with which to attack one of man's most dreaded diseases, syphilis.

Treponema pallidum was first reported by Schaudinn and Hoffmann in 1905 as the etiological agent in syphilis, a disease recognized in Europe during the latter part of the fifteenth century. Reports indicate that this malady was unknown in America until the visit to our shores by Columbus and his crew. The generic and specific names of the microbe literally translated mean "pale thread," an apt description for the delicate corkscrew-shaped organism with a low index of light refraction.

The magic arsenical, *606* or *salvarsan,* was found to exhibit specific affinity for spiral-shaped organisms. Ehrlich's initial successes came with studies conducted on trypanosomes, and when Fritz Schaudinn announced his discovery of the etiological agent of syphilis, Ehrlich was struck by the similarity in both shape and movement of these venereal pathogens and trypanosomes. These facts spurred his experiments on apes and eventually on human beings, which finally led to a practical technique for treatment. Since his breakthrough in chemotherapy, additional investigations have resulted in the development of neoarsphenamine and mepharsen which have shown even greater promise than 606 in the fight against syphilis.

Sulfa Drugs

A quarter of a century slipped by after Ehrlich's pioneer discovery before another significant step forward in the area of chemotherapy was announced to the world. Domagk discovered in 1935 that *Prontosil,* which breaks down into sulfanilamide in the tissues, exhibited remarkable cures when employed against infections caused by beta hemolytic streptococci in human beings. During the ten years following Domagk's announcement some 5000 derivatives of sulfanilamide were synthesized. Many of these were too toxic or otherwise useless in medicine, but a few of them showed great promise in man's ceaseless attack on pathogenic marauders. In contrast to the specific and relatively narrow spectrum of activity displayed by the arsenicals, sulfonamides were found to be effective against a wider variety of bacteria. An ideal chemotherapeutic agent is one that is extremely lethal to many species of bacteria *in vivo,* and at the same time is harmless to the host. Research continues in an endeavor to find such ideal chemicals to which microorganisms will not become resistant.

Sulfa drugs, as they are popularly known, are aimed principally at inhibiting growth and multiplication by striking at vital reactions in the metabolism of microbes. Once this has been achieved, the natural defense mechanisms of the body are in a better position to destroy or remove the invading cells. Successful application of sulfa drugs appears to bear some relationship to their early administration during the time when the invading pathogens are in the logarithmic phase of their multiplication. Organisms apparently are more susceptible to the action of these drugs during this particular period.

Of the thousands of sulfa drugs discovered since 1935, the following list is representative of those that have been employed most successfully against the organisms listed. Changes in resistance of microbes through the intervening years, however, have necessitated considerable modification in their use in clinical practice.

Sulfanilamide:	streptococci
Sulfapyridine:	pneumococci
Sulfathiazole:	staphylococci and gonococci
Sulfaguanidine:	some of the enterics
Sulfadiazine:	pneumococci, meningococci, beta hemolytic streptococci, gonococci, and some of the gas gangrene group. There have also been reports of successful prophylactic injections of this drug in controlling the spread of meningococci to persons who have been exposed to active cases.

The normal arsenal of external and internal defenses with which man is endowed is eminently successful in protecting us from frequent invasion by pathogenic microbes that are everywhere about us. But when the sum total of our resistance factors is unable to cope with the stronger forces of large numbers of virulent pathogens, man falls victim to disease, a word which literally means "uncomfortable" (*dis-ease*). When this unhappy situation develops, our bodies call forth the reserve potentials built into our complex biological systems. If these fall short of required needs, artificial outside help in the form of drugs or anti-microbial agents must be introduced to stem the unfavorable tide by interfering with the normal function of the enzyme complex of the cells. Once the forward rush of bacterial multiplication has been checked, then the normal disposal systems of our body take over and help to get rid of the foreign cells. If the chemotherapeutic agents are administered "too little or too late," or if they are ineffective against the specific pathogens, microscopic invaders eventually are able to destroy a human being billions of times larger than themselves.

Antibiotics

History is filled with accounts of many unusual techniques and treatments for curing infections. As science has moved forward on a broad front many of these apparently weird "witch doctor" treatments have turned out to be based upon sound scientific reasoning. Molds were employed by the early Chinese to relieve the symptoms of boils, and sandals covered with a mat of mold growth were worn to control foot infections. Chewing the bark of the cinchona tree was found to relieve the fever of malaria, and we now realize that quinine was the active ingredient of this bark. Metchnikoff's recommendation that cultures of lactobacilli might be ingested in the treatment of dysentery was put on a commercial basis in the 1920's with the marketing of acidophilus milk for the relief of intestinal disorders. Many other accounts of similar applications of microbes and higher plants in promoting human health are available, but the real foundation of modern antibiotic therapy dates from the work of a British investigator, Alexander Fleming, in 1929.

Fleming had committed a cardinal sin in microbiology. He had allowed his culture dish containing *Staphylococcus aureus* to become contaminated with a mold. This leak in his technique ushered in the era of antibiotics. When the staphylococcus culture grew, Fleming was struck by the appearance of a wide, clear-cut zone—a lack of bacterial growth—adjacent to the mold contaminant. Without doubt others before him had observed similar reactions, but Fleming possessed that added measure of scientific curiosity which prompted him to pursue his observation further. He isolated and identified the mold as *Penicillium notatum* and the active principle that was responsible for the inhibitory action he named *penicillin,* the first offspring in the "miracle drug" family.

It was indeed most fortunate that subsequent pharmacological and clinical studies indicated that the by-product of Fleming's mold, in addition to being remarkably inhibitory to a number of bacteria, was relatively nontoxic to human beings injected with the drug. Had the *notatum* culture turned out to be relatively poisonous to animals, perhaps the search for effective antibiotics might have died in infancy.

FIG. 13.1. *Penicillium chrysogenum.* (Courtesy Chas. Pfizer and Company, Inc., New York, N. Y.)

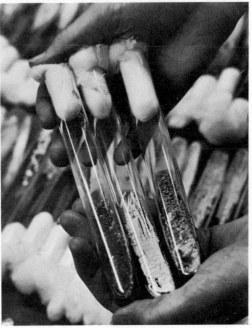

FIG. 13.2. A microbial culture library. (Courtesy Chas. Pfizer and Company, Inc., New York, N. Y.)

FIG. 13.3. Soil cultures to be screened for antibiotic activity. (Courtesy Eli Lilly and Company, Indianapolis, Indiana.)

FIG. 13.4. In producing antibiotics, liquid media contained in these fermentation tanks are inoculated with mold cultures. Constant agitation and aeration promote rapid growth throughout the liquid. (Courtesy Eli Lilly and Company, Indianapolis, Indiana.)

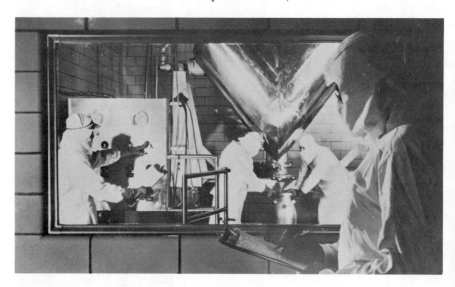

FIG. 13.5. Antibiotic compounding operation. (Courtesy Squibb, Division of Olin Mathieson Chemical Corporation, New York, N. Y.)

FIG. 13.6. Clear zones around discs impregnated with antibiotic indicate zones of microbial inhibition. (Courtesy Eli Lilly and Company, Indianapolis, Indiana.)

Later studies have indicated that *Penicillium chrysogenum* is a better species of mold to employ for commercial production of penicillin. Florey and his associates working at Oxford University did a great deal of follow-up work after Fleming's discovery, and in 1940 penicillin was put to clinical tests with marked success. The massive field trials afforded by thousands of patients during World War II proved beyond a doubt that medical science had at its disposal a powerful new ally.

Millions of people have been spared severe and prolonged illnesses and premature death because of the miraculous power packed within penicillin molecules and the dozens of other antibiotics that came into being as a direct aftermath of the work of Fleming and Florey. Combinations of antibiotics and sulfonamides have been shown, in some instances, to be more effective in combatting some stubborn infections than has the use of either drug alone.

Resistance to Antibiotics

After initial successes with penicillin, the word **panacea** began to be heard with increased frequency. Bacteria, many believed, were no longer to be a medical problem. But before too long the medical world began to be faced with disappointments and outright failures in therapy with the "wonder drugs." Microbes were becoming refractory and were refusing to play dead in the face of the mighty miracle chemicals. The specter of **resistance** began to rear its ugly head, and efforts had to be redoubled to step up the potency of antibiotics and to find new untried microbes that might provide even stronger by-products with which to combat other organisms.

Following the use of any antibiotic a certain proportion of viable organisms will usually remain. Many relapses can be accounted for when therapy is concluded too soon, before the defenses of the host can subdue the invaders.

What had brought about the sudden reversal in activity? The answer appears to lie primarily in the development of **mutants**—those sudden changes in offspring which fail to mimic the parent cells in one characteristic or another. In this case the mutants were able to by-pass the usual metabolic block induced by antibiotics in the enzyme systems of microorganisms, and even increasing the dosage many-fold had little or no effect in turning back infections.

Part of this trouble had its origin during the exploratory years when doctors had an incomplete understanding of the necessary dosage of the new weapon required to complete the job effectively. Administration of sub-effective amounts merely allowed resistant strains of bacteria to build up even more resistance to action by the injected drug. Another important contributing factor to this problem has been the indiscriminate use of antibiotics. Too often they have been employed unnecessarily as a routine prophylactic measure or in minor infections where conventional treatments might better have been used. Demand on the part of the public for administration of antibiotics by their physicians cannot be dismissed without a statement that this pressure has also contributed its share to the problem.

Sufficient, but not excessive, amounts of antibiotics must be administered to overpower microbes quickly before selected mutants have an opportunity to build up within an infection. Unfortunately, the ability to develop drug resistance has been most noticeable with virulent staphylococci, and new strains of this troublesome organism have developed a punch that appears to exceed that which existed prior to the antibiotic era.

It cannot be said too many times that at least part of the battle to regain control over microbes revolves around the practice of strict asepsis —a technique that may have been glossed over during the last twenty years when antibiotics too often were allowed to serve as poor substitutes for cleanliness.

Representative Antibiotics

A natural outgrowth of a discovery as significant as penicillin was the initiation of a virtual crash program, financed principally by industrial concerns, to find additional antibiotics possessing even wider spectra of antimicrobial activity than that demonstrated by penicillin. The scientific literature soon became liberally sprinkled with announcements of reported successes, and the following list is representative of some of the antibiotics marketed in recent years.

Name of Antibiotic	Source
Bacitracin	*Bacillus licheniformis*
Carbomycin (Magnamycin)	*Streptomyces halstedii*
Chloramphenicol (Chloromycetin)	*Streptomyces venezuelae*
Chlortetracycline (Aureomycin)	*Streptomyces aureofaciens*
Cycloserine	*Streptomyces orchidaceus*
Dihydrostreptomycin	Catalytic hydrogenation of streptomycin
Erythromycin	*Streptomyces erythraeus*
Neomycin	*Streptomyces fradiae*
Novobiocin	*Streptomyces niveus* and *Streptomyces spheroides*
Oxytetracycline (Terramycin)	*Streptomyces rimosus*
Penicillin	*Penicillium notatum* and *Penicillium chrysogenum*
Streptomycin	*Streptomyces griseus*
Tetracycline	Catalytic hydrogenation of chlortetracycline
Viomycin	*Actinomyces vinaceus*

Miscellaneous Uses of Antibiotics

Feed Supplements

The discovery of the growth-promoting properties of mash wastes from fermentation procedures employed in production of antibiotics was, like a number of findings in science, purely an accident. When these wastes were added as supplements to feeds for poultry and other food-producing animals, marked growth stimulation was observed. Because of this discovery pure antibiotics are being added to feeds today in carefully calculated portions as a routine commercial practice. Amounts as small as 5 to 20 grams of antibiotic (chloramphenicol, tetracyclines, or penicillin) per ton of feed may increase the growth rate of poultry and swine from 10 per cent to as high as 50 per cent—a significant consideration when it comes to cutting down on feeding costs and feeding time before marketing such animals.

The exact mechanism of growth stimulation by antibiotics is far from clear, but several interesting theories have been proposed to help explain the phenomenon. One group suggests that certain undesirable intestinal bacteria which drain away some of the energies of the host are suppressed or even killed within the body of the animal. The minute amounts being added to feeds, however, would hardly seem to be enough to accomplish this. Some nutritionists indicate that antibiotics are involved in some manner with the metabolism of vitamins, particularly vitamin B_{12}. Undoubtedly the total growth-stimulating reaction is a combination of factors, some recognized and others still obscure.

Virology

Virologists employ antibiotics rather extensively for retarding bacterial growth in their virus cultures. The resistance of these ultramicroscopic forms to most antibiotics, even in relatively high concentration, allows suppression of the ever-present threat of bacterial contamination.

Food Preservation

Preservation of foods, especially poultry, by dipping them into antibiotic-containing solutions to improve shelf life is another application of these drugs for inhibition of bacterial growth. In the opinion of the writer this is an undesirable practice, since it might be one more means by which organisms can acquire resistance to antibiotics. Sub-effective doses merely provide a training ground for the development of drug-resistant mutants that are bound to come back and haunt us one way or another in years to come. The same disapproval must be expressed for the use of certain medicated throat lozenges being sold over the counter in pharmacies. If the amount of antibiotic in the lozenge is insufficient to warrant placing the item on prescription, the small dose of the drug probably is merely adding to the resistance being built up by microorganisms.

Chemotherapy in Malaria

Any discussion of chemotherapy should make at least passing reference to quinine and to some of the synthetic drugs designed to fight the *Plasmodium* of malaria. Quinine has been employed against this widespread disease since at least 1630, although the bark of the cinchona tree apparently had been used as a medicine by South American Indians well before that date. Massive doses of quinine over a short period appear to produce less favorable results in the treatment of malaria than smaller doses taken over an extended period. Quinine destroys only the asexual forms of the malaria parasite found in the bloodstream, and the drug provides temporary relief from chills and fever, but parasites lodged deep in the tissues and the sexual forms of the parasite are not destroyed. This accounts for the numerous relapses encountered in this disease. *Atabrine,* a synthetic compound, acts in a manner similar to quinine.

When the supply of quinine was cut off during World War II, the pressures and necessities of war spurred an intensive search for suitable substitutes. Such drugs as atabrine, totaquine, and plasmoquin were called upon to fill the void, and each drug possesses specific advantages and disadvantages.

Atabrine proved to be an effective prophylactic in the South Pacific during World War II. Before its use in 1943 the military casualties from malaria in New Guinea amounted to 740 cases per 1000 men per year, a staggering morbidity rate. After the administration of atabrine became mandatory in the military forces, the case rate dropped to 26. The ideal drug for prophylaxis and for cure of malaria remains to be found.

Tests for Antibiotic Activity

The ability of an antibiotic to inhibit growth or to kill an organism can be assayed by either chemical or biological means. Chemical evaluation may be more accurate, especially where the antibiotic is in pure chemical form and strengths can be expressed in terms of micrograms of active agent per unit volume of specimen. However, laboratory findings of effectiveness of a drug may not necessarily be correlated with the effectiveness of that drug against given microorganisms *in vivo.*

In biological assays, the results are expressed in terms of effectiveness compared with a standard under strict conditions of testing, and although this *in vitro* evaluation may not always check exactly with expected clinical results, *in vivo* experience in general tends to bear out the laboratory findings. International standards have been approved for some antibiotics such as penicillin where one unit is the activity produced under prescribed conditions by 0.5988 micrograms of the International Standard of pure benzylpenicillin.

Cylinder Technique

The cylinder technique consists of measuring the activity of an antibiotic placed in a cylinder made of stainless steel, glass, or porcelain which is embedded in a seeded agar medium. After suitable incubation, the zone of clearing (bacterial inhibition) adjacent to the cylinder provides some indication of the diffusability of the drug and its ability to affect growth of the organisms. Unless all test conditions are highly standardized, including such factors as the amount of the test antibiotic, the numbers of bacteria per unit of agar, temperature of incubation, etc., results may not be reproduceable. For the sake of accuracy, all tests should include a standard of known potency to be used as a reference.

Broth Turbidity Technique

Inhibition of microbial growth in broth containing various amounts of antibiotics will be reflected in turbidity differences in the medium after a few hours of incubation. This method possesses the advantage of speed in arriving at results as compared with readings made by the cylinder technique.

Some laboratories feel that inhibition of growth in the initial stages of incubation, followed by an overgrowth of organisms later in the incubation period might have some bearing on the effectiveness of therapy with the given antibiotic. If resistant cells are able to survive contact with the drug, the same type of action might be expected when the antibiotic is employed on a patient, and relapses could occur.

To determine whether the zone of clearing around a cylinder represents mere inhibition (static action) or actual killing (cidal action), portions of agar taken from the clear zone can be subcultured into tubes or flasks of suitable broth, and any growth in this subculture would indicate that at least some cells were still viable and had resisted the action of the test drug under a given set of conditions.

Filter Paper Disc Technique

Discs of filter paper impregnated with the test antibiotics may be placed on the surface of agar plates that have been streaked with the test bacteria. Following suitable incubation the results can be interpreted, with the same limitations that hold true for the cylinders. Supply houses have developed testing kits of discs containing different antibiotics in varying concentrations as a means of obtaining semiquantitative evaluations of a given drug against specific organisms. When these discs were first marketed clinical laboratories tended to report their results in terms of degrees of microbial sensitivity (slight, moderate, very), but the trend in recent years has been to report the microbes as *sensitive* or *resistant* to the antibiotics without attempting to express results in any order of activity. As some workers have pointed out, if the antibiotic is to be injected into a patient, it will find its way into the circulation and be carried to every tissue of the body, provided the dosage is great enough.

Diffusability measured as a zone on an agar plate is not the important criterion. Whether or not the drug can adversely affect the test organisms is the real factor to be determined.

A physician naturally wants to treat a patient with an antibiotic that is most likely to be effective in the shortest space of time. For aid in making a decision, he must have some laboratory confirmation of the relative sensitivity of the pathogens in the particular infection to the antibiotic he plans to use for therapy. Since time is of the essence in speeding the recovery of a patient, quick and relatively reliable tests must be available to the clinical laboratory. Crude or mixed specimens taken directly from infected patients can be tested directly, or more time-consuming pure culture studies can be conducted. Many infections tend to be caused by a single organism, and in the interest of saving time, many laboratories prefer to conduct an evaluation on an unpurified specimen in order to give the physician a preliminary sensitivity report. In the meantime pure culture studies can be run and if the patient does not respond to one of the wide-spectrum antibiotics initially administered, the later lab report may provide the physician with a fuller evaluation of specific antibiotics as tested with the pure culture isolations a day or two later. There are advantages in each approach to the problem.

There are times when findings of the laboratory sensitivity tests, even with pure culture studies, are not borne out in clinical application. The physician must always bear in mind that laboratory findings are only a guide. Naturally he must use his judgment in switching drugs, depending upon the clinical response of the patient. Different injections located in different areas may demand variations in drug administration, and it may be necessary to use combined antibiotics or even sulfa drugs in conjunction with antibiotics.

Review Questions

1. Distinguish between an antibiotic and some of the other commonly employed chemotherapeutic agents.
2. If microbes continue to build up resistance to antibiotics, what would appear to be the long-range solution to the problem?
3. Are sulfa drugs antibiotics? chemotherapeutic agents?
4. Based upon the experience of the last two decades, can penicillin still be considered a "miracle" drug?
5. What is the mechanism by which microbes gradually develop resistance to drugs?
6. Is there any danger that widespread use of antibiotics in food industries might eventually have deleterious effects on those who consume such treated foods?

14 | MODES OF TRANSMISSION OF MICROBIAL DISEASES

PUBLIC HEALTH AUTHORITIES GENERALLY ATTRIBUTE THE SPREAD of most microbial diseases to the four F's: *fingers, flies, fomites,* and *food,* and by broadening each of these categories somewhat, it would be possible to include practically all means by which biological diseases are spread from person to person and from animal to animal.

The Human Body

Fingers, Hands, and Carriers

A number of pathogens can be transmitted to individuals only by direct contact of the microbes with susceptible body surfaces, but the majority of organisms can be carried on contaminated hands or be transmitted indirectly through food, drink, and animate or inanimate objects. The skin of our hands, even after it is thoroughly scrubbed with germical soaps and hot water, is far from microbe-free. Were this not so, the surgeon would have no need for rubber gloves for protection of the patient during an operation. It is virtually impossible to sterilize the human skin without killing the living tissue. The skin, which is made up of many layers of cells, has a surface that is relatively rough; the pore spaces and hair follicles provide ideal locations in which microbes can lodge and multiply.

The importance, especially for food handlers, of maintaining clean hands, has already been stressed in Chapter 12 and the details need not be repeated. However the potential for spreading virulent organisms other than those implicated in food poisoning outbreaks has particular significance for individuals whose work necessitates close contact with patients. There is little or no excuse for a patient who has entered a hospital for surgery to correct a condition of nonmicrobial origin to acquire an infection because someone foolishly cut a few corners and failed to take prescribed sanitary precautions when moving from one patient to another. Unfortunately, this may happen in situations where there is a lack of complete understanding and appreciation of microbiology and its practical applications.

It is only natural that the instructor of each discipline should feel that his or her science is one of the most important for medical and paramedical students to master, but wide experience in both military and civilian hospitals has convinced this writer that the training received in microbiology by most of these individuals could be strengthened. We all tend to become rusty rather quickly unless we keep up with the literature being published in our fields, and periodic refresher courses may be necessary to bring personnel up to date on the rapid advances being made in all sciences.

There are a number of suitable microbicides available on the market today for use as hand rinses by persons who have either direct or indirect contact with infected and noninfected patients. Mercuric chloride (bichloride of mercury) 1:1000 is one such chemical that can be recommended to reduce microbial populations. The usual tests employed for measuring effectiveness of disinfectants confirms the fact that mercuric chloride can be relied upon to do an effective job on the skin when this chemical is employed as a hand rinse. Because of its corrosive action, however, mercuric chloride cannot be used on metal surfaces.

Each hospital or laboratory generally has its own favorite disinfectant solutions, but periodic checks should be carried out to substantiate the continued effectiveness of a particular germicide. The relative value of compounds has changed through the years as bacterial resistance has increased. Never take a compound for granted.

Green soap has been a standard solution used in and in conjunction with operating rooms. A few years ago one of the leading hospitals on the east coast of the United States was experiencing a disproportionate number of postoperative *Staphylococcus* infections. The usual battery of screening tests failed to pinpoint the source of the infections until the difficulty was finally traced to the green soap that was found to be harboring millions of viable staphylococci per milliliter. Such solutions are now routinely autoclaved in many hospitals before use to prevent a recurrence of the difficulty, but one can't help asking himself how effective green soap is if the most common cause of infections in humans can survive (or multiply?) in this supposedly germicidal solution.

Progress does not always involve development of new techniques. There are times when it becomes prudent for us to go backward if we expect to move forward. Our changing biological world may call for a return to practices that proved to be relatively effective in the preantibiotic era. Not all of these abandoned procedures and practices were necessarily bad.

Hands play an increasingly important function in the spread of microorganisms, especially when the hands belong to a **carrier.** These persons may display no outward sign of illness, yet they harbor and excrete virulent microbes which, if they can find a suitable portal of entry on a susceptible host, can initiate infection.

If we recognize portals of entry by which pathogens gain admittance to our bodies, tighter controls can be instituted and eradication of some diseases becomes a theoretical possibility. The usual routes of invasion are the respiratory tract, breaks in the skin, the digestive tract, and in certain cases possibly the unbroken skin. Proving beyond a doubt that an organism has penetrated nature's thick physical and chemical barrier of intact skin tissue probably is not possible. Skin could appear to be whole to the human eye, but microscopic examination might reveal it to be otherwise. Such diseases as tularemia (rabbit fever) caused by *Pasteurella tularensis* and brucellosis (undulant fever) caused by members of the *Brucella* genus have occurred so frequently among experienced laboratory workers that the suggestion has been put forth that these particular minute microbes might possess some means by which they are able to penetrate unbroken skin. The possibility of an aerosol-spread infection in these cases should not be ruled out, however. Studies of techniques by high-speed photography reveal the potential hazard that exists in transferring organisms by pipetting and in the shaking and blending operations so commonly accepted as routine practice in our laboratories.

Individuals may be *convalescent carriers* or recent victims of a microbial disease, and only bacteriological tests can definitely confirm the carrier state. There are also *contact carriers* who pick up viable organisms from active cases and then spread the pathogens to other individuals without themselves ever developing clinical symptoms. But perhaps the greatest threat to human health is the *chronic carrier* who may harbor and discharge virulent microbes for months, years, or even a lifetime. These persons serve as reservoirs of infection and prevent certain diseases from dying out. Typhoid Mary (Mary Mallon) is a classic example of a chronic carrier. She is known to have caused at least 50 cases of typhoid fever between 1900 and 1915. She knew she was a dangerous typhoid carrier, but she chose to ignore specific medical advice that she refrain from preparing food for consumption by others. She left a trail of disease and death wherever she went. Mary's final undoing came about when she found a position in the kitchen of a hospital where she caused 25 cases of the disease before the State of New York "tucked her away" (probably illegally) for safekeeping. Unfortunately, the law does not permit the arrest of dangerous carriers who persist in ignoring medical warnings. These persons spreading microbial bullets are murderers in every sense of the word, but the punishment fails to fit the crime for those who elude public health enforcement agents and who continue to spread disease and kill their fellow men.

Carriers remain as a major means by which enteric diseases are transmitted, with food serving as the most common vehicle for dissemination. Physical examination of food handlers, including a complete bacteriological examination of their stools, is still one of our logical approaches to elimination of dangerous carriers. Advances in sanitary control of water and milk supplies have reduced typhoid fever to the status of a minor public health problem as far as numbers of cases in the statistical tables are concerned, but the rare human carrier, as long as one remains, cannot be forgotten, or explosive epidemics could once more be upon us.

Droplet Dissemination

A breath quietly exhaled through the nose is usually free of living organisms, but every time we open our mouths to whisper, talk, shout, sing, cough, or sneeze we spray the atmosphere with microbe-laden particles. Some of the larger droplets are visible to the eye, whereas many others may be microscopic in size. Even the bark of a dog, the meow or hiss of a household cat will add moisture particles to the atmosphere. Because these animals discharge their droplets close to the floor or ground, however, few microbes of this origin are ever inhaled by humans who probably are affected little, if at all, by the microbial flora of such lower animals.

Figures 14.1, 14.2, 14.3, 14.4, and 14.5, illustrate the magnitude of the discharge that occurs with an explosive sneeze, but the number of droplets expelled through ordinary conversation is also rather impressive. An unstifled sneeze may propel moisture particles as far as ten feet from the mouth, while moderate volume talking shoots aerosols up to a distance of three feet.

Droplet contamination of the air has much more public health signifi-

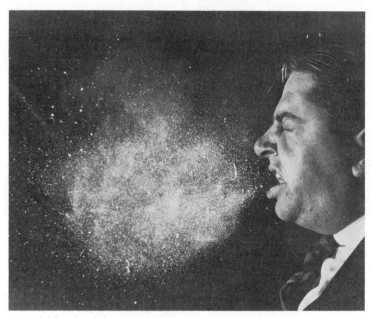

FIG. 14.1. A violent unstifled sneeze. (LS-5 Courtesy American Society for Microbiology.)

FIG. 14.2. A sneeze stifled with the bare hand. (LS-9 Courtesy American Society for Microbiology.)

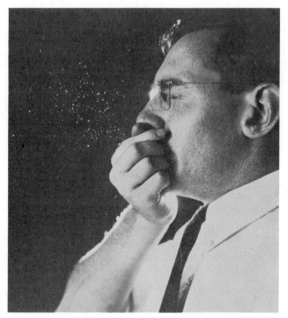

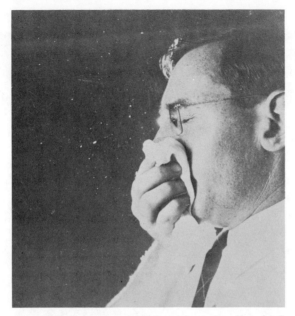

FIG. 14.3. A sneeze stifled with a handkerchief.
(LS-10 Courtesy American Society for Microbiology.)

FIG. 14.4. Sneezing onto a culture dish containing nutrient agar.
(LS-17 Courtesy American Society for Microbiology.)

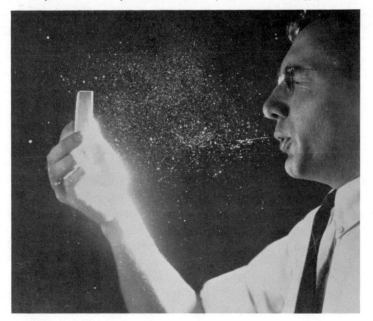

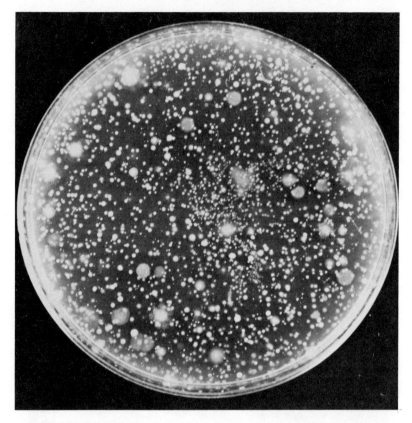

FIG. 14.5. Colonies of bacteria which have developed during incubation of the culture plate inoculated with sneeze droplets. (LS-18 Courtesy American Society for Microbiology.)

cance than pollution of the atmosphere by most dust particles, although in some dusty trades (stonecutting, for example) the sharp pieces of material, when inhaled, must be considered a real threat to human health, particularly as a cause of silicosis. Saliva and mucus provide a protective layer for trapped organisms which may float around in a viable state for minutes or even hours. Large moisture droplets (100 microns and larger) fall rather quickly in quiet air, whereas smaller particles may remain in suspension for periods dependent upon relative humidity of the atmosphere, particle size, air temperature, rate of movement of air, and other less well-defined factors. When small droplets dry out, the solid residues that remain are called **droplet nuclei.** These bits of material containing a cargo of microbes may waft about and be inhaled or they may settle out and become part of the dust that could eventually be forced back up into the air. Standard counts of house dust reveal the presence of millions of bacteria, many of them of human origin.

The mouth, nose, and upper respiratory tract contain enormous numbers of microorganisms, some of which are relatively pathogenic for susceptible individuals. We learn to live in relative harmony with our own hordes of organisms most of the time, but these same cells are capable of causing serious infections when inhaled by a less resistant individual. When our own microbes get out of hand and cause infections in our bodies, especially in the respiratory tract in the form of a sore throat, cold, or pneumonia, then our mouth and nasal discharges become even more dangerous for those about us. The added virulence of our microbes under these circumstances encourages rapid spread of our ailments to others, and a chain reaction causes epidemics of varying proportions. The common cold is an example of this type of reaction. It is primarily a respiratory disease with the number of cases reaching a peak during the colder months of the year when people spend more time indoors in dry, over-heated rooms in close contact with others who are also doing their share to raise the microbial population of the air.

Couples who spend a great deal of time together will gradually build up a relative resistance to the organisms they each expel into the air. Contact of their lips during kissing will make the microbial transfer even more direct, and without some preliminary gradual resistance having been established, such contact could precipitate respiratory infections. Students report that when they leave a college campus where they have remained for some time and go home for a vacation, the new contacts they make at home may possess a microbial flora to which the students have little or no resistance, and frequently they "catch a cold." Changes in both their physical and biological environment undoubtedly play a part in causing such an illness.

Covering your mouth and nose with a tissue or a handkerchief during a cough or a sneeze will not trap all of the expelled organisms, but the precautionary measure should not be abandoned just because it is not fool-proof. Minimizing the spray of organisms is certainly better than doing nothing about it.

When droplets are given off into the air outdoors, the danger to other persons is naturally less than it would be indoors. The dilution factor, evaporation of the moisture, and to some extent the lethal effect of ultra-violet radiation on the microbes, all combine to minimize the potential hazard to human health. When the pathogens eventually fall to the ground, the antagonistic action of organisms in the soil usually results in the pathogens coming out second best in the struggle for survival.

Sanitary Disposal of Body Wastes

The very fact that our body eliminates wastes in the form of urine and feces should indicate that these discharged materials probably contain chemicals or biological agents that are no longer required or that might actually inflict harm were they to be retained in our systems.

Urine, as it is given off by the kidneys and the bladder, is microbe-free in healthy individuals, but during elimination the liquid comes in contact with the urethra where it becomes contaminated with the normal flora of staphylococci and other bacteria common to the region. It is for this reason that physicians collect catheterized specimens for bacteriological examination to determine whether an individual is harboring organisms in the bladder or in the kidneys. Voided samples would be meaningless for such determinations. Inflammation of the bladder is termed **cystitis;** a similar reaction in the kidneys is known as **pyelitis.** Safe disposal of urine is decidedly less of a problem than is true of fecal discharges which are composed of as much as 25 per cent bacteria on a dry-weight basis.
. Most of the bacterial species found in the intestine are not pathogenic should they be ingested in small numbers as pure cultures, but the danger to human health about which sanitarians must be concerned lies with the unknown microbes that might be associated with the normal fecal flora. In public health it is customary to be super-cautious when deciding whether something is safe or potentially hazardous, and by this cautious attitude authorities avoid playing roulette with human lives. It is wiser to condemn more items than might seem necessary than to bend in the other direction and declare something safe that might not be so in all circumstances.

In order to avoid the creation of health problems fecal material must be disposed of in a manner that is scientifically sound. A review of the accepted procedures was presented in a previous discussion on sewage (Chapter 9). The greatest potential danger of contamination with intestinal wastes lies in the area of private water supplies that are located too close to raw sewage outlets. Enteric pathogens against which we possess little or no natural resistance must be denied access to our food and drink, and the dramatic drop in the incidence of typhoid fever and similar diseases paralleled closely the institution of pasteurization of milk and other foods and the chlorination of public water supplies. If the carrier of enteric pathogens could be eliminated, this group of diseases might well disappear, at least in certain areas of the world.

The presence in a water supply of *Escherichia coli,* the index organism of sewage pollution, does not in itself condemn the water. Rather, it is the company that *coli* might be keeping that is the important public health factor to be considered. To phrase this another way, the presence of *E. coli* in water represents guilt by association. The possibility that people who are carriers of enteric diseases *might* have contributed to the pollution is what must be guarded against whenever a water supply is declared unfit for human consumption.

Venereal Disease Transmission

The term *venereal* is derived from Venus, the Goddess of Love. This may seem like an unfortunate association, but venereal diseases are contracted almost exclusively by sexual contact.

A number of microbial diseases may be acquired in this manner, but the four most commonly encountered and their microbial agents are gonorrhea (*Neisseria gonorrheae*), syphilis (*Treponema pallidum*), chancroid (*Hemophilus ducreyi*), and lymphogranuloma venereum (a virus). The first two will be discussed in greater detail in Chapter 15, but some of their characteristics are discussed below. The incidence of these venereal diseases is generally in the order listed.

GONORRHEA

It has been estimated that about 10 per cent of our population suffers from one or more venereal diseases, and each year a million new cases are acquired—an appalling statistic. Ten million females in the child-bearing age are victims of this affliction. Nearly 6 per cent of all males examined for military service in World War II were found to be infected.

To many teenagers gonorrhea, which goes under a number of unscientific pseudonyms, is considered to be no more serious than a common cold. This gross untruth merely adds to the difficulty experienced by health authorities who are trying to reduce the incidence of this serious affliction, which unfortunately is once more on the increase after a hopeful downward trend for a number of years. One of the tragedies we face is the tendency for gonorrhea to show up in increasing numbers in our early teenage population as sexual promiscuity increases. Much of the careless attitude associated with this disease stems from the quick cures that chemotherapeutic agents have been able to bring about. One or two "shots" of penicillin could effect a remarkably quick disappearance in symptoms of the disease. However, the appearance of an increasing number of stubborn infections that are refusing to respond to the usual treatment should serve as ample warning that our society may be on the threshold of a more alarming problem than that experienced with antibiotic-resistant staphylococci.

The crippling effects of gonorrhea are rarely brought to the attention of our youth. Local as well as general complications develop in some

30 per cent of infected individuals, and subclinical cases may smolder for years, with hosts unknowingly serving as dangerous unrecognized carriers. Except for very young females in whom this disease has been shown to be transmitted through the use of contaminated common towels, undergarments, or bedclothing, gonorrhea is acquired almost exclusively through direct sexual contact with an infected individual. Prostitutes are responsible for a high proportion of these cases.

It is unfortunate that in spite of an apparent let-down in moral values and an increase in juvenile delinquency in recent years, society still considers it poor taste to publish pictures showing unsightly physical destruction of human bodies afflicted with the so-called "social diseases." It does not seem appropriate to bestow on venereal diseases the cloak of respectability implied by such an innocuous designation, when in reality these infections must be looked upon as definitely antisocial.

Some of our present-day venereal disease problems undoubtedly stem from ignorance, but to the majority of individuals who cannot be classed as innocent in these matters, the application of some type of fear technique might not be out of order. Gonorrhea is a ghastly disease capable of causing unbelievably serious consequences not only to those who acquire the infection through sexual promiscuity, but to innocent unborn babies who must suffer for the sins of those responsible for their creation.

The etiological agents in most venereal diseases cannot withstand any degree of drying or temperature change even for relatively brief periods without losing their viability. With these facts in mind it becomes apparent that the "myth of the toilet seat," so frequently used as a refuge when an infection develops, will not stand up under scientific scrutiny, especially with modern open-end construction of these seats developed as an outgrowth of public health studies of venereal disease control.

The religious and moral issues involved in the employment of prophylactic techniques to reduce opportunities for acquiring venereal diseases will be left for others to discuss.

SYPHILIS

Perhaps no known bacterial disease can wreck a person's health in so many ways as syphilis. It is called "the great imitator," because its clinical manifestations are so variable, especially after the initial stage, that they can resemble any number of organic disturbances. Syphilis is a contact venereal disease caused by a corkscrew-shaped spirochete, *Treponema pallidum,* that is highly motile and can penetrate areas of delicate skin and mucous membranes. Although sexual intercourse is the most frequent mode of transmission, a kiss or bite by an infected individual may also spread the deadly microbes. In pregnant females the spirochetes can migrate through the placenta and localize within a developing fetus, resulting in congenital syphilis. If the organisms do not cause death of the fetus, which must then be expelled, babies born with congenital syphilis may display all degrees of physical and mental damage.

Few microbes are more sensitive than *Treponema pallidum* to the environmental factors of drying, temperature changes, and the presence of chemicals. The toilet seat, therefore, can virtually be ruled out as a means for transmission of this disease, but it is conceivable that the spirochetes could be acquired from contact with a common drinking cup immediately after it had been used by an infected individual suffering with open mouth lesions of syphilis.

CHANCROID

The microbe *Hemophilus ducreyi* is the etiological agent in this venereal disease, which is also known as "soft chancre" to differentiate it from the hard chancre of syphilis. The gram negative rod-shaped organism gains entrance to the tissues during sexual contact with an infected person.

A soft ragged-edged ulcer appears in from 3 to 21 days (usually within one week) somewhere on the genitalia, and the infection spreads itself by contact of the running discharge onto other skin surfaces so that multiple sores develop. A common companion of these lesions is a swelling of the inguinal glands, which may progress to form deep-seated "boils" which rupture and must be drained to relieve pressure created within the pus pockets. The whole process is most painful for the patient.

Any article containing pus or fluids drained from chancroid lesions must be treated promptly and effectively. Bandages, dressings, clothing, instruments, towels, wash cloths, toilet seats, and bath tubs must be disinfected to minimize further transmission of the disease.

This infection does not spread throughout the body the way the syphilis spirochetes do. In cases of chancroid the neighboring lymphatics may become infected and form secondary **buboes,** but that is as far as these bacteria tend to migrate. There is no immunity to chancroid, just as there is no resistance to the other venereal diseases.

LYMPHOGRANULOMA VENEREUM (LYMPHOGRANULOMA INGUINALE)

The causative microbe in this less common, yet important, venereal disease is a large (250 to 350 millimicrons) virus that appears to be closely related to the infectious agent in parrot fever (psittacosis). It is a more difficult disease to treat than the other three that have been discussed.

The initial lesion on the genitalia may be a small pimple or ulcer, but in many cases the first apparent sign of infection is painful swelling of the lymph glands in the groin. The overlying skin becomes hard and red, and the glands dissolve into foul-smelling pus which breaks through to the surface in many places and drains for months. Rheumatism and painful deformities are common complications of this disease once the swelling has subsided.

The incubation period of the primary lesion is from 6 to 21 days, and inflammation of the lymph nodes occurs within 10 to 30 days after contact with an infected individual. Combinations of sulfa drugs and some of the wide-spectrum antibiotics may be employed for therapy, but results tend to be slow and are not always satisfactory. The disease has a low incidence in America and in most of Europe, but it occurs frequently among Negroes in the tropics, especially among those with a low standard of living.

Arthropods and Other Vermin

The normal microbial flora of arthropods (members of the phylum *Arthropoda,* which possess an articulated body and jointed limbs) reflect their living habits. The peculiar attraction filth has for flies and roaches makes them particularly dangerous from a health standpoint. Their rough, hairy bodies provide ideal conditions for picking up and retaining "dirty" debris and its microbial cargo.

Any public health approach to environmental sanitation must include a reduction in fly and roach populations. The importance of denying these arthropods access to fecal deposits of human origin and wastes from lower animals is not simply a matter of aesthetics, it is also of extreme biological importance. Food to be eaten by human beings should be protected from contamination by flies, roaches, mice, and other vermin. The presence of flies, even in small numbers, should not be tolerated in eating establishments. Patrons should take it upon themselves to indicate feelings of disapproval to the management when these threats to health exist. If people would do this and refuse to patronize a restaurant until the condition was corrected, fewer digestive upsets of microbial origin would be encountered.

Contamination of the surfaces of nuisance arthropods is bad enough in itself, but when the fecal discharges visited by the flies and roaches have come from carriers of enteric diseases, the public health hazard is doubled. Recent controlled studies on insects in the author's laboratories have indicated that the number of enteric bacteria that must be ingested before the fly or roach can serve as a culture reservoir and excrete these pathogens appears to lie in the range of ten to twelve thousand cells. However, certain species of roaches, particularly *Blaberus craniifer,* can be fed massive doses containing billions of typhoid cells without any detectable excretion of these human pathogens. When these roaches are fed about twelve thousand paratyphoid cells, members of the same *Salmonella* genus to which typhoid belongs, not only are the fed organisms excreted, but the host serves as an incubator and the paratyphoid organisms multiply enormously within the gut of the roach.

A great deal of human misery throughout the world has its origin in arthropod-borne diseases. Justice cannot be done in an elementary textbook to a topic of such wide interest and significance, but the reader should at least gain some insight into the problem, and those with more than a passing interest can enlarge their knowledge in this area by collateral readings. Control of these vicious afflictions depends upon breaking the cycle of infection. The weakest link in the chain may vary with individual diseases.

Any consideration of biological transmission of diseases by arthropods should include mention of mosquitoes as vectors of malaria and of yellow fever. Accounts of discovery of the cause of these widespread maladies and the search for prophylactic measures and reliable cures make fascinating reading.

Biological transmission generally implies that the organisms must undergo at least one stage within the insect and another stage in man. The pioneer efforts of Theobald Smith in 1893 revealed the role played by ticks in the transmission of Texas fever. A few years later, in 1898, Sir Ronald Ross demonstrated the relationship between the bite of infected *Anopheles* mosquitoes and the spread of malaria. Walter Reed is given major credit for the discovery in 1900 that *Aedes aegypti* mosquitoes were the culprits responsible for yellow fever; and the list could go on and on.

The increasing realization of the relationship between arthropods and many of man's afflictions, especially in the warmer areas of the globe, stimulated an ever-widening search for causes and for specific cures. Some of the diseases acquired by man through bites of insects and other arthropods and the etiological agents responsible for the clinical symptoms will be found in the following abbreviated list.

FLEAS

Bubonic plague—*Pasteurella pestis* (bacteria)
Endemic (murine) typhus—*Rickettsia typhi* (rickettsia)
Tularemia—*Pasteurella tularensis* (bacteria)

LICE

Typhus fever (epidemic) —*Rickettsia prowazeki* (rickettsia)
Trench fever—*Rickettsia quintana* (rickettsia)

MITES

Rickettsial pox—*Rickettsia akari* (rickettsia)
Tsutsugamushi group—*Rickettsia tsutsugamushi* (rickettsia)

MOSQUITOES

Dengue—A virus transmitted by *Aedes aegypti*
Malaria—*Plasmodium* spp. (protozoa) transmitted by *Anopheles* mosquitoes
Yellow fever—A virus transmitted by *Aedes aegypti*

TICKS

Q fever—*Coxiella burnetii* (rickettsia)
Relapsing fever—*Borrelia recurrentis* (spirochete)
Rocky Mountain spotted fever—*Rickettsia rickettsii* (rickettsia)
Texas fever—*Piroplasma* sp. (protozoa)
Tularemia—*Pasteurella tularensis* (bacteria)

Fomites

Fomites are inanimate objects other than food and water. The relative importance of some fomites in the dissemination of human diseases has undoubtedly been overemphasized, whereas others of great sanitary significance may require more consideration than they are being accorded at the present time. The following items are obviously important with respect to the spread of harmful microbes: eating utensils, drinking cups and glasses, pencils, bedding, paper money and coins, books, doorknobs, strap hangers in public conveyances, toys, handkerchiefs, drinking fountains, bed pans, thermometers, floors, walls, and furniture.

A primary consideration in this area of sanitation and its relationship to disease transmission must, of necessity, include the relative resistance of pathogens to such environmental factors as drying, pH, humidity, presence of chemicals, and other still unrecognized factors. Spore-forming cells, by their very nature, are equipped to survive under adverse conditions, whereas some of the more fastidious spirochetes die off within seconds or minutes after leaving the protective environment of the host. Microbes causing diphtheria, tuberculosis, and staphylococcus infections, in spite of their lack of spores, may withstand the rigors of a dry atmosphere for surprisingly long periods.

The length of time that pathogens are in contact with fomites is another consideration. The sooner an individual's hands or some susceptible body surface come in contact with the viable microbes after they have been deposited by an infected person on the inanimate object, the more likely are the pathogens to find their way into the new host through an appropriate portal of entry. Our hands and our mouths serve as active agents in picking up and spreading microbes.

The passing from the scene of the common drinking cup on the village green did not come about without opposition from those who thought such a change was downright unnecessary. A few of our churches still cling to the tradition of the common Communion Cup in their services of worship. The trend in recent times, however, has been toward individual glasses and to move away from use of the silver chalice except as a symbol of the Lord's Supper. The writer remembers well the objections voiced by his parents to the common cup. The mental image of what might be coming along on the rim of the chalice eventually came to overshadow the religious significance of this important symbol of church doctrine, and in time enough support was mustered for conversion to individual glasses for each communicant.

As potential health hazards drinking fountains should receive more attention than they have to date. It would appear that very few architects and designers have ever been exposed to a formal presentation of microbiology, and many of their artistically acceptable fountains are an abomination to an observant bacteriologist. The recent trend has been to get away from the bubbler that merely shoots the water up an inch or so, permitting mouth rinsings to drop back into the flow or onto the bubbling device itself. The newer innovation of an "angle shot" of water gets away from this objection, *if* the water pressure is great enough to permit a person to quench his thirst without having to put his lips or face on the "sanitary" guard which too often turns out to be more of a hindrance to sanitation than a help. Take time to observe the construction and operation of drinking fountains for a while and see if you can't prepare recommendations for improvement. The fact that moisture is provided on these fountain surfaces helps microorganisms to survive for considerable periods of time.

Fomites are particularly dangerous when they have been contaminated by carriers of enteric pathogens. When the interval between contamination and contact by another is brief, indirect transmission of organisms is essentially the same as a direct contact. Intestinal and respiratory diseases rank high on the list of ailments that are disseminated through fomites. A brief consideration of a few objects and their relative importance in the spread of pathogenic organisms will be presented.

Coins

The metals of which money is made, especially silver-containing coins, do not favor the survival of microbes for a very long period. The oligodynamic action of silver has already been discussed in Chapter 6. Unless the coins are grossly contaminated, are passed almost immediately to a susceptible individual, and the organisms get into the new host quickly (fingers put in the mouth, for example), public health authorities need not be overly concerned with this mode of disease transmission.

Paper Money

Not only are paper bills too dry to allow for prolonged microbial survival, but the very ink with which the money is printed tends to be relatively bacteriostatic and even bactericidal to some species of organisms. "Filthy lucre," as it is sometimes called, may be physically unattractive when it is wrinkled and dirty, but we can probably dismiss paper money as one of the fomites serving as a serious threat to human health.

Books

Unless books are handled by patients who have contagious diseases such as tuberculosis, there is not too great an opportunity under normal circumstances for books handled by healthy individuals to be dangerous fomites. It might be wise, nevertheless, to use paper-back books for patients on the contagion ward and to burn such books after use, because cells of *Mycobacterium tuberculosis* and some of the other pathogens can withstand drying for some time, and books could serve to spread these biological agents.

Bed Pans

These items should be given careful treatment after use, especially when enteric diseases are involved. If a steamer is not available to sterilize the pans after they have been washed, a suitable disinfectant must be employed to minimize the chance spread of pathogens through these vehicles.

Thermometers

Without doubt, thermometer sanitation has left much to be desired. It goes without saying that each hospitalized patient should have his own thermometer, but cleaning and disinfection procedures need to be reviewed and strengthened in some hospitals and in physician's offices. A number of so-called germicides being employed for this purpose do not kill bacteria as quickly as one might suspect. Contact time with microorganisms is an important consideration, but if the germicidal solution is weak or ineffective, the hocus-pocus soaking is all for naught. Solutions should be checked frequently for their effectiveness. Hospitals routinely test the efficiency of the autoclaves in Central Supply, Pediatrics, and Surgery, but it is equally important that the laboratory be instructed to check thermometer sanitation on just as strict a basis.

If most disinfectants are to get at the thermometer itself, organic debris must first be wiped away with cotton or a tissue before the thermometer is placed in a germicidal soak. Using 70 per cent alcohol for this task is not suitable; it will not do the job effectively. A number of compounds are available from hospital supply houses that will be found upon analysis to be reliable. Don't let thermometers be a weak link in the chain of asepsis.

Bedding

Many recent publications have stressed that bedding can be one of the primary sources of *Staphylococcus* infections from previous patients and from hospital personnel. Techniques are being worked out for gaseous sterilization of blankets, pillows, and mattresses with ethylene oxide and other similar compounds. Sterilizing chambers in which the relative humidity, temperature, and gas pressure can be controlled have been found to be completely reliable in freeing bedding of living microbes. With the disturbing rise in *Staphylococcus* infections, not only in hospitals but in private homes, more attention must be paid to better disinfection of bedding.

Floors, Walls, and Furniture

It is the dust that gathers on these areas that must be combatted, since dust can harbor impressive numbers of potentially dangerous organisms. In addition to physical removal of dirt, germicidal solutions should be employed to keep microbial populations to a minimum on these inanimate objects.

Towels and Washcloths

Many "staph" infections are undoubtedly contracted through foolish use of a common towel in many homes. Impetigo, sometimes referred to as a filth disease, is a most unpleasant type of skin infection and it is probably spread more by common towels and washcloths than by any other means. Gonorrhea may be contracted, especially in young females, by immediate contact with a moist towel previously used by an infected individual. Institutions must be on the alert at all times to prevent this type of practice.

Cups and Glasses

Because the lips of these vessels can remain moist for some time, cups and glasses are particularly important in the spread of such diseases as trench mouth, streptococcal sore throats, common colds, and other respiratory infections. Syphilis could conceivably be contracted through this means. Although the bartender might raise an eyebrow when you ask for a straw with your beer, your beverage might contain less saliva, lipstick, and armies of microbes were you to sip it through a straw rather than to touch your lips to the rim of the glass. Sanitation of glasses in beer halls and soda fountains leaves much to be desired.

It would be a distinct shock to many if they could see the amount of saliva and traces of fecal contamination found on common objects with which we come in daily contact. Were these unpleasant microbe-laden materials colored a deep red or purple to make them more readily visible, our surroundings would indeed be in technicolor, and we might possibly be more discriminating in our habits.

Our fingers touch our lips, mouths, and noses much more frequently than most of us realize. All of these areas harbor potentially dangerous microbes. A housewife tastes the soup she is cooking to see if it requires more seasoning, and after sipping a sample from the spoon that she has sprayed with her saliva by blowing on it during cooling, she returns the remainder to the pot. But don't worry; any saliva that might have found its way back into the pot has a fair chance of being heated sufficiently to kill the organisms before the soup is finally served! Are you naive enough to believe this practice does not take place in the kitchens of what we consider to be our finest restaurants?

Did you blow out the candles at your last birthday party and then serve your guests the aerosol-sprayed slices of cake? Have you moistened your fingers to turn a single page of this book?

When the postal clerk dispenses stamps he has been instructed to put them on the counter with the gummed side up. This practice is designed to assure you that your stamps will not become contaminated by whatever happens to be on the surface of the soiled counter at the time. Instead, you may have to settle for some fresh saliva from his fingers which he moistened when he tried to separate the sheets of stamps. When you send a letter, whether it be to a loved one or to the department store to pay for that new garment, you ship along a saliva sample under the stamp and under the gummed flap of the envelope for good measure.

Aren't needles difficult to thread at times? But if you put the thread into your mouth and bite down on the strands of cotton or silk before you twirl them in your fingers, the pointed end is much easier to coax through the eye of the needle. Of course the saliva that remains on your fingers may on occasion find its way to the bread, rolls, or drinking glass you are setting up for lunch. Do you *always* wash your hands thoroughly before handling foods for yourself or for others?

Did you ever see a mother "clean" away the spot on baby's face with a saliva-moistened finger or handkerchief just before someone kissed the little darling?

Standards of cleanliness in restaurants were mentioned in the chapter on food poisoning, and in that discussion it was pointed out that not many folks keep their hands immaculate—at least to the eyes of a bacteriologist. Some workers don't even bother to wash their hands after visiting the toilet, in spite of posted signs that admonish them to do so. These signs would not be necessary were it not true that many grown people must be reminded of this simple elementary sanitary precaution they were taught as youngsters. Others who do wash their hands may not be very thorough in this ritual, and without the application of a stiff scrub brush much organic debris can remain lodged under the fingernails, especially when the nails are not kept short or clean.

How many waitresses and waiters handle the "business end" of eating utensils as they prepare to serve you? The napkins they brought might have been difficult to separate from the stack, but a quick trip of their fingers to their mouths probably took care of that! Isn't it easier to carry four glasses by slipping your fingers down inside them? Did you ever see them carried that way in public eating establishments?

These few examples will suffice to indicate some of the widespread unsanitary practices with saliva we see on every hand, and perhaps the discussion has been enlightening to some readers who may never have given them a second thought. Other readers may need a sharp reminder that much remains to be done in educating people in personal hygiene if the number of cases of diseases of microbial etiology are to be reduced still further.

Some fomites employed in nursing and in medical practice, as well as in the instruction of individuals preparing to enter these professions, must be looked upon as potential troublemakers unless proper sterilization techniques are employed.

When a class of students is being taught the art and science of blood typing for example, the lancet employed for drawing the blood sample must not be an instrument for the passive transfer of malaria, jaundice, or contagious diseases of other types. Aseptic techniques must be stressed and practiced. Sterile, individually wrapped disposable lancets should be used. The old-fashioned spring-type lancet employed so frequently for classroom instruction in years gone by may have been responsible for the spread of microbes from one student to another when the device was improperly disinfected between uses on different individuals. Soaking in 70 per cent alcohol for a few seconds, or even for a few minutes, cannot be relied upon to insure inactivation of organisms before the incision is made in the finger of the next individual. The writer sees a real danger in the routine drawing of blood samples from the ear lobe for hemoglobin tests or for blood typing. Since skin cannot be sterilized, there may be an opportunity for an infection to become established at the site, and being that close to the brain it can be a decided hazard. Pathologists have expressed such a concern.

The common practice of boiling or steaming needles and syringes in physicians' and dentists' offices is certainly not as reliable as employing steam under pressure in an autoclave, but if the exposure to moist heat is long enough (at least ten minutes at 100°C), experience indicates that there is little need for concern about passive transfer of living organisms from one patient to the next. Bear in mind, however, that boiling occurs at a lower temperature than 100°C as the elevation increases, and at very high altitudes (over 10,000 feet) a longer exposure period may be required to accomplish the same killing action that one might expect at sea level.

Food and Water

The solids and fluids we take into our body for energy and survival are far from sterile, and nature would probably prefer to have it that way. Constant stimulation of our antibody-producing mechanisms, triggered by ingested organisms serving as antigens, undoubtedly assists us in maintaining a relatively effective resistance to many common diseases. When the number of microbes and their metabolic products become excessive, man reacts with predictable symptoms, frequently in the form of gastrointestinal upsets. A few highly pathogenic enteric organisms to which we possess little or no resistance, can set in motion a number of serious clinical responses that can, if allowed to go unchecked, result in death of the host.

Separate chapters (8 and 12) have been devoted to considerations of food and water as vehicles for the transmission of disease organisms, and the student is referred to these readings for a review of the facts.

Review Questions

1. If known carriers of serious enteric pathogens cannot be locked up to keep them from spreading their lethal cargo, what approaches should be used by public health officials to minimize the menace presented by carriers to their fellow men?
2. List diseases that might be disseminated through each of the four "F's" (flies, fingers, fomites, and food).
3. What can be done to improve the sanitation of thermometers in our hospitals? Is it feasible to sterilize them?
4. What might be done to decrease the use of saliva in many everyday practices?
5. How does one decide how many organisms should be ingested each day to keep his antibody-producing mechanisms active?

15 PATHOGENIC BACTERIA

THE PRECEDING FOURTEEN CHAPTERS HAVE BEEN DESIGNED TO present the fundamentals of our present-day science of microbiology. We are now prepared to discuss representative diseases of microbial etiology in order that personnel who will be coming in contact with infected patients will find themselves better equipped to comprehend specific characteristics of microbes and the means by which their numbers may be minimized and controlled. In earlier discussions the names and certain pertinent features of a few pathogens have been woven into the text to make specific points somewhat clearer.

Although the present discussion of disease-inciting microbes cannot be complete in every detail, and need not be at this level of instruction, it should suffice to provide a working knowledge of the more common microbial diseases encountered in hospital and public health practices. Excellent textbooks written specifically for premedical and medical students are available to those interested in widening their sphere of knowledge of the microbiology of pathogenic organisms.

Bergey's Manual of Determinative Bacteriology (7th edition, 1957) serves as the standard reference work and "bible" in bacteriology. It contains a rather detailed listing of the characteristics and biochemical reactions of the bacteria described up to the time of its publication, and condensed listings of pertinent characteristics of individual species presented in this chapter have been distilled from the master reference work.

Gram Positive Bacteria
Spheres

ORGANISM: *Diplococcus pneumoniae*

DISEASE: *Pneumonia*

CHARACTERISTICS: Young cells are gram positive and measure about 0.5 to 1.25 microns, occur as oval or spherical forms typically in pairs, occasionally singly or in short chains. The distal end of each pair of organisms tends to be lancet-shaped. Non-sporing. Nonmotile. Faculative. Produce alpha type of hemolysis on blood agar media. Encapsulated. Optimum temperature is 37°C. Normally parasitic and the most common cause of lobar pneumonia. Habitat is respiratory tract of man and animals.

The word *pneumonia* literally means "inflammation of the lung," and when the term is employed without qualification it implies lobar pneumonia, an acute infection in which the **alveoli** become filled with an exudate consisting of bacteria, leucocytes, and fluid. Any number of microorganisms—bacteria, rickettsia, and viruses—can cause pneumonia, but this discussion will focus on *Diplococcus pneumoniae,* the etiological agent in up to 90 per cent of the cases of lobar pneumonia. Bronchopneumonia involves multiple areas of the lungs. This same diplococcus can cause blood poisoning (**septicemia**), inflammation of the lining of the abdomen (**peritonitis**), middle ear infection (**otitis media**), infection of the pleural cavity (**empyema**), inflammation of the spinal cord and the brain (**meningitis**), and other less frequent infections.

Prior to the era of sulfonamides and antibiotics a diagnosis of pneumonia justifiably struck fear into the hearts of many individuals, because the prognosis in very young children and in elderly persons generally was poor. Double pneumonia (involvement of both lungs) was particularly serious. In the older age group pneumonia was one of the most common terminal illnesses. Although this disease is still serious, chemotherapy provides a relatively effective treatment, and the outlook for recovery of pneumonia patients today is markedly more optimistic.

Most of us harbor significant numbers of pneumococci in our upper respiratory tract at all times, and when conditions become favorable through a lowering of resistance (lack of proper rest, poor diet, exposure to the elements, etc.), these pathogens are able to descend into the lungs where they may set up an inflammation. Pneumococci are most commonly transmitted from one individual to another through expelled droplets, and no lasting immunity is built up by recovering from a bout with this disease. In fact, increased susceptibility to future attacks is

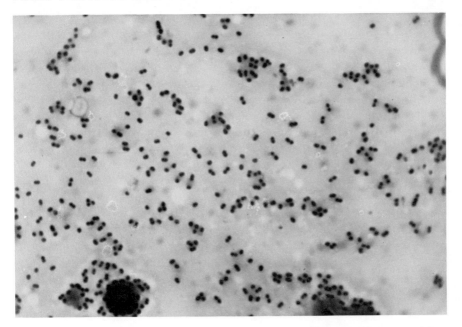

FIG. 15.1. *Diplococcus pneumoniae.* (Courtesy General Biological Supply House, Inc., Chicago, Ill.)

probably more likely since the lungs are damaged to varying degrees and they may not be able to ward off infections as readily.

The outstanding biochemical characteristics that set the pneumococci apart from the streptococci, which they may closely resemble morphologically, include fermentation of inulin and solubility of the pneumococci in bile or in other surface tension depressants.

Virulence of the pneumococcus is imparted to it principally through its polysaccharide capsule, which also endows the organism with serological identity upon injection of the whole cell into an animal. When stripped from its underlying cells, the capsule in itself is nonantigenic. Such a nonprotein substance capable of imparting specificity to an antigen is termed a **haptene,** and in the case of the pneumococcus the capsule also contains SSS, which is an abbreviation for *Soluble Specific Substance.*

Serological classification of at least 75 recognized types of pneumococci is based upon the marked swelling of their capsule as observed under the microscope when the bacteria are placed in contact with specific antiserum. This visible morphological change is known as the *Neufeld* or the *Quellung Reaction.*

The mouse is highly susceptible to *Diplococcus pneumoniae,* and even though sputum (which is a complex mixture of microbes and nonliving organic matter) is injected intra-peritoneally, this animal possesses the remarkable ability to digest the bulk of the sputum, and the unaffected virulent pneumococci then proceed to kill their new host in about twenty-four hours. If the animal is not dead at the end of this time, it can be sacrificed for further study by anaesthetizing with chloroform or ether. Autopsy will reveal an almost pure culture of the pathogenic diplococci which can then be washed from the body cavity with saline and be subjected to the Neufeld typing test or other diagnostic determinations.

Since these organisms respond only to their specific antiserum, it was imperative in the pre-antibiotic era for the attending physician to know the specific type of pneumococci involved in a given case before administering antitoxin, a therapeutic agent produced in horses or, better still, in rabbits. The smaller-sized protein molecules in rabbits make this antiserum superior to that produced in horses, and fewer side effects may be experienced with serum from the smaller animal. Physicians "in the old days" frequently were forced to resort to stop-gap measures while waiting for laboratory findings that might require up to twenty-four hours to complete. Injections of polyvalent antiserum composed of a mixture of anti-pneumococcus serum for the more prevalent types of pneumonia might be initiated, and as soon as the laboratory typing procedure was completed, administration of type specific serum could be substituted for the less effective polyvalent serum.

In advanced cases of pneumonia it is possible to conduct a Neufeld typing directly on a fresh sputum specimen, but in many cases this procedure is more difficult than if the determination were conducted using saline washings of the peritoneal cavity of an injected mouse. Not only will such washings generally be found to have a heavier concentration of bacteria, but mouse passage tends to enhance development of capsules, making them easier to observe in a Neufeld test.

Sulfonamides and antibiotics now make pneumococcus typing unnecessary except from the standpoint of academic interest. Costly time delays before initiating therapy can thus be eliminated. Many of the newer drugs are decidedly more effective than specific antiserum, and frequently the expense to the patient may be considerably less.

ORGANISM: *Staphylococcus aureus*

DISEASES: A wide variety of afflictions including furuncles, carbuncles, abscesses, wound infections, osteomyelitis, respiratory tract infections, septicemia, food poisoning, etc.

CHARACTERISTICS: Gram positive spherical cells 0.8 to 1.0 micron in diameter. Non-sporing. Nonmotile. Aerobic, facultative, anaerobic. Clear-cut hemolysis normally produced on blood agar. Optimum temperature is 37°C. Habitat is skin, nasal and other mucous membranes of warm-blooded animals.

Pasteur observed cocci in pus as early as 1880. The organisms were isolated in pure culture three years later by Becker, and in 1884 Rosenbach showed their relationship to suppuration in wounds and to osteomyelitis. The golden-colored colonial pigment of *Staphylococcus aureus* has generally been associated with virulence, but it should be made clear that white (*albus*) varieties have also been isolated from serious infections. Staphylococci as a group are not fastidious in their growth requirements, and undoubtedly this helps to explain in part why they are so widespread and why they are implicated as often as they are in so many infections and food poisonings.

Staphylococci are endowed with surprising resistance to the usual unfavorable environmental factors that cause so many other non-sporing organisms to lose their viability. They have a growth temperature span of

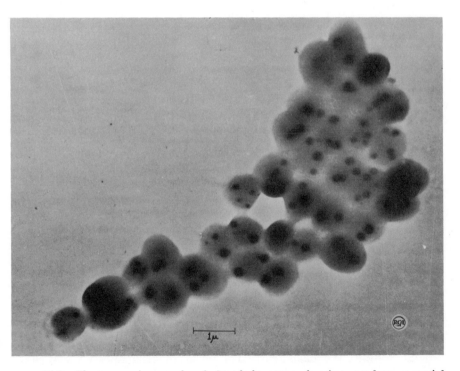

FIG. 15.2. Electron micrograph of *Staphylococcus* showing nuclear material. (LS-89 Courtesy American Society for Microbiology.)

about 10–42°C, but species causing human infections prefer to grow close to body temperature (37°C).

Most non-sporing bacteria are killed by an exposure to 60°C for about 30 minutes, but many staphylococci can withstand 80°C for 20 minutes or longer—a rather significant consideration in the inactivation of suspensions to be employed as vaccines. Any technique designed to kill staphylococci will usually destroy all but the spore-forming pathogens.

Staphylococci have been responsible for more than their share of human misery through the years, and it would appear from the increased resistance to antibiotics being displayed by these microbes that our troubles are far from over. The gamut of afflictions they cause range from troublesome skin blemishes of teenagers to septicemia and death when these organisms gain superiority in the body and microbial multiplication is not checked. Some of their effects in food poisoning were described in Chapter 12.

Some people believe that pimples and other ugly skin blemishes are caused by "bad" blood, but this is scientifically incorrect. Were these staphs circulating in our bloodstream, we would indeed be in serious trouble. Other factors, principally physiological ones induced by the action of hormones, can cause changes in the skin which allow bacteria, particularly staphylococci which are normally found in substantial numbers on human skin, to set up pockets of infection. These organisms, it should be recognized, do not come from within the body proper or from the blood (except in cases of blood poisoning); they enter from the outer skin surface which is their normal habitat. A simple localized infection may progress from a pimple or ingrown hair to a more painful and potentially serious boil, carbuncle, or septicemia.

One treatment for deep-seated localized infections is the injection of an **autogenous vaccine** prepared from a saline suspension of a pure culture of the bacteria obtained from the patient's own infection. After standardizing the concentration of cells and heat-killing them for prescribed periods, graded doses are injected into the patient, who responds by producing specific antibodies to the injected antigenic cells. This old-fashioned approach to the treatment of such infections is regaining some of its former stature, especially in the light of the increased resistance to drugs being displayed by stubborn staphylococci.

A marked increase in resistance has followed the general and oftentimes indiscriminate use of antibiotics, particularly penicillin. This drug may be at the forefront of the resistance parade but other antibiotics are not too far behind. We have reached a point that suggests we may have regressed to the pre-penicillin era as far as treatment of staphylococcus infections is concerned.

Penicillin is inactivated by the enzyme *penicillinase* which is produced by a number of bacteria, and unfortunately some *Staphylococcus* cultures can also neutralize the lethal effect of penicillin by means of this enzyme system. There is probably no group of common pathogenic organisms with a wider and more vicious striking power than the staphylococci, and everyone connected with medicine, either directly or indirectly in the paramedical sciences, has in recent years become painfully aware of today's number one bacteriological problem.

Individuals are cautioned not to attempt self-treatment of localized skin infections, but especially those on the upper section of the head above the nose line. Put yourself in the hands of a competent physician who can treat your ailment properly. Too often the well-built barriers provided in the tissues by nature for walling off infections are broken down by well-meaning but uninformed lay individuals who too frequently end up with serious infections, some of which unfortunately prove to be fatal.

Upon primary isolation from a wound staphylococci will usually display clear-cut zones of hemolysis when colonies develop on blood agar plates. Even in the absence of cells, broth culture filtrates of these microbes can dissolve (*lyse*) erythrocytes, and at least five different types of lysins have been described based upon serological differences and the types of animal red blood cells they can attack.

COAGULASE

One of the more important physiological reactions displayed by pathogenic staphylococci is demonstrated by the **coagulase test,** an *in vitro* reaction that correlates closely with pathogenicity. Virulent staphylococci are capable of clotting citrated or oxalated blood plasma which gels in less than three hours at body temperature. Reference to a coagulase-positive staphylococcus is meant to imply virulence. Coagulase also aids in the clotting of blood and may be instrumental in the formation of clots (**thrombi**) in certain types of staphylococcus infections.

The presence of coagulase liberated by these bacteria tends to localize *staph* infections. The purulent nature of the lesions is probably tied in with the destructive activity of lysin. Fibrin appears to be deposited on the surface of the bacteria and this in turn may interfere somewhat with phagocytosis, thus allowing staphylococci to remain viable after they have been taken in by the leucocytes.

FIBRINOLYSIN

Virulent streptococci are capable of dissolving fibrin clots through the action of **fibrinolysin,** and the bulk of observations with this technique have been conducted with these gram positive cocci that are typically arranged in chains. But virulent staphylococci may also cause plasma clots to dissolve if the plasma comes from the blood of dogs, guinea pigs, or rabbits; human and cow plasma are not satisfactory for this test.

ENTEROTOXIN

The importance of staphylococci in food-borne outbreaks has been discussed in Chapter 12, and the active principle that triggers this unpleasant reaction in man (and possibly in kittens and rhesus monkeys) is an **enterotoxin.** Opinions differ somewhat as to the susceptibility of these lower animals to these poisons.

Because of the rather violent nature of the physiological response, most of the ingested toxin is probably eliminated in a matter of a few hours—indeed moments to remember, or perhaps better to forget! Virulent *Staphylococcus aureus* strains are not only coagulase positive, but in addition they produce a potent enterotoxin. However there are no reliable *in vitro* tests to indicate which cultures are enterotoxinogenic. Human volunteers (usually involuntary volunteers) are the surest means by which to determine the vomit-triggering potential of these microscopic poison generators.

PHAGE TYPING

Viruses capable of attacking bacteria and lysing them are called **bacteriophages** ("bacteria-eaters"), and they might be considered to be a disease of bacteria.

In England in 1915 Twort first observed this curious dissolving action while he was working with cowpox vaccine that had become contaminated with staphylococci. (Just because Fleming's discovery of penicillin and Twort's detection of bacteriophage came about through contamination with staphylococci, students should not get the mistaken notion that instructors encourage poor laboratory habits in anticipation that someone will make another great finding through a leak in his technique!) Twort noticed a degenerative change in the bacterial colonies as evidenced by a nibbled or moth-eaten appearance. The French microbiologist, D'Herelle, rediscovered this transmissible lysis two years later, and he named the filterable agent *bacteriophage,* which is frequently abbreviated to *phage.* Workers in the field honor both discoverers by referring to the lytic reaction as the *Twort-d'Herelle Phenomenon.*

Phage particles range in size from about 10 to 150 millimicrons, and electron micrographs of these viruses show some of them to be cubical in shape; others are round and may be characterized by the presence of a tail-like appendage which gives them an appearance similar to spermatozoa. Phage exhibits cell specificity and can be employed to separate

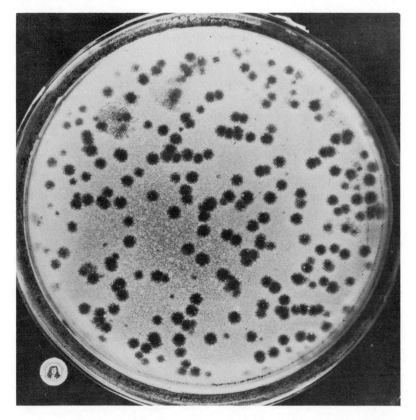

FIG. 15.3. Plaques of *Rhizobium* bacteriophage. (LS-145 Courtesy American Society for Microbiology.)

closely related cultures of what, by the usual criteria of identification, may appear to be identical organisms.

One might be tempted to consider single-celled plants such as bacteria to be rather simple, but a species can possess differences in chemical makeup detectable only by unique methods. Phage typing is one valuable tool at our command to locate these apparently minor differences and to aid in epidemiological studies. It is generally accepted that viruses are specific in their actions, and bacteriophages are no exception.

When staphylococci are typed using bacteriophage, one obtains what is known as a phage pattern rather than a single phage that attacks only one particular strain of bacteria. Cell fractions (molecular configurations) are shared in common by a number of bacteria, and these minute targets may be attacked by such phages.

The exact mechanism by which viruses destroy bacteria is not fully understood. If spot inoculations of an organism, such as *Staphylococcus aureus,* are prepared on a solid agar medium and a small drop of specific phage is placed in contact with these cells, when the bacterial colony develops during suitable incubation there will appear on the visible growth clear areas called **plaques,** which will vary in size and shape depending upon the specific virus involved.

Staphs of the same phage pattern may become dominant in the nasal passages of hospital patients and in their environment (dust, bedding, and other fomites). In general, bacteria tend to become resistant to the antibiotics most frequently employed in a hospital. By use of the phage typing technique epidemiologists can determine whether staph cultures isolated from lesions during outbreaks are similar to those strains harbored by hospital personnel or in the patients' surroundings.

As studies expand in this interesting and relatively new approach to epidemiology, an increasing number of phage types are being discovered. The Communicable Disease Center of the U.S. Public Health Service acts

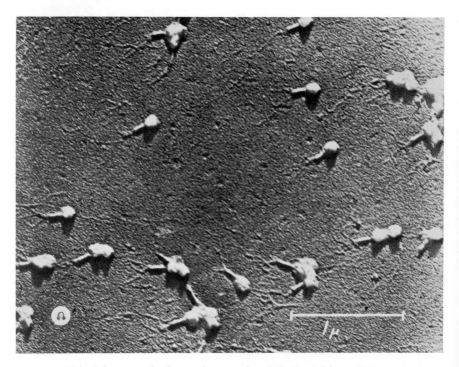

FIG. 15.4. Electron shadow micrograph of *Escherichia coli* bacteriophage. (LS-138 Courtesy American Society for Microbiology.)

as a clearing house and national reference laboratory from which regional laboratories may obtain known specific phages for local investigations of *Staphylococcus* outbreaks. Quantitative counts of phage particles may be made in a manner similar to that employed for bacteria, but it must be remembered that plaques are areas of *no growth* rather than visible masses of colonies.

Phages are widely distributed in nature. They abound in sewage. Because of their filthy habits, flies and roaches serve as excellent reservoirs of a number of phages, and students who choose to isolate these fascinating agents for study will find directions for their separation in a number of virology textbooks.

ORGANISM: *Streptococcus pyogenes*

DISEASES: Infections of the throat and respiratory tract, infected lesions producing inflammatory exudates, blood stream infections, and occasionally mastitis in cows

CHARACTERISTICS: Gram positive, spherical to ovoid cells 0.6 to 1.0 micron in diameter, occurring as long chains in broth. Non-sporing. Nonmotile. Surface and submerged colonies are beta hemolytic. Facultative anaerobic to strictly anaerobic. Optimum temperature approximately 37°C. Habitat is primarily the human body where it causes the formation of pus or even fatal septicemias.

A typical streptococcus (frequently abbreviated to *strep*) divides in only one plane and the cells tend to remain united, giving them the appearance of a string of beads. However, the spacing between cells is such that the string looks more like chains of diplococci than a necklace of similar-sized pearls, and the belief once held that the length of the chain bears a direct relationship to virulence apparently is not based upon scientific fact.

Many of these chainlike cocci are saprophytes—perfectly harmless to man and to lower animals, even in large numbers. Our mouths and intestines are well populated with streptococci, many of which are considered to be part of the normal microbial flora of these body regions. Healthy skin does not harbor streptococci, at least in significant numbers, as it does staphylococci. One member of the genus, *Streptococcus pyogenes,* is the cause of a number of serious and sometimes fatal diseases. Ogsten, Fehleisen, and Rosenbach in the early 1880's first indicated the frequency of these cocci in pathological processes.

When cultivated on solid media, even those containing a diet considered to be rich for most bacteria, streptococcus colonies never are very large. They are small, convex, and entire. Pyogenic streptococci are restricted in their growth requirements to a temperature close to that of the human body, and some of the lactic acid group may flourish within the range of from 10° to 37°C. Most streptococci are facultative anaerobes, but frequently pathogenic strains may be strict anaerobes and isolations are missed unless cultures are incubated in an environment lacking free oxygen.

As a group, the streptococci are relatively fastidious in their nutritive requirements, but pathogenic species display a marked need for enriched diets. Superior growth-promoting media are prepared from infusions rather than from standard meat extract, and the addition of blood in a concentration up to 10 per cent favors their development, especially in the presence of a phosphate buffer and a small amount of glucose.

TOXINS

The types of poisonous metabolic end products produced by strepto-cocci vary widely with different species. **Endotoxins** (sometimes referred to as insoluble toxins) are poisons that are intimately bound to the cell protoplasm and are not liberated until after the cells die and break up by autolysis or are shattered through the use of physical forces. Soluble toxins, on the other hand, are given off into the surrounding medium during metabolism of cells, and these poisons are called **exotoxins** or *true toxins*. Endotoxins, as we generally consider them, are not produced by streptococci. At least upon injection or ingestion of these substances the clinical symptoms of the host are not typical of those accepted for "ordi-nary" endotoxins. The question of the ability of these cocci to produce exotoxins may also be debatable, although the poison associated with scarlet fever resembles exotoxins to some extent. Some investigators report that this metabolic product is thermostable, whereas others claim it is inactivated by heat, a characteristic usually associated with true toxins. Since an antitoxin is available to combat scarlet fever toxin, perhaps it is not incorrect to state that an exotoxin, or something closely resembling it, is produced by the streptococci associated with this particular disease.

In addition to this poison, streptococci produce a number of curious end products that undoubtedly affect the ability of the microbes to incite and to spread infections. Some of these recognized substances will be dis-cussed briefly.

ERYTHROGENIC TOXIN

When this chemical fraction produced by some virulent streptococci is injected intradermally (*into* the skin), it gives rise to a marked local red-dening of the skin technically called **erythema**. Large doses of this mate-rial may cause a similar reaction when injected into the skin of rabbits, but laboratory animals in general are resistant to its action. The presence of erythrogenic toxin is the basis of the *Dick Test* developed in 1924 by two Chicago physicians, George and Gladys Dick, for measuring an individual's susceptibility to scarlet fever. This determination is similar to the technique introduced in 1913 by Bela Schick to detect the relative resistance of an individual to diphtheria toxin. Following an intradermal injection of a minute amount of exotoxin, usually in the forearm, persons possessing sufficient circulating antitoxin to neutralize the injected poison will display no marked reaction at the site of the inoculation. In the absence of sufficient antibody, however, a typical reddened, swollen, inflammatory area appears on the arm. It fades within a few days and leaves no permanent scar.

The value of such skin tests lies in their use for mass surveys of populations during a threatened epidemic to determine which members of a community require immunization or "booster shots."

HYALURONIDASE

This substance, discovered in 1928 by Duran-Reynals, is also known as **spreading factor.** It bears some relationship to the ability of streptococci to penetrate tissues of a host by the dissolving action it has on hyaluronic acid which serves as a gelatinous cell-binder in tissues. It should be stated, however, that *in vitro* tests and *in vivo* activity are far from parallel, and the exact mechanism of its action in disease is not clear cut. By diffusion through tissues it appears to increase the spread of the streptococci, as well as to increase migration potential of toxic by-products of microbes. This could represent a significant difference between infections caused by staphylococci, which tend to remain localized, and those caused by streptococci, which frequently cause diffuse infections.

HEMOLYSINS

The use of blood agar plates for the cultivation of pathogenic organisms was introduced by Schottmüller in 1903, and various modifications have naturally been introduced since that time. Not only does blood support the growth of fastidious organisms, but it also provides a visible means by which colonies may be separated and classified.

Some species of bacteria growing on blood agar plates produce a lysis of the erythrocytes as evidenced by a clear, colorless zone adjacent to the developing colonies. This is *beta hemolysis,* and in the case of streptococci, this type of blood reaction is correlated with virulence of the organisms. Another type of reaction seen on blood agar plates is termed *alpha hemolysis,* which appears as a greenish halo around colonies caused by a reduction of hemoglobin to methemaglobin. Alpha streptococci frequently are culturally indistinguishable from pneumococci on blood agar, but the inability of streptococci to ferment inulin or to be dissolved by bile or other surface tension depressants sets them apart from *Diplococcus pneumoniae*. A gamma type colony shows no visible change in the blood medium as far as the eye can detect, and this is typical of saprophytic streptococci.

Lancefield proposed a classification of the beta hemolytic streptococci into a number of distinct groups based upon antigenic differences as shown by the precipitin test. For example, her Group A includes those streptococci pathogenic for humans; members of Group B are involved in bovine infections, particularly mastitis; and Group C consists of streptococci responsible primarily for infections of lower animals. To date at least nine different antigenic groupings have been proposed by various investigators. Considerable discussion still revolves around whether some of these groups should be combined or whether additional splinter groups should be formed.

A single species of Group A streptococcus may be responsible for more than one clinical manifestation in human beings. In contrast, the hemolytic species affecting lower animals generally exhibit a high degree of specificity and are the cause of only a single disease. Human beta streptococci rarely affect lower animals, except perhaps in cases where the udder of a cow may become infected from a human carrier and result in milkborne septic sore throat of other persons. Such other diseases as scarlet fever, tonsillitis, rheumatic fever, erysipelas, localized abscesses (especially in teeth), and septicemia may also be caused by these chainlike spheres.

Members of the younger age group in a population appear to be relatively more susceptible to streptococcus infections than are older individuals. Infants may display prolonged infections with suppurative complications, but rheumatic fever and nephritis are less likely to follow such an attack. Older children and adults, on the other hand, tend to contract acute, localized infections without the suppurative complications.

STREPTOKINASE

Pathogenic species of streptococci are notable for their ability to dissolve fibrin clots or to inhibit the clotting of plasma. This activity was originally described in 1933 by Tillett and Garner and the active principle has been called **fibrinolysin.** But more recent investigations indicate this particular factor produced by streptococci is not lytic in itself, but rather that it is a **kinase** that serves to activate a precursor of a plasma protease called **plasmin,** which is the actual dissolving agent. Such an activator produced by streptococci is called **streptokinase.**

Clots of human plasma will be lysed by pathogenic streptococci, but when these cells are tested against the plasma of other animals, the reaction is usually not reliable. Animal fibrin is susceptible to lysis if it is clotted with human thrombin, and human fibrin may still be broken down even if it is clotted with animal thrombin. The whole reaction is a complex one, and this discussion could not bring out all of the interesting chemical reactions involved, even if they were known. But the test is so widespread that the student should be familiar with its use as a diagnostic tool in medical practice.

As was pointed out in the discussion of staphylococci and their role in disease, the body attempts to wall off an infected region by a number of physiological processes, and staphylococci aid in this process by releasing coagulase which clots plasma in the immediate area of the infection. Streptococci, on the other hand, are among the most invasive pathogens with which man must deal, and undoubtedly some of the damage they inflict may be attributed to the extensive tissue invasion encouraged by fibrinolytic activity.

LEUCOCIDIN

Leucocidin is an antigenic toxin produced by some bacteria, including staphylococci and streptococci, capable of killing leucocytes, primarily polymorphonuclear cells, when tested *in vitro*. It might appear from this statement that streptococci could protect themselves and aid their own cause by destroying the very cells designed by nature to engulf the bacteria through phagocytosis. However, this engulfment is not of major importance to the polymorphonuclear leucocytes, and just how effective leucocidin is in destroying other white cells (particularly monocytes and histiocytes) is not clear.

The basis of the test for leucocidin activity is the ability of white blood cells to reduce the oxidation–reduction indicator, methylene blue. Dead leucocytes are incapable of reducing this indicator. An antitoxin can be produced to combat leucocidin produced by staphylococci, but this antibody is unable to neutralize the leucocidin liberated by streptococci— definite evidence that the substances are immunologically distinct.

Miscellaneous Cocci

Gaffkya tetragena (also known as *Micrococcus tetragenus*) are bacteria that divide characteristically by splitting at right angles to their long axis, a process known as binary fission. But since spheres have no long axis, the number of possible arrangements they can assume is somewhat greater than is true for rod-shaped organisms. *Gaffkya tetragena* is a common skin contaminant that is found with the cells arranged typically in groups of four. It is mentioned here only because its presence may confuse inexperienced laboratory personnel who must make meaningful decisions relative to the various cultures they isolate from patients.

In drawing a blood sample for bacteriological examination, for example, it is sometimes not possible to avoid picking up gram positive cocci that are ordinary skin contaminants and have no bearing on the patient's disease. These cells lodge beyond reach of the chemical employed to disinfect the skin just before collection of the blood sample.

Members of the genus *Gaffkya* are pathogenic for mice and guinea pigs, and less so for rabbits, but they are not the cause of human infections. In fluid cultures they may be recognized by their tetrad appearance, and experienced technicians may be able to recognize their enamel-white colonial growth with a fair degree of accuracy. In many respects *Gaffkya* colonies tend to resemble rather closely the growth of albus varieties of staphylococci, but their differences in pathogenicity should be realized.

Sarcina lutea is another coccus that is a common culture contaminant from the air, but it produces a lemon-yellow, water-insoluble pigment when growing on solid media, and in fluid cultures the cells are found arranged in packets of eight (four on top of four). Other species of *Sarcina* produce orange or red pigments, but none of them are pathogenic. Their significance also lies in the area of contamination, unless accepted bacteriological techniques are practiced in the preparation of cultures made from clinical material.

Rod-shaped Bacteria

ORGANISM: *Bacillus anthracis*

DISEASE: Anthrax

CHARACTERISTICS: Gram positive spore-forming rods, 1.0 to 1.3 by 3.0 to 10 microns, with square or concave ends, occurring in long chains. Nonmotile. Aerobic, facultative anaerobic, or anaerobic. Optimum temperature is about 35°C. Causes anthrax in man, cattle, swine, sheep, rabbits, guinea pigs, mice, etc. Habitat is man and animals suffering from anthrax.

Koch's early work in demonstrating the causal relationship between infectious diseases and microorganisms was conducted with anthrax as the test organism. The German bacteriologist was not the first person to observe these gram positive cells, but he contributed fundamental observations in 1877 when he successfully grew the microbes in aqueous humor of the eye of an ox and then reproduced anthrax by inoculating the isolates into animals. Experiments of this nature led Koch to propose his germ theory of disease and to present in 1882 what have since been labeled *Koch's Postulates*. Before a microbe can be said to be the etiological agent of a specific disease, the following requirements must be fulfilled:

1. The organism must always be found in association with the particular disease. This poses certain problems in connection with mixed flora which may sometimes confuse the biological picture, but by appropriate isolation techniques each species can be set apart from its neighbors for pure culture studies.

2. The suspected organism must be isolated and grown in pure culture. As some writers have pointed out, this requirement has not been met with the leprosy bacillus. It can be seen in enormous numbers as acid-fast rods (*Mycobacterium leprae*) in infected tissues, but to date cultivation of these pathogens has not been successful in any type of media—living or dead. The spirochete of syphilis (*Treponema pallidum*) fails to grow on nonliving substrates, but its relationship to this serious venereal disease can no longer be questioned.

3. The isolated organisms must be able to reproduce the disease when inoculated into a susceptible host. The key word here is *susceptible* since many animals are refractory to specific microbes that are deadly to other animals. Mice, for example, do not contract mumps, nor do horses "catch" chicken pox or whooping cough. Therefore, unless an appropriate animal is chosen for the fulfillment of the third postulate, the required proof of relationship of the microbe to a given disease may fail. Another curious fact is that a single species of organism may manifest itself in apparently unrelated diseases insofar as clinical symptoms are concerned. Undulant fever in man, to cite one example, is caused by the same gram negative rods (*Brucella*) that induce contagious abortion in cattle. Koch's third postulate is a vital link in the chain of events necessary to prove that a given organism is without doubt the etiological agent in a specific disease.

4. Once the disease has become established in the susceptible test animal injected with the isolated pure culture, the organism must be reisolated in pure culture and must prove to be the same species of microbe found in postulate 2.

The ability of exotoxins liberated by certain pathogenic organisms to produce typical symptoms of disease in selected animals has been suggested as a possible fifth postulate, but the idea has not gained much support.

It might appear that this discussion has strayed somewhat from the intended characterization of specific rod-shaped bacteria, in this case *Bacillus anthracis,* but the importance of this particular bacillus in the history of microbiology needed to be brought out through a brief review of the ground rules presented by Koch in support of his *germ theory of disease*.

Anthrax bacilli are some of the largest pathogenic bacteria known, and the appearance of flat or even concave ends on these rods is rather characteristic. Capsules are difficult to demonstrate when the organisms are grown on artificial media, unless such foods are rich in animal proteins. Blood-containing media may enhance capsule development, as will animal passage. Aerobic incubation encourages the production of spores which appear as refractile bodies located almost centrally within the cell, but when cultures are isolated from animals, the rods are devoid of spores.

No measurable toxin appears to develop from *B. anthracis* grown in test tubes, and yet symptoms of toxemia appear within animals infected with these cells. The exact mechanism of this toxic reaction remains to be discovered, but the tissues themselves undoubtedly figure in the reaction in some manner.

How many readers of this book have ever heard of a case of anthrax in the area where they reside? Probably not many, and yet during the period from 1945 to 1952 this disease appeared in thirty-eight states, causing a loss of 14,708 domestic animals in a total of 2784 separate outbreaks. Although anthrax is primarily a disease of sheep, cattle, and horses, the World Health Organization (WHO) has estimated that there are between 20,000 and 100,000 human cases annually throughout the world. In fact, during the decade extending from 1945 to 1955 there were 400 recognized human cases in the United States. Fatality rates in man average about 20 per cent. Such startling statistics cannot and should not be dismissed as being unimportant.

Anthrax is an occupational disease striking most frequently those individuals whose duties bring them into close contact with infected animals or their hides and wool: shepherds; slaughterhouse workers; herdsmen; handlers of hides, fleeces, and hair, etc. An occasional laboratory infection is acquired by technicians working with *B. anthracis* cultures. This disease is not contagious in the sense that one person can acquire it from another; it is almost always picked up, by one means or another, from lower animals.

Shaving brushes manufactured from unsterilized bristles contaminated with anthrax spores have been implicated in some outbreaks. Readers will note that when they purchase brushes of various types, the label on the container will frequently state that the brush has been sterilized. That should not be interpreted to mean that the brush is sterile at the time of purchase, but at least the buyer has the assurance that in some step along the line the bristles have been treated with heat or some other suitable sterilizing agent that minimizes opportunity for harmful living agents to be passed on to the purchaser.

There are three principal types of anthrax: skin, pulmonary, and alimentary. Each will be reviewed briefly.

SKIN INFECTION

This is the most common form of the disease in man, and the infection takes on the appearance of unpleasant abscesses called **inflamed** or **malignant pustules.** In fact, the word "anthrax" is derived from the Greek and means **boil** or **carbuncle.** Tannery employees carrying hides on their shoulders are potential targets for skin anthrax on their faces or necks where the bacteria, if present, may find breaks in the skin caused by shaving or close haircuts. With such a portal of entry provided through an otherwise intact barrier, anthrax cells or their spores have little difficulty in becoming established and setting up foci of infection. The head of such a pustule generally appears as an ugly-looking, black, crusty sore which may sometimes heal spontaneously or which may progress into a more widespread infection.

PULMONARY INFECTION

Although this is the least common type of anthrax encountered, it has the highest mortality rate. Anthrax cells or their spores may be inhaled by those working with contaminated material, and the development of pneumonia with extensive hemorrhagic lesions and an overpowering septicemia generally leads to the death of the patient. In Great Britain this is called *Wool-sorters' disease.* Virulent spores have been isolated from the nasal passage of apparently healthy carriers employed in the hide and wool industries, but there is no concrete evidence that other persons acquire the disease through droplets expelled by such carriers. Perhaps they do.

ALIMENTARY INFECTION

This manifestation of the disease is rare in human beings, but when they do contract it the fatality rate is high. Lower animals, particularly grazing animals, probably pick up most cases of anthrax by ingesting spores found on fodder taken from soil previously contaminated with feces or carcasses of diseased animals.

Specific antiserum, arsenicals, and sulfonamides have all been employed for treatment of anthrax infections in human beings, but today antibiotics (penicillin and more recently tetracyclines) are being used more widely for therapy. Prophylactic measures date to the work of Louis Pasteur who injected vaccines attenuated with heat and initially tested in a dramatic public demonstration in 1881 at Pouilly-le-Fort, France. Today, in that country and others, hundreds of thousands of animals are vaccinated each year with some form of anthrax vaccine, because of the hazard that still exists when animals graze on pasture lands where infected carcasses were buried in years gone by. Cremation of all infected animals is one of the few recommended safe techniques for disposing of contaminated animals.

Before the classic work of Pasteur and his colleagues, anthrax spread in frightening epidemics that literally obliterated whole herds of animals or flocks of sheep. Although the application of preventative measures has helped to reduce the hazard both to man and to domestic animals, anthrax is far from being eradicated, and research must continue for still more effective means for obliterating this disease throughout the world.

ORGANISM: *Corynebacterium diphtheriae*

DISEASE: Diphtheria

CHARACTERISTICS: Non-sporing gram positive rods showing marked diversity of form, varying greatly in dimensions, 0.3 to 0.8 by 1.0 to 8.0 microns, occurring singly. Nonmotile. Aerobic to facultative. Optimum temperature about 34–36°C. The cause of diphtheria in man, but may be pathogenic for guinea pigs, kittens, and rabbits. Incubation period of the disease ranges from one to ten days, usually from two to five days. Habitat is membranes in the pharynx, larynx, trachea, and nose of infected human beings.

Before science developed effective prophylactic techniques diphtheria was one of man's most feared diseases, particularly since its principal target was young children below the age of five years. In recent decades, however, prevention of diphtheria has been remarkably effective, and by having children submit to properly timed immunizations, parents today in vast areas of the world can almost dismiss this disease from their minds.

Diphtheria is worldwide in distribution, but is most common in temperate climates, reaching its peak of incidence in late autumn or early winter.

During the latter stages of World War II in the European Theater of Operations diphtheria appeared and became a real concern to health authorities. As contacts with the disease diminish, our relative immunity tends to lessen; in time an adult population can become susceptible to attack when virulent strains of the bacteria appear in the population. Vigilance must be never-ending.

Diphtheria has had an interesting history dating back to 1826 when Bretonneau first described it as a clinical entity, but it was not until 1883–

84 that Klebs and Löffler detected the microbes and isolated them in pure culture. Since Löffler observed these same organisms in the throat of a healthy child, he was unwilling to state that these particular bacteria were definitely the cause of diphtheria. In support of his reluctance was the further fact that he was unable to isolate corynebacteria from all cases of apparent clinical diphtheria. We suspect that the inflammatory reaction he observed in the throats of healthy persons might well have been caused by streptococci which produce symptoms not too unlike those of diphtheria in some cases. It is also recognized today that healthy carriers do exist, and no doubt some such individuals were seen by Löffler during the course of his extensive studies.

In 1888 Roux and Yersin demonstrated a soluble (exo-)toxin produced by virulent *C. diphtheriae* capable of producing typical clinical symptoms of the disease. This is one of the three most powerful biological poisons known to man. These highly granular cells are still called "K–L bacilli" in honor of Klebs and Löffler, but the writer objects to the term *bacillus* to describe non-sporing rods.

In addition to their marked diversity in form and size (pleomorphism), these bacterial cells exhibit a strong tendency to stain unevenly. A single cell may contain dark bands or irregular bits of dark-staining granules (**metachromatic** or Babes-Ernst **granules**) especially when cultures are stained with Löffler's alkaline methylene blue or with Albert's stain (toluidine blue). Such concentrations within the cells have been described as reserve food materials or wastes, and they aid in preliminary microscopic recognition of *C. diphtheriae,* but final identification and determination of pathogenicity naturally have greater significance. Löffler developed a blood serum medium for the cultivation of these bacteria, and although modifications in the formula have been proposed and introduced through the years, the original composition suggested by Löffler, whose name the medium bears, has not changed materially.

Dozens of media have been developed to aid in the screening of suspects, and in recent years the addition of potassium tellurite to basic serum media has gained favor. Possible explanations of the mechanism of action of tellurite will be left to advanced textbooks.

Diphtheria is an acute infection generally localized in the upper respiratory tract, but wound infections and body ulcers displaying a gray-colored base are not uncommon in the tropics. The powerful toxins produced by the bacteria spread throughout the body via the bloodstream and lymph channels. When small children develop a laryngeal infection it may be termed **membranous croup,** and if the membrane (composed of tissue debris, fibrin, leucocytes, and bacteria) becomes extensive, it may become necessary to place a small tube in the larynx (tracheotomy) and introduce an air vent to permit the patient to breathe. Diphtheria toxin has a particular predilection for nerve and cardiac muscle tissue, but kidney damage and changes in other organs are also part of the clinical picture.

Personnel working with and near diphtheria patients frequently become contact carriers, and great care should be taken to insure that these ambulatory individuals are free of virulent *C. diphtheriae,* as evidenced by a series of negative cultures, before they are permitted to minister to the needs of other patients. Droplet contamination of the atmosphere by active cases, missed cases, and healthy carriers undoubtedly explains why this disease does not die out. The Schick test, described earlier in this chapter, is a valuable guide for physicians who must determine susceptible members of a given population who should be given prophylactic immunizations. Recovery from an attack of the disease usually provides a lifelong immunity to diphtheria.

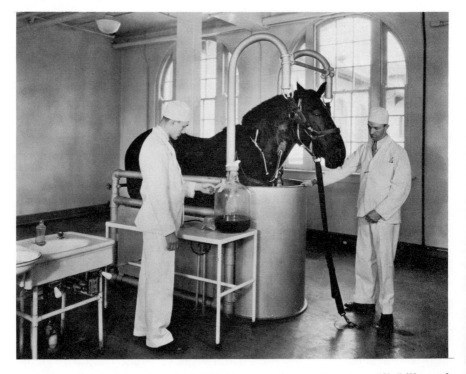

FIG. 15.5. Antitoxin production. Bleeding the horse. (Courtesy Eli Lilly and Company, Indianapolis, Indiana.)

Prevention of diphtheria hinges upon artificial active immunization of all or nearly all infants and children, coupled with the pasteurization of milk. Concurrent and terminal disinfection of the sickroom with chemical compounds and techniques that have proven to be effective naturally should be practiced. Each hospital has its own Standard Operating Procedure (S.O.P.) for treating the contents of wards and private rooms.

Immunity to diphtheria is aimed at the exotoxins rather than at the organisms themselves. Because the poison is so powerful, it cannot be safely injected unless it is first modified. The addition of a small quantity of formalin to diphtheria toxin converts the poison into a **toxoid,** which when injected into animals will induce active immunity. The formalin inactivates the lethal fraction of the exotoxin without destroying the immunizing (antigenic) ability of the protein. An antigen triggers the body to manufacture antibodies against the injected foreign material, and in this case the protective antibodies are **antitoxins.**

Injection of toxoid stimulates the body to produce an **active immunity** which is longer lasting in its effects than **passive immunity,** to be mentioned later. The body requires about a week to "tool up" when antigens are introduced into the system before the manufactured antitoxin finds its way into the general circulation where its potency can be evaluated. Therefore toxoid has its greatest value in protecting us from some future possible contact with the soluble waste products of *C. diphtheriae.*

Once the clinical symptoms of this disease have developed in a patient, toxoid will do little, if any, good in therapy. In fact the time lag before antibodies spilled over into the circulation would undoubtedly prove disastrous. In such cases the introduction of therapeutic doses of antitoxin previously produced in other animals (usually horses) should be administered to neutralize as quickly as possible any circulating toxins before they can attack and damage vital organs of the body.

Antitoxins for use in passive immunization (where the patient plays a passive role) is prepared by injecting horses with repeated doses of toxoid. After the animal has developed a hyperimmunity, blood is withdrawn; the cell-free portion is fractionated, purified, and standardized before being used for therapy in patients. This type of immunity is short in duration since the injected antibodies are excreted by the body, but the reaction is a valuable one for treating cases where the poison is already in the patient's system and needs to be neutralized. By combination of antitoxins and antibiotics, a two-pronged attack is aimed at the exotoxin and at the bacterial cells producing the poisons. Time is of the essence in treating diphtheria, and physicians cannot sit back and wait for laboratory confirmation of the disease before treatment is commenced.

ORGANISM: *Mycobacterium tuberculosis*

DISEASE: Tuberculosis

CHARACTERISTICS: Non-sporing, acid-fast slender rods, straight or slightly curved, ranging in size from 0.3 to 0.6 by 0.5 to 4.0 microns, occurring singly and in occasional threads. Facultative. Optimum temperature 37°C. Produces tuberculosis in man, monkey, dog, and parrot. Experimentally, it is highly pathogenic for guinea pigs but not for rabbits, cats, goats, oxen, or domestic fowl. Habitat is lesions in human tuberculosis.

The pulmonary form of tuberculosis is by far the most common type, and it causes 90 per cent of the tuberculosis deaths in the United States. Droplet infection through inhalation of air-borne organisms is undoubtedly the major means by which these virulent microbes are transmitted from an infected individual to other susceptible persons. The remaining 10 per cent of the deaths are the result of nonpulmonary infections, generally of bovine origin. *M. tuberculosis* is capable of surviving for long periods outside its hosts, particularly when the organisms are embedded in a shielding coat of pus or sputum. Although these cells contain no spores to protect them from unfavorable environmental conditions (drying, presence of chemicals, etc.), they nevertheless can remain viable in dust and on fomites for days, weeks, or even months. This characteristic adds materially to the hazards presented by this disease.

In 1882 Robert Koch was able to reproduce tuberculosis with pure cultures and to fulfill his postulates. Reports published in 1895 by Theobald Smith, the American bacteriologist, pointed out the differences between human and bovine varieties of mycobacteria. Human varieties tend to be more slender and longer than the short, plump cells of the bovine type.

Much difficulty was encountered by these early investigators in attempting to find the etiological agent in tuberculosis, which was at that time the leading cause of death. In the light of present-day knowledge their trouble can be attributed to the resistance displayed by members of the *Mycobacterium* genus to staining techniques that had proved so effective with other types of microbes. Tuberculosis cells contain a high percentage of unsaponified wax which retards or prevents penetration of dyes into the cells, but once the bacteria have been stained, they are reluctant to release their color even in the presence of alcohol and dilute mineral acids. It is this unusual characteristic that is the basis for their being called **acid-fast** bacteria.

Ziehl-Neelsen developed a staining technique employing hot carbol fuchsin which successfully overcomes the dye-resistance of mycobacteria.

When a stained smear is dipped in acid-alcohol for a few seconds, all extraneous organisms and organic debris give up their carbol fuchsin, while the acid-fast cells are relatively unaffected by such a decolorizing procedure. A suitable counterstain (methylene blue, picric acid, or Bismarck brown) may be used to restain the decolorized material against which the pink *M. tuberculosis* cells are clearly visible. A number of modifications of the Ziehl-Neelsen technique have been proposed to circumvent the need for the application of heat in the staining process. Kinyoun's modification involves tripling the concentration of carbol fuchsin in the Ziehl-Neelsen formula, and increasing both the phenol and the alcohol content. With this procedure the smears can be stained without the aid of heat.

Gram positive materials known as Much's granules have been demonstrated in exudates removed from cold abscesses and other sources in which no acid-fast rods could be demonstrated but which, nevertheless, were infective when injected into appropriate hosts. The nature and the significance of these particles in producing the disease are still not clear.

The local lesion of tuberculosis is the **tubercle** which is formed through a build-up involving a series of biological events. Monocytic blood cells are attracted to the area and they gather at the site of the infection. As the lesion enlarges, epithelioid cells and multinucleated giant cells appear in characteristic arrangements. In time, if the tissue succumbs to the infection, the central portion of the tubercle breaks down, releasing a cheeselike mass loaded with organisms that may escape as pus and be discharged with sputum through coughing. In the advanced stages of the disease enormous cavities are left behind as mute evidence of the destructive force of these slow-growing but deadly microbes.

If the tissues exhibit resistance to the bacterial invasion, which is more commonly the case, a wall of connective tissue forms while the lesion is still quite small, and further extension of the tubercle is prevented. Calcium salts may eventually be deposited in the immediate area of the infection, forming **calcified tubercles.** But it should be borne in mind that within these "calcified coffins" lie viable cells of *M. tuberculosis,* since calcification merely represents an arrested infection, not a healed or cured case. During times of prolonged stress, overexertion, and substandard nutrition, especially during war and postwar periods, these tubercles have a tendency to break down with a subsequent release of their virulent cargo, and active tuberculosis follows.

Tuberculosis is not an inherited disease any more than any other bacterial disease is transmitted through genes, but a tendency toward the infection can be passed on from one generation to another by the inheritage of an organically weak lung structure, for example. In the same manner, a greater than average resistance to tuberculosis may be exhibited by those fortunate enough to be born with strong bodies.

By the time the majority of us have reached middle age, perhaps even earlier, we probably have successfully warded off at least one attack by these acid-fast bacteria. Autopsy records tend to bear this out. Individuals engaged in so-called "dusty trades" (stone cutters and workers in quarries) have a higher than normal incidence of lung infections, including tuberculosis, since they develop a fibrosis of the lungs called **silicosis,** and their resistance to lung infections is definitely lowered by the shearing action of the inhaled sharp particles of stone.

Artificial immunization against tuberculosis has, in general, been disappointing. But the French bacteriologists Calmette and Guérin developed an attenuated culture by growing the bovine type of *M. tuberculosis* for thirteen years on a bile medium which removed the virulent characteristics of the cells without materially impairing their antigenic qualities. This preparation which has undergone extensive field trials in a few countries (over 100 million cases by 1961) is called *BCG vaccine* in honor of its discoverers. BCG-treated individuals in France, Scandinavia, New York City, and certain American Indian reservations have experienced a tuberculosis incidence only about one-fourth that of control populations in the same areas. Early reports from France where many trials got underway after World War I were sufficiently encouraging to stimulate the World Health Organization to attempt vast immunization programs involving millions of children in Europe. Because of one notably unfortunate experience in Lübeck, Germany when, through a human error, a virulent culture of *M. tuberculosis* was employed to inoculate a group of children, with a number of subsequent deaths from the disease, acceptance of BCG vaccine has met with understandable resistance. However this feeling is gradually being broken down as reports of encouraging results continue to come in from widely scattered areas.

Tuberculosis is still an important public health problem even in countries where sanitation and education are considered to be at a high level. The thousands of deaths reported annually in the United States alone make it painfully clear that we cannot dismiss this disease as being no longer important.

Control of this disease lies in early diagnosis and treatment before droplets can be transmitted from infected persons to the many susceptible individuals in their environment. Hospitalization with its isolation practices and controlled medication procedures can help to minimize spread of tuberculosis. Coupled with this must be a never-ending educational program to keep the public informed of its responsibilities and to maintain an awareness of the presence of the disease in our communities. The concept of the minuteness of microbes, their mode of action, and the common means for their dissemination are not easy matters to impart to laymen, even to the educated, who may find it difficult to comprehend "all this business about germs" when they have never been privileged to view such microscopic forms of life under the revealing lenses of a modern microscope.

THE TUBERCULIN TEST

One of the most commonly employed reactions for detection of the presence of *M. tuberculosis* in the body is the *tuberculin test*. In contrast to the Dick and the Schick tests it does not measure an individual's susceptibility to the disease; rather, it is an allergic response alerting us to the presence within the body of specific protein of which the tuberculosis cells are composed. Once tuberculo-protein has found it way into our systems, we build up a definite hypersensitivity to this substance which can be detected by means of skin reactions.

Robert Koch introduced a skin test in 1890 when he discovered that an intradermal injection of a filtrate prepared from a heat-killed extract of *M. tuberculosis* grown in a glycerinated veal broth provoked a reaction in previously infected animals. Noninfected animals failed to respond in the same manner. His rather crude preparation (known as *O.T.*, which stands for "original" or "old" tuberculin) has been largely replaced in recent years by relatively pure extracts prepared by growing the organisms in a synthetic, protein-free medium. As the microbes grow they give rise to tuberculo-protein which is precipitated from the broth by the addition of trichloracetic acid. This concentrated preparation is called *PPD* (purified protein derivative).

Tuberculin tests are conducted using the following three principal methods:

1. *Mantoux Test:* This test involves the intradermal (*into* the skin) injection of graded doses of tuberculin; it appears to be the most reliable.
2. *Von Pirquet Test:* Tuberculin is rubbed into scarified skin. This is one of the older methods.
3. *Vollmer Test:* A patch of filter paper or other suitable material impregnated with concentrated tuberculin is taped to the relatively sensitive skin of the forearm. Although the findings are not as accurate as those obtained with the Mantoux procedure, the patch technique is much easier to conduct on large groups of children who, as a rule, don't exactly leap for joy at either the sight or the feel of a needle.

A positive tuberculin response is indicated by an area of redness and swelling at the point of application. It progresses from a simple edema within a few hours to a maximum degree of inflammation in from 15 to 48 hours, followed by a gradual fading of the reaction a few days later. It should be understood that a positive reaction does not mean the individual has an active case of tuberculosis. It could indicate either a present or a past infection. Somewhere within the body there are tuberculosis organisms with their characteristic tuberculo-protein. They may be walled off in calcified tubercles, or they could be in open lesions.

In cattle a positive tuberculin test means an active case of the disease, and such animals should be separated from the rest of the herd and slaughtered as soon as possible to prevent further spread of their microbes to other cattle—to say nothing of preventing the dissemination of tuberculosis to human beings through contaminated raw milk.

Treatment for this ancient disease is being studied extensively on a wide front, with conflicting reports as to the relative merits of sulfones, streptomycin, para-aminosalicylic acid, isoniazid, and other drugs.

Any discussion of the genus *Mycobacterium* would be incomplete without a few comments about leprosy, a disease that dates back to at least 600 B.C. and is described in the Old Testament. These acid-fast bacilli were first reported in about 1874 by Hansen who observed them in the round epithelioid cells of lesions. Leprosy is also known as *Hansen's disease*.

In many respects these cells resemble the tuberculosis organisms, but since no one has successfully cultivated them, it has not been possible to subject pure cultures to the customary cultural and biochemical tests employed in the study of other bacteria, or to apply Koch's postulates. According to *Bergey's Manual* the habitat of leprosy bacilli is confined to the skin, testes, and peripheral nerves of the body. They probably do not grow in the internal organs.

There are an estimated 500 to 1000 cases of leprosy in the United States, many of them confined to the National Leprosarium in Carville, Louisiana. The incidence of the disease in certain other countries is relatively high. Man appears to exhibit a high degree of resistance to infection with leprosy bacilli, and little is understood about transmission of these microbes. Many uninfected individuals have worked for years in relatively close contact with leprosy patients without ever contracting the disease, whereas other persons after, supposedly, a single exposure have come down with the disease, sometimes years later. Nasal mucus can be shown to harbor acid-fast bacilli in active cases of leprosy, and droplet infection from this source cannot be dismissed as a possibility.

Chemotherapy for leprosy parallels that for tuberculosis, with some drugs yielding promising results for the one disease and other drugs apparently attacking the other disease. Once leprosy cells can be grown *in vitro,* it would seem a reasonable hope that in time cures might be found for this severe affliction.

This is one frontier of microbiology that awaits the inspiration and good fortune of another Pasteur, Koch, or Lister to provide a breakthrough in our understanding of a baffling disease that has long tortured the best minds of science. Anyone who feels that all of the great biological discoveries have already been made is sadly misinformed. Man has hardly scratched the surface of the mysteries locked within living cells. For those of you who possess a hunger for knowledge and discovery, the world is still your oyster. Start nibbling!

ORGANISM: *Actinomyces bovis*

DISEASE: Actinomycosis

CHARACTERISTICS: Variable lengths of branching hyphae less than 1.0 micron in diameter. No aerial hyphae. Large club-shaped cells seen in morbid tissues. Mycelium undergoes fragmentation very rapidly but extensive branching is rare. Not acid-fast. Nonmotile. Anaerobic to microaerophilic. Optimum temperature is 37°C. Originally found in "lumpy jaw" of cattle. Frequently found in and around the mouths of cattle and probably other animals. Possibly also found in human mouths.

Actinomycosis was first recognized as a parasitic affliction in 1877 by Bollinger who persuaded Harz, a botanist, to study the characteristics of the organism found in the diseased tissues. Members of the order *Actinomycetales,* to which these organisms belong, might be looked upon as transition forms midway between the true bacteria and complex molds. The generic name *Actinomyces* was given by Harz to these organisms when he described the forms seen in "lumpy jaw" of cattle. The word literally means "ray fungus," a designation suggested by the sunray-like arrangement of threads which make up the granules found in lesions. Subsequent studies, however, have revealed that this cell arrangement is not characteristic for saprophytic members of the group that assist in the decomposition of organic matter in the soil. The characteristic odor of soil associated with newly plowed fields is due in part to the volatile compounds produced during metabolism of *Actinomyces* in the earth.

Actinomycosis is an endogenous infection of man and certain lower animals. Man-to-man or animal-to-man transmission of organisms apparently has not been satisfactorily established. The question has been raised, might not *Actinomyces* represent part of the normal flora of the mouth of some individuals? One, apparently, never finds *A. bovis* in pure culture when infectious material is subjected to microbiological scrutiny. They appear to be always found in association with other microbes of different types. Carious teeth and the crypts of the tonsils have been found to harbor *Actinomyces.* The need for necrotic tissue coupled with a symbiotic relationship with selected bacteria might be one explanation of why more cases of actinomycosis are not seen—or, at least, not recognized. Perhaps some of the conflicting reports concerning the difficulties encountered in trying to cure cases may be due to differences in resistance of the associated organisms rather than to the *Actinomyces* themselves.

A second species, *A. israeli,* described in *Bergey's Manual,* was reported in 1891 by Wolf and Israel who isolated it from a human case of actinomycosis. Opinions are divided as to whether *A. bovis* or *A. israeli* is the more pathogenic for man. Some prefer to consider them as a single species, one being merely a variant of the other.

One notable characteristic of *Actinomyces* is their relative resistance to drying, an important consideration for anyone coming in contact with discharges from patients suffering with actinomycosis. Reports indicate that at room temperature these organisms can remain viable up to 22 days. Exposure to 60°C for one hour normally kills the cells, but according to some investigators cultures may resist this temperature for as long as three hours. Penicillin still appears to be the drug of choice for combating this type of infection. Oxytetracycline also displays promising results, but streptomycin can be dismissed as almost completely ineffective against these cells.

Up to 1923 there had been some 700 reported cases of actinomycosis in the United States. Three principal types of infections are found in man: cervicofacial, thoracic, and abdominal. About 60 per cent of the cases are of the first type, involving the jaw and tissues of the face and neck. Thoracic infections appear in the lungs and the thoracic cage, and abdominal infections originate in the area of the cecum with symptoms not unlike those associated with appendicitis. Following surgery in the latter cases, however, the wound fails to heal and irregular tender masses appear in the abdomen.

Actinomycosis is characterized by multiple draining sinuses with tangled mycelial masses or "granules" being found in the draining pus or in tissue sections. When these granules are crushed between slides the material will be found to contain gram positive branching filaments, short diphtheroids, and coccoid bodies.

It is difficult to know how to prevent a disease when so little is known about its exact mode of transmission. Studies indicate that persons who are engaged in agricultural pursuits, especially those individuals working around cattle, have a disproportionately large share of the total reported cases of actinomycosis. Some workers go so far as to suggest that persons who make a practice of chewing on blades of grass or pieces of straw might be predisposing themselves to possible infections of this type, although *A. bovis* apparently has never been found as a saprophyte in nature.

ORGANISM: *Clostridium botulinum*

DISEASE: Botulism

CHARACTERISTICS: Gram positive rods 0.5 to 0.8 by 0.3 to 8.0 microns with rounded ends, occurring singly, in pairs, and in short to occasionally long chains. Spores ovoid, central, subterminal, terminal at maturation, swelling the cells to make them resemble snowshoes. Motile by means of peritrichous flagella. Strictly anaerobic. Optimum temperature between 20° and 30°C. Produces a powerful exotoxin. Habitat appears to be the soil. Pathogenic for a number of animals, including man.

Botulism, an infrequent but fatal type of food poisoning, was first observed and reported in Germany in 1785, but the organism was not isolated until 1896 by Van Ermengem who named it *Bacillus botulinus*. The organism is now called *Clostridium botulinum*. The organisms are essentially saprophytic and are unable to multiply within the body of warm-blooded animals.

Some of the characteristic features of botulism as it relates to food poisoning have already been discussed in Chapter 12, but a few additional facts will be brought out here. *Clostridium botulinum* produces what Lamanna has called "the most poisonous poison," and according to Raffel, "the disease represents the extreme in remoteness of relationship of etiologic parasite to host." Before 1945 relatively little was known about the chemical nature of botulinus toxins, but since then various military agencies have expended great sums of money on research to study this poison as a possible lethal agent in biological warfare.

There exist at least five well-defined antigenic types of botulinus toxin (A through E), each of which is highly specific for its own antitoxin which is generally produced in horses. This makes the neurotoxins antigenically distinguishable, since cross-neutralization between types does not occur. It has been postulated that one milligram of type "A" toxin could theoretically kill ten million mice. The minimum lethal dose for a human being cannot be stated with any degree of certainty, but it has been estimated by some investigators that as little as 0.00001 gram might prove fatal for an average-sized man. The toxic principle is a protein and when crystallized it is reported to have a molecular weight of about 900,000. Authors do not completely agree on this matter however.

One of the curious features of botulism is that it is caused by an oral poison that to be effective must successfully pass through the alimentary tract where digestive enzymes capable of attacking proteins are present in substantial amounts. Theoretically these proteolytic juices should destroy the toxin which is protein, but if the rate of destruction is slow enough, apparently some of the molecules of botulinus toxin get through the physical and biological traps and gain entrance to the circulation, probably into the lymph rather than directly into the blood. The size of the molecules of absorbed toxin may not necessarily be as great as the molecular weight of 900,000 mentioned previously, and with a potency of this magnitude not all of the molecules of poison need to breach the intestinal barrier to set up typical clinical symptoms of botulism.

Botulism involves a paralysis of the efferent autonomic nervous system; sensory nerves are not harmed. The immediate cause of death is usually a paralysis of the skeletal musculature causing an interference with breathing that eventually leads to terminal asphyxia. With such a high mortality rate, it is indeed fortunate that the incidence of this disease is low. Because of the low case rate, prophylactic immunization on any mass scale is not warranted, but protection of laboratory personnel who handle cultures of these bacteria and their toxins is undoubtedly a wise precautionary measure. Protection of fur-bearing animals (mink, fox, etc.) through prophylactic immunization procedures is a common practice on many farms, and it has served to minimize the costly epidemics that formerly swept through such groups of animals.

This disease gained its name from sausages which were implicated in the early outbreaks of botulism described by Van Ermengem. Today these same foods, together with brined meats, continue to lead the botulism hit parade in Europe. Most cases in the United States have been traced to home-canned neutral, high-protein foods (olives, string beans, spinach, peas, corn) which have not been adequately processed under steam pressure. Spores of *Cl. botulinum* are some of the most resistant known. Some writers claim that up to 20 hours of boiling may be required to inactivate these resistant bodies, but the majority are of the opinion that five or six hours may be the outside limit of resistance. When subjected to 15 pounds steam pressure (about 121°C) for a minimum of 15 minutes, however, even the most resistant spores are killed in small volumes of substrate. As the volume of material to be sterilized increases in bulk, however, the exposure period naturally must be increased to allow the desired moist heat to reach the core of the mass. Canning directions accompanying pressure cookers will generally indicate what these times should be for specific foods to be processed in various-sized containers.

Whereas the spores of *Cl. botulinum* are extremely resistant to heat, exotoxins produced by these bacteria are relatively thermolabile and can be inactivated within 10 minutes at 100°C. *Never taste home-canned neutral, high-protein foods that smell "off" or that look the least bit unnatural until they first have been adequately cooked!* There are cases on record where individuals have foolishly tasted such foods. Even though they spit them out almost immediately because of their bitter taste, and did not actually swallow any of the particles, such persons have succumbed to botulism within a few days. Apparently sufficient toxin was absorbed through the tissues of the mouth to bring about eventual death.

Heavily manured and acid soils have the highest count of clostridia per gram, but the numbers of *Cl. botulinum* cells vary widely in different sections of the country. Since these microbes are strict anaerobes, the better job the housewife does to keep out unwanted air in her canning jars, the more successful she may be in creating ideal conditions for the undesirable anaerobes to flourish unless the jars are processed in a steam pressure cooker for prescribed times. Botulism is not a disease spread through the ingestion of fresh foods, nor would frozen foods be expected to be implicated unless the toxin was formed in the foods prior to their being frozen, and this is rather unlikely.

When the clinical symptoms of double vision, swelling of the tongue, difficulty in swallowing, and general weakness appear (usually in less than 24 hours), the amount of good that can be done for the victim by injection of specific antitoxin is debatable. At this stage in the disease nerve damage has already taken place, but it is still highly recommended that antitoxin be administered to halt further damage to tissues by circulating toxin.

Ducks, chickens, horses, and cattle may contract botulism from eating spoiled grass, fodder, and silage. In poultry the disease is called **limberneck** which characterizes the clinical symptoms associated with loss of control of neck muscles.

ORGANISM: *Clostridium perfringens*

DISEASE: Gas gangrene

CHARACTERISTICS: Short, thick, encapsulated gram positive rods 1.0 to 1.5 by 4.0 to 8.0 microns, occurring singly and in pairs, less frequently in short chains. Spores ovoid, central to eccentric, not swelling the cells. Nonmotile. Anaerobic. Optimum temperature between 35° and 37°C, but growth occurs as high as 50°C. Pathogenic for guinea pigs, pigeons, mice, and human beings. Habitat is feces, sewage, and soil.

This gram positive spore-forming anaerobe was first cultivated by Achalme in 1891, but others rediscovered it several times in association with a number of diseases. Welch and Nuttal isolated the bacillus in 1892 from the foamy organs of a cadaver. For years the pathogen bore the name of *Cl. welchii* in honor of Welch, but the present edition of *Bergey's Manual* lists it as *Cl. perfringens* (Latin: "breaking through"), a name that it may well lose if certain taxonomists have their way. Some prefer to return the name to its former designation of *Cl. welchii*. The fact that the organism is nonmotile sets it apart from other pathogenic clostridia, and its **stormy fermentation** of milk is particularly characteristic. As it grows in this medium the violent fermentation of lactose spatters the shredded acid clot around in the tube and gives the culture a "stormy" appearance.

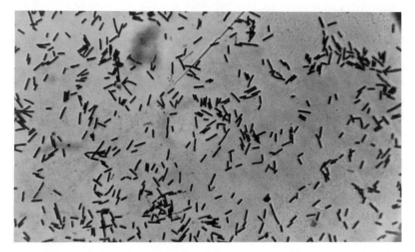

FIG. 15.6. *Clostridium perfringens.* (Courtesy Armed Forces Institute of Pathology, negative #50340.)

More than 70 per cent of the cases of gas gangrene encountered during World Wars I and II showed the presence of *Cl. perfringens,* with *Cl. novyi, Cl. septicum,* and *Cl. histolyticum* in other cases. Gas gangrene becomes established when deep, dirty wounds are contaminated with fertilized soil or with fecal matter, and the presence of mixed cultures of aerobes as well as anaerobes in such infections favors the development of gangrene. While *Cl. perfringens* is an anaerobe, its environmental gaseous requirements are far less strict than those for *Cl. tetani,* the so-called "lockjaw" organism. When the free oxygen in a wound has been used up by the aerobes present, conditions become favorable for the multiplication of clostridia, and unless medication (sulfa drugs, antitoxins, antibiotics) is given to stop the reaction or to reverse it, extensive destruction of flesh will occur, frequently necessitating amputation of limbs.

Dry gangrene, a disease of nonmicrobial etiology, may develop when the blood supply is cut off from a given tissue for prolonged periods of time. Trench foot, seen so frequently in soldiers compelled to stand in cold water or mud for long periods, involves tissue death and the flesh may turn very dark in color before amputation becomes necessary in severe cases. Leaving a tourniquet on a limb for too long could result in the development of gangrene.

Clostridium perfringens forms a number of distinct toxins that can cause anemia through gross blood destruction in addition to the proteolytic reactions responsible for tissue breakdown. These anaerobes release hyaluronidase *(spreading factor)* which may help to speed the spread of this infection. They also produce **collagenase,** an enzyme that destroys collagen, a supporting substance in muscles, bone, and cartilage, and this reaction contributes to the invasiveness of the organisms.

As tissue sugars are fermented and gas is liberated the pressure produced will clamp off the blood supply in capillaries, eventually leading to necrosis which in turn contributes more fuel for the gangrene fire. Tissue destruction under these conditions progresses at an alarming rate, but prompt surgical removal of dead flesh tends to limit the spread of this reaction by reducing the available food supply.

Clostridium perfringens is a normal inhabitant of our intestines and it undoubtedly contributes to the toxemia associated with the peritonitis that follows rupture of an appendix. In Great Britain sanitarians and bacteriologists use this spore-forming organism as an index of water pollution in preference to *E. coli* which they feel does not persist as long in water as do the clostridia or some of the enteric streptococci. Because the toxin generated by *Cl. perfringens* is a true poison, specific antitoxins have been developed, and they are included in the polyvalent antisera administered in cases of gas gangrene. This exotoxin is not considered to be particularly powerful if *Cl. botulinum* is used as a standard, but it is still a force with which to reckon. Toxoids may be employed to induce active immunity, and when combined with tetanus toxoid they provide protection for individuals who are likely to be exposed to physical risks that could lead to possible gangrene.

ORGANISM: *Clostridium tetani*

DISEASE: Tetanus (lockjaw)

CHARACTERISTICS: Gram positive rods 0.4 to 0.6 by 4.0 to 8.0 microns, rounded ends, occurring singly, in pairs, and often in long chains and filaments. Spores spherical, terminal, and swelling the cells to impart a drumstick-like appearance. Motile by peritrichous flagella. Strictly anaerobic. Optimum temperature 37°C. Highly toxic. Habitat is soil, human and horse intestines, and feces.

Nicolaier first described the tetanus bacillus in 1884 in pus taken from mice and other animals injected with soil samples. Pure cultures were isolated in 1899 by Kitasato who demonstrated the relationship to "lockjaw" and the intoxication produced in the body. The disease is characterized by spasms of the voluntary muscles, particularly those of the jaw and neck, caused by **tetanospasmin.** Another metabolic product, **tetanolysin,** is a hemolysin, but there is no evidence to indicate that it is toxic in the same sense as tetanospasmin.

Severity of this disease is greatest in infants and in adults but it is relatively low during childhood. The "sardonic smile," so characteristic of tetanus, is due to spasm of the facial muscles, particularly the masseter. Differentiation between tetanus and strychnine poisoning may be difficult at certain stages in the development of the disease, but pure culture isolation of cells of *Cl. tetani* with their typical terminal swollen spores should remove all doubts as to which disease is involved.

Tetanus toxin is one of the more potent biological poisons known to man. Death of its victims occurs from asphyxia due to spasms of the respiratory muscles. The incubation period (from 2 to 50 days) before symptoms appear is the time required for the poison to be absorbed by the end organs of the motor nerves and to travel to the ganglion cells of the central nervous system along the axis cylinders of the peripheral nerves. The longer the incubation period (more chronic?) the more favorable is the prognosis. In fact, the statement made centuries ago by Hippocrates still seems to be scientifically sound: "Such persons as are seized with tetanus die within four days, or if they pass these they recover."

Lockjaw is essentially an intoxication with the etiological microbes remaining localized while their toxins circulate throughout the body until they come in contact with appropriate cells of the central nervous system. Fatality rates in man run about 60 per cent. Up to 1925 as many as 10 per cent of tetanus cases observed were due to postoperative or surgical causes. *Tetanus neonatorum,* an infection of the umbilicus usually brought about through septic midwifery, is especially common in areas of the world where strict sanitary standards are not maintained during delivery of babies.

No gaping wound is necessary to cause tetanus. A splinter, a thorn, an insect bite, or even a vaccination might be responsible. Surgical attention to the wound coupled with the use of antibiotics may be required to remove the focus of infection. Curare, a resinoid extract prepared by South American Indians as an arrow poison which paralyzes the motor nerves, has shown some promise as a muscle-relaxing agent. One deadly poison may thus oppose or modify the effects of another toxin.

Some rather interesting cases of tetanus occurred during a smallpox scare in the 1920's when some individuals recommended covering vaccinations with a collodion compound "to keep out germs." Unfortunately in these cases the protective air-tight covering also kept undesirable bacteria in, and by cutting off the supply of air, presented anaerobes with ideal growth conditions. The patients involved never did contract smallpox because they died first from lockjaw!

The highly fertilized soil of Flanders Fields, about which John McRae wrote his well-known poem, is rich in tetanus spores. It is not surprising, therefore, that gas gangrene and tetanus were rampant during the trench warfare of World War I. It is unfortunate that progress in science frequently must be given the impetus of urgency by the necessities of war, but what was learned about anaerobic infections during World War I and in the years that followed resulted in the saving of untold numbers of lives and limbs in subsequent conflicts. World War II was the first conflict in which more men died from enemy action than from microbial diseases. Now isn't that progress in our civilized society?

Anyone whose responsibilities entail the maintenance of athletic fields, either directly or indirectly, should remember that such grassy areas must not be fertilized with manure, especially horse manure, which contains significant numbers of *Cl. tetani* cells as well as other pathogenic anaerobes. Should one of the players sustain any type of laceration or deep, dirty penetrating wound while engaged in sports, it could lead to serious consequences unless prophylactic injections are administered. Athletic fields, therefore, should be treated with commercial fertilizers to avoid this potential hazard.

Effective antitoxins for tetanus are available both for prophylactic use and for therapeutic inoculations, but in the latter cases the material is of limited value. Once the toxin has come in contact with nerve tissue, for which it has remarkable affinity, nerve damage is permanent and the administration of antitoxin will not reverse the lethal action of the toxin. Effects of the poison on nerve tissues are not visible as far as pathologic alteration is concerned. Reports may vary concerning therapeutic use of these biologicals, but the majority opinion supports the conclusion that little or no good is accomplished by their injection.

Tetanus toxin converts spontaneously and rather rapidly into toxoid, but by the addition of a minute amount of formalin, the toxic fraction of the poison is detoxified almost immediately without any impairment to the antigenic qualities of the toxin. Toxoid can be employed to produce active immunity that remains effective for several years. The U.S. Army requires that military personnel be given a booster "shot" once every four years after completion of the initial series of injections, and statistics bear out the value of such measures in reducing the number of cases of tetanus. In fact, a booster can set off such a rapid rise in anti-

body titer that toxoid is even recommended by some as a possible substitute for prophylactic antitoxin when the use of the latter is indicated.
The prompt elevation in blood level antitoxin is due to a recall response
known as an **anamnestic reaction.** The body "remembers" how to manufacture this antitoxin quickly once it has "tooled up" to produce it
through the stimulus of the original series of injections. Chemotherapy
in tetanus is generally aimed at the specific toxin rather than at the
anaerobic bacilli that create the poison.

Antitoxin may be given both intramuscularly and intravenously in
doses varying between 30,000 and 40,000 units. Sensitivity to the horse
serum from which the antitoxin is derived must be watched, or the
adverse reactions in some hypersensitive patients may be so pronounced
that serum sickness or more serious allergic reactions bordering on anaphy-
lactic shock might occur.

Gram Negative Bacteria

Spheres

ORGANISM: *Neisseria meningitidis (N. intracellularis)*

DISEASE: Epidemic meningitis

CHARACTERISTICS: Gram negative cocci 0.6 to 1.0 micron in diameter, occurring
singly and in pairs with adjacent sides flattened. Occasionally found in tetrads.
Nonsporing. Nonmotile. Aerobic. Optimum temperature between 36°C and
37°C. Cause of epidemic cerebrospinal fever. Habitat is the nasopharynx of
man.

Meningitis (also called brain fever), a disease affecting the meninges
(covering) of the brain and spinal cord, may be caused by a wide
variety of pathogenic microbes including streptococci, staphylococci, *M.
tuberculosis, H. influenzae,* salmonellae, syphilis, pneumoniae, and meningococci, but the meningococcus (*N. meningitidis*) is the only organism
exhibiting epidemic characteristics. The incubation period is generally
about one week, but it may vary between two and ten days after contact.
The disease is characterized by fever, muscular pains, severe headaches,
stiff neck, malaise, nausea, and vomiting. Delirium and loss of consciousness are not uncommon. Microbial invasion of the blood stream—a true
septicemia—may persist for a matter of only a few hours or for days,
and in a fulminating (galloping) case the individual may expire within
as short a period as four hours following the appearance of symptoms.
A rash and skin hemorrhages called **petechiae** appear characteristically
on the wrists and ankles, but they may also be evident on other areas

of the body. Such spots may be caused, at least in part, by the blocking action presented by concentrated foci of organisms. For this reason petechiae are a good source for cultures when the skin is broken directly above one of the hemorrhagic spots. Direct smears of this blood can be prepared on slides or a drop of the blood may be subcultured onto the surface of a warm, solid, blood-containing medium.

Fulminating meningococcemia (the Waterhouse-Friderichsen syndrome) usually culminates in adrenal apoplexy. This manifestation of the disease is usually more prevalent in infants and in older individuals, with the age group in between being more or less refractory. According to published records slightly more than 200 such major acute cases have been reported in the United States. The number of cases of all types of meningitis reaches a peak in winter, with the low point generally experienced in late summer. Before modern chemotherapy, fatality rates ran as high as 70 or 80 per cent. Today the figure is somewhat under 5 per cent, with deaths in this group taking place among those patients who become stricken with an overwhelming infection that is not diagnosed or treated early enough.

In laboratory confirmation of meningitis a sample of spinal fluid obtained by lumbar puncture is subjected to microscopic examination for the presence of leucocytes and microorganisms. Spinal fluid normally is crystal clear, but in cases of meningitis it becomes turbid, almost milklike in some cases. A white blood cell count may reveal 20,000 leucocytes or more per cubic millimeter with a predominance of polymorphonuclear cells containing gram negative diplococci both intracellularly and extracellularly.

The physician may make a preliminary diagnosis of meningitis based upon microscopic examination of stained spinal fluid specimens, particularly when the fluid is spun down in a centrifuge tube to concentrate the cellular elements present. But until the microbes have been isolated and identified through biochemical reactions, the preliminary diagnosis must remain tentative.

Four distinct serological types of *N. meningitidis* have been described, with various combinations of numbers and letters suggested in typing schemes dating back to 1914. The designation that has been in most common use for a number of years lists in the four types as I, II, II alpha, and III, although the recommended classification proposed by the Nomenclature Committee of the International Association of Microbiologists lists the four types as A, B, C, and D, respectively.

The typing procedure can be carried out by several techniques, one of which is the Quellung reaction described earlier for the differentiation of pneumococci. In addition, an agglutination test can be conducted by adding specific antisera to saline suspensions of the bacteria and shaking the tubes on a Kahn shaker for a few minutes to increase the speed of contact between the cells and their specific antibodies. Up to 90 per cent of the reported cases of meningitis in the United States belong to type I (or type A), according to a number of studies.

Neisseria meningitidis was first isolated by Weichselbaum in 1887, although the German bacteriologist Neisser had observed similar diplococci in gonorrheal pus in 1879. The genus into which these two gram negative species were eventually placed honors the name of Neisser. In general, these fastidious microbes require rich media containing blood, serum, or other body fluids, especially on primary isolation. *Neisseria meningitidis* cells are some of the most sensitive bacteria known. Even minor deviations in temperature, humidity, and light may cause their death. When cultivating pathogenic *Neisseria* the addition of 10 per cent carbon dioxide to the atmosphere favors their growth. According to some investigators these cells grow slowly anaerobically, but they must still be considered to be essentially aerobic with slight leanings toward being microaerophilic. Maintaining stock cultures of meningococci is fraught with difficulties unless the cells are subjected to carefully controlled freeze-drying techniques **(lyophilization)** which may permit the microorganisms to be maintained for indefinite periods with their characteristics virtually unchanged.

Direct contact with infected individuals, probably through droplet dissemination, is the recognized mode of spread for this respiratory infection, and man appears to be the sole natural reservoir and host for meningococci, although symptoms of the disease can be produced experimentally in monkeys. The carrier rate may run as high as 50 per cent (perhaps higher), but the case rate of less than 5 per cent would indicate a relatively strong natural immunity of human beings to the disease. The cells normally enter the body through the nasopharynx and reach the meninges through the bloodstream.

Epidemics have appeared in four major waves since World War I, with the last peak experienced in 1944. Meningitis is particularly troublesome in military camps, compounds for refugees, and institutions where individuals live in close proximity with relatively large numbers of other persons gathered from widespread areas. Fomites can probably be dismissed as a means for the spread of *N. meningitidis* because of the extreme sensitivity of these pathogens to drying.

In military barracks an attempt is made to reduce chances for the spread of upper respiratory infections by employing so-called head-to-foot sleeping, with bunks about $2\frac{1}{2}$ to 3 feet apart. Microbes expelled through talking, coughing, or sneezing of one individual must whiz over the feet of the man in the adjacent bunk before they find a target "once removed" that can inhale the expelled droplets.

Military statistics during World War II indicate that susceptibility of Negro troops to meningitis is about twice that of white soldiers. A number of plausible explanations have been put forth in an attempt to explain these significant differences. One theory proposed that Southern Negroes being sent to Northern camps, especially in late autumn or in winter, were not immunologically prepared for the requirements imposed on their bodies by the cold, damp, changeable climate. The longer the Negro troops were stationed up north, the less likely it would appear that they might fall heir to this particular disease.

Many of the unpleasant symptoms of meningitis arise from the toxemia generated by these fastidious bacteria. This is not a soluble toxin and it is thermostable at 100°C for 30 minutes, but the endotoxin is probably composed of at least two major fractions that are not equally resistant to heat.

Sulfadiazine is still the treatment of choice for this disease, both as a prophylactic measure to reduce the carrier rate and as a therapeutic measure once the symptoms put in their appearance. The injection of killed suspensions of monovalent or polyvalent vaccines does not seem to yield results sufficiently promising to warrant their use in any widespread immunization programs. Antisera are employed only when other chemotherapy cannot be tolerated or when the patient fails to respond to treatment.

All of the usual established precautions taken to protect personnel from any communicable respiratory infection must be carried out, and administration of prophylactic doses of sulfadiazine can remove at least part of the hazard involved.

ORGANISM: *Neisseria gonorrhoeae*

DISEASE: Gonorrhea

CHARACTERISTICS: Gram negative cocci 0.6 to 1.0 micron in diameter occurring singly and in pairs, the sides flattened where they are in contact. Nonsporing. Nonmotile. Aerobic to anaerobic. Optimum temperature is 37°C. Found only in infections of man.

Gonorrhea has already been discussed in the portion of Chapter 14 dealing with venereal diseases, and some rather startling statistics were presented as to the prevalence of this common disease. Morphologically the bacteria are practically indistinguishable from those involved in epidemic meningitis, but their biochemical reactions and their pathogenic effects on the body are quite different.

The name *gonorrhea* was introduced by Galen about A.D. 130, but if the written records of the Chinese and the Hebrews are interpreted correctly, the disease was not uncommon long before this date. Some authorities claim that gonorrhea is second only to tuberculosis among infections that give rise to serious aftereffects (sequelae) including conjunctivitis, septicemia, arthritis, osteomyelitis, endocarditis, and meningitis.

Although Neisser called these cells to the attention of the medical world in 1879, it was not until 1885 that Bumm succeeded in demonstrating their etiological relationship to the disease we know as gonorrhea. This he did by the use of human volunteers. *Bergey's Manual* spells the specific name *gonorrhoeae*, but most textbooks omit the last "o" in the spelling.

Microscopic examination of smears made from pus taken from acute cases reveals the typical coffee-bean-shaped gram negative diplococci within the leucocytes, but some of the microbes are also found extracellularly; this latter location becomes more pronounced in chronic cases of long standing. Like meningococci the gonococci have complex nutritional requirements, with chocolate agar (heated blood) one of the most widely used media for their cultivation. A moist atmosphere coupled with about 10 per cent added carbon dioxide are prerequisites for successful growth of *N. gonorrheae*, particularly on primary isolation.

Gonococci display a pronounced sensitivity to drying, heat, dyes, and chemicals (2% tincture of iodine, 0.5% Lysol, 0.5% phenol, 70% alcohol, 1:4000 silver nitrate, and just plain soap and warm water), but it has been reported that cells have remained viable in masses of dried pus for weeks. This may be somewhat unusual.

Some public health workers are of the opinion that less than 20 per cent of the cases of gonorrhea ever come to the attention of physicians, and thus are not reported in health statistics. This, then, becomes of primary concern in the problem of effective control. Too many laymen are trying to practice medicine on themselves and their acquaintances. Many individuals who have worked in hospitals or in clinics in the military service or in civilian life have learned just enough about sulfonamides and antibiotics to give them confidence in their own ability to diagnose and prescribe for some diseases, particularly the venereal diseases. This is a prime example of a little learning being a mighty dangerous thing, and without question a great deal of our present difficulties with drug-resistant bacteria stem from the practices of these pseudo-physicians who may gain confidence by what they consider to be a flush of successful "cures."

Penicillin has been a true wonder drug in its action on the gonococci, but its hoped-for panacea effect is showing definite indications of fading, and other antibiotics, including tetracyclines, are being employed to treat resistant and persistent cases. Drug therapy changes quickly in this era of widespread research, and one chemical that may be in vogue today may find itself standing at the post a few years hence while other drugs are rounding the far turn and running well.

Development of a satisfactory vaccine to build up an active immunity against gonorrhea has not been feasible. Little or no protection is afforded an individual by having an active case of the disease which manifests itself as a suppurative infection of the mucous surfaces and glandular structures of the urogenital tract of both men and women. In the acute stage of the infection a white to slightly yellow-colored pus is discharged from the genitalia, and untreated cases frequently terminate in sterility of the host. Scar tissue obstructs the fallopian tubes of the female and the vas deferens of the male by the formation of **strictures.** In males these contractions of the tissues may interfere with urination and surgical treatment may be required to correct the condition. Invasion of the body by the microbes with localization in joints (gonorrheal arthritis or rheumatism) and in heart valves occurs more frequently than most promiscuous individuals care to realize, resulting in painful and crippling diseases. Childless marriages too often are caused by previous gonorrheal infections of one or both partners.

Gonococci in the eyes (ophthalmia neonatorum) of newborn infants cause blindness. With an estimated ten million females in the child-bearing age afflicted with this venereal disease, the instillation of either silver nitrate solution (1%) or penicillin is required by most states to destroy the diplococci the infant may acquire as its head passes through the infected genital tract of the mother during delivery. This is called the Credé process in honor of Karl Credé, a professor of obstetrics in Leipzig, Germany. He introduced the use of silver nitrate in an attempt to halt the appalling number of cases of blindness in newborn, and the dramatic drop in the number of cases following the adoption of the Credé process attests to the significant contribution this obstetrician has made to human health.

Relatively asymptomatic female carriers may serve as undiagnosed reservoirs of infection, and cures in females are generally more difficult than is true in males. There is no such thing as a "safe" prostitute, and they represent the greatest potential sources of venereal disease infection. Gonorrhea is found all over the world, and unfortunately in recent years there has been a tendency for the age of individuals acquiring the disease to drop into the lower teenage brackets as sexual promiscuity becomes more widespread. Increased resistance of the gonococcus to once-effective doses of antibiotics is another great concern to public health authorities. Penicillin in doses of about 300,000 units administered within an hour after exposure has usually been found to prevent most infections, but once the clinical symptoms appear, it may require up to 1,200,000 units to effect a cure in most males if the bacteria are not resistant to the drug, and this is the uncontrolled factor.

When grown on chocolate agar the colonies of *N. gonorrheae* may be differentiated from saprophytic contaminants usually found in cultures made from urethral discharges by spraying or flooding the plate with a 1 per cent solution of dimethyl-para-phenylenediamine hydrochloride (oxidase reagent). *Neisseria* colonies, which liberate the enzyme **oxidase** turn first pink, then maroon, and finally black. If such colonies are fished from the chocolate agar surface while still in the pink stage, the gonococci will be found to be still viable and they can be cultivated on other media for further biochemical studies. Other bacteria may also produce oxidase, but an experienced technician can generally choose colonies typical of *Neisseria*, ignoring the colonies that have no significance in this case.

Great care must be exercised by nurses, physicians, and attendants when they handle articles soiled by persons infected with gonorrhea. Patients should be taught the means for preventing the spread of their own infection to their eyes through contaminated hands and the dissemination of virulent organisms to others about them. Laundry from these patients should be boiled before it is added to the family wash, and obviously individual towels, bedding, and clothes must be used by infected individuals. The average citizen knows little or nothing about microbes and their mode of spread, and for this reason instructions given to him must be simple and clear down to the most minute detail. If education of a patient was ever needed, it certainly is for those suffering from venereal diseases. Public ignorance, together with indifference, makes the battle to overcome gonorrhea an uphill struggle all the way. In public health work one cannot afford to give up when the battle is only partly won.

Rods

ORGANISMS: *Brucella melitensis, Br. abortus,* and *Br. suis*

DISEASES: Undulant fever in man and contagious abortion in certain lower animals

CHARACTERISTICS: Short gram negative ellipsoidal rods 0.5 by 0.5 to 2.0 microns in length, occurring singly, in pairs, and rarely in short chains. Encapsulated. Non-sporing. Nonmotile. Aerobic. Optimum temperature 37°C. Habitat is the milch goat (*caprine*), the milch cow (*bovine*), and the hog (*porcine*).

The generic designation of these pathogens honors Sir David Bruce, a British colonel, who in 1887 first recognized the organisms causing undulant fever in man when he examined the spleens of persons infected by organisms acquired through drinking contaminated goat's milk. A Danish veterinarian, Bang, described the *abortus* species in 1897, and in 1914 an American named Traum reported the *suis* type organism. The fact that all three of these microbes are closely related was revealed in 1918 in the United States by Alice Evans.

The following table indicates some of the reactions generally employed to separate the three species which morphologically are so similar, but the list is not meant to be complete. Growth on appropriate media containing selected concentrations of dyes varies between the species which have different sensitivities as indicated.

	Br. abortus	*Br. melitensis*	*Br. suis*
CO$_2$ required	+	−	−
H$_2$S produced	+	−	+
Basic fuchsin			
1:200	growth	growth	no growth
Crystal violet			
1:400	growth	growth	no growth
Pyronine			
1:8000	growth	growth	no growth
Thionine			
1:800	no growth	growth	growth

Members of the *Brucella* genus are interesting in that they produce one set of disease symptoms in lower animals, namely contagious abortion, while these same bacteria cause undulant fever in man who is susceptible to all three species. Prevalence of each type is related to geographical areas, with *Br. abortus* most frequently being encountered in dairy states, while the *suis* type is more prevalent in the corn belt. The latter organisms cause more severe symptoms in humans than either the more common *Br. abortus* or *Br. melitensis* which is rarer in the United States where fewer goats are raised. These distributions of types will naturally vary in other countries where relative numbers of cattle, pigs, and goats differ from those in our own country. The Island of Malta where Bruce carried out his studies was called *Melita* because of the fine honey (*mel*) found there, and this is how the caprine species of *Brucella* happened to acquire its name.

In addition to being a public health problem brucellosis is of great economic importance in the cattle industry, where an estimated annual monetary loss in excess of one hundred million dollars is incurred in the United States alone from loss of milk production and from abortions. Cattle are relatively resistant to infections with these gram negative pathogens during the first three to six months of their lives owing, undoubtedly, to a strong natural passive immunity, but these animals are most susceptible to infections during their first pregnancy. Organisms localize in the uterus, fetus, fetal membranes, lacteal ducts, and the udder which permits contamination of the milk, and udder infections may persist throughout the life of the animal. Bacterial invasion of the lymphatics is what presents the greatest potential hazard to slaughterhouse workers who may come in contact with massive numbers of aerosolized *Brucella*.

Because of the highly contagious nature of this disease, animals should be segregated and slaughtered as soon as brucellosis has been diagnosed. Humans contract the disease by ingestion of raw milk and unpasteurized dairy products; farmers and veterinarians face the additional risk of inhalation of droplets originating within infected animals. There is also evidence to support the contention that *Brucella* may pass through the skin either through minor cuts or through what appears to be intact skin. Symptoms of undulant fever vary so widely in humans that many cases probably are never recognized.

The incubation period in man may vary from 5 to 30 or more days with clinical symptoms including generalized aches and pains of muscles and joints, progressive weight loss, chills and night sweats, and a remittent daily fever. Symptoms may continue for from three to five days, then abate, only to return. The average duration of the disease is three months, but some chronic cases may persist for years—even decades. Since 1945 there have been over 4000 new cases reported annually in the United States, but some statisticians are convinced that the unreported and unrecognized cases could well increase this figure tenfold. Death rates run under 3 per cent. As the number of infected animals decreases, so should the number of human cases of undulant fever. This is demonstrated by the results of effective control measures instituted in New York State where the number of human infections fell from 138 in 1949 to only 10 in 1958—an encouraging trend.

Diagnosis of brucellosis in man may be accomplished through a number of tests, but the following four are perhaps the most commonly employed: isolation of the organisms from blood cultures, opsonocytophagic tests, agglutination reactions, and skin tests. Each of these will be described briefly.

BLOOD CULTURES

Blood cultures may be positive for *Brucella* one day and negative the next. For this reason a number of samples should be drawn at different times of the day and at various stages of the fever cycle on a number of successive days. Some of the most fruitful results have come from the use of liver infusion or media containing trypticase soy or tryptone peptones on primary isolation of *Brucella*. Blood cultures should not be considered to be negative until at least three weeks of incubation have elapsed; during this period streak plates can be prepared at intervals from the blood culture flasks to see if organisms have grown out.

OPSONOCYTOPHAGIC INDEX

This test is conducted by adding a suspension of the bacteria to anti-serum and leucocytes (or whole blood) in a test tube. After a suitable incubation period smears are prepared from this mixture and stained with appropriate dyes. The polymorphonuclear leucocytes are then examined for their numerical count of ingested organisms. A control tube consisting of a parallel preparation in which "normal" serum or blood is substituted for antiserum is used as a standard comparison. The **phagocytic index** is expressed as the average number of phagocytized bacteria per leucocyte in the test sample and in the control. The **opsonic index** is the ratio of the immune to the control phagocytic index. If, for example, the immune serum reveals an average of twenty-five organisms per leucocyte with only five bacteria in the control preparation, the opsonic index would be five (25 divided by 5). This figure represents the degree of resistance acquired against the invading organisms, and the findings in this particular test have some value when interpreted in the light of other determinations.

Definite phagocytosis in up to 40 per cent of the leucocytes is considered to represent an active infection, but when a figure over 40 per cent is reached, it is believed to denote immunity and probably some previous infection. Not all investigators subscribe to this conclusion, however.

AGGLUTINATION TESTS

When the blood serum of a patient is placed in contact with a saline suspension of test bacteria, if specific antibodies are present in the serum they will cause the suspended bacteria to adhere to one another until clumps become large enough to fall by the force of gravity to the bottom of the tube. Such a reaction is called **agglutination.** When the antibody (**agglutinin**) concentration (**titer**) exceeds 1:80, it is usually diagnostic. A titer of 1:80 means that the serum can be diluted 80 times and still cause clumping of the cells. In some active cases of brucellosis the titer may rise to as high as 1:5000.

SKIN TESTS

Bacteria and their products may sometimes be employed for detecting the presence of microbes within the body. The tuberculin test discussed earlier (p. 291) is one such reaction. A preparation called *brucellergen* may be used for a preliminary skin test for brucellosis, and *brucellin* may be employed for desensitization. These reactions may have some value in diagnostic procedures.

Treatment of undulant fever takes on many different forms. Good temporary results have been reported by using chlortetracycline, chloramphenicol, and oxytetracycline; unfortunately, relapses may run as high as 40 per cent. Streptomycin in combination with other drugs may be somewhat better than single drugs, but relapses still occur in a high percentage of cases. With great differences in resistance to drugs being displayed by members of the *Brucella* genus, there probably is some virtue in "shotgun therapy" in which the microbial target is sprayed with more than one chemical in anticipation that if one fails to inactivate the organism perhaps the second drug will be more effective. Although vaccines are of some prophylactic value in calves, their usefulness in treating humans must be questioned.

Undulant fever patients are not highly infectious unless there are draining lesions. In such cases the dressings are best incinerated, and body wastes (urine and feces) should be disinfected. *Brucella* have been reported to have remained viable for ten days in refrigerated milk, two months in roquefort cheese, and four months in refrigerated butter. Cold storage, therefore, would not appear to be the answer to freeing dairy products of these pathogenic bacteria, but we do know that proper pasteurization will make milk and its by-products safe for human consumption.

ORGANISM: *Bordetella pertussis*

DISEASE: Whooping cough

CHARACTERISTICS: Gram negative minute coccobacteria 0.2 to 0.3 by 1.0 micron, occurring singly, in pairs, and occasionally in short chains. Non-sporing. Non-motile. Aerobic. Optimum temperature between 35° and 37°C. Habitat: etiologically associated with whooping cough.

The specific name of these bacteria is derived from Latin and means "very severe cough." The generic designation honors Bordet, a Belgian scientist who made great contributions to our understanding of the disease. Until relatively recently these microbes were classified as members of the *Hemophilus* ("blood-loving") genus, but since the organisms do not require certain growth factors known as "X" and "V," *B. pertussis* has been removed from the *Hemophilus* group and has been placed in the genus *Bordetella*.

In 1906 Bordet and his colleague Gengou first observed the ovoid rods in stained smears made from material taken from a child suffering from whooping cough, but it was six years before they were able to cultivate the bacteria which have since been subjected to Koch's postulates to prove their etiology in whooping cough (pertussis). This disease may be separated into three periods of from two to three weeks each, the length of time varying with individuals.

Following an incubation period of from 7 to 14 days the *catarrhal* stage sets in with sneezing and coughing which might very well be mistaken for an ordinary cold, although the symptoms may also resemble those associated with measles or scarlet fever. This phase is followed by the *paroxysmal* stage which usually is the most easily recognized period of the disease. A series of explosive coughs come close together, with the air being pushed out of the lungs in such a manner that the cough is followed by a tell-tale "whoop" or forceful inspiration of air. The paroxysm may be accompanied by vomiting, cyanosis, and even hemorrhages of the eyes, nose, and sometimes the brain. Weakness brought on by loss of sleep and diminished appetite may predispose the patient to secondary infections leading to bronchopneumonia or deafness. *Convalescence,* the third stage in the disease, may vary widely both in length and in symptomatology.

While choking during a paroxysm is no doubt the immediate cause of death of some very young infants, bronchopneumonia caused by *B. pertussis* or other microbes exacts a much higher toll of lives. The younger the child the higher is the mortality rate which averages more than the combined totals of scarlet fever and measles. About 97 per cent of the deaths occur in youngsters under the age of five, but 70 per cent of these deaths are in those under the age of one year, although the latter group represents less than 10 per cent of the total number of cases involved. The second month of life exhibits the highest fatality rate from pertussis.

The most contagious period in a case of whooping cough occurs during the first few weeks, and recognized cases should therefore be compelled to remain away from school and its reservoir of susceptible hosts. Isolation of expelled bacteria, which lodge in the ciliated lining of the bronchi and trachea, may be accomplished by use of a "cough plate" held about five inches away from the patient's mouth during a paroxysm. The sprayed aerosols may contain great numbers of the etiological microorganisms. The medium of choice for such a test is the one originally proposed by Bordet and Gengou whose names the medium bears. It consists of glycerine-potato-blood agar, but instead of the usual 3 to 5 per cent blood added to most blood agar plates, B-G medium contains between 15 and 20 per cent blood, which appears to be necessary to support good growth of members of the *Bordetella* genus.

After incubation at 37°C for three or four days positive cough plates will reveal the presence of dome-shaped colonies resembling tiny droplets of mercury surrounded by slight zones of hemolysis. Other writers describe the colonies as looking like halves of gray pearls. Minute coccobacteria resembling *Hemophilus influenzae* in morphology can be observed on smears made from typical colonies after staining the preparation by Gram's technique, with alkaline methylene blue, dilute carbolfuchsin, or carbonated toluidine blue. It may be necessary to expose *Bordetella* cells to these dyes for longer periods than is customary for most bacteria if the pathogens are to be seen clearly under the oil immersion objective of a microscope. In addition to the cough plate procedure, nasopharyngeal swabs yield an even higher percentage of positive cultures on Bordet-Gengou medium, but sputum specimens are not, in general, satisfactory for such studies.

The peak of incidence for whooping cough, which appears in epidemic waves, is late winter and spring, with the low point being reached some time in summer. One attack of the disease generally protects most individuals from future infections, but if an adult contracts pertussis for a second time, it may be quite severe. This is not usually the case with children who suffer from a recurrence. There is no evidence that healthy carriers exist. Most cases are acquired from others who are in the catarrhal stage of the disease when enormous numbers of *Bordetella* may be expelled in a single explosive cough. Only measles and chickenpox (*Varicella*) appear to have a higher rate of communicability. Although the trend in morbidity has been downward since the introduction of vaccination and the use of antibiotics, statistics seem to indicate that whooping cough may be on the rise again.

Injection of *B. pertussis* vaccine together with diphtheria and tetanus toxoids has become a routine practice when infants reach the age of about three months. Polio virus is being incorporated as a fourth component of these vaccines, and investigators have suggested that the pertussis organisms may act as an adjuvant for the other antigens in the mixture. It is recognized that until an individual reaches a certain age, and this varies for different diseases, his body is incapable of manufacturing substantial amounts of antibody. But even though so-called serological maturity has not yet been attained by these youngsters, the little antibody response that does occur appears to justify the early injection. The degree of protection can be materially enhanced by booster doses as the baby gets older.

A certain amount of passive protection against whooping cough is conferred on the developing fetus by the mother, and attempts to jack up the concentration of these circulating substances through hyperimmunizing the mother during pregnancy have met with mixed success. Some research workers are of the firm opinion that injecting these antibodies directly into the newborn child affords a much greater degree of protection during the first few months after birth than can possibly be attained by using the mother as an intermediary.

Sulfonamides and penicillin are of little or no value in the treatment of whooping cough, but the administration of broad-spectrum antibiotics, including tetracycline, chlortetracycline, and chloramphenicol alone or in association with other drugs, produces encouraging results. Some of the clinical symptoms of pertussis remain in spite of antibiotic therapy, but the etiological bacteria disappear.

The use of convalescent sera or whole blood transfusions may prove decidedly helpful in severe cases of the disease, but the main value of antibiotic therapy lies in the area of diminishing the incidence of secondary infections through shortening the course of the disease. Whooping cough is not the threat that it was in years gone by, but it would be folly to let down our guard even for brief periods. The same precautions employed against any droplet-borne infections should be practiced by those who are engaged in the care and treatment of patients who have whooping cough.

ORGANISM: *Pasteurella pestis*

DISEASE: Plague

CHARACTERISTICS: Gram negative encapsulated rods 1.0 by 2.0 microns, occurring singly. Safety-pin and ringlike involution forms are common. Nonsporing. Nonmotile. Aerobic and facultative anaerobic. Optimum temperature between 25° and 30°C. Habitat: the causative organisms of plague in man and ground squirrels, rats, and other rodents.

These interesting microbes are named for Louis Pasteur in honor of his fundamental studies on the immunology of *P. avicida,* the etiological agent in fowl cholera. Many fascinating accounts have been compiled through the years describing the impact that plague has had on the course of human history, but it is difficult to know just when the disease was first recognized. The plague of the Philistines in 1320 B.C. may or may not have been the same disease that we call "plague" today, but the extensive epidemic (**pandemic**) of "black death" that raged from A.D. 1348 to 1349 and killed an estimated twenty-five million people in Europe (one-fourth of all the inhabitants) was unquestionably plague as we know it.

A number of severe outbreaks have occurred since then, including one in London in 1665 when 70,000 victims perished. Hong Kong was the target in 1893, and Bombay suffered an outbreak in 1896. More than ten million died between 1896 and 1918 in British India. Plague first reached our American shores in 1900 in San Francisco, and in the following half decade (1900–1951) there were 523 cases diagnosed in the United States with a mortality rate of about 65 per cent. The microbes undoubtedly arrived with fleas found on infected rats who had "hitchhiked" a boat ride from the Orient.

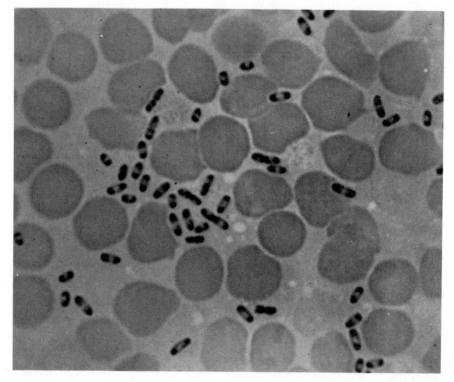

FIG. 15.7. *Pasteurella pestis.* (Courtesy Naval Biological Laboratory, School of Public Health, University of California.)

The typical bipolar-staining, sometimes pleomorphic rods were recognized almost simultaneously by the Swiss scientist, Yersin, and Kitasato, a Japanese investigator. *Pasteurella pestis* is not considered to be a particularly fastidious organism as far as its growth requirements are concerned. It grows slowly on standard nutrient agar, but its cultivation may be enhanced on blood-containing media. Hemolysis is absent. Old broth cultures overlaid with sterile oil will show a characteristic streamer-type effect, somewhat similar to stalactites, suspended from the surface pellicle.

Curiously enough the optimum temperature for growth of *P. pestis* is well below that of the human body. In fact, the cells may grow up to five times as rapidly at 28° as at 37°C.

Susceptible animals (in addition to man) include rats and guinea pigs which die within two to five days after inoculation. Postmortem examination reveals pleural effusion and a congested spleen and liver. Because of the high levels of hazard involved in handling cultures and infected tissues from individuals or experimental animals, workers are warned to take superprecautionary measures to prevent the creation of aerosols. Efficient masks, rubber gloves free of defects, and complete surgical-type gowns must be worn. Accidental laboratory infections in Vienna in 1898 put Koch's postulates to the test, and his germ theory of disease came through with flying colors, much to the sorrow of the unfortunate victims.

Plague is a disease primarily of rats and other rodents, with the bacteria multiplying within the digestive tract of the rat flea (*Xenopsylla cheopis*) which regurgitates the cells when it bites a victim. These fleas are responsible for the spread of plague among rodents and from infected rodents to man. As many as 100 million *P. pestis* cells may be found per milliliter of blood of an infected rat. Evidence points to the fact that when man is bitten by an infected flea, the flea regurgitates and defecates on the site, and through rubbing and scratching the irritation man drives the pathogenic microbes into the skin lesion, from which the bacteria spread throughout the body at an alarming rate.

In man plague can assume three distinct forms: *bubonic* (glandular), *pneumonic,* and *septicemic.* In bubonic plague the fleas generally bite the lower extremities of man and the bacteria gain entrance to the lymphatics, causing an enlargement of the nodes in the groin termed **buboes.** Abscess formation and necrosis occur followed by an escape of the microbes from the area to other parts of the body through the bloodstream. During the first three days of the disease up to 75 per cent of the blood cultures may be positive. Secondary foci of infection then become established in the spleen, lungs, and meninges of the victim.

Massive invasion of the bloodstream with its accompanying hemorrhages in the skin and mucous membranes is termed septicemic plague. The dark appearance of these spots gave rise to the term "black death."

The pneumonic type of plague is practically 100 per cent fatal. It may be acquired directly through droplet infection or as a secondary phase in the glandular type of the disease. When the pneumonic infection struck Manchuria in 1910–1912, apparently every single one of the 60,000 infected individuals died. When aerosols are breathed into the lungs the virulent microorganisms multiply rapidly and quickly invade the lymphatics. The entire lung becomes hemorrhagic, terminating in suffocation of the individual. Just prior to death cyanosis becomes extreme and it contributes to the symptomatology that helped to give this disease its name of black death.

History reveals that just before any massive human outbreaks of plague, extensive epidemics had taken place in the rat population, and the two epidemic waves tended to overlap one another. When rats die and their bodies cool off, fleas seek new warm hosts, and man serves this function very well. The black rat is the most dangerous insofar as plague is concerned, since it prefers to nest in the upper floors of houses, and when the infected rats die the houses become invaded with hungry infected fleas. Epidemiologists theorize that one reason (possibly the primary reason) why the plague of the Middle Ages died out in Europe was a shift in the rodent population to the more vicious gray rat that practically wiped out the black rats. Gray rats do not tend to live in human habitations.

Control measures for plague include the eradication of rats and rodents that can harbor infected fleas. Not only are rats a health menace, but they represent a significant economic drain on a community. It is estimated that the number of rats in the world far exceeds that of the human population, and even at a cost of only a few cents a day (it is probably higher) the bill to feed these rats is staggering. The liberal use of DDT to kill fleas on man and on rodents is another line of attack. As fleas develop a resistance to DDT, other compounds must be found to destroy the fleas. Strict enforcement of regulations at ports where ships arrive from countries in which these diseases are endemic can help to prevent rodents from stepping on our shores. Special baffle plates on ropes used to tie boats to the dock can block foreign rats that attempt to "jump ship." Early recognition and treatment of cases is imperative. Finally, aggressive immunization programs can help to reduce the hazard.

During World War II U.S. military troops were given prophylactic vaccinations with formalin-killed suspensions of *P. pestis* (about two billion cells per ml). Anyone whose duties compel him to be in areas of the world where plague is endemic should be actively immunized against this severe disease, with booster doses administered at four- to six-month intervals since the protection, as measured by antibody titer, is not as long-lasting as that of some of the other vaccines, including typhoid and cholera. Dead rats should be avoided like the plague!

Medical personnel working with patients suffering from this highly contagious disease should employ great precaution to protect themselves from infections. One careless mistake can prove fatal. Clothing taken from patients should be placed in an air-tight bag and treated to kill all of the fleas. Fomites coming in direct or indirect contact with a patient must always be treated with suspicion. In private homes the attack must be a vigorous one aimed at elimination of rats and free-lance fleas through the use of traps, gas, poison bait, and insecticides. All body wastes and discharges from patients must be disposed of in a sanitary manner. Only by adherence to the strictest type of vigilance can epidemics be kept in check. It is easy to fall victim to plague during a rampaging outbreak, but it takes skill and understanding to escape this horrible death. The major areas of the world where *P. pestis* must be considered to be endemic and therefore has the potential to leap from a smouldering situation to a raging fire include: Argentina, Bolivia, Brazil, Burma, China, Hawaii, India, Manchuria, Peru, Russia, and the western United States.

Sulfadiazine and streptomycin appear to be the drugs of choice for treating cases of plague, and they may be given alternately in series. In critical cases tetracycline, chloramphenicol, and even rabbit antiserum may be employed to supplement the usually preferred drugs. A person who is fortunate enough to recover from an infection with *P. pestis* may be endowed with a lifelong immunity to the disease.

Laboratory confirmation consists of isolating from pus or sputum gram negative rods displaying decided bipolar staining, and the pure cultures must then be subjected to animal tests and biochemical reactions. Agglutination of the cells by homologous antiserum will offer additional confirmation of plague.

ORGANISM: *Pasteurella tularensis*

DISEASE: Tularemia (rabbit or deerfly fever)

CHARACTERISTICS: Gram negative pleomorphic bacteria occurring as cocci and bizarre-shaped rods 0.2 by 0.2 to 0.7 micron in singles. Non-sporing. Non-motile. May display bipolar staining. Aerobic. No growth anaerobically. Optimum temperature 37°C. Survives best at low temperature, even at minus 70° C. Habitat: the cause of tularemia in man; transmitted from wild animals to man by blood-sucking insects, by contact with infected animals, or by drinking water contaminated by infected animals.

The specific name of this pathogen is derived from Tulare County in California where the disease was originally observed in 1911. It is an affliction primarily of rabbits, but it may also be found in rodents and birds. Man happens to be an accidental host. Between 2000 and 3000 human cases of tularemia are reported each year in the United States, primarily in the western half of the country, although cases have been found in 49 of the 50 states. The mortality rate rarely exceeds 5 per cent in any one year.

Isolation and identification of the etiological organism were accomplished in 1912 by McCoy and Chapin who worked with ground squirrels afflicted with a plaguelike disease, but it was not until 1919 that Francis provided the fundamental knowledge that linked these findings in animals to human infections. He named the human infection *tularemia* which combines the name of the area where the disease was discovered and the clinical symptoms of septicemia. When examined under the oil immersion objective the cells in young cultures are found to be extremely pleomorphic: dumb-bells, L-shapes, knobs, coccoid bodies, and even some forms resembling spermatozoa with pseudoflagella. These bizarre shapes are somewhat less pronounced in older cultures.

Pasteurella tularensis does not grow on standard nutrient agar or in nutrient broth; it requires a richer diet consisting of blood-glucose-cystine (or cysteine) to support its growth, and in this regard *tularensis* differs sharply from other species in the genus *Pasteurella*. These pathogens are not particularly hardy to changes in the environment, although one report states that they survived for two years in a refrigerated infected rabbit. Frequent transfer—once every three to four days—may be necessary to maintain viable cultures. Lyophilization, when properly carried out, will apparently maintain them for several years.

Many taxonomists are of the opinion that tularemia organisms are misplaced in the classification scheme. The British workers feel they are more like members of the *Brucella* genus in their characteristics, and have classified them as such. *Pasteurella tularensis* differs from other bacteria in that budding and filament formation take place in addition to the customary binary fission. In this they resemble members of the pleuropneumonia group of microbes.

More than 90 per cent of human cases of tularemia in the United States are caused by infected wild rabbits. Domestic rabbits have never been found to be naturally infected, nor has man-to-man infection ever been shown to occur. At least thirty forms of wild life harbor *P. tularensis,* and the disease may be transmitted to man by blood-sucking fleas, lice, ticks, mosquitoes, and flies. *Dermacentor andersoni* is an important vector, since that tick can remain infected over the winter months and pass the organisms on to offspring, thus maintaining a constant reservoir of infection. In parts of our country the deerfly, *Chrysops discalis,* serves as another important vector, as does the mosquito *Aedes cinereus.*

Bites of cats, dogs, and even nonpoisonous snakes who have come in contact with or have fed on the carcasses of animals that have died from tularemia may also be responsible for cases of this disease in man. Drinking water contaminated by infected beavers has been linked with still other outbreaks. Well-documented cases show that undercooked contaminated meat, especially from rabbits, has also caused infections. Hunters, butchers, and housewives handling carcasses of wild animals may be exposed to infection if the animals are contaminated with *P. tularensis,* since the microorganisms may be able to penetrate unbroken skin.

The incubation period for tularemia varies from one to ten days before a papule forms at the site of the infection. Chills, fever, severe headache, and muscular pains are typical symptoms, but since these reactions are characteristic of a number of diseases, early exact diagnosis may be extremely difficult.

Ulceroglandular type of tularemia is the most prevalent form contracted through touching infected tissues or fluids. Sick animals should, therefore, not be handled unless protective gloves are worn. Hunters would be wise to heed this warning and not handle rabbits that appear to have been sick before they were trapped or shot.

The papule, generally found on the hands, progresses to an ulcer, and this is followed by the appearance of painful and swollen satellite lymph nodes which may eventually discharge a purulent material, but the prognosis for this type of tularemia is favorable if the disease is recognized early and treatment promptly instituted.

Should aerosols containing *P. tularensis* from infected animals or from laboratory cultures get into a person's eyes, ulcers develop on the eyelids with subsequent involvement of cervical glands. This type of infection is called *oculoglandular,* and, again, if it is recognized and treated properly the prognosis for the patient is good.

Should the etiological agent be ingested the disease symptoms resemble in many respects the reactions associated with typhoid fever, and for this reason it is referred to as the *typhoidal* type of tularemia. A septicemia generally follows, but attempts to culture *Pasteurella* from the blood of such patients may not be too successful. Clinical material injected into guinea pigs will usually result in the formation of distinct lesions in the animal's liver, spleen, and lungs from which the pathogenic bacteria can be cultivated on appropriate media.

Streptomycin has been found to be the antibiotic of choice for therapy, with chlortetracycline showing promise. Sulfonamides do not appear to be of any particular value in treatment of active cases. Recovery from tularemia generally imparts a lifelong immunity to the disease, but several documented cases report repeated laboratory infections in laboratory workers within a few years following an original infection.

ORGANISM: *Pseudomonas aeruginosa*

DISEASE: Formation of blue-green pus

CHARACTERISTICS: Gram negative rods 0.5 to 0.6 by 1.5 microns, occurring singly, in pairs, and in short chains. Non-sporing. Motile, possessing one to three polar flagella. Aerobic, facultative. Optimum temperature 37°C. Generally hemolytic. Cause of various human and animal lesions. Found in polluted water and in sewage.

Bergey's Manual (1957) lists 149 different species of *Pseudomonas,* but from the standpoint of human disease we shall be concerned only with *Ps. aeruginosa* which was first isolated in pure culture by Gessard in 1882. This genus is characterized by water-soluble pigments produced by the cells, and the colors diffuse into the adjacent medium. These pigments include *pyocyanine* (bluish-green), *pyorubin* (red), and *fluorescein* (yellowish-green fluorescent pigment), but some 4 per cent of the species produce no detectable colors.

Pseudomonas aeruginosa is an aggressive secondary invader (or opportunist) whose importance in medicine has mounted sharply since the advent of sulfonamides and antibiotics. Even though the cells are non-sporing and may be inactivated by an exposure to 55°C for one hour, they are, nevertheless, relatively resistant to the usual antimicrobial agents, particularly antibiotics. Polymyxin B appears to be the most effective drug for therapy, but neomycin, streptomycin, and oxytetracycline also show some promise.

Long before penicillin got off the launching pad investigators had speculated about the possibility of harnessing the antagonistic properties of selected microbes in the treatment of bacterial diseases, and members of the *Pseudomonas* genus were seriously considered as possibilities. Emmerich and Low reported in 1899 that a by-product called **pyocyanase** displayed significant antagonistic action on a number of bacteria *in vitro,* but the extreme toxicity of this material eliminated its possible use *in vivo* and the matter was dropped. Perhaps part of the aggressiveness of *Ps. aeruginosa* can be attributed to pyocyanase which may help to eliminate some of the microbial competitors in a mixed wound.

These gram negative bacteria which are generally considered to be common saprophytes may be associated with or may even be the primary cause of conjunctivitis, otitis media, enteritis in infants, infections following extensive burns, septicemia, pneumonia, endocarditis, mastitis in cows, a fatal disease in poultry, and leaf rot in tobacco and lettuce. Unfortunately, *Pseudomonas* infections appear to be on the rise. Apparently with competition being reduced in mixed infections through antibiotic therapy, members of the *Pseudomonas* group are becoming more prevalent, and their stubbornness in the face of accepted treatment techniques is of growing concern to physicians.

Eye infections caused by *Pseudomonas* may have as serious consequences as those caused by the gonococcus which frequently leads to blindness. Rubbing the eyes with contaminated hands or swimming in bodies of polluted water may be responsible for initiating such pathological conditions. Swimming in stagnant pools where rats and other animals have discharged their wastes may account for the rash of middle ear infections that seem to be a reliable harbinger of spring or early summer when the call of the "ole swimming hole" becomes strong for the young in heart. Unfortunately some cases of middle ear infection may become chronic when antibiotic-resistant strains of microorganisms are encountered.

Urinary tract involvement with species of *Pseudomonas* also appears to be on the increase, and some of these cases display strong resistance to chemotherapy. Extensive burns often become infected with these gram negative bacteria that seem to thrive on dead skin and the underlying tissues. Should septicemia develop—and some clinicians feel that *Pseudomonas* infections could well surpass staphylococci in this regard—foci of infection may become established in the lungs, resulting in pneumonia, or in the heart, causing endocarditis.

The usual precautions taken by personnel in handling contaminated dressings from any wound must be practiced with materials from infections caused by *Pseudomonas,* and extra care is advised when it comes to disinfecting hands after working with or near patients who have blue-green pus infections.

ORGANISM: *Proteus vulgaris*

DISEASES: Abscesses and other infections of the urinary tract, middle ear, and wounds

CHARACTERISTICS: Gram negative pleomorphic rods 0.5 to 1.0 by 3.0 microns, occurring singly, in pairs, and frequently in long chains. Actively motile by peritrichous flagella. Aerobic, facultative anaerobic. Optimum temperature 37°C. Pathogenic for fish, dogs, guinea pigs, mice, and man. Habitat is putrefying material.

Proteus vulgaris organisms were first isolated by Hauser in 1885 from sewage and decomposing matter; *Bergey's Manual* (1957) lists five species. Proteus was an ocean god who took many shapes, and *vulgaris* means "common." The description fits this particular organism rather well. Many of the previous statements made about *Pseudomonas* species and the problems they are creating in medicine since the introduction of wonder drugs hold true for members of the *Proteus* group and need not be reiterated in detail. It might be stated, however, that *Proteus* probably ranks second only to *E. coli* as the cause of cystitis, and patients undergoing prolonged treatment with antibiotics are frequently found to be harboring greater numbers of *Proteus* organisms in their stools than was true prior to antibiotic therapy.

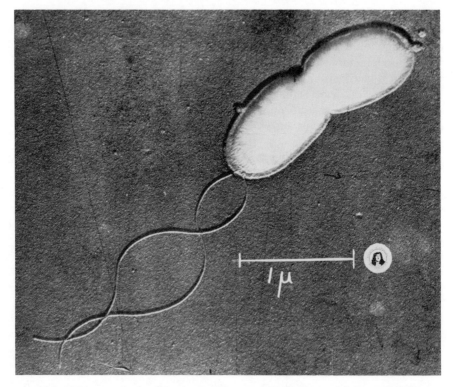

FIG. 15.8.   Electron shadowed micrograph of *Pseudomonas* species. (LS-275 Courtesy American Society for Microbiology.)

Motility of these bacteria appears to be encouraged considerably when cultures are incubated at about 25 to 30°C rather than at 37°C, which is considered to be optimum for most rapid growth of these cells. Identification of *Proteus vulgaris* colonies as they develop on moist agar surfaces is frequently aided by the appearance of a characteristic film or spreading type of growth, called a **swarming reaction,** which generally appears as ripples or distinct waves of bacterial growth. The spreading phenomenon is caused by the pronounced extension of the margin of colonies by cells swimming out into the adjacent moisture. The exact explanation of why the growth appears in waves is not clear in view of the fact that the entire surface of the plate may appear to be equally moist. On some plates the organism may exhibit a bluish-gray confluent growth. The swarming tendency of these cultures poses a number of problems for clinical bacteriologists trying to isolate minority bacteria in mixed cultures that are contaminated with *Proteus,* but techniques have been devised to minimize, or in some cases to prevent, the overgrowth of plates by these microorganisms.

Discrete colonies are more likely to develop when agar plates are incubated at temperatures somewhat above 37°C. Part of this alteration in colony form may be attributed to the drying effect such elevated temperatures might exert on the surface of the culture media. Cultivating *Proteus* on media in which the agar concentration has been raised from the customary 1.5 or 2 per cent to about 5 per cent also retards or eliminates the swarming effect, as will growing the organisms on eosine methylene blue milk or desoxycholate agar. The addition of a small quantity of chloral hydrate ("knockout drops") to agar-containing media serves a similar function. Should one desire to isolate streptococci from a *Proteus*-containing mixture, the addition of 0.01 per cent sodium azide to the medium will retard the growth of gram negative bacteria, including *Proteus,* permitting the gram positive microorganisms to flourish. This then becomes a **selective medium.**

Flagellated actively growing cells are referred to as organisms of the *H-type,* derived from the German word **Hauch,** meaning a film or veil. When a nonflagellated *Proteus* grows on an agar surface no swarming effect occurs and the colonies develop as small, rounded, discrete growths known as *O-type (ohne Hauch,* "without film"). In serology an "H" antigen refers to the flagella, whereas an "O" antigen means the somatic or body portion of the organism.

One of the characteristic physiological reactions of *Proteus* that sets it apart from other gram negative rods that are also able to attack glucose with the formation of acid and gas is the ability of *Proteus* to break down urea with the production of ammonia. When phenol red is added as an indicator, if the enzyme urease is active in a tube of urea broth it will liberate ammonia and the medium will turn a red color as the pH of the medium rises to the alkaline side of neutrality.

An interesting heterogenetic antigen exists in members of the *Proteus* genus linking these cells with certain rickettsiae. Weil and Felix isolated from a typhus fever patient a particular culture designated as *Proteus OX-19,* and even though *Proteus* has no known clinical relationship to typhus fever which has a rickettsial etiology, these two types of microorganisms possess a common antigen or antigens capable of being detected through agglutination reactions. Blood serum from a typhus fever patient is capable of causing a saline suspension of *Proteus OX-19* cells to clump, or agglutinate. Since antibodies react only with their specific antigens, the common relationship can be detected. Such a test affords the physician a reliable method for the laboratory diagnosis of typhus fever. Two additional strains designated *Proteus OX-2* and *OX-K* also bear some relationship to rickettsiae-causing diseases other than typhus fever. The following table presents the agglutination reactions one might expect with these three species of *Proteus* and the diseases listed. A four plus reading indicates a strong reaction; weaker reactions are shown by proportionately fewer plus signs.

Rickettsial Disease	Proteus OX-19	Proteus OX-2	Proteus OX-K
Typhus fever	++++	+	negative
Rocky Mountain spotted fever	++	++	?
Tsutsugamushi disease (Scrub typhus)	?	negative	++++
"Q" fever	negative	negative	negative

When the above *in vitro* tests are expanded to include the **complement fixation reaction** (which will be discussed in Chapter 19), the physician has at his command additional confirmation of his clinical findings in diagnosing diseases of rickettsial origin.

ORGANISM: *Shigella* species

DISEASE: Bacterial dysentery

CHARACTERISTICS: Gram negative rods, 0.4 to 0.6 by 1.0 to 3.0 microns, occurring singly. Non-sporing. Nonmotile. Aerobic, facultative anaerobic. Optimum temperature 37°C. Habitat: found in the feces of infected individuals.

Dysentery has been a scourge throughout history in both military and civilian populations. The genus *Shigella* derives its name from the Japanese investigator, Shiga, who first discovered these organisms in 1898. Dysentery should be thought of as a clinical entity causing inflammation of the lower bowel as the result of action by bacteria, protozoa, and in all likelihood by filterable agents such as viruses. Although a number of different types of bacteria may be implicated, members of the *Shigella* group are the most frequent offenders. They cause painful abdominal cramps; severe diarrhea with blood, mucus, and pus in the stools; and ulceration of the large intestine.

Eight distinct species of *Shigella* are described, although it should be recognized that there are a number of subgroups within species differing from one another in antigenic makeup. These microbes are not fastidious in their growth requirements, but their recognition may be made easier by cultivating clinical material on selective and differential media including S.S. (*Salmonella-Shigella*) agar, desoxycholate-citrate agar, endo agar, and E.M.B. (eosine-methylene blue) agar.

Wherever sanitation standards are low, the incidence of dysentery can be expected to be high. Countries located in warmer climates have a much higher case rate than do those in temperate climates where the disease is more or less seasonal, reaching a peak during the summer months. The human carrier and missed cases account for the greatest reservoir of infection. Dissemination of organisms is through the stools of infected individuals either directly or by fomites, or through living agents such as flies, roaches, and other vermin. Symptoms may vary from mild diarrhea to acute dysentery with prostration and death. Polluted water may be responsible for some cases, but statistics seem to indicate that more typhoid than dysentery is spread through this vehicle. The really serious threat to public health comes from carriers, many of whom are unaware of their carrier state, and from improper disposal of wastes from infected individuals. The rise in dysentery in temperate climates may be correlated with the population of flies, since their filthy living habits lead them to human excrement that is not adequately covered. Flies and other vermin can carry these enteric pathogens on their hairy bodies to kitchens where food is exposed, and this type of transmission naturally is seasonal.

Institutions, particularly those housing the mentally ill, frequently have more than their share of dysentery outbreaks with the convalescent carrier commonly serving as the culprit. While most carriers remain so for only a matter of a few weeks, there are reported cases where individuals have been shown to excrete *Shigella* for as long as four years after recovery from an attack of the disease.

Epidemic outbreaks of dysentery are a constant threat in military forces where only through rigid control can catastrophic epidemics be avoided. Many a battle has been won not by enemy hardware, but by microbes only 1/25,000 of an inch long. The mortality rate is generally low but the disability is so great that entire armies have been rendered ineffective. General Montgomery's forces at El Alamein appear to have been given a significant assist by dysentery running rampant at the time in the Italian and German armies. Microbes can serve as powerful allies or merciless enemies. How much deliberate bacterial warfare has been waged in armed conflicts is difficult to assess, but oftentimes carelessness in sanitation practices on the part of soldiers is just as effective a boomerang as enemy sabotage with living microbial agents or attacks with bullets and shells.

As was stated previously in this book, World War II was the first armed conflict where disease caused fewer casualties than enemy action. Man may be learning more about sanitation but he has a long way to go before he learns to prevent war with all of its horrible consequences.

Shigella species are classified into two major groupings based upon fermentation of mannitol, and the distinction has considerable significance insofar as severity of symptoms is concerned. *Shigella shigae* was the first species isolated by Shiga; two years later Kruse isolated the same organism from a case in Germany. This species is unable to ferment mannitol, and it produces a much more severe type of dysentery with a higher mortality rate than is true of the species that do attack mannitol.

Shigella shigae produces two major types of poisons, one an endotoxin that is composed of a polysaccharide-lipid-polypeptide that acts on the digestive tract, and the other a true soluble exotoxin that has an affinity for nerve tissue (neurotoxin) and causes paralysis. In many respects this exotoxin resembles that liberated by *C. diphtheriae*. This type of dysentery has the highest incidence in Asia (India, Japan, and China) and is rarely encountered in the United States.

The two other non-mannitol fermenters are *Sh. parashigae* and *Sh. ambigua* which differ from *Sh. shigae* immunologically and in certain biochemical reactions. They tend not to produce symptoms as severe.

The mannitol-fermenting *Shigellae* include *Sh. flexneri* (also known as *paradysenteriae*) which was originally discovered by Flexner in the Philippines but which has since been encountered practically all over the world. This species produces an endotoxin but no soluble toxin. *Shigella boydii*, another mannitol fermenter, closely resembles *Sh. flexneri* biochemically, but its antigenic makeup is distinct. It too is distributed throughout the world and is composed of a number of subgroups varying in antigenic composition.

There is also a group of slow lactose-fermenting species called *Sh. sonnei* discovered in 1904 by Duval who found that up to ten days may be required for evidence of fermentation of this sugar. Since laboratories customarily do not incubate subcultures for this long a period, many cases reported as *Sh. flexneri* might well have been *sonnei* species. A number of other dysentery bacteria have been described, and eventually the classification of these microbes may have to undergo revision.

The incubation period for bacillary dysentery is approximately 48 hours, and the disease may be extremely acute with prostration or it may run a chronic course. Blood cultures are not too helpful in diagnosis since a bacteremia is not characteristic of this disease, but stools will routinely yield positive results. In fact, in severe cases *Shigellae* appear to be the only bacteria present. Stools or material recovered on rectal swabs are generally streaked on one or more selective media including *Salmonella-Shigella* agar (S.S. agar), desoxycholate-citrate agar, endo agar, or eosine-methylene blue agar (E.M.B.). Characteristic colonies are fished from these plates and are subjected to a series of biochemical tests which the reader can find listed in *Bergey's Manual*. The use of enrichment media, including tetrathionate broth, is recommended to increase the number of positive cultures. Serological confirmation may be necessary, employing specific antisera in agglutination tests. The antibody titer may rise markedly in individuals suffering with an acute case of dysentery, and this finding also helps in determining the specific cause of the disease.

Dysentery is a disease that must be combatted without letup. As recently as 1945 there were over 33,000 cases and 400 deaths reported in the United States where we like to believe standards of sanitation are higher than in many areas of the world. Man is the sole source of these organisms. The disease may be reproduced in monkeys, but these animals do not contract the disease naturally and they possess such a high degree of resistance to this type of infection that large doses must be employed to induce clinical symptoms. Control measures, therefore, must be focused on breaking the chain of events that permit dissemination of enteric pathogens from infected individuals or from carriers to other persons. One study in Georgia and New Mexico revealed that for every recognized case of dysentery there were over nine convalescent carriers. Only two out of 380 carriers investigated were under any medical supervision. When one considers how few individuals have even the haziest concept of what microbes are and their modes of action and means for spread, the potential sources of infection become frightening. We might well marvel that the disease is not *more* prevalent.

Fatality rates are correlated with the species implicated, but *Sh. shigae* may kill up to 20 per cent of the patients in any given outbreak in Asia. The mortality rate drops to about one-tenth this number in the United States where other less powerful bacteria are involved and many of these are cases of dysentery in very young children. Scrupulous cleanliness, particularly on the part of food handlers, when coupled with pasteurization of dairy products and chlorination of water supplies have proven to be effective weapons in the never-ending struggle by health authorities to keep dysentery from a disastrous rampage.

Shigella may resist contact with 0.5 per cent phenol for up to five hours, according to some reports, and the organisms may remain viable for as long as six months in tap water, from two to five months in sea water, and up to two months in ice.

In general, sulfonamides are effective for chemotherapy, but resistant strains of *Shigella* do exist and must be attacked with such antibiotics as streptomycin, chloramphenicol, and the tetracyclines. Penicillin fails to be effective in the treatment of bacterial dysentery. Immunity through vaccination is not feasible in that these bacteria are extremely toxic even in small doses and they do not appear to serve as useful antigens for stimulating significant antibody production.

ORGANISM: *Salmonella* species

DISEASE: Gastroenteritis and enteric fever in man

CHARACTERISTICS: Gram negative rods 0.5 to 0.7 by 2.0 to 3.0 microns, occurring singly. Motile by peritrichous flagella. Non-sporing. Aerobic, facultative anaerobic. Optimum temperature 37°C. A natural pathogen for man, causing enteric fever. Some species pathogenic for lower animals including reptiles, birds, and mammals.

The generic name honors D. E. Salmon, an American bacteriologist and former head of the U.S. Public Health Service. He isolated the first member of the group in 1885 from a case of hog cholera. Species are named for their discoverers (*S. schottmulleri*), for patients (*S. thompson*), for specific diseases (*S. cholerasuis*), or, as has been true in later years, for places where the particular species was originally isolated (*S. hartford, S. california, S. panama,* etc.). *Bergey's Manual* (1957) lists nearly 250 different species differing from each other in antigenic makeup in the *O,* or somatic fraction, and in the *H,* or flagellar components. This scheme was originally proposed by Kauffman and White, and it has been further developed and expanded through the efforts of Edwards, Ewing, and others. Although morphology and biochemical reactions tend to bring these species together, the heart of classification of the *Salmonella* group is based upon serological findings through antigenic analyses. The present scheme is the result of an agreement by a group of international experts who in 1955 published the *Kauffmann-White Schema* that has since become the standard reference work in the field.

This group of organisms may manifest its presence by producing paratyphoid fever, food infections, or salmonellosis of animals. Paratyphoid may be caused by any number of species, and food infection is frequently from animal sources or carriers. Salmonellosis is reflected in such diseases as pullorum of chickens, hog cholera, or contagious abortion of horses and sheep.

Symptoms of *Salmonella* infection may vary from mild enteritis to fatal septicemia, and unfortunately we have a plentiful supply of healthy carriers, walking cases, and infected rodents serving as reservoirs of potential infection.

For many years the typhoid organism was known as *Eberthella typhosa* after Eberth who in 1880 found the organisms in the mesentery and the spleen of infected individuals. Since it was found to be antigenically related to members of the *Salmonella* group, however, this pathogen has been placed in the latter group by taxonomists, in spite of the objections of some investigators who feel that differences in certain biochemical reactions are sufficiently important to exclude the typhoid organism as a *Salmonella* species. For example, *S. typhosa* fails to produce gas in glucose whereas other *Salmonellae* produce both acid and gas from the breakdown of glucose. Lactose, sucrose, and salicin are not fermented by members of the group. The **incubation period** for typhoid fever is generally 10 to 14 days.

These bacteria produce a potent endotoxin but no demonstrable exotoxin. When the microbes are taken into the digestive tract by way of contaminated food or drink, the bacteria multiply rapidly within the intestines. Clinical symptoms may appear within 3 to 36 hours after intake, but the most common incubation period is 12 to 24 hours, although delays beyond this limit may occur. The characteristics of *Salmonella* food infection are not unlike those of dysentery with severe abdominal cramps and painful evacuations with blood, mucus, and pus in the unformed stools. Some types of this disease may be typhoidal in character, with septicemia and high fever which may persist with or without gastrointestinal symptoms. The death rate in this more severe type of paratyphoid fever may run as high as 25 per cent with such species as *S. paratyphi A*, *S. schottmulleri* (paratyphoid B), *S. hirschfeldii* (paratyphoid C), or *S. typhimurium* (mouse typhoid) being implicated. Whenever these microbes get into the bloodstream, foci of infection frequently become established in susceptible areas of the body causing endocarditis, meningitis, pneumonia, and abscesses.

The wide distribution of human carriers makes control of this disease rather difficult, and the same precautions outlined for the control of dysentery hold true for the *Salmonella* species. Public health authorities should continue to concentrate their efforts in the area of early detection of carriers and development of a program to educate these individuals as to their potential danger to others unless they practice habits of good sanitation. Examinations of food handlers, particularly tests involving periodic bacteriological studies of stool specimens, must be unrelenting, especially since the turnover of personnel in food establishments tends to be high.

Food may also become contaminated by infected mice, rats, roaches, and flies, and drinking water may contain excreta of infected rodents. Dried eggs have been implicated in many outbreaks of *Salmonella* food infection, with rodents responsible in many instances. Since dried eggs are frequently used in the preparation of salad dressings and desserts without sufficient heating to inactivate the pathogens, it is of paramount importance that the dried eggs be protected from contamination.

The incidence of salmonellosis in dogs has been described as being as high as 15 per cent, and this fruitful source of infection could have a greater significance for public health than has been realized up to this point. Bacillary white diarrhea in chicks caused by *S. pullorum* is of extreme importance in the poultry industry, and if pullorum is allowed to go unchecked, the high mortality rate might easily bankrupt a poultry farmer. The bacteria localize in the liver, but especially in the ovaries through which the disease is transmitted to the developing chicks. People who enjoy raw eggs, either by sucking the contents directly through holes in the shell or by consuming undercooked eggs, may be inviting infection with a member of the *Salmonella* group.

Diseases caused by *Salmonella* species are known as paratyphoid (typhoid-like) fevers, but in general they are considerably milder. Fatal paratyphoid cases do occur, however. Nursing precautions are essentially the same for all enteric fevers, with extreme care being taken to dispose of body wastes as promptly as possible and in a proper manner. The incubation period for paratyphoid may extend up to ten days, but it is usually nearer 48 hours. Typhoid fever generally takes a week to ten days before the onset of clinical symptoms.

Bacteriological diagnosis consists of isolation and identification of the gram negative rods from blood or stools. In addition to preparing streak plates directly from clinical material, it is strongly advised that technicians utilize enrichment media (either selenite-F broth or tetrathionate broth) which inhibit the growth of saprophytic bacteria and permit enteric pathogens to multiply. After incubation of such enrichment for about twelve hours, appropriate streak platings should be prepared on selective and differential media including S.S. agar and MacConkey agar. Nonlactose-fermenting bacteria appear as colorless colonies in contrast to the red growth of organisms that attack lactose. Endo and E.M.B. agars may also be employed for the cultivation of *Salmonella* species, but they are not nearly as effective as the other media recommended. *Salmonella typhosa* grows especially well on Wilson and Blair medium which contains bismuth-sulfite, but because of the powerful inhibitory action of the medium, inocula must be relatively heavy.

Since these non-sporing bacteria are inactivated by exposure to a temperature of 60–65°C within a few minutes, it becomes evident that undercooking must be blamed for some infections, although contamination of the unprotected food after cooking by carriers, walking cases, and vermin should not be overlooked.

Treatment of patients suffering with *Salmonella* infections involves attempts to restore the electrolyte balance that may become severely disrupted through extensive vomiting and diarrhea. Unconsciousness may occur in severe cases unless intravenous injections of physiological saline or glucose-saline solutions are initiated.

Prophylactic measures aimed at typhoid fever revolve around immunization with a vaccine composed of a suspension of bacteria in a concentration of about one billion cells per milliliter. In reality it is a triple vaccine composed of a mixture of three bacteria: *S. typhosa* (about 500 million cells/ml), and approximately 250 million cells each of paratyphoid A and paratyphoid B. This vaccine is frequently referred to as T.A.B. vaccine. The immunization consists of three weekly injections beginning with 0.5 ml of the mixture and working up to 1.0 ml. Booster shots every three years are recommended to maintain a suitable blood level of antibodies. Students should bear in mind that such a vaccine imparts only relative immunity, not complete protection. Ingestion of large numbers of typhoid organisms will still result in the development of typhoid fever, but contact with minimal numbers may thwart the bacteria before they have an opportunity to become firmly entrenched within the digestive tract.

Spirals

ORGANISM: *Vibrio comma*

DISEASE: Asiatic cholera

CHARACTERISTICS: Gram negative slightly curved rods 0.3 to 0.6 by 1.0 to 5.0 microns, occurring singly and in spiral chains. Cells may lose their curved form on artificial cultivation. Motile by means of a single polar flagellum. Aerobic. Optimum temperature 37°C. Habitat: found in the intestinal contents of cholera patients and carriers.

Vibrio comes from the Latin and means "to move rapidly to and fro" or "to vibrate," and the specific name *comma* indicates the morphology of the cells. Man is the only animal susceptible to this infection. Although cholera is not a major concern to health authorities in the United States, it is a disease of extreme importance in other areas of the world, particularly in Asia, and as such it must be considered in this jet age by tourists who may find themselves in endemic areas within a matter of hours after take-off. Proper self-protection through active prophylactic immunization becomes imperative. It should be made clear that hog cholera is caused by a viscerotropic virus and bears no relationship to Asiatic cholera of bacterial etiology.

History records a series of devastating epidemics and pandemics between 1817 and 1910, and when cholera is on the rampage only plague holds more terror for a susceptible population. The Yangtse River in China and the delta of the Ganges in India have been described as the homes of endemic cholera. India has known the horrors of this disease for centuries, but it was not until 1832 that cholera was detected in the United States in Irish emigrants who brought the disease with them to New York. New Orleans in 1848 was another port of entry, and at that time the disease spread rapidly up the Mississippi Valley. Persons arriving at United States ports of entry today from countries where cholera is endemic must present evidence of vaccination within six months beginning six days after the initial injection. Only through strict quarantine enforcement has cholera been kept in check in areas other than those where it is commonly found. This precaution, in conjunction with other measures, has proved to be effective, and no cases have been reported in the United States since 1913.

Koch discovered these curious organisms in 1883 while examining the intestinal discharges of cholera patients. Two persons (Pettenkofer and Emmerich) who doubted the relationship between these bacteria and the clinical symptoms of the disease ventured to swallow a broth culture of the organisms to disprove Koch's claims; they were easier to convince thereafter! Remarkable differences in individual resistance to cholera exist, but exactly what underlies these variations is still a matter of conjecture; fatigue and excessive use of alcohol have been suggested as two possibilities to explain lowered resistance.

The incubation period before clinical symptoms appear is generally from three to five days after ingestion of the microbes, but massive doses of cells may bring on the reactions in as short a time as 24 hours. Mild cases of cholera may be clinically indistinguishable from mild food poisoning or food infection, but laboratory examination of stools will readily differentiate them from one another. Not until massive numbers of bacteria have developed within the intestine and have autolyzed, releasing their endotoxins, do clinical symptoms become apparent. The illness may be marked by two stages. In the first there is loss of large volumes of fluid through vomiting and diarrhea with the discharge of characteristic "rice water stools" containing mucus and gross flakes of epithelial cells packed with practically pure cultures of vibrios. The second stage results from serious fluid loss and dehydration. Severe disruption of the salt balance of the body leads to shock, collapse, circulatory failure, and subnormal body temperature. The resulting increased blood acidity is a factor contributing to death. Fatality rates run about 50 per cent in untreated cases, but 30 per cent of individuals may survive if they receive replacement injections of fluid, salt, and alkali before the imbalance is maintained too long. At autopsy in fatal cases the intestinal wall is found to be highly **edematous** with the epithelial lining severely injured and ulcerated. Since the cholera organisms remain within the lumen of the intestine, it would appear the disease is largely a toxemia terminating in impairment of renal function through nephritis.

Laboratory confirmation of cholera is made by inoculating a few drops of the stool specimen in peptone water at a pH of from 8.0 to 9.0. Most other bacterial growth is markedly retarded by the highly alkaline medium, and cholera cells grow rapidly. Because of their aerobic nature they develop into a film on the surface of the alkaline peptone water within six to eight hours. A stain made from such a pellicle reveals cells whose morphology is typical of *Vibrio comma*. A number of biochemical tests may then be employed to confirm these morphological findings and to separate the pathogens from saprophytic spirals sometimes encountered.

The carrier state does not persist nearly as long in cholera as in some other enteric diseases. Stool cultures generally become negative within two weeks, but there is always the exceptional individual who may continue to excrete viable cells for some time thereafter. True chronic carriers, however, do not appear to exist. Without doubt, a dangerous phase in cholera must be considered to be the incubation period when the individual may not even be aware that he is discharging the virulent microorganisms.

Contaminated water and unwashed fruits and vegetables are major vehicles for the transmission of this disease, but in areas where the sewage systems are well constructed, the water supplies are amply protected and treated, and the population is actively immunized, cholera need not be a problem. Seasonal outbreaks in India are almost predictable, and each year cholera occurs in epidemic form, varying in severity, as it radiates from the endemic area through predetermined communities as summer wears on. Interestingly enough, cholera was the first disease shown to be water-borne. This finding by John Snow in 1854 in the Broadstreet Pump epidemic in London has become a classic in epidemiology.

Recovery from cholera imparts some degree of immunity to the individual as indicated by the observation that second attacks rarely occur within a year or two after recovery from an infection. Allied armies in Asiatic countries proved the effectiveness of vaccines made from killed suspensions (8–10 billion cells per ml) of virulent *Vibrio comma*. An initial injection of 0.5 ml of such a bacterial suspension followed in from seven to ten days by a second dose of 1.0 ml of vaccine offers an active immunity that generally persists for about six months, at the end of which time a booster dose of 1.0 ml should be administered. Booster injections must be repeated semiannually for the individual to maintain adequate protection. One study showed that immunized persons were 12 to 14 times less likely to contract cholera than unvaccinated subjects. Cholera cells die in water and in soil in a very few days; hence, infections are usually acquired from freshly contaminated sources.

Administration of sulfonamides, particularly sulfadiazine, may tend to shorten the duration of the clinical symptoms, but the number of vibrios in the stools may not be materially affected. Streptomycin, on the other hand, is reported to speed recovery in addition to reducing the cholera population in the intestines.

Any discussion of cholera would be incomplete without at least mentioning the **Pfeiffer phenomenon.** Pfeiffer noticed that guinea pigs did not succumb to massive doses of cholera organisms if they had previously been given a sublethal injection of the pathogens. Pasteur and others had made similar observations, but Pfeiffer wondered why this should be so and proceeded to find out. Upon opening the peritoneal cavity of such animals and examining some of the exudate under a microscope, instead of finding the live motile bacteria he had injected, Pfeiffer discovered only fragments of organisms. They were literally being dissolved *in vivo,* and this reaction became known as **bacteriolysis.** Further studies revealed that before such a change could take place, not only was it necessary to have cells and their specific antibodies in the animal, but a third component called **complement** is required. This is a heat-labile fraction found in the serum of all warm-blooded animals. The significance of complement in serology will become more apparent in the discussion (see pp. 424–425) of the *Complement Fixation Test* employed in the Wassermann technique for detecting syphilis.

ORGANISM: *Borrelia vincentii*

DISEASE: Associated with *Fusobacterium fusiforme* in cases of Vincent's angina, or trench mouth

CHARACTERISTICS: Gram negative cells 0.3 by 8.0 to 12.0 microns with three to eight irregular, shallow spirals. Motile with a rapid, progressive, vibratory motion. Anaerobic. Optimum temperature 37°C. Habitat: found in normal respiratory mucous membranes.

Earlier in this text it was pointed out that before an organism can be said to be the cause of a specific disease it must fulfill postulates formulated by Koch to prove his microbial theory of disease. However there is no provision in his postulates for diseases caused by the symbiotic action of two or more organisms. Vincent's angina is an example of such a unique biological arrangement wherein loosely coiled spirochetes and rod-shaped cells with pointed ends called *fusiform bacteria* act in symbiosis with vibrios and cocci. Alone, no single organism can produce the clinical symptoms of this disease, even in a susceptible host. All four microbes are required to yield a typical case of Vincent's angina, and apparently this occurs only when there is trauma (damage) or a vitamin deficiency. Fusospirochetal diseases are not found only in the mouth, however. Lesions may develop in such diverse areas as the brain and the genitalia.

Fusiform bacteria can be cultivated under anaerobic conditions in association with *Borrelia,* and a mixture of pure cultures of all four species implicated has been found to reproduce the disease. In this respect Koch's modified postulates may be fulfilled.

The tonsils are the most commonly affected tissue, and as the microbial growth progresses the area may become covered with a grayish pseudomembrane resembling somewhat the type formed in cases of diphtheria. The membrane may become necrotic and impart a foul breath to the host. Ulcers, sometimes mistaken for syphilis, may develop in the tonsils. This clinical picture was so common during World War I that it came to be known as trench mouth, but more scientific names include ulceromembraneous stomatitis and ulcerative stomatitis.

Sensible oral hygiene coupled with a balanced diet eaten with clean utensils appear to be the best means for preventing trench mouth. Authorities seem to differ as to the contagiousness of this disease, but as a result of his experience on a university campus, the author is inclined to believe that once the glasses and silverware in a given dining hall become contaminated through an infected individual, other persons will contract the condition very readily unless extreme care is taken to rinse these items in hot water at 180°F for 20 seconds. Penicillin and arsenicals may be employed to combat such infections, and dentists frequently prescribe hydrogen peroxide as a mouth rinse in addition to any injections given.

ORGANISM: *Leptospira icterihaemorrhagiae*

DISEASE: Infectious jaundice (Weil's disease)

CHARACTERISTICS: Spiral cells 0.25 to 0.3 by 6.0 to 9.0 microns. Some may extend to 25 microns in length. Best stained with silver nitrate stains or examined as a wet preparation under a dark-field microscope. One or more gentle waves occur throughout the entire length. In liquid media one or both ends may be semicircularly hooked; in semisolid media, the organisms appear serpentine, waved, or bent. Very active flexibility. Flagella are absent. Aerobic to microaerophilic. Temperature range for growth is 25° to 37°C, but motility is most active at 25°C. Habitat: found in kidneys and urine of wild rats.

There are a dozen or more pathogenic leptospira capable of causing hemorrhagic jaundice, but it should be borne in mind that viruses are also involved in some types of infectious jaundice. When the disease is caused by bacteria the condition is known as leptospirosis. *Lepto* comes from the Greek adjective *leptus* meaning "thin" or "small," and *icterus* means "jaundice."

The disease was recognized as far back as 1886 by Weil, but the microbes were not successfully cultivated until 1915 in Japan. Although wild rats must be considered the principal reservoir of infection, many other animals including cats, dogs, horses, field mice, pigs, and poultry may transmit the organisms to human beings. The urine of these animals may contain leptospira, and these organisms may persist in water for weeks after being excreted. Polluted shallow wells, therefore, may be one source of infection. The infectivity rate for rats has been found to vary from 4 per cent in New York to as high as 40 per cent in Holland. As many as 32 per cent of dogs examined have been found to be seropositive for leptospira, and they could be more important in the dissemination of these organisms than has been realized. Washing the dog's dishes with those of the family could conceivably be one mode of transmission of this disease, but if dishwashing machines are operating properly, the final hot water rinse should inactivate any *Leptospira canicola* present.

Weil's disease has an incubation period that may vary from one to three weeks, but in most cases symptoms appear within ten days. The leptospira get into the body through the digestive tract, but many infections are caused by invasion through breaks in the skin when individuals come in contact with urine from infected animals. Coal miners, for example, standing in rat-contaminated water without proper foot protection have been shown to pick up leptospirosis. Persons bathing in pools of stagnant water where rats are commonly found may not only contract leptospirosis, but in some cases *Pseudomonas* infections of the ears as well.

Cultivation of these spiral-shaped microbes may be effected on media containing ascitic fluid or fresh rabbit serum. One of the earlier media was that recommended by Noguchi and it included serum and hemoglobin. The living membrane of a developing chick embryo affords an excellent natural medium in a normally bacterial-free package.

After an initial period of fever, Weil's disease is characterized by icterus, associated with liver damage, hemorrhages of the skin, enlargement of the spleen, chills, fever, intestinal upsets, muscular pain, headache, and albumin in the urine. The spirochetes are circulating in the blood during the first week of the disease, and injection of a guinea pig with a few milliliters of such blood will generally induce typical reactions in the test animal. After a week the leptospira may be found in the urine. A solid immunity is provided by recovery from this disease, which has an average mortality rate of about 10 per cent with variations in particular outbreaks.

Although penicillin is moderately effective in treating infections of leptospiral etiology, chlortetracycline yields more promising results if the drug is administered early in the course of the disease. Prevention of leptospirosis lies mainly in the area of rat eradication and in the wearing of protective clothing by persons engaged in hazardous occupations which expose the individuals to the wastes of infected animals.

ORGANISM: *Treponema pallidum*

DISEASE: Syphilis (sometimes euphemistically called "lues")

CHARACTERISTICS: Very fine protoplasmic spirals 0.25 to 3.0 by 6.0 to 14.0 microns coiled in 8 to 14 regular rigid spirals with an amplitude of about 1.0 micron. Weakly refractive in the living state by dark-field illumination. The cells rotate rapidly but progress slowly in a stiffly flexible manner. Stain with difficulty except with Giemsa's stain by which they appear a pale pink or rose. They are black when treated with Levaditi's silver impregnation technique. Optimum temperature about 37°C. Habitat: man, but can be transmitted experimentally to anthropoid apes and to rabbits.

The word *syphilis* comes from the name of an infected hero in a poem written by Fracastorius in 1530. *Treponema* means a turning thread, and *pallidum* indicates pale, an apt description for an organism with such a low index of light refraction. In many respects *Treponema* more nearly resembles the protozoa than the bacteria. Because of their poor light refraction, hanging drop preparations are useless for their demonstration and dark-field illumination must be employed to demonstrate the motion of these pathogenic organisms discovered in 1905 by Schaudinn and Hoffmann. Multiplication is by transverse fission with a division time of about 30 hours under optimum conditions.

Syphilis, the most dreaded of the venereal diseases, unfortunately is believed to strike about one person in ten. Transmission is almost exclusively (99.9 per cent) by sexual contact, kissing, or abnormal sexual practices; the remaining 0.1 per cent must be considered an occupational disease for those persons who must deal with syphilitics—nurses, physicians, midwives, and dentists. Extreme caution must be exercised by medical and paramedical personnel in the proper disposal of bedding, linen, dishes, and other objects that might have been freshly contaminated by discharges from syphilitic lesions.

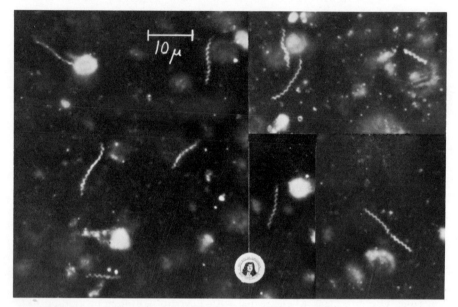

FIG. 15.9.   Dark field photomicrograph of *Treponema pallidum*. (LS-327 Courtesy American Society for Microbiology.)

The biblical plague of Moab is believed by some historians to have been syphilis. History suggests that Europe knew little or nothing of this disease until Columbus and his crew returned from their trip to the New World. (Still others suggest that the direction was the reverse!) There are presently some two million persons in the United States undergoing treatment for syphilis, and one-third of them are destined to suffer permanent disabling effects. Some will end up as hopeless mental patients with paralysis and insanity brought about by diffuse spirochetosis of the brain with its concomitant tissue destruction. Ignorance and indifference—the usual obstacles to progress—continue to make this a disease of paramount importance in public health.

Treponema pallidum is one of the most delicate microbes known, insofar as its resistance to external factors is concerned. Even slight drying, contact with atmospheric concentrations of oxygen, soap, or other chemicals capable of lowering surface tension, or mild disinfectants will rapidly immobilize and kill these spirochetes. They have the ability to penetrate what appears to be intact skin. Blood to be used for transfusion purposes is routinely screened by serological tests to eliminate any chance for passive transfer of syphilis, but three days of storage in a refrigerator will insure the death of all *Treponema pallidum* cells. It is unfortunate that the same thing does not hold true for the viruses that seem to be implicated in the spread of infectious jaundice.

The incubation period for syphilis may vary widely from about ten days to three months, with an average of about three weeks. During this period the spirochetes are multiplying locally as well as in the lymphatics and in the blood stream. The primary lesion is a *hard chancre,* but at times this lesion is so insignificant that it could be mistaken for a pimple, and its customary location on the cervix of the uterus in the female or in the urethra of the male may cause it to escape detection. Clinical diagnosis is confirmed upon finding of the living *Treponema* in fluid taken from the chancre and examined under dark-field illumination. Such a microscopic examination should be conducted prior to chemotherapy, since the spirochetes leave the local area within the first 24 hours of such treatment.

Even without any medication the primary lesion may spontaneously disappear in from 10 to 40 days, probably as the result of the build-up of local tissue immunity. Secondary lesions may "pop out" as the original ones disappear or they may be delayed, and the patient may remain asymptomatic for from two to six months. The symptoms of secondary syphilis include anemia, enlarged glands in the inguinal region, copper-colored rash on the skin of the trunk, arms, and legs, and the presence of peculiar grayish patches inside the mouth. These manifestations of the disease may appear singly or in various combinations. In the late manifestations of syphilis the cardiovascular and nervous systems become involved; frequently the disease is not infectious even by sexual contact at this stage. The liver becomes scarred and damaged (cirrhosis) and bulges appear in the aorta where layers of lesions have weakened this vessel that is so vital in blood circulation. These bulges are termed **aneurisms** and when they burst, prompt death is a certainty.

Treatment techniques for one of man's most vicious diseases date to the pioneer work of Paul Ehrlich in his laborious development of "606," the arsenical magic bullet that introduced the practice of chemotherapy. This was the hoped-for breakthrough in the all-out attack on a horrible disease. Bismuth was later added to treat syphilis, but penicillin is the drug of choice for combatting most infections with *Treponema* today. Sensitivity to this antibiotic restricts its use in some patients, and other techniques must be employed. The build-up in resistance to this drug has not yet become evident as it has with the gonococcus. Active immunity through inoculations with vaccines has not yet become feasible, but infected mothers can be kept on antibiotics during pregnancy to forestall congenital syphilis in the fetus.

A number of serological tests based upon precipitation reactions and the complement fixation reaction have been developed to aid in the detection of this venereal disease. Such names as Kahn, Hinton, Kline, Mazzini, Eagle, and Wassermann come to mind, since they developed *in vitro* techniques for detecting the presence of serological changes in the blood reflecting a response of the body to stimulation induced by invading foreign protein in the nature of *Treponema pallidum*. Chapter 19, dealing with serology and immune responses, will discuss the theory and the mechanics of these antigen–antibody reactions.

The prevention of venereal diseases is largely a matter of education, and by early recognition and treatment of syphilis the entries on the public health statistics can be made to shrink in the direction of eradication of these misnamed "social diseases." In the 1930's the Surgeon General of the United States took a bold step forward when he published in a national widely read magazine a frank discussion of syphilis as a "kick-off" in his campaign to do something about the mounting problem of venereal disease in the United States. He received some (anticipated) criticism for his boldness in discussing a condition that for too long had been hushed up, but his courage brought results. The figures began to show an encouraging decline in the number of cases of syphilis, and by warnings to the public of the serious dangers of not seeking prompt treatment for their condition, more early cases were detected and treatment instituted. After a steadily declining rate, the statistics once more seem to be on the rise as our youth mistakenly assume the attitude that with a quick easy cure, venereal disease is no longer a sword hanging over sexual promiscuity. If these misguided souls could see at first hand what havoc is wrought on human bodies, minds, and family units by syphilis and other venereal diseases, they might give thought to the consequences of one misstep for a few moments of carnal pleasure with an individual of questionable health.

This chapter was never intended to present a complete listing of all pathogenic bacteria, but probably enough representative samples have been given for an introductory course for which this book has been prepared.

Review Questions

1. Of what value is a classification scheme in biology?
2. Although pneumococcus typing is no longer of importance in the treatment of patients suffering with pneumonia, is there any reason why the typing procedure should be eliminated in a clinical laboratory?
3. Which is the more serious infection, staphylococcus or streptococcus?
4. What laboratory tests bear the most weight in deciding the pathogenicity of staphylococci?
5. What differences and similarities exist between toxins produced by streptococci and staphylococci?
6. Compare the Dick test, Schick test, and tuberculin test.
7. Differentiate between alpha hemolysis exhibited by streptococci and by staphylococci.
8. How serious a disease is anthrax throughout the world?
9. Has diphtheria been controlled throughout the world? When does the disease tend to become epidemic in countries where it normally is practically nonexistent?
10. What significance do granules have in the recognition of pathogenic organisms under the oil immersion objective?
11. What public health measures are being taken to reduce the morbidity rate from tuberculosis?
12. What is the nature of the acid-fast reaction?
13. What is the status of BCG vaccination in the United States?
14. Would it be your judgment that more diseases are caused by gram positive or by gram negative species of bacteria?
15. Name several pathogenic microbes that exhibit different clinical symptoms in man and in lower animals.
16. What diseases can man contract from drinking unpasteurized milk?
17. What types of infections might one contract from swimming in polluted water?
18. Which *Salmonella* species are most frequently implicated in human infections?
19. Should cholera be considered as a potential threat in any parts of the United States?
20. Is there any single serological test that can be relied upon to confirm a diagnosis of syphilis?

16 | FUNGI

The Yeasts

ALTHOUGH YEASTS HAVE BEEN MAN'S UNSEEN SERVANTS FOR CEN-
turies, it was not until 1680 that the pioneer Leeuwenhoek first described
these curious cells. Some species of yeasts possess the potential for causing
disease in man, whereas others are instrumental in enriching his food
and drink and adding variety to his diet. In 1885, 205 years after
Leeuwenhoek's study, Louis Pasteur through his fundamental studies
conducted with yeast cells firmly established the biological theory of
fermentation in marked opposition to the mechanistic concept so rigidly
adhered to by the leading scientists of his day. Microbiologists are proud
that Pasteur, an eminent chemist, "changed his major" and contributed
so widely to fundamental understandings of our science.

The word "yeast" is a common term that has no significance in classification schemes. A suitable definition for the term is difficult to come
by, but yeasts are generally considered to be those unicellular, chlorophyll-free fungi which possess a demonstrable nucleus, multiply by budding, and ferment simple sugars with the liberation of carbon dioxide
and alcohol. Henrici stated that yeasts are fungi that permanently maintain a unicellular growth form, not developing mycelia. Not all yeasts
may fit either of these definitions exactly.

Much has been said about "good" yeasts, but the "bad" ones are perhaps of more direct importance in medical practice. Although yeasts,

like bacteria, are unicellular plants that lack chlorophyll, the former are classified primarily on the basis of methods of reproduction as indicated in the following abbreviated scheme of taxonomy.

Kingdom: *Plant*
Phylum: *Thallophyta* (Simple plants lacking roots, stems, leaves)
    Subphylum: *Fungi* (unicellular *yeasts* and multicellular *molds*)
        Class: *Ascomycetes.* Produce sexual spores in an ascus
            Order: *Endomycetales.* Zygote or single cell transformed into an ascus
                Genus: *Saccharomyces*
        Class: *Fungi Imperfecti.* Do not produce sexual spores
            Order: *Moniliales.* Reproduce by fission, budding, or formation of asexual spores
                Genus: *Cryptococcus*
                      Candida

Habitat

Yeasts are found in nature on the skins of fruit, particularly grapes; their presence accounts for the spontaneous fermentation underlying production of wine, vinegar, and other fermented products. Insects may play some part in transporting yeast cells from their bodies to the fruit which may in turn supply sufficient nutrients, particularly sugars, to permit the yeasts to remain viable on the outer surface of the insects until they visit another fruit and "inoculate" it by contact. Soil, as a rule, is not a rich source of yeasts, except perhaps in orchards or vineyards where they may be washed off the fruit by rain or be blown off by wind.

Structure

Yeast cells tend to be oval or ellipsoidal, although some forms are cylindrical and even filamentous in the group of so-called **false yeasts.** They commonly reproduce vegetatively by budding and by transverse fission (*Schizosaccharomyces*), and sexually by production of **ascospores** (*Saccharomyces*). A cell containing a sexual spore is called an **ascus** and the spores are called ascospores.

The wall of a yeast cell is a more or less rigid membrane composed of pseudochitin which differs from the usual cellulose of higher plants. Protoplasm of these fungi contains the usual fats, proteins, carbohydrates, and enzymes through which these microbes are capable of accomplishing a prodigious amount of work in the biological process of fermentation. The central controlling mechanism, the *nucleus,* is vital to the operation and survival of yeasts as it is in all cells. Granules of glycogen appear to serve as reserve food material, and fat globules increase in numbers and in volume when yeasts are cultivated on a carbohydrate-rich diet. **Vacuoles** are also present within the organisms, but their exact responsibilities in the welfare of the cells are not fully understood.

Yeasts are gram positive in their staining reaction; they accept a number of dyes, including methylene blue. When a small amount of this dye is added to a water suspension of yeasts, dead cells have a greater affinity for the methylene blue than do live cells, and this provides a means of determining the relative number of viable cells in a given mixture.

Cultivation

The ability of yeasts to tolerate a relatively high acidity (low pH) and osmotic pressure provides a basis for aiding in their separation from less resistant bacteria. A number of derived media have been proposed for growing these microscopic plants. Some of these substrates are tomato agar, Sabouraud's sugar agar, infusions of corn meal or potatoes enriched with glucose, wort agar, Littman's oxgall agar, and other sugar-containing compounds and mixtures adjusted to a pH on the acid side of neutrality. Most free-living yeasts have an optimum growth temperature of between 25° and 30°C. Being chlorophyll-free they must secure their energy from higher plants and animals through aerobic oxidative dissimilation or by anaerobic fermentation. Most species are saprophytes, and some are important parasites.

Ascospores in true yeasts do not seem to form so long as cells are growing in a favorable medium, but a useful substrate to encourage development of these structures is Maneval's agar which is composed of beef extract, sodium chloride, glucose, and agar adjusted to a pH of 7.2. The combination of a pH that is relatively high for yeasts coupled with the poor nitrogen source supplied by Maneval's agar favors ascospore formation. Incubation at about 30°C for four days generally yields favorable findings when stains are examined under a microscope.

A number of techniques commonly employed for staining bacterial spores also work well with yeasts. One method, for example, is to heat a smear in steaming malachite green for about one minute, followed by counterstaining in safranin for a few minutes. Green ascospores stand out clearly within pink cells. Yeast spores are somewhat more resistant to heat and other unfavorable factors than are vegetative cells, but the spores are not nearly as tolerant at the tougher bacterial spores.

Uses of Yeasts

Beer, a product of fermentation by yeasts, is a very ancient drink dating back at least 6000 years when it was brewed in Mesopotamia, and records indicate that this beverage was consumed in ancient Babylon and in Egypt during the times of the pharaohs. Yeast cultures employed in the fermentation of beer may yield from 4 to 6 per cent alcohol, and certain strains of *Saccharomyces ellipsoideus* may produce as high as 16 per cent alcohol in some wines. Cultures that grow on the bottom of the fermentation tank in the brewing of lager beer are called "bottom yeasts," whereas ales are produced through the action of "top yeasts." Brewing high-quality beer is probably more an art than a science, and expert brewmasters jealously guard the secrets of their technique as well as the particular strains of yeast they employ for developing distinctive flavors and aromas.

Vinegar is generally manufactured from apple juice (cider vinegar) by an initial alcoholic fermentation brought about by yeasts; bacteria (*Acetobacter*) then step in and oxidize the alcohol to acetic acid.

Yeasts have been used for centuries to make breads "rise." Some writings suggest that unleavened bread dates from the time Moses led his people into the wilderness in such haste that they forgot to take yeast along. Our ancestors discovered that by retaining a small portion of unbaked leavened dough from each batch of bread and using it as an inoculum in the next mixture of dough, leavening could be encouraged. The biscuits baked by Alaskan "sourdoughs" were prepared in a similar manner. Sugar added to the flour dough is fermented by *Saccharomyces cereviseae* with the liberation of carbon dioxide which puffs up the dough and improves its texture. The heat of baking further expands the trapped gas pockets and leaves the desired air spaces. The small amount of alcohol produced by the fermentation is driven off by the heat of baking.

A whole industry eventually came to be established to supply commercial establishments and housewives with yeasts, and presently more than 100,000 tons are produced annually in the United States. The residue remaining after recovery of crystalline sucrose from concentrated sugar cane or beet sugar juice is called "blackstrap" molasses, and it contains sucrose as well as its two component monosaccharides, glucose and fructose. This residue is diluted to yield a sugar concentration of between 7 and 9 per cent. Ammonium salts are added as a nitrogen source to supplement the organic nitrogen present, and the mixture is acidified to a pH of about 4.5. After addition of the desired amount of yeast culture, the liquid medium is aerated to stimulate rapid multiplication of the cells, and when the maxiumum stationary phase of growth has been attained, the yeasts are drawn off through centrifugation. The cell harvest is squeezed to reduce the moisture content, mixed with about 5 per cent starch and edible oil to serve as a binder, and the product is then pressed into cakes and packaged. Rigid asepsis must be practiced throughout manufacture, and storage at from 0°C to 5°C is required to maintain viability of the cells.

To be effective the yeast culture must serve as an active leavening agent, i.e., one which produces carbon dioxide rapidly in bread dough. Coagulation of the grain proteins during baking traps the gas bubbles and makes the bread light. The desirable sourness of some rye breads is attributed to the acids released through bacterial action that occurs when the dough is kept at a temperature too cool for rapid multiplication of yeasts but favorable for the bacteria.

Yeasts may also be cultivated on sugar-containing media prepared through hydrolysis of wood or other cellulose-containing materials. By the addition of selected chemicals to the mixture, the end product of yeast fermentation may be glycerine which has a number of commercial uses as a solvent, an antifreeze, a sweetening agent, an antiseptic, adhesive, ink, and even explosives when converted into nitroglycerine.

Yeasts can bring about the synthesis of certain vitamins of the B complex, and some individuals eat these microorganisms as a regular part of their diet. Some years ago a manufacturer even incorporated yeasts into a candy bar!

Saccharomyces SPECIES

This ascospore-producing true yeast is usually called bread or brewer's yeast, and different species of this genus are employed in the manufacture of ethyl alcohol and distilled liquors. The amount of alcohol produced varies with the particular species of *Saccharomyces* used, but yields much over 15 per cent cannot be expected. For this reason hard liquors must be distilled to concentrate their alcoholic content.

Alcoholic fermentation is anaerobic. In the early stages of the process aerobic conditions are maintained to promote rapid multiplication of yeast cells, but little alcohol is produced until the air supply is cut off. A maximum concentration of about 15 per cent alcohol is reached in from two to three days at which time the yeasts are killed off by the product of their own creation. Fractional distillation separates the alcohol from the other ingredients and yields a final product containing about 95 per cent alcohol. It is estimated that over a dozen enzymes are involved in the conversion of simple sugars (monosaccharides) into ethyl alcohol and carbon dioxide. This organic complex is *zymase* which formerly was considered to be a single enzyme.

When grains are employed as a substrate the enzyme *diastase* found in sprouting seeds converts the starch to sugar which in turn is attacked by yeasts to form alcohol. Sugar beets, rice, potatoes, and molasses are other substrates used in commercial manufacture of alcohol.

Saccharomyces ellipsoideus, an elliptical-shaped yeast, is capable of producing higher alcohol yields than the bread or beer yeast, *Sacch. cereviseae,* and for this reason wines, which have an alcoholic content of 10 per cent or more, are made with the stronger yeast cultures.

Bottom yeasts ferment sugar more slowly and are employed in the brewing of lager beer. *Saccharomyces carlsbergensis* is an example of such a bottom yeast. These species have been "taught" to live under the relatively anaerobic conditions that exist at the bottom of the vat. Fermentation of the **wort** is generally completed within 72 hours from the time of "pitching" (when the yeast culture is added). The large volume of carbon dioxide evolved may be collected and used for carbonating the beer later in the process. After vat fermentation is completed the beer is stored in tanks close to the freezing point to allow the product to mature for a matter of months before it is "racked" into bottles, cans, or barrels. Carbonation may be accomplished by the addition of carbon dioxide to the containers, or by a "krausening process" in which a small amount of wort that is still fermenting is allowed to mix with the finished beer in the maturing tank. Thus the mixture carbonates itself as the wort ferments.

Mild ale may contain 3 per cent alcohol by volume, but some of the best pale ales may run as high as 4.5 per cent. Port wine contains up to 20 per cent alcohol, and Scotch whiskey contains about 40 per cent alcohol. A small yeast may pack a powerful potential!

Gin is no more than a water solution of alcohol obtained from the fermentation of grain. "Botanicals" are added to impart flavors; the most common ones are juniper berries, orange peel, cassia bark, coriander seed, caraway seed, and others. Each distillery has its own "secret" formula.

Cryptococcus neoformans

This organism is a highly pathogenic yeast-like fungus that causes fatal infections in man and in other animals. Unfortunately there is no known cure for this disease that goes under a number of different designations including torulosis, cryptococcosis, and European blastomycosis; the etiological agent may also be listed as *Torula histolytica*. Cryptococcosis is sporadic throughout the world, exhibiting no particular affinity for any given race, but young men appear to have a disproportionately high percentage of the total cases reported. Many infections undoubtedly go unrecognized; were they accurately diagnosed, statistics for this disease might be markedly different.

In Europe cryptococcosis is found most frequently in the form of abscesses and nodules in the skin, lymphatics, lungs, bones, and deep tissues, whereas in the United States physicians see more cases involving the brain and meninges. Because of the clinical symptoms produced, such infections are sometimes erroneously diagnosed as brain tumors or as tubercular meningitis. In spinal fluid the yeast cells, which measure from about 5 to 15 microns in diameter, may be mistaken by the untrained observer for lymphocytes. Yet careful microscopic examination would disclose the presence of budding, and culturing some of the fresh clinical material would remove any doubt as to the nature of the cells observed. *Cryptococcus neoformans* is not resistant to heat, and exposure to 60°C fòr as short a time as five minutes will inactivate the cells.

A drop of India ink mixed with spinal fluid from an infected individual will reveal clear hyaline capsules ranging up to twice the size of the underlying cells. A Quellung reaction similar to that described for *D. pneumoniae* (see p. 267) can be prepared by treating the yeast cells with specific rabbit antiserum and observing the preparation under the oil immersion objective.

Infusion blood agar is a suitable medium for the cultivation of these pathogenic fungi, and when the transplants are stored at 37°C, visible growth generally appears on the medium in from two to four days. Sabouraud's agar is another suitable substrate which is generally incubated at room temperature. Growth of cryptococci even on what seems to be the best of media may be delayed for periods ranging up to a week or more. After the appearance of an initial yeast-like growth, colonies may become slimy, mucoid, creamy to brownish in color, and if cultivated on agar slants the viscous microbial mass may slide to the bottom of the tube. *Cryptococcus neoformans* is the only yeast-like fungus that produces the enzyme **urease** which will yield a positive urea test and turn the medium red in the presence of the alkali indicator, phenol red. This is of decided diagnostic value.

The European and the American types òf the disease were believed to be of entirely separate origin until 1934 when Benham showed them to be caused by substantially identical strains of yeast. The major difference lay in the area of pathogenicity. Unfortunately, as stated earlier, there is no effective cure for this affliction. Animal tests showed some promise with the antibiotic cycloheximide, but this drug is highly toxic for humans in doses required to inhibit effectively the growth of these microbes.

Laboratory confirmation of *Cryptococcus* infections entails the intraperitoneal injection of white mice with 1.0 ml of a saline suspension of the yeast cells or the intracerebral inoculation of 0.02 ml to distinguish between the pathogenic and saprophytic members of this genus. The latter species generally fail to grow at 37°C. The intraperitoneal route of the injection is usually fatal to mice within three weeks. Typical brain lesions are observed at autopsy. The intracerebral route may cut the death time to a week, at the end of which the body cavity is found to contain gelatinous masses with lung and brain involvement. An India ink preparation of material taken from such mice should exhibit characteristic budding of cells coupled with pronounced capsules. At least three distinct serological types of *Cryptococcus neoformans* have been described to date, and as research progresses with additional isolations of members of this interesting group of pathogens, further antigenic groupings will undoubtedly emerge.

Methods by which these fungi are transmitted are not understood, although claims are made that spread from animal to man or from man to man does not exist. There might even be spontaneous cures in mild unrecognized cases. In any event, those individuals whose activities bring them in direct or indirect contact with infected patients would do well to practice the precautionary techniques accepted for dealing with communicable diseases. Soiled fomites and body discharges should be handled with extreme care.

Before leaving this discussion we should mention that not all members of the genus *Cryptococcus* are pathogenic. One species is employed in the manufacture of fermented milks in Asia and in eastern Europe, and other members have been reported as apparently natural flora of the gastrointestinal tract in supposedly healthy individuals.

Candida albicans (Monilia albicans)

These yeast-like fungi, which masquerade under a reported 88 synonyms, are the most common cause of subacute or acute mycotic infections in man. Some are mild, whereas others inflict a high mortality rate. When lesions develop due to tissue injury or malnutrition they vary in severity in the mouth, skin, nails, vagina, bronchi, or lungs. Septicemia and endocarditis (especially in drug addicts) have been reported. The fact that *Candida albicans* is normally found so frequently in the mouth, stools, and vagina adds considerable confusion to diagnosis of the disease which is known by such titles as moniliasis, candidiasis, thrush, and sprue. When this fungus condition was first described in 1839 by Langenbeck who discovered the cells in mouth cultures, the organisms were called *Oidium albicans* whose generic designation later became *Monilia* and eventually *Candida*.

One of the cultural characteristics of this fungus is the formation of a *mycelium* (a mass of filaments) when the organism grows under reduced oxygen tension in submerged cultures or in tissues. When conditions for growth are optimum, a yeast-like colony predominates.

With the advent of antibiotic therapy and the accompanying reduction in competition by bacteria, fungus infections have come to the forefront, and the serious conditions thus created bear a direct relationship to prolonged administration of chemotherapeutic agents.

When mucous membranes become affected by *C. albicans* the condition is termed *thrush*. This symptom is found more commonly in neglected bottle-fed babies than in breast-fed infants. Chronically ill adults suffering with debilitating diseases tend to develop thrush unless they are given proper nursing care to maintain a healthy condition within the mouth. Ill-fitting dentures appear to be a precipitating factor. Throat infections with these fungi resemble somewhat the membrane that develops in cases of diphtheria, but a microscopic examination of some of the stained material from the growth will readily differentiate the two conditions.

Candida infections of the intestines cause an ulcerative condition accompanied by diarrhea, and this is called sprue, a deficiency disease found most frequently among non-natives in tropical countries.

Individuals whose occupations demand that their hands be kept wet a good deal of the time are particularly prone to develop eczema-like lesions of the skin with eventual involvement of the fingernails which may thicken and turn a brown color. Scrapings of such nails treated with 10 per cent sodium hydroxide, which serves as a clearing agent, will bring out not only budding cells but also threadlike projections called *hyphae* when the preparation is subjected to microscopic examination.

The majority of cases of moniliasis tend to remain mild and localized, but the yeasts may spread to other membranes followed by the appearance of generalized lesions in the skin. Diabetes is a predisposing factor in cutaneous moniliasis, and abscesses in the viscera are also characteristic. Pregnant women frequently develop mild vaginal infections with these fungi, and during delivery infants may pick up the organisms as they pass through the birth canal.

Bronchomoniliasis is a respiratory infection that has been observed in both Europe and the United States, but this type of infection appears more frequently in the tropics. The mild form of respiratory involvement is an irritant and causes coughing, but when the mycotic infection becomes acute, lungs are damaged and the fatality rate runs high.

Diagnosis of *Candida* infections is complicated by the presence of these organisms as common inhabitants of the mouths of so many persons. Only by repeated isolation of the organisms from sputum samples obtained after the patient has rinsed his mouth with a suitable antiseptic, and only when the yeast cells are found in significant numbers, can one definitely confirm this type of respiratory mycotic infection.

When the skin becomes involved in *Candida* infections, it can generally be attributed to chafing at points wherever two areas of skin are in constant contact; folds of the groin, folds of the neck of infants, under the breasts of nursing mothers, etc. Since this disease is preventable through good nursing care, its occurrence in this form in a modern hospital must be looked upon as unnecessary and a direct reflection on the treatment being given the patient.

To isolate the etiological fungi from sites of infection Sabouraud's agar containing chloramphenicol and cycloheximide should be inoculated in duplicate with one set of tubes incubated at 37°C and the other cultures maintained at room temperature. If yeast-like organisms are present, they will produce visible growth in about four days. The intravenous injection of a rabbit with about 1 ml of a 1 per cent suspension of the cells will generally bring about death of the animal in from 72 to 96 hours. At autopsy the kidneys will show abscesses which when stained will be found to contain gram positive yeast cells.

Molds

The word "mold" has no more taxonomic meaning than the term "yeast," but it is a convenient designation to describe a heterogeneous group of multicellular, filamentous organisms that lack chlorophyll and are widely distributed under varied environmental conditions. Fungi may be either unicellular, as exemplified by the yeasts, or multicellular in the manner of molds, but it should be recognized, especially among the pathogenic fungi, that some of the plants may be dimorphic. That is, they may be unicellular in the tissues and multicellular in artificial cultures.

Morphology

Mold plants consist of cells attached in such a manner that they form filaments, or **hyphae.** An entire plant is called a **thallus,** and a mass of hyphae visible to the unaided eye is a **mycelium.** Some hyphae exhibit cross walls called **septa,** whereas the filaments in nonseptate molds may be multinuclear without septa and contain protoplasm in a continuous mass. Each nucleus together with its surrounding protoplasm may be considered as a cell.

Further major subdivisions of the mycelium are apparent. One type, the *vegetative hyphae,* grow into the substrate and are primarily concerned with obtaining food for the plant; aerial hyphae are involved in multiplication and are called *fertile* or *reproductive hyphae.* It is on these elevated structures that spores are borne. Classification of molds is largely based upon differences observed in the hyphae, particularly in the reproductive segments. In other words, morphology rather than physiology primarily differentiates molds from each other.

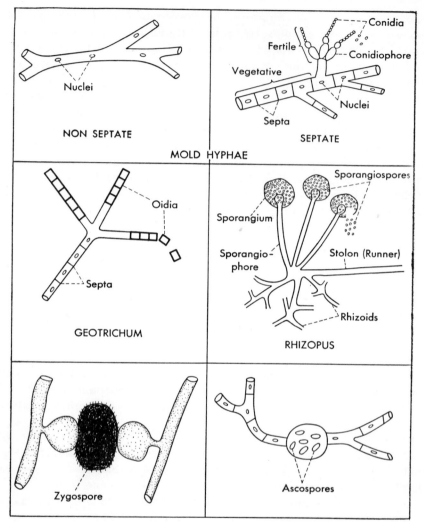

FIG. 16.1. Mold structures. (Reprinted from S. E. Wedberg, *Microbes and You,* 1954, with permission of The Macmillan Company, New York, N. Y.)

Reproduction

The colors associated with various molds are imparted to the growth by the reproductive bodies, or spores, which appear in many arrangements and are carried in a number of structures. Molds belonging to the class *Phycomycetes* produce enormous numbers of asexual spores in cases known as *sporangia* (from the Greek *angium,* "bag" or "envelope") formed at the tips of fertile hyphae. *Rhizopus nigricans,* the common bread mold, is an example of this type, and it grows profusely as a cottony gray mass on barnyard manure, fruits, and starchy foods. The generic name points out one of its characteristic growth features, namely that it sends out stolons resembling those found on strawberry plants, and these runners produce rootlike hyphae (*rhizoids*) wherever they touch the substrate, thus increasing the rate of spread of this mold which produces black asexual spores.

Ascomycetes form spores which are not encased but rather appear as projections from the tips of the fertile hyphae, and these spores are called **conidia** (from the Greek *conidio,* "dust") which may grow as singles or in chains. The genus *Aspergillus* which is included in the Ascomycetes possesses a septate mycelium and reproduction is chiefly by conidia. The *niger* species produces jet-black spores that are wafted about on air currents and carried to foodstuffs which they attack.

In some species of molds the mycelium may thicken and form a spore-like body called a **chlamydospore.** Other molds may indicate a fragmentation of the mycelium with a release of rectangular-shaped free cells called **oidia** (from the Greek root of "egg"), and each cell is capable of giving rise to a new mycelium when a suitable substrate becomes available.

Sexual spores produced by molds form through the fusion of two cells, generally called plus and minus rather than male and female. Cells involved in fertilization in which two cells or two nuclei fuse are called **gametes.** If the gametes are similar they are referred to as **isogametes** in contrast to the **heterogametes** which are morphologically dissimilar. Sexual spores are known as **zygospores** in the genera *Mucor* and *Rhizopus,* but when they are borne within a sac, or ascus, in *Penicillium* and *Aspergillus* species, the sexual spores are called *ascospores.* The name "perfect fungi" is given to those molds which exhibit both sexual and asexual forms of reproduction. Pathogenic molds as a group lack a demonstrable sexual phase, and for this reason they are classified as *Fungi Imperfecti.*

Cultivation

Molds, like yeasts, can tolerate and actually prefer an acid pH. Their nutritive requirements are not demanding, especially if small amounts of sugar are provided in the substrate. Pathogenic fungi tend to grow more slowly than saprophytic species, even on the best media devised. Morphology of the plant is markedly influenced by the substrate upon which molds are cultivated, and descriptions may vary on this account.

Tomato agar is suitable for the growth of most nonpathogenic fungi, but it appears less useful in the field of medical mycology where Sabouraud's agar, a neopeptone-maltose compound, is the medium of choice.

Czapek-Dox medium, a synthetic preparation containing saccharose, sodium nitrate, dipotassium phosphate, magnesium sulfate, potassium chloride, and ferrous sulfate, is another widely employed substrate for the cultivation of fungi.

Being aerobic, molds must have free access to uncombined atmospheric oxygen if they are to grow. It is for this reason that these fungi develop at the surface rather than deep in substrates. Molds are ubiquitous since their light spores can be carried long distances without material loss of viability, and they represent an ever-present threat as contaminants in bacterial cultures. Mold spores possess a tough wall which helps them to resist drying, but they are not nearly as resistant to heat as are bacterial spores.

Uses of Molds

The economy of nature is markedly influenced by mold action. These organisms are responsible for enormous amounts of food spoilage, to be sure, but the positive side of the ledger makes good reading and should not be minimized. Molds play a vital role in the soil where they materially assist in the decomposition of cellulose, an organic plant residue that is not readily attacked by many bacteria. If the carbon cycle is to continue in operation, elements bound up in cellulose must be released, and mold action carries a major part of this burden. Since molds are aerobic, their decomposition is in the form of *decay*. Bacteria may break down cellulose either aerobically or anaerobically. The latter process is termed *putrefaction*. Some mold decay may be merely troublesome in the form of growth in improperly sealed jars of jam, jelly, or fruit, but destruction of leather goods, canvas, books, and bread has considerably more economic significance.

The delicate texture, flavor, and aroma of roquefort and camembert cheeses that delight the palates of connoisseurs are attributed to the activity of specific molds which are employed for what one might consider "controlled spoilage." The species involved belong to the genus *Penicillium,* which gets its name from the Latin and means "little brush," a morphological feature imparted to the plants through growth of the fingerlike branches of conidia on the fertile hyphae.

Enzymatic breakdown of fats, carbohydrates, and proteins in cheeses imparts the characteristic flavors which differ with the species used. *Penicillium roqueforti* is a blue-green mold employed in the manufacture of roquefort cheese. By means of a special pointed instrument spores of this mold are driven into blocks of cheese, and sufficient oxygen is thus provided to permit the mold to grow and to produce the colored veins and the characteristic flavor of this cheese through the breakdown of butterfat into caproic acid. Ripening proceeds from the inside toward the outside of the cheese mass, and this particular species is somewhat less fastidious in its oxygen requirements than is *P. camemberti* which must be inoculated on the outside of the cheese where free access to oxygen is available. Spores of this mold are seeded on the outside and ripening of camembert cheese proceeds inward.

Retting of flax entails the freeing of fibers from the binding agent, pectin, and this important industrial procedure in the manufacture of linen is carried out through the action of molds belonging to the genus *Mucor* as well as by the enzymatic forces of bacteria. The manufacture of diastase from starch is dependent upon the mold *Aspergillus oryzae*.

Before 1923 up to 90 per cent of commercial citric acid came from the extraction of citrous fruits in Italy, the remainder being produced from lemons, limes, and pineapples in California, Hawaii, and the West Indies. A factory was then established in New York State to produce citric acid by the action of molds on sugar-containing substrates, and this industry has an interesting history. Species of *Penicillium* and *Mucor* had been under study, and *Aspergillus niger* was found to produce the less valuable oxalic acid. However, by controlling conditions of growth, and by selecting a specific strain of *Asp. niger,* it was discovered that citric acid could be produced; this is the technique employed today. Sucrose from beet or cane sugar in a concentration of from 12 to 20 per cent appears to be the best substrate, and when the pH is adjusted to about 3.5 and the temperature maintained at 30°C, citric acid can be produced in from seven to nine days. If the temperature is lower than this, fermentation proceeds slowly and favors the production of oxalic acid. The iron content must be kept at an extremely low level, and the addition of certain inorganic salts will increase the yield of citric acid. The fungus grows as a mat on shallow layers of substrate. Deep culture in aerated vats appears to present certain technical difficulties, and this method has not been widely adopted.

Similar utilization is made of molds in the manufacture of gluconic acid, fumaric acid, and gallic acid. The latter product is used in preparing inks, dyes, and pharmaceuticals.

Medicine owes a staggering debt of gratitude to the molds, particularly those species of *Penicillium* (*P. notatum, P. chrysogenum*) from which our first useful antibiotics were derived. A group of moldlike organisms, the Streptomyces, provide additional antibiotics and a host of valuable by-products, including vitamin B_{12}.

Pathogenic Molds

Medical mycology is one of the more rapidly expanding fields of biological science. When biological competition is reduced through chemotherapy aimed at controlling bacterial infections, mycotic infections are provided with an easier opportunity to flourish, and the search has been stepped up to find fungicides and antibiotics that can be taken internally to combat the rising menace of resistant fungus infections.

Even prior to the advent of "wonder drugs" a disease of the ear caused by various species of *Aspergillus* molds was a common problem. This otomycosis involves a plugging of the external meatus with an extensive growth of mycelium or an ulceration of the middle ear. This particular type of infection appears to be most prevalent in India, although cases have been reported from all over the world. Aspergillosis of the lungs is sometimes observed among bird fanciers, especially in connection with pigeons who seem to be able to transmit the disease to man.

The most commonly encountered fungus diseases in man are caused by dermatophytes, those moldlike fungi classified as *Fungi Imperfecti*. Some 200 species have been reported belonging to the three principal genera: *Epidermophyton, Microsporum,* and *Trichophyton.* These mycotic infections cause such conditions as ringworm and "athlete's foot." Any number of different treatments have been tried to clear up these superficial infections of the skin, hair, and fingernails, including iodine, copper, salicylic acid, benzoic acid, Roentgen epilation, and surgical removal, but results vary widely, and frequently a series of different treatments may be necessary before the condition clears up. The fungi that attack hair and nails have a peculiar attraction for the highly insoluble scleroprotein, keratin, for their metabolism.

Medical mycology is much too broad a field to be covered in an introductory presentation of this type, and the reader is encouraged to supplement his reading in textbooks in this area of science or in certain fuller treatments of medical microbiology for details concerning mycotic infections.

Review Questions

1. What tests are employed to differentiate true yeasts from false yeasts?
2. Does the commercial value of yeasts outweigh their importance as pathogenic organisms?
3. Why are some fungus diseases on the ascendancy?
4. What laboratory techniques can be employed to separate yeasts and molds from bacteria?
5. Name some useful and some harmful species of molds.

17 | THE RICKETTSIAE

Historical Background

THE RICKETTSIAE, MINUTE (0.2 TO 0.6 BY 0.3 MICRON) COCCUS-like rods, were originally observed in 1909 by Howard Ricketts (1871–1910) in association with cases of Rocky Mountain spotted fever. Similar organisms were seen in the bodies of lice removed from typhus fever patients by Da Rocha-Lima in 1916, and he named his microbes *Rickettsia prowazekii* in honor of the American medical scientist, Ricketts, and the Austrian, Von Prowazek, both of whom fell victim to typhus fever which they were investigating. A year before his death Ricketts, together with Wilder, demonstrated that typhus fever and Rocky Mountain spotted fever were two separate diseases caused by similar organisms. (The reader is reminded that *typhoid fever* is a bacterial disease and should not be confused with *typhus fever* of rickettsial etiology.)

If the descriptions of illnesses reported by early historians have been interpreted correctly, typhus fever must have been prevalent at least as far back as 400 B.C. The pestilence referred to in *The Four Horsemen of the Apocalypse* undoubtedly was typhus or a typhuslike disease. Ferdinand of Spain lost some 20,000 of his men—not to the Moors, but rather to rickettsiae, and the mortality rate from typhus during the Thirty Years' War was also extremely high. A book recommended for those who are interested in learning more about the historical role of disease is Hans Zinsser's classic, *Rats, Lice, and History* which states with reference to

FIG. 17.1. Howard Taylor Ricketts (1870–1910). (Courtesy National Library of Medicine, Washington, D. C.)

Serbia in 1915: "Typhus may not have won the war, but it certainly helped."

Veterans of World War I can hardly forget the louse, or "cootie," that made life so miserable during the trench warfare. A rickettsial disease called *trench fever* was prevalent during the war (second only to influenza) and lice were responsible. This ailment does not have a high mortality rate but it incapacitates its victims for weeks with extreme pain in the back and lower legs. The etiological agent, *Rickettsia quintana*, was not recognized until 1917, and the species name *quintana* reflects the characteristic "five-day fever" which was the doughboys' designation for the affliction.

Characteristics

Bergey's Manual (1957), which lists rickettsiae under the class, *Microtatobiotes,* describes these organisms as small, gram negative, nonmotile, rod-shaped coccoid and often pleomorphic microorganisms occurring as elementary bodies which are usually intracellular but which may occasionally be facultatively or exclusively extracellular. They are considered nonfilterable and may be cultivated outside the host only in living tissues, embryonated eggs, or rarely in media containing body fluids. The species which are pathogenic for vertebrates, however, have not been grown in a cell-free medium. They are usually transmitted by such vectors as lice, fleas, ticks, and mites, to cause the following diseases:

Insect-borne:	Typhus fever group
Tick-borne:	Rocky Mountain spotted fever and Q fever
Mite-borne:	Scrub typhus (Tsutsugamushi) and rickettsialpox

Rickettsiae may resemble some of the smaller bacteria morphologically. They appear to multiply by fission and the cells are not too unlike vegetative bacteria in their resistance to heat, light, drying, and chemicals. Phase contrast microscopy reveals internal structures suggesting nucleus-like bodies. Rickettsiae stain well with Giemsa's stain, but poorly with aniline dyes. Some of the smaller members of the group are of a size close to that of the larger viruses, which they resemble biologically. In many respects rickettsiae might be considered to represent a living bridge connecting ultramicroscopic viruses with the bacteria.

Cultivation Techniques

Rickettsiae may live as commensals or as symbionts in the intestinal epithelium of arthropod hosts, and in the case of ticks the microbes are transmitted through their eggs to succeeding generations. In vertebrate hosts the organisms invade the cells lining the blood and lymph vessels and the serous cavities.

Before an effective prophylactic vaccine could be produced to combat such infections, methods had to be developed to cultivate rickettsiae in volume. Initial attempts involved grinding up the viscera of infected vectors and inactivating the released rickettsiae with phenol. In fact, at the close of World War I some laboratories were producing commercial vaccines for armed forces in Europe by the intrarectal injection of lice on a production line basis! Later when tissue culture techniques were developed employing the yolk sac of developing chicks, the infected embryonic tissues were ground up to separate the abundant rickettsial bodies, which were then suspended in saline and treated with formalin to inactivate the pathogenic microorganisms which were to serve as the antigen in vaccines. Persons who are allergic to egg protein should have a sensitivity test conducted prior to typhus vaccination, since deaths have been reported in hypersensitive individuals.

Diseases

Epidemic Typhus

Epidemic typhus is caused by *R. prowazekii* transmitted principally through the body louse, *Pediculus corporis,* but the head louse, *P. capitus,* may also transmit the disease. When a louse bites a victim it defecates at the same time and the wound becomes infected from this contamination. The lesion itches and the person tends to scratch the area, thus driving the microbes into the break in the skin. Bedbugs and ticks may be experimentally infected with these rickettsiae, but there is no indication that they represent a natural reservoir for typhus. The disease, which is more severe in adults than in children, is associated with overcrowding and lack of sanitation, and through the centuries classical typhus has killed millions of human beings. Between 1917 and 1922 an estimated 25 million cases of typhus occurred in Europe. Mortality rates run as high as 70 per cent in some outbreaks, whereas in other epidemics this rate may drop by half. The disease tends to flourish in colder weather when lice adopt a human host for warmth and blood. Zinsser made the interesting observation that Napoleon's retreat from Moscow "was started by a louse." It was not until World War II that the efficacy of typhus vaccine was proved in North Africa and in Italy during threatened outbreaks so characteristic of wartime. Even the Korean conflict was not without its typhus attack in 1951 when the North Koreans and the Chinese felt its impact.

These rickettsiae are intracellular parasites, but oddly enough they prefer slowly metabolizing cells, a characteristic which differentiates them from viruses which tend to propagate better in young, actively growing cells. Typhus organisms when cultivated in embryonated eggs grow more rapidly in cells which line the yolk sac than they do in the chorioallantoic membrane. This discovery by Cox paved the way for the eventual commercial production of effective vaccines.

The incubation period for epidemic typhus in man varies from 5 to 21 days after the victim has been bitten by an infected louse, and the initial symptoms are not unlike those of acute influenza, with fevers running as high as 103° to 104°F, accompanied by chills, marked weakness, and pains in the head and limbs. Characteristic skin eruptions appear on the fourth or fifth day following onset of symptoms, and one of the rather unusual features of some rickettsial diseases, including typhus, is that the palms of the hands and the soles of the feet become spotted. These areas generally escape any rash in other diseases, but in typhus fever it is the face and forehead that might be spared. The original pink eruptions turn purplish and then brown, and hemorrhagic centers may remain for some time. Blood cell pictures are not particularly helpful to a diagnostician since the leucocyte count may rise little, if at all, and the differential count is typically normal.

The severe headaches during the peak of the disease are usually accompanied by delirium, but death rarely occurs during the first week. If a crisis occurs, it can be expected on about the twelfth day, and should the patient survive, bronchitis and a persistent cough may continue for weeks. Complications include encephalitis, parotitis, otitis media, and mastoiditis. In cold weather gangrene of the feet may be a typical symptom as the aftermath of localization of the rickettsial bodies in the capillaries.

Recovery from an attack of typhus imparts a permanent immunity to this disease, but immune individuals have been known to contract spotted fevers, indicating a lack of cross protection between these two types of disease.

Prevention of typhus fever rests in the destruction of lice by liberal applications of DDT as a dusting agent for the body and clothes of individuals in endemic areas. When this technique is coupled with prophylactic vaccination of the population, the disease can be controlled. Once an individual becomes infected, however, para-aminobenzoic acid may be administered to decrease the severity of the symptoms, but chloramphenicol is the drug of choice.

Laboratory confirmation of this disease is conducted on blood samples subjected to the Weil-Felix reaction which is a cross-agglutination test with *Proteus* species serving as diagnostic antigens. Strong serological specificity occurs with Proteus OX-19, a slight reaction takes place with *Proteus* OX-2, and Proteus OX-K is negative when placed in contact with serum from an infected typhus fever patient. The reader is referred to the discussion of these curious bacterial-rickettsial relationships in the section of Chapter 15 that deals with the *Proteus* genus.

A number of cases of Brill's disease reported between 1910 and 1930 were probably reactivated manifestations of old typhus fever infections sometimes years or even decades following original attacks.

Endemic or Murine Typhus

The "murine" title for this disease stems from the fact that it is primarily a disease of rats (Latin: *mus, muris*) transmitted to man by the rat flea, *Xenopsylla cheopis,* that carries pathogenic *Rickettsia typhi.* Although the usual mode of transmission is through the bite of infected fleas, evidence points to the inhalation of dust carrying flea feces and the ingestion of food containing contaminated urine as other potential sources of this disease which is usually less severe than the louse-borne epidemic typhus.

Endemic typhus is widespread throughout Europe and Asia, and in the United States over 36,000 cases were reported between 1913 and 1944. Most of these were concentrated in eight Southern states, fanning out from granary and warehouse workers employed in rat-infested areas.

Murine typhus fever patients develop agglutinins to *Proteus* OX-19 and OX-2, but the complement-fixation test, a more sensitive serological reaction, may be required to separate endemic typhus from some of the other rickettsial infections. A vaccine prepared from embryonated eggs by Cox's method offers protection against murine typhus, but booster doses should be administered annually to maintain the recommended concentration (titer) of antibodies. Although flea control naturally is important, a relentless fight against rats—house, barn, and sewer—will get at the base of the problem. Para-aminobenzoic acid will tend to shorten and to modify the symptoms once the disease has become established in humans, but chloramphenicol appears to be the superior antibiotic for treatment of endemic typhus.

Rocky Mountain Spotted Fever
(American Spotted Fever)

Spotted fevers caused by *Rickettsia rickettsii* are transmitted by the wood tick *Dermacentor andersoni* in Western states and by *Dermacentor variabilis,* the dog tick, along the East Coast of the United States. The rabbit tick is naturally infected in nature but does not bite man and thus is of little or no hazard to human beings unless the vector is crushed on the skin, which might permit the rickettsiae to enter the body. A number of other ticks are implicated in spreading this disease among lower animals.

In the case of *D. andersoni* the infectious agents are carried from one generation of ticks to the next either transovarially or by copulation, and rickettsiae invade practically every tissue, although ticks do not appear to suffer from their presence. When humans are infected the mortality rates will vary with the geographical location of the vectors and will range from a low of about 4 per cent in sections of Idaho to as high as 90 per cent in the Bitter Root Valley of Montana. The over-all fatality rate is slightly below 20 per cent for the 500 or so cases reported annually in the United States. Although this disease was originally recognized in the Rocky Mountain regions in about 1899, cases have been reported in every state except Maine, Vermont, Rhode Island, and Kansas, but no doubt these areas eventually will be added to the roster. Similar, if not identical, spotted fevers occur in South American countries.

In 1909 Ricketts and King independently reported that the wood tick was the primary vector of Rocky Mountain spotted fever in the Western states, particularly among the adult population of hunters, sheepherders, and ranchers. In the absence of suitable repellants for ticks, proper clothing, including high boots and shirts fastened at the neck, should be worn. This precaution must be coupled with careful inspection of exposed areas of the body every two or three hours to ascertain the presence of any ticks that might be enjoying a free blood meal. The possibility that they might have worked their way to "protected" areas of the body should not be overlooked, and after a day outdoors the evening inspection should be a thorough one.

Should ticks be found with their heads buried in the skin of a host, individuals are advised not to try to pry the invader loose, or the buried head could become severed from the rest of the body, and this foreign substance is capable of setting up an uncomfortable and sometimes fatal infection. Some ranchers recommend holding a lighted cigarette "near the posterior end of the tick," and this may encourage them to back out! Others claim that the application of a minute drop of kerosene or gasoline to the same portion of the tick will also produce the desired effect. In any event the tick should not be handled with bare fingers; diseases have been acquired by this means when the infectious contents of a tick spilled on the skin. Once tick feces have dried out they are no longer infectious. This is in direct contrast to typhus fever rickettsiae which may remain viable in the dried feces of lice and fleas for some time after elimination from infected vectors. A pair of forceps or fingers covered with paper or rubber gloves are recommended for handling ticks before they are incinerated—a wise precaution to follow.

Adult ticks prefer to feed on deer, cattle, dogs, and human beings, but man presumably is the only host that suffers from the transferred rickettsiae. Children acquire the greatest number of cases of spotted fever on the East Coast because they come in more intimate contact with dogs who frequently harbor *D. variabilis,* the common carrier of spotted fever in this area. Parents in rural areas where this disease is known to be present should examine their children at frequent intervals for the presence of ticks if the youngsters spend a great deal of time with dogs.

When man is bitten by an infected tick, there is a recognized delay of several hours during which time the feeding tick is not infectious, but after this initial period, what has been termed a *rejuvenation reaction* occurs. Investigators have not ascertained whether this lag is required by the tick to build up the number or the virulence of rickettsiae to trigger an infection in man. Perhaps it is a combination of factors. Whatever the reason, this noninfectious period should be taken advantage of by all exposed persons to examine their bodies and to remove any "hitch-hikers."

After an incubation period of from 3 to 12 days, the clinical symptoms put in their appearance and include a fever of 104° to 105°F accompanied by severe chills, sharp headaches, and prolonged pains in the joints and muscles. The characteristic rash appears between the second and the fifth days, beginning on the wrists, ankles, forehead, hands, and feet. This extremity pattern of skin involvement aids in differentiating spotted fever from typhus where the trunk and body serve as initial sites of rash formation. The *Rickettsia rickettsii* exhibit a marked preference for nuclear material of the cells they invade, whereas other rickettsiae are primarily intracytoplasmic in their growth requirements.

In acute cases of Rocky Mountain spotted fever the leucocyte count may be elevated to between 12,000 and 15,000, accompanied by an enlargement of the spleen. Antibodies specific for *Proteus* species of bacteria, with which they react, appear on about the fifth day with a continuing rise in titer during convalescence. Death, if it claims a victim of this disease, can be expected during the second week of infection when hemorrhages and thromboses become too overpowering for the host.

A high level of immunity is acquired after one attack of spotted fever, but second attacks have occasionally been reported in the literature. The persistence of low-grade unrecognized infections in man after "recovery" from the disease has been postulated by some investigators as a possible explanation for the relatively high degree of protection this disease imparts.

It was at the United States Public Health Service Laboratory in Hamilton, Montana, that the first successful vaccine was prepared to combat spotted fevers. It consisted of infected tick tissue inactivated with phenol. However, this original preparation which was in use for over a decade has now been replaced by a more effective suspension made from formalin-inactivated rickettsiae grown in yolk sac cultures. Following a primary series of injections, annual booster doses are recommended in "dangerous areas" where the infected tick population is high. An interesting account of this early struggle to perfect rickettsial vaccines has been recorded in *Man Against Death* by DeKruif.

Spraying infected areas with DDT from airplanes has been found useful in localized pockets of high tick population, but complete eradication of Rocky Mountain spotted fever still seems remote.

Laboratory evidence to support clinical cases of suspected spotted fever may be gathered by using the Weil-Felix test on patients' blood serum. This agglutination reaction is strong against *Proteus* OX-19, weak with OX-2, and absent when OX-K is the antigen. Since these findings parallel those of typhus fever, complement-fixation tests are recommended to differentiate the two diseases. The antibiotics chloramphenicol and tetracycline give promising results in the treatment of spotted fevers when administered in full therapeutic doses until several days after the fever has disappeared.

Q Fever

Q fever was first described in 1937 among slaughterhouse workers in Queensland, Australia and was originally called "query fever" because of its questionable origin. The name has since been shortened to Q fever, and the disease has been recognized in the United States, Europe, Asia, and Africa. Because of marked differences in characteristics from those usually associated with other rickettsiae, a new genus, *Coxiella,* was proposed in honor of Herald R. Cox who was a co-discoverer of the agent of Q fever in America, and the specific name *burnetti* is for Burnet who first studied the disease in Australia. *Coxiella* can pass through Berkefeld N and W filters which hold back other rickettsiae and the bacteria. They are relatively stable to heat and drying, and the disease produces no rash and no agglutinins for any *Proteus* species.

The exact mechanism by which human beings become infected with these agents is not fully understood, but it has been established that arthropod transmission is not a required intermediary step, although at least seventeen species of ticks have been found to harbor these rickettsiae in nature. Other ticks can be infected experimentally, and transovarial survival has been demonstrated in *D. andersoni*. The bandicoot (*Isoodon macrourus*) appears to be the natural reservoir of *Coxiella* in Australia.

Milk from infected animals may contain significant numbers of *Coxiella,* and because of the somewhat higher resistance displayed by these microorganisms to heat, the time-honored technique of pasteurizing milk and dairy products at from 142° to 145°F for thirty minutes has recently been modified to a *minimum* of 145°F to insure inactivation of Q fever organisms that might be present.

Although it is true that infected ticks might bite man and cause this disease, evidence weighs heavily in favor of the concept that inhalation of dust contaminated with *Coxiella* from a number of sources is probably the most common mode of dissemination, with milk consumption also high on the list. Patients suffering from Q fever generally show a history of contact with sheep, cattle, goats, or ticks. According to one study in northern California, Q fever shows a seasonal increase on ranches during the lambing period when infected placentas are most abundant, and dust-borne contamination is probably involved.

A particularly high incidence of this type of rickettsial infection occurs among individuals engaged in dairying, slaughterhouse operations, wool and hair industries, diagnostic laboratory procedures, and laundry operators who serve laboratories where Q fever is under investigation. At least one nurse and two hospital workers are believed somehow to have contracted this disease from an infected patient. Over 1000 Americans were afflicted with Q fever in the Mediterranean area during World War II. These rickettsiae are treacherous to work with in a laboratory, and even when supposedly iron-clad techniques were practiced, experienced technicians have acquired the disease. Prophylactic vaccination should become a routine practice for anyone working in these hazardous occupations; killed vaccines prepared from yolk-sac cultures of embryonated eggs offer adequate protection.

One attack of Q fever, which happens to have a relatively low mortality rate, imparts a high degree of immunity, but there is little, if any, cross-protection with other rickettsiae. As is true of other rickettsial diseases, Q fever responds to treatment with chloramphenicol and the tetracyclines, but *Coxiellae* are somewhat more resistant and require heavier doses over a longer period to accomplish equivalent results.

The incubation period is usually two or three weeks before the customary rickettsial symptoms—malaise, headache, severe chills and sweats, fever, and weakness—appear, and they remain for periods up to ten days. In the absence of suitable laboratory confirmation, particularly the complement-fixation test, the atypical pneumonia (pneumonitis) characteristic of Q fever is undoubtedly mistaken for influenza in some cases. A mild, annoying cough may persist for some weeks after the clinical symptoms subside.

Scrub Typhus (*Tsutsugamushi*)

This form of typhus is transmitted by *Rickettsia tsutsugamushi* (meaning "of a dangerous mite") by mites of the genus *Trombicula*, particularly in the rural population and among agricultural workers in the jungle and scrub area of the Philippines, Japan, Burma, Malaya, and other islands of the southwest Pacific where the disease has been recognized since 1879. Field voles, shrews, mice, and rats are reservoir hosts. More than 6000 personnel of the United States armed forces contracted scrub typhus during World War II in these regions, and some 1300 cases were reported in one British army corps in Burma. Mortality rates range from zero to as high as 44 per cent in different outbreaks.

Morphologically these rickettsiae appear to be somewhat less pleomorphic than other species, with a predominance of diplococci and short rods. They grow well in the cytoplasm of cells in the yolk sac of embryonated eggs as well as in agar tissue cultures. The usual cycle involves both mites and a vertebrate host, although transovarial passage is also possible.

The incubation period for tsutsugamushi disease is from 7 to 21 days (usually no longer than 14 days, however) after customary bites on ankles and legs produce a local lesion called an **eschar** which progresses to a necrotic ulcer. Clinical symptoms follow the appearance of local lesions, and they may be gradual or acute with severe malaise, chills, vomiting, and head pains. The temperature rises in steplike fashion while the pulse rate remains low. Between the fifth and the eighth day a red macular, or maculopapular, rash may appear, although not all patients exhibit it. Death, if it occurs, generally takes place toward the end of the second week from complications of encephalitis, bacterial pneumonia, or circulation failure. Those who successfully pass the second week of the disease may undergo a gradual and prolonged convalescence that may last for months.

Agglutinins for *Proteus* OX-K appear at about the end of two weeks, but the level of antibodies (the **titer**) never becomes high. There is no serological cross-reaction between scrub typhus and other rickettsial diseases. The local eschar may be caused by the peculiar technique employed by the larval mites who form small liquefied areas in the skin of their human victim from which they drain off their food requirements by means of a sucking tube. Enlargement of regional lymph nodes, another characteristic finding in scrub typhus, may also be associated with this type of feeding on the part of the mites.

Some investigators advocate the wearing of protective clothing impregnated with dimethylphthalate to repel *Trombicula* mites in known contaminated areas. Vaccines prepared from tissue cultures or yolk sacs do not appear to be as effective for preventing scrub typhus as some of the other rickettsial vaccines. The three antibiotics that have shown the most promise in the treatment of established infections include chlortetracycline, oxytetracycline, and chloramphenicol.

Rickettsialpox

This relatively mild, nonfatal, febrile, rickettsial disease was first reported in an outbreak involving 124 individuals in a housing development in New York City in 1946; within one year over 300 cases had been reported along the Eastern seaboard. Cases of this disease have also been found in urban centers in the U.S.S.R.

The etiological agents are *Rickettsia akari* which are minute diplobacilli that frequently exhibit bipolar staining and are carried by the mite *Allodermanyssus sanguineus*. The generic name of these rickettsiae is derived from the resemblance of the disease to chickenpox, and the specific name comes from the Greek word meaning "mite."

Transmission to man occurs through the bite of a mite that has fed on an infected house mouse, *Mus musculis,* which serves as an intermediate host. *Rickettsia akari* are unable to grow on artificial media, but when cultivated in embryonated eggs the organisms are found both intranuclearly and intracytoplasmically in the cells of the yolk sac and the amniotic sac which they invade.

In man the microorganisms cause an initial erythematous focal lesion at the site of the mite bite; this reaction is followed by fever which lasts for about one week and, finally, a macular rash appears. The original bite on the skin evolves into a vesicle not too unlike that seen with vaccinia, and this is followed by the development of a black eschar which may persist for the better part of a month.

In the original New York outbreak the mites were found on the warm walls through which the heat ducts passed to upper floors, and the mouse population in the basement of this apartment house was high. Mouse-to-mouse transmission of this rickettsial disease has been well established.

The Weil-Felix test is negative when blood sera from infected patients are tested against members of the *Proteus* genus, but laboratory confirmation of rickettsialpox can be made either by isolation of the etiological microorganisms from the blood of infected individuals or by the complement-fixation test which yields some cross reactions with *R. rickettsii,* the cause of spotted fever.

Prevention and control of this disease involves the elimination of rodents which serve as hosts for the infected mites, and this can be accomplished largely through denying mice attractive environments by the frequent disposal of garbage and rubbish at central incinerators so often seen in apartment houses and housing developments.

The usual antibiotics employed for the treatment of rickettsiae work well with rickettsialpox, but in view of the limited distribution of the disease, the development of a vaccine for prophylactic vaccination does not seem to be warranted.

Review Questions

1. What are the major differences between rickettsiae and viruses?
2. What are the underlying differences between rickettsiae and bacteria which determine the techniques employed for their cultivation?
3. Is typhus fever a potential threat in the United States?
4. Are rickettsial diseases becoming more or less of a public health problem throughout the world? What are some of the active means for their control?
5. Is there any difference between vaccination against a rickettsial disease and a bacterial disease?

18 | VIRUSES

Historical Review

SOME OF THE MOST SIGNIFICANT ADVANCES MADE IN MICROBIOLOGY during the last decade have been in the area of virology, and this chapter can do little more than point out a few of the fundamentals of this science that has moved forward with the development of tools and techniques. The major instrument that has made progress possible has been the electron microscope with which man can view viruses, and the techniques include cultivation of these parasitic agents in embryonated eggs and in tissue cultures. Without the able assistance of antibiotics to inhibit unwanted bacteria, however, growth of viruses *in vitro* was dealt a delaying blow that impeded progress in this field.

Salle defines a virus as an exogenous submicroscopic unit capable of multiplication only inside specific cells. The word *virus* is derived from Latin and means a slimy poisonous liquid. (In recent years the word has also come to mean anything that poisons the mind or the soul of man.) Viruses are etiological agents of disease, typically are of small size and often are capable of passing through filters that retain bacteria. But the older designation of "filterable viruses" is no longer felt to be a reliable differentiating criterion for these microorganisms, since so many factors influence filterability. In fact, the virus of cowpox and rabies may not always pass through the usual types of filters.

FIG. 18.1. Electron microscope. (Courtesy Radio Corporation of America, Camden, N. J.)

In 1892 Iwanowski demonstrated that the sap from a diseased plant run through the finest filter available at that time was still capable of transmitting the disease to healthy susceptible plants, but progress in recognizing viruses was gradual. Foot and mouth disease of cattle was shown in 1897–98 to be of virus etiology, and in 1901 Walter Reed reported a similar type of agent in yellow fever in man. Viruses capable of attacking specific bacteria were first described in 1915 by Twort whose findings were substantiated by D'Herelle who gave this filterable material the name *bacteriophage,* which literally means "bacteria-eater." *Bergey's Manual* (1957) lists viruses under the class *Microtatobiotes,* derived from the Greek words *microtatus* and *biote,* meaning "smallest life."

Physical Characteristics of Viruses

A great deal was known about the size and the shape of some viruses before they were ever observed with the aid of an electron microscope. By employing collodion membranes with predetermined porosities, size limits of these microorganisms were calculated on the basis of whether the resulting filtrate was capable of causing specific infections in known hosts. If the virus breached the membrane of one pore size and not another, the general limits of size of the filterable "things" could be established. Later electron scope observations proved these early calculations to be remarkably accurate. Shapes of viruses have been found to include spheres, rods, ovals, and tadpole-like objects with sizes ranging from about 10 to 300 millimicrons. The agent in foot and mouth disease is at the small end of the scale (10) together with yellow fever (22) and polio (from 22–32). Smallpox virus is relatively large (250); as a point of reference, red blood cells measure 7500 millimicrons in diameter. As many as a million virus particles can fit into a single bacterial cell.

Not only must viruses be provided with living cells if they are to remain active, but the degree of cell specificity is so exacting in many cases that the requirement becomes a definite limiting factor in controlling the population of virus particles. This prerequisite would appear to be a handicap for the viruses but a fortunate circumstance for man, other animals, and plants for which these agents are pathogenic.

A convenient but by no means iron-clad scheme for grouping viruses is presented in the following framework, together with representative examples:

Dermotropic viruses (skin):   chickenpox and smallpox
Pneumotropic viruses (lungs):   influenza and virus pneumonia
Neurotropic viruses (nerves):   poliomyelitis and rabies
Viscerotropic viruses (vital organs):   yellow fever

Man has been able to "train" certain viruses to grow in cells and tissues which do not correspond with the above general scheme of cell affinity, and it is indeed fortunate, insofar as vaccine production is concerned, that such adaptations are feasible. The breakthrough in the development of Salk vaccine for the neurotropic poliomyelitis virus came with the announcement by Enders and his colleagues in 1950 that monkey kidney tissue could be employed for production of relatively large amounts of virus.

It is customary to make the broad statement that viruses cannot be viewed under an "ordinary" type of light microscope, but this assertion should be qualified. Some of the larger viruses, including vaccinia (cowpox), when suitably treated with appropriate dyes can be viewed as distinct dots under the oil immersion objective of better microscopes. The first pictures of viruses taken by an electron scope were published in 1938 in Berlin by Von Borries and Ruzka, and since then electron micrographs have become a routine part of studies in virology. Attempts to purify and to identify viruses reached a significant milestone with the crystallization of tobacco mosaic virus for which Wendell M. Stanley was awarded the Nobel prize in chemistry in 1946. Perhaps we are not as much concerned today with what viruses are as we are with what they do, but these two aspects of research in this field of science cannot be sharply separated. Both are important to an over-all understanding of· these minute microbes.

There are technical difficulties that must be faced when objects are to be examined under an electron scope. First of all, the preparation must be extremely thin. After being placed on a layer of nitrocellulose in a carrier consisting of a disc made of fine wire mesh, the preparation is inserted within an airtight chamber and the entire system is put under a high vacuum, a technique that dehydrates the film and undoubtedly distorts morphology of the particles being examined. Some increase in sharpness of the image can be attained by impregnating the particles with various chemicals to increase their opacity.

The technique known as "shadowing" is carried out by bombarding the preparation at an angle with free atoms of gold, silver, or other metals. The sprayed atoms adhere to all surfaces that are not protected and the objects (viruses, etc.) throw a shadow where the atoms have failed to strike the surface of the film. Photographic techniques will reveal white areas that were heavily coated, whereas the uncoated shadowed areas are dark and yield a three-dimensional effect which enhances the sharpness of the objects being examined.

Cultivation

Because viruses must have specific living cells in which to grow, the methods employed for their cultivation differ markedly from those used for growing bacteria, yeasts, and molds. In general there are three principal methods using live animals such as mice or hamsters, developing chick embryos, or tissue cultures. In each technique results are determined by noting changes brought about in host cells. Not all living cells, whether in the body of a living animal or bits of tissue placed in a suitable medium *in vitro,* serve as suitable hosts for all viruses. Trial and error has been the means by which suitable substrates have been determined. If a neurotropic virus is being investigated, the required portal of entry might be directly into the brain of anaesthetized mice. Histological changes may be the criterion of whether the viruses have attacked specific cells; death of the animal may be employed in other determinations, with the customary statistical allowances being made for physical injury (trauma) which sometimes results during inoculation.

Fertile Eggs

Fertilized hen eggs were suggested by Goodpasture and Woodruff in 1931 as a suitable substrate for the cultivation of selected viruses, and with this announcement dawned a new era in microbiology. The advantages presented by embryonated eggs are many and include the following: readily available; reasonable cost; relatively little care when compared with the feeding of animals and the cleaning of cages; usually free of bacteria, other viruses, and antibodies; and they contain a number of cell layers suitable for inoculation and study of a wide variety of viruses. Students of embryology understand the general stages through which a fertilized egg passes during the 21-day development while the egg is incubated at from 38° to 39°C. Almost all parts of the developing chick may be useful in growing one or more types of viruses. Some prefer the allantoic cavity; others have an affinity for the amniotic cavity, the yolk sac, or various organs of the embryo itself. The age of the embryo·may be a critical factor, with 6 to 13 days the usual limits for optimum multiplication of the parasites.

The allantoic membrane serves as the respiratory organ for the developing chick, and gaseous exchange takes place between the blood of the capillaries and the atmosphere through the various porous membranes and the outer shell itself. These blood-filled vessels are a sign of viability and they can be viewed directly through the shell when the egg is placed before a strong light in the candling process. Such an examination also serves to position the embryo for the technician who can draw legends and sketches on the. shell for reference purposes. Such markings aid in determining the precise point at which inoculations of viruses should take place with the least possible damage to the underlying living embryo.

Rapid multiplication of viruses takes place in an embryonated egg because of the high degree of susceptibility of specific cells lining the various cavities, and this characteristic makes the egg technique extremely useful in virology. Through suitable dilution of test fluids, graded doses of viruses can be sprayed or pipetted onto membrane surfaces, particularly the chorioallantoic membrane, and lesions (pocks) that develop serve as a means for counting the number of virus particles in a given suspension. This method is not too unlike colony counts of bacteria on agar-containing substrates. The membrane can be "dropped" before inoculation by drilling a small hole in the air sac (blunt end) of the egg and applying gentle but firm suction. This procedure causes the choriolallantoic membrane to pull away from the shell membrane, and facilitates inoculation of the surface by means of a hypodermic syringe. Seeding the membrane with virus is made through a second "window" carefully drilled through the shell to avoid rupturing any blood vessels. This is where previous candling of the egg serves as a useful guide during the drilling operation. Some technicians prefer to drill triangular openings in the egg shell by means of an oxy-hydrogen blowtorch which, in the hands of a skilled operator, is superior to the dentist's drill so frequently employed. The torch not only cuts a suitable hole, but the heat also serves to maintain sterility in the area. Great care must be exercised, however, to avoid any heat damage to the embryo.

Once the seeding of the membrane surfaces has been completed, the opening in the shell may be sealed with a cover slip window held in position by a sterile mixture of vaseline and paraffin. Some workers prefer gummed cellophane or similar seals. Throat and nasal washings from patients suspected of having influenza should be mixed with appropriate amounts of wide-spectrum antibiotics prior to inoculation to retard the growth of bacterial contaminants and to provide the viruses with suitable conditions for their growth and multiplication. This use of antibiotics has become routine whenever possible bacterial contamination is a factor. The particular portion of the embryonated egg that may best serve to initiate growth of viruses being isolated from clinical material may not be the same tissue that will provide optimum conditions for an egg-adapted virus. For example, the washings from a patient with influenza may develop virus populations better in the amniotic cavity, but once the virus has been isolated, further egg transfers are best via the allantoic route of inoculation.

Tissue Culture

It has been known since shortly after the turn of the twentieth century that selected bits of tissue separated from the animals that produced them can be made to grow in tubes, flasks, or bottles when the cells are suspended in a suitable fluid medium and stored at an appropriate temperature. New cells grow out of these tissue fragments and develop into a thin sheet in which viruses can live and multiply. One type of cell that is widely employed in tissue culture work was originally obtained from a human tumor and is known as the **HeLa cell.** When viruses attack these or other cells growing *in vitro* the damage inflicted by the parasites can be seen by examining the host cells under a microscope. Tissue specificity

FIG. 18.2. Virus-containing tissue culture growing under controlled conditions. (Courtesy Eli Lilly and Company, Indianapolis, Indiana.)

and host specificity are maintained through tissue culture cultivation, and this has more than passing significance in virology investigations.

Minced chick embryo suspended in serum or in a complete salt solution, such as Tyrode's or similar mixtures, constituted the original tissue culture, and step by step the technique developed whereby single types

FIG. 18.3. Tissue cultures are gently rocked for six days at 36°C. (Courtesy Eli Lilly and Company, Indianapolis, Indiana.)

FIG. 18.4. During inactivation of the viruses, tubes are slowly rolled in circular machines so that tissue cells are immersed intermittently in the nutrient medium. (Courtesy Eli Lilly and Company, Indianapolis, Indiana.)

of tissues were selected on the basis of virus preferences. The monkey kidney cells upon which Salk depended for his polio viruses are a direct outgrowth of success in this approach to virus cultivation. HeLa cells have been found particularly useful in the growth of a wide variety of viruses that have rejected a number of other cells as hosts.

Bacteriophages are extremely specific in their bacterial host requirements, and this restriction serves as a valuable diagnostic tool in identifying particular strains of bacteria from suspected human carriers who might be implicated in particular outbreaks. Much of the detective work involved in tracking down the causes of *Staphylococcus* infections in hospitals and institutions is based upon the bacteriophage approach.

Among advances made in tissue culture techniques in recent years has been the introduction of "roller tubes." Tissue fragments are held in place by plasma on the walls of test tubes that are slowly rotated in or on a drum to increase the oxygen level of the nutrient fluid. This method permits longer growth periods and greater harvests without the necessity for frequent transfers of cultures to maintain viability. The type of cells employed is naturally dependent upon the virus being studied. Muscle tissue, glandular epithelia, and differentiated nerve tissue fail to produce offshoots of cells in tissue cultures even though physiological tests indicate that the cells are alive and metabolizing. Tissue survival is not enough; active multiplication must take place.

The speed of virus multiplication in tissue cultures is impressive. For example, vaccinia virus in a flask culture may in 48 hours produce up to 100,000 times as much virus as was in the original inoculum, and this is a paramount consideration in volume production of vaccines. The speed of virus multiplication, however, does not parallel the speed of cell growth. One decided advantage of *in vitro* growth of viruses over the egg method for vaccine production is that tissue cultures eliminate the need for concern over egg protein sensitivity in injected individuals.

Dermotropic Viruses

Varicella (Chickenpox) and Herpes Zoster (Shingles)

Varicella, an acute, extremely contagious disease contracted primarily by young children, has an incubation period of from 14 to 16 days. The infection involves the upper layers of the skin, causing eruptions that are found most abundantly on the trunk of the patient, although lesions may also appear on the scalp and mucous membranes of the upper respiratory tract. The virus apparently enters by way of the nose and mouth, and the widespread distribution of skin lesions suggests an initial viremia.

Symptoms persist for about three or four days. Chickenpox strikes relatively infrequently after the age of twenty, but when adults become infected, the clinical symptoms tend to be severe. Orchitis and testicular atrophy may occasionally occur in males.

Varicella is characterized by a sudden onset of fever with marked itching of the skin eruptions. Within about 24 hours papules appear on the skin and they eventually progress to vesicles surrounded by erythema. These lesions are called *pocks*.

The virus particles are brick-shaped and measure about 210 by 240 millimicrons in size. They initiate formation of acidic inclusions within the nuclei of epithelial cells in both diseased animals and human tissue cultures, but chickenpox viruses cannot be cultivated in chick embryos.

The relationship between chickenpox and herpes zoster (shingles) has provided ground for much speculation, but indications point strongly to the possibility that herpes zoster may represent a varicella infection with the clinical symptoms modified by some pre-existing host immunity. Chickenpox is primarily a disease of children, with over 70 per cent of the population contracting the disease before the age of fifteen. Shingles is almost exclusively an adult disease, yet a close connection between the two clinical responses is supported on a number of grounds. Varicella was first transmitted experimentally in 1875 when the fluid from chickenpox vesicles was transferred to human volunteers. However, if fluid from herpes lesions is injected into children, some contract varicella and others come down with herpes. Adults suffering from shingles have been known to initiate epidemics of chickenpox through contact with susceptible children.

Morphologically the viruses from the two diseases appear to be identical, and evidence points strongly to the probability that the symptoms represent different phases of a single disease with factors, probably antibodies, within the host being responsible for the clinical modifications observed. One attack of either disease generally provides permanent immunity. Active artificial immunization procedures are not practiced, because chickenpox is considered to be a rather benign disease. The administration of gamma globulin that modifies the severity of a number of other virus infections has yielded disappointing results in cases of chickenpox. When deaths do occur from this disease, usually in young infants, they may be attributed to a rare fulminating hemorrhagic form of varicella pneumonia or encephalitis. This neurotropic tendency may conceivably be correlated with high virulence of the viruses, low resistance of the host, or possibly a combination of these two factors. Chemotherapy has its greatest value in preventing secondary bacterial infections, but no

antibiotic or other drug has been found effective in preventing or modifying either varicella or herpes infections.

The virus of herpes zoster causes an inflammation of dorsal-root ganglia
or ganglia of cranial nerves accompanied by crops of vesicles indistinguishable from varicella in areas supplied by affected sensory nerves.
Anyone who has ever gone through the extreme discomfort of shingles
can attest to the acute localized pain associated with this affliction.

Variola (Smallpox)

Louis Pasteur claimed that in time certain microbial diseases could
theoretically be wiped from the face of the earth, and although smallpox
has not yet been eradicated, it represents an excellent example of what
can be done to reduce cases of a given disease to a minimum through
application of rigid quarantine practices and widespread prophylactic
vaccination. Compulsory legislation in this instance is entirely justified
from a health standpoint, and any relaxation on the part of official health
agencies is followed by outbreaks of smallpox.

Epidemics of this dreaded disease occurred in China as early as the
twelfth century B.C., and smallpox became widespread throughout all
of Europe during the Crusades. It was introduced into the Western
Hemisphere in the sixteenth century, probably reaching the United
States during slave-trading operations. Smallpox was once one of the
most prevalent diseases of the world. In some areas as many as 95 out of
100 persons contracted it, with a mortality rate of at least 25 per cent.
Many of those who survived were left blinded and disfigured. According
to figures of the World Health Organization (WHO) there were over
70,000 deaths from smallpox in 1961 throughout the world, and the
1960's have been designated by this health group as the decade of
development, with smallpox one of the prime targets.

As recently as 1943 there were 789 cases in the United States, but less
than ten deaths occurred. In this age of jet travel when persons can reach
our shores within a matter of a few hours from any point in the world,
it is indeed a tribute to the vigilance of our public health authorities that
smallpox has been kept remarkably in check. No cases of endemic origin
have been reported in the United States since 1949, and precise requirements with respect to vaccination can be given credit for this fine record.

When cases do occur in countries where strict quarantine is practiced,
they can generally be traced either to lack of acceptance or failure to
practice vaccination in certain backward communities. Rejection of this
prophylactic practice on religious grounds on the part of certain religious
groups has also been responsible for some cases of this preventable
disease.

Smallpox, which is transmitted by direct contact with an infected individual or with material from a smallpox lesion, has an incubation period of about twelve days. It is an acute infection characterized by sudden onset, severe chills, rapidly rising temperature, followed by a skin eruption that passes through three stages—papular, vesicular, and pustular. The trunk of the body tends to display fewer eruptions than the limbs. The frequency of smallpox reaches its peak in winter and the distribution is practically universal unless active programs are in force to keep the disease in check. Recovery imparts a permanent immunity; artificial immunity may be effective for about three years. Some individuals apparently remain relatively immune for life following a single vaccination.

It was recognized centuries ago that one attack of smallpox conferred permanent immunity. The Chinese, according to some records, used to breathe upon dried scabs taken from smallpox patients as an immunizing procedure. Before Jenner substituted a modified cowpox virus for that of smallpox, the British as early as 1718 introduced smallpox virus into the skin and they reported some success. Today's vaccinia virus, while not identical with Jenner's cowpox virus, is produced with glycerolated calf lymph. Postvaccinal encephalomyelitis may occur in about one person in 100,000 following primary vaccination. This type of complication occurs with natural infections of both variola and cowpox.

Persons entering the United States must present proof of recent vaccination before they can clear customs, and the only acceptable document for international travel is the *International Certificate of Vaccination* obtainable from passport agencies, travel bureaus, local and state health departments, physicians, and the U.S. Public Health Service. Travel to most foreign countries requires evidence of vaccination within three years beginning eight days after vaccination.

Historically smallpox is interesting in that it was the first disease in which vaccination was successfully employed through artificial means. Edward Jenner, a country apothecary and naturalist from Gloucestershire, England, conducted these pioneer experiments in 1796–98. He had observed that dairymaids who contracted cowpox were spared the dreaded smallpox. We have since learned that cowpox is in all likelihood a modified (attenuated) form of smallpox. Jenner postulated that some cross-relationship existed between these two diseases, and his theory was put to the test using an eight-year-old boy, James Phipps, whose parents, we assume, were willing to sacrifice the young lad to science! A small amount of cowpox virus was rubbed into an area of his skin, and after a suitable incubation period, the boy was exposed to viable smallpox virus, but he failed to contract the disease.

When Jenner sent his original paper on this subject to the Royal Society, it was returned with the advice that he might better confine his research to the habits of the cuckoo, a study that had gained him his membership as a Fellow in the Society. But Jenner felt strongly enough about his theories to publish them in pamphlet form in 1798. One critic wrote that this paper was "just the sort of rambling discursive essay containing acute observations mixed up with mere conjectures which an unsystematic field naturalist might be expected to produce." Persistence on the part of the country apothecary, however, eventually culminated in development of a successful technique for saving untold numbers of lives, and his fundamental contribution became one of the significant milestones in microbiology. Today's vaccinia virus employed in the manufacture of smallpox vaccines is a lineal descendant of Jenner's original strains obtained from cows and dairymaids around 1796.

Vaccination against this widespread disease was introduced into America in 1800 by Dr. Benjamin Waterhouse, a Boston physician, who obtained vaccinia virus from Europe. He vaccinated his five-year-old son and two of his servants, and when they were subsequently exposed to smallpox they were found to be immune. This revolutionary practice was quickly adopted by many physicians with dramatic results. Thomas Jefferson paid Jenner a fine tribute in a letter written in 1806 when he stated "Future nations will know by human history only that the loathsome smallpox existed and by you has been extirpated."

Most communities and public health experts encourage vaccination when a child is less than one year old, with a revaccination required prior to entry into school, usually at the age of about five. Such vaccination is considered effective for a period up to three years. Before a person enters a country where smallpox is endemic, however, a repeat vaccination is recommended, even if the three-year "safe" period has not expired, and during impending epidemics mass vaccination of all persons is advised. Naturally all those engaged in the healing arts should keep their immunizations up to date.

After initial vaccination there is a period of three or four days during which time no clinical changes are evident, but then an eruption takes place at the site of vaccination, and this lesion then passes through a series of predictable changes culminating in a characteristic scar. On about the seventh day following introduction of the virus into the skin there is for most individuals a systemic reaction consisting of fever, headache, loss of appetite, and a general lack of well-being apparently correlating with the release of protective antibodies into the circulation. This is known as *active immunity* since the person plays an active part in building up his own antibodies in response to the introduction of foreign protein in the vaccine. *Passive immunity,* on the other hand, may be acquired for some diseases by receiving injections of anti-bodies produced in another person or animal, but this technique is not effective for preventing smallpox.

Various methods of immunization have been recommended through the years, but one of the most common procedures—the *multiple pressure technique*—is to place a drop of vaccine about one centimeter in diameter on a properly cleansed area of the skin. The skin is pressed repeatedly with a sharp needle to breach the superficial epidermis and to allow introduction of the virus. These punctures should not be deep enough to draw blood, however. Any type of tight bandage or protective device that might tend to exclude air should be avoided once the pustule appears. Contaminated dressings should not be handled without some protection and they should be disposed of by burning. Since both respiratory and skin discharges may contain infectious agents, great care must be exercised by those working with smallpox patients to prevent careless spread of this serious disease.

Smallpox vaccine may be prepared from calf lymph obtained by rubbing the virus into a scarified abdomen of a six-month-old calf, or by growing the organisms in living tissue cultures composed of minced chick embryo suspended in Tyrode's solution. The finished preparation must be stored at a very low temperature, preferably in the frozen state, to maintain viability, and expiration dates printed on the packages should be honored if best results are to be attained. Freeze-drying of the vaccine has made immunization programs much more effective in under-developed countries where refrigeration facilities are minimal or absent.

An individual being vaccinated for the first time (*primary reaction*) will display the usual three stages of the lesion: papule (third or fourth day), vesicle (sixth or seventh day), pustule (tenth to twelfth day), and finally a white scar sometime after the scab falls off. But when a person is partially immune from previous vaccinations, the responses are accel-erated and less severe with a maximum response on the seventh day called a *vaccinoid reaction.* A fully immune individual will display only a mild reddening of the area with little or no other reaction, and this is known as an *immune response.*

Antibiotics have no direct effect on smallpox virus, but they do tend to decrease the severity of any secondary bacterial infections.

Rubeola (Measles)

Measles is perhaps the most infectious of the known specific human diseases, and people of all ages and all races appear to be susceptible to even casual exposure to the virus which was first pinpointed in 1940. We think of measles as being a childhood disease but this is so only because youngsters are originally exposed to the disease by their close association with so many others who are also susceptible. Most individuals have had the disease before they reach the age of twenty, but if adults have escaped exposure in the early stages of their lives, frequently their children or grandchildren may bring measles home and older individuals then have a good chance of contracting it.

City dwellers appear to have a higher morbidity rate than their country cousins, and this fact was brought into sharp focus in 1916 when widespread epidemics occurred among young army recruits from rural areas. Barracks living apparently had provided them with their first exposure to measles virus, and the effects were most severe—a common finding in adults. When measles was brought to the Fiji Islands, the natives died like flies since they possessed no immunity whatsoever to the disease which was not endemic in their area.

Measles is a generalized disease caused by a dermotropic virus that is probably inhaled through droplet dissemination by carriers. The incubation period is from 10 to 14 days, with early symptoms not unlike those of a cold. The conjunctiva frequently become reddened and skin eruptions appear at the height of the fever which may reach 104 to 105°F. The characterisitc small white spots on the membranes of the pharynx are called **Koplik's spots,** and they develop several days prior to the skin rash and aid in the diagnosis of the disease.

Although measles probably does not in itself cause death of the patient, it is a disease that may exhibit serious sequelae, and these aftereffects are brought about through a general weakened resistance of the mucous membranes and the pulmonary tissues, making them susceptible to invasion by a wide variety of pathogenic bacteria and leading to pneumonia, middle-ear infections, and meningitis. About one patient in 1000 develops encephalitis or encephalomeningitis. Recovery from measles confers a permanent immunity, but it does not afford cross-protection for German measles.

At the time of this writing preliminary announcements have been made to the effect that successful measles vaccines have been produced and tried on an experimental basis. The early results sound highly encouraging, and within a few years massive immunization against measles may become as commonplace as polio vaccination is today.

If a mother has had measles, her newborn child is protected through passive transfer of antibodies, and this immunity may last for several months. Convalescent serum and gamma globulin preparations are presently being administered to exposed individuals as a means of modifying the course of measles. The injection of from 0.1 to 0.2 ml of gamma globulin per pound of body weight given during the first five days of the incubation period may prevent the disease from ever developing. A similar injection after the first five days and before clinical symptoms become apparent may not prevent the disease but may modify its severity, and the individual then builds up his own active immunity through having an active case of the disease.

German measles (rubella) had for many years been regarded as a benign disease, but in 1941 Gregg reported that when a woman, during the first three months of pregnancy, suffers an attack of rubella, severe congenital damage frequently occurs in the developing embryo.

Eye opacities (congenital cataract), heart damage, congenital deafness accompanied by failure to talk, and other serious effects appear to bear a direct relationship to such virus attacks. Some authorities claim that abnormalities may occur in up to 85 per cent of such individuals, and they even raise the question of the advisability of terminating pregnancies in women who develop German measles during the first trimester of pregnancy.

Figures vary as to the effectiveness of gamma globulin in such individuals. In any event, every effort should be made by all pregnant women to remain away from active cases of German measles and all known contacts. Young girls should probably not be prevented from contacting individuals infected with these viruses. In fact, some informed mothers even make a sincere effort to expose their young daughters to German measles before the youngsters reach the age of puberty.

Pneumotropic Viruses

Influenza

Influenza has been called the "modern plague" by some writers, and in many respects this is an apt description. The frightening part of widespread influenza epidemics is the large number of individuals who become incapacitated in a relatively short space of time. The worst pandemic occurred at the close of World War I when an estimated 20 million people succumbed to influenza, directly or indirectly. About 50 per cent of the world's population was infected, with a case fatality rate of about 3 per cent in most countries. However in India, where the mortality was greatest, the outbreak was sufficient to wipe out the entire population increase for the previous ten-year period! Other extensive epidemics of this disease have taken place since 1918–19 but the great flu pandemic has never been surpassed in intensity. Mass infections appear to be the result of antigenic changes in the virus, or viruses, which attack the vast reservoir of nonimmune individuals who possess neither natural nor artificially-induced immunity to the specific microorganisms.

Recognizing an infectious disease is the first essential to understanding it, and with the many types of respiratory diseases to which man is susceptible, it is not always easy to pinpoint "true flu" from similar clinical conditions. Early studies of this disease suggested that the etiological agent was a gram negative rod named *Haemophilus influenzae*. This microbe was isolated in 1892 by Pfeiffer who found it associated with the respiratory symptoms we call "influenza." In the early 1930's, however, the causative agent was discovered to be a virus; the blood-loving *Haemophilus* species has been accepted as an opportunist that appears as a secondary bacterial invader once the tissues have been attacked and weakend through the action of viruses. Influenza viruses are typically spherical with a diameter of between 80 and 100 millimicrons, but when the organisms are cultivated in embryonated eggs it is not unusual to observe filamentous forms of the virus.

In temperate climates influenza reaches its peak during the winter months, but in the tropics epidemics occur irregularly with no apparent seasonal correlation. Epidemics, in order to flourish in our North American climate, require a combination of the right season and the correct proportion of susceptible individuals to serve as hosts for the viruses.

The symptoms of influenza are acute, displaying a sudden onset, a fever of from 101° to 104°F lasting from one to four days, catarrh, pains in the head and muscles, sore throat, bronchitis, extreme prostration, and a decided tendency to pneumonic complications. Once the virus gains entrance to the respiratory tract of man the incubation period is less than 48 hours, and the number of cases can snowball at an alarming rate in just a few weeks. Recovery affords some immunity to the specific virus implicated, but the level of antibody production does not tend to be very high unless an individual has been exposed repeatedly.

Influenza viruses attack the epithelial cells lining the respiratory passages and the damage they cause favors invasion by virulent bacteria, particularly staphylococci, streptococci, and pneumococci. Staphylococci are by far the most serious secondary invaders and most deaths from influenza can probably be attributed to these organisms. There are two principal types of influenza virus, type A (PR8) and type B (Lee). The type A strains cause epidemics once in about every two or three years; outbreaks from B virus tend to be less severe and reach peak waves spaced at intervals of from three to five years.

If deaths are primarily the result of bacterial invasion of the respiratory tract rather than being attributable to the viruses themselves, the question might well be raised as to how effective antibiotics might be were mankind to be afflicted with another massive flu attack of 1918–19 proportions. In the early days of penicillin high hopes could have been held for the use of this drug in combatting infections caused by gram positive cocci, but since an increasing number of bacteria are developing a marked resistance to antibiotics, particularly to penicillin, how much better off would we be than the victims at the close of World War I prior to the discovery of antibiotics? The young adult population was the primary target in that epidemic, but some authorities in the field of virology are of the opinion that progress made in the understanding of the pituitary and adrenal hormones (cortisone and adreno-cortico-tropic hormone, or ACTH) in certain types of therapy could spell the difference in the outcome of a modern outbreak even if antibiotics failed to check the secondary bacterial invaders. The search continues for new and more effective drugs to combat antibiotic-resistant bacteria, and significant discoveries are being made in this area of research.

The employment of vaccines designed to ward off influenza or to modify its effects in human beings has undergone active evaluation in recent years. Such preparations are polyvalent suspensions of formalin-inactivated viruses that have been cultivated in fertile eggs and subsequently purified to remove the egg protein which, if present, would sensitize injected individuals and cause serious allergic reactions.

Since strains of viruses are constantly undergoing change and mutation from one outbreak to another and even during a single epidemic, the specific virus make-up of the vaccines must remain one jump ahead of the prevalent epidemic strains, if possible. In an attempt to control pandemics the World Health Organization has established a central laboratory in London to which specimens may be sent for identification and correlation. By this means it is anticipated that vaccines can be kept current by incorporating new prevalent strains of the virus as epidemics progress.

Experience has varied from one year to the next insofar as successful artificial protection is concerned, but from 40 to 70 per cent effectiveness has been the general experience; varying degrees of immunity may persist for from six to eight months following injection. Since there is a lag of a week or more after inoculation before measurable protection against influenza virus is apparent, the timing of injections as well as the combination of strains being employed in the vaccine have a direct bearing on the degree of protection afforded the individual. General immunity of human beings is another unpredictable factor, and those with a high level of over-all resistance would be expected to present an additional barrier to any invading microbes—viruses or bacteria.

Many respiratory conditions are probably never diagnosed as true influenza owing to lack of laboratory confirmation, and some individuals may serve as carriers of the virus which cannot survive for too long a period away from a living host. They make up the reservoir from which infectious droplets are disseminated to susceptible persons and from which epidemics arise.

Laboratory confirmation of influenza consists of inoculating nasal washings mixed with appropriate antibiotics (usually a combination of penicillin and streptomycin) into the amniotic cavity of 12- to 14-day-old embryonated eggs. More than one egg should be employed in each determination to allow for a certain amount of embryo mortality. If the virus is present in the amniotic fluid it can be detected within four days by its unique ability to agglutinate suspensions of chicken erythrocytes. This is the *Hirst Test* which serves as an *in vitro* means for a quantitative evaluation of both virus and antibodies. It is one of the best diagnostic tools available for confirmation of clinical cases of influenza. By mixing specific antiserum with virus suspensions, a so-called *hemagglutination–inhibition* test can be performed on a quantitative basis.

If the virus cannot successfully be cultivated by this means, there is an indirect approach to diagnosing influenza. Blood samples are collected from the patient during the acute stage (up to the fifth day) of the disease and during the convalescent period (fourteenth to twentieth day). If the later blood sample is able to inhibit agglutination of the red cells in the presence of specific virus by a fourfold or greater rise in antibody titer when compared with the acute specimen of blood, this is considered diagnostic.

One of the more recent techniques for detecting the presence of influenza virus is to mix with nasal smears a preparation of fluorescein dye linked with specific antibody. If the epithelial cells from the patient contain virus, the "tagged" antibody is precipitated and may be viewed as glowing areas under a fluorescence microscope. The speed of this type of diagnosis presents great advantages to the clinician.

Hospital personnel working with or near flu patients should be immunized with the most effective vaccines available, and patients must be protected from bacterial infections arising from other patients and from medical personnel. Although gauze face masks as presently constructed have limited value in preventing droplet infections, they do represent one step in control that should be taken nevertheless. This area of asepsis has been neglected and more originality and imagination should be devoted to creating masks that are more effective. Treatment of the air in confined areas with glycol vapors or similar germicidal substances might also be given some consideration for helping to control bacterial infections in patients whose resistance has been dealt a severe blow by toxic viruses. Wide spacing of beds with head-to-foot sleeping coupled with segregation of the most severe cases should be considered as part of the medical care of such respiratory infections. Frequent disinfection of hands should become a routine practice for all who come in contact with flu patients or with fomites that might have been contaminated by their respiratory discharges.

Neurotropic Viruses

Poliomyelitis

This disease is also known as *infantile paralysis,* but the designation is not completely accurate and it has been gradually discarded in favor of the more scientific name *poliomyelitis.* This word is derived from the Greek, *polios,* meaning "gray," and *myelitis* which literally means "inflammation of the spinal cord." The virus attacks the gray matter of the cord, especially the anterior horn in which the motor cells are located. Man is apparently the only natural reservoir of infection, although chimpanzees can be experimentally infected and may become "healthy carriers."

The history of this disease, especially its early history, is difficult to document. One reference calls attention to a skeleton unearthed in Cairo dating back to about 3700 B.C. It showed a decided shortening of one leg similar to what one might expect in certain types of paralytic polio, but this deformity may or may not have been the result of such a virus attack. Until the nineteenth century the medical literature is sketchy when it comes to descriptions of paralytic-type diseases that could be surmised to be polio. Perhaps physicians were too concerned with overwhelming numbers of such frightful diseases as plague, smallpox, and typhus to notice if polio existed, since it is doubtful that the number of cases, if any, ever reached significant proportions.

Modern epidemics date to about 1836 when Swedish and English physicians described outbreaks of paralysis which clinically resemble polio as we know it today. Microscopic changes seen in the spinal cord in later cases led to the designation of *acute anterior poliomyelitis,* and it was during this period that the infectious nature of the disease was recognized.

Strangely enough improvements in personal hygiene, sanitation, and standards of living failed to decrease the incidence of this mounting scourge; in fact, the number of cases of polio actually rose alarmingly. In the tropics, where sanitary practices and hygiene in general leave much to be desired by our standards, children apparently are exposed to sub-clinical doses of ingested virus from human excrement, and these indi-viduals gain immunity to polio early in life if they do not first succumb to other diseases. More careful disposal of human wastes and stricter attention to handwashing in other areas of the world have cut down on possible contacts with polio virus and necessitates mass vaccination of young children as a substitute for natural exposure.

In 1909 the spinal cord of a child dead from what was then known as "infantile paralysis" was found to contain a virus which when inoculated into the brain of a monkey produced a similar fatal disease.

Polio viruses are extremely minute. Published figures vary somewhat, but the stated range is from about 10 to 35 millimicrons with most par-ticles in the 22–32 millimicron category. They are composed of nucleo-proteins and the nucleic acids constitute one-fourth to one-third of the mass of the virus particle. These viruses display an unusual resistance to desiccation, freezing, and exposure to 5 per cent phenol, but the agent is thermolabile and is inactivated by a temperature of 45°C. Typing of the viruses is based upon a neutralization of cytopathogenic effects in tissue culture by specific antisera, and three antigenic types have been described: Type I (prototype Brunhilda), Type II (prototype Lansing), and Type III (prototype Leon). Other strains are being discovered and are being placed in appropriate groups.

Theories as to how the virus gains access to the motor nerves vary somewhat. One group postulates that the particles multiply in the oro-pharynx and intestinal tissues; from there they get into the blood stream (viremia) by which they are carried to the central nervous system where they somehow manage to breach the "blood-brain barrier," a major ob-stacle. Another group maintains that the virus is strictly neurotropic *in vivo* and can propagate only in nerve tissue. Its initial course is the inva-sion of peripheral nerves with eventual progression to peripheral ganglia where the virus multiplies. From this site the virus travels via neural pathways to the central nervous system. Once the motor cells of the an-terior horn have been damaged, voluntary movements dependent upon nerve impulses carried to the muscles are blocked, and paralysis follows. Perhaps the mechanism of virus transport is a combination of these two or of as yet unrecognized pathways.

Paralytic cases are more prevalent in temperate climates, with a peak incidence in late summer or in early autumn. Children under the age of sixteen are the prime targets. The overwhelming pattern of victims under the age of five no longer holds true. A number of factors determine whether a given individual will contract polio; included in the list are such considerations as the antigenic make-up and virulence of the virus, the age of the host, the vulnerability of the motor nerve cells at the time of invasion by the virus, and the general over-all resistance of the host at the time of contact. Precipitating factors might include a broken limb, removal of tonsils during the "polio season," and even immunizing injections other than polio vaccine.

Possible sources of the microbes include stools of patients just before and during acute stages of the disease, and droplets from the nasopharynx for several days prior to and directly after the onset of symptoms. Communicability appears greatest during late incubation and the early stages of acute illness when viruses are particularly prevalent in the nasopharynx. The existence of healthy carriers is debatable.

Since polio virus has been isolated from flies, roaches, and mosquitoes these vectors cannot be dismissed entirely as possible sources of human infection, although there is no undisputed evidence that they have been directly involved in any documented cases. There is some indication that milk might be implicated as a possible agent for transmission, but the possibility of contracting polio by swimming in polluted water containing viable virus has been questioned.

The initial symptoms of poliomyelitis are not unlike those of a number of other unrelated diseases: fever, sore throat, gastrointestinal upsets, and headache. Unless there are other cases of polio in the community, a physician could hardly be expected to diagnose this disease until the clinical picture comes into sharper focus. After the first few days the headache becomes more severe and stiffness of the neck and spine put in their appearance with accompanying muscular pain and tightness of the hamstring muscles.

It has been estimated that for every clinically recognized case of polio there are probably hundreds of mild missed cases if the level of antibody titers in adults can be taken as a criterion. It is for this reason that pooled blood samples are a valuable source of precious gamma globulin which offers passive protection to individuals who have been exposed to active cases of the disease. Even a single injection of this antibody-containing preparation in the amount of 0.1 ml per pound of body weight has been found to offer good protection up to six weeks. Supplies of globulin are limited, however, and prophylactic active immunization with such preparations as Salk's vaccine has largely replaced passive protection techniques employing antibodies built up in other individuals.

One of the great advances in polio research came with the announcement in 1949 by Enders, Weller, and Robbins that this neurotropic virus could be cultivated in extraneural tissue. Cells from monkey kidney and those from a human carcinoma of the cervix (HeLa cells) are widely employed today in many phases of virus investigations.

Salk's vaccine is propagated in monkey kidney tissue culture and is inactivated with the addition of carefully controlled amounts of formalin which destroys virus infectivity without seriously impairing antigenicity (immunizing ability). The delicate balance between too little or too much formalin is a critical step in the preparation of this vaccine. Monkey kidney tissue produces virus in a higher titer than nerve tissue, and the smaller quantity of extraneous protein in the kidney tissue makes inactivation with formalin more uniform. Allergic encephalitis can also be avoided.

An analysis of statistics gathered during extensive field trials conducted in 1954 by Salk and his colleagues indicated that the rate of paralytic polio could be reduced by as much as 80 per cent with the use of the vaccine as it was then constituted. Subsequent improvements have raised the effectiveness of the immunizing agent considerably.

The present recommended series of four shots of 1.0 ml each involves a second injection administered four weeks after the primary dose, with the third injection in about seven months, and the fourth booster a year or more later. Salk has expressed the opinion and the hope that after completing such a program an individual coming in contact with polio virus in later years will respond by a prompt recall of antibody titer, called an *anamnestic reaction,* to provide sufficient protection to ward off the disease.

The live attenuated oral polio vaccine recommended by Sabin and others has undergone extensive field trials in many parts of the world, but whether this preparation will ever replace Salk vaccine is difficult to predict. Its supporters claim a higher degree of immunizing power for the live vaccine without the need for the unpopular needle that is feared by so many children—and adults. What effect combining the two techniques will have on increasing immunizing power is unknown at this writing, but in all likelihood the Salk vaccine will continue to be employed extensively with the Sabin vaccine complementing it.

One attack of polio confers lasting immunity—probably for life in most individuals. A number of research workers who had been afflicted with polio in earlier years felt safe when they worked with these viruses in the development of vaccines. There are rare cases, however, where persons have apparently contracted the disease a second time, but the etiological agent was undoubtedly a different antigenic strain.

Antibiotics are ineffective in the treatment of poliomyelitis, and no chemotherapeutic agent has been found to alter the course of the disease once it has become established. Gamma globulin can serve as a deterrent, but it will not act as a therapeutic agent. Treatment of polio patients centers around attempts to relieve pain caused by muscle spasms, to offer relief during breathing difficulties, and to assist in the rehabilitation of damaged limbs. During the acute stages of the disease patients should be isolated in separate cubicles.

Since stools contain viable viruses for six weeks or more after an attack, extreme care must be used in the proper disposal of body wastes, and the same precautions employed in dealing with any respiratory infection must be followed while working with polio patients. As stated earlier in this chapter, medical personnel would be unwise to expose themselves to possible infection until they had completed the recommended series of vaccinations.

Rabies

Rabies, also known as hydrophobia, is caused by one of the larger neurotropic viruses which measure from 100 to 150 millimicrons in diameter. The virus appears to be a single antigenic type except for minor variations in composition detected by carefully controlled serological studies. The infectious agent was found to be filterable in 1903 by Remlinger. The designation, *hydrophobia,* stems not from an outright "fear of water" as the name implies, but rather from the tendency of victims to shy away from food or water which precipitate extreme spasms and convulsions during attempts to swallow. Terror and extreme depression are spasmodic and, at times, particularly during the terminal stages of the disease, the patient may lose all control and literally go berserk.

The disease was recognized at least 4000 years ago when a recorded law required all mad dogs to be caged. If such an animal bit a human being, the dog's owner was fined 40 shekels of silver. A Roman physician named Celsus was the first person to report that hydrophobia in man was the consequence of a bite by a rabid animal. It is customary today for health authorities to detain and to observe animals suspected of having rabies, and if no signs of the disease appear for at least ten days, the animals may be released from quarantine.

Once the rabies virus gets into the body and finds suitable host nerve cells, there is an incubation period varying from about two weeks in victims suffering from multiple bites around the head to as long as eight months when the bites are minor and in the lower extremities. The most common period is from four to twelve weeks before clinical signs of the disease become apparent. Infections have even been recorded when wounds of nonbite origin have been exposed to saliva from infected animals. Bites through clothing are less likely to develop into clinical rabies because the saliva and its lethal virus may be absorbed by the fabric before it can come into contact with open lesions of the broken flesh.

Rabies is an overwhelming encephalomyelitis which begins as a head-ache and fever with sensory changes and feelings of apprehension fol-lowed by spasms and finally death. As virulent as these viruses are, however, only about 25 per cent of all persons bitten by rabid animals contract the disease. The other 75 per cent are spared, probably because of the strict need for nerve cells in which the virus can flourish. Some-times this requirement apparently is not fulfilled and the virus is eventu-ally disposed of within the body and eliminated. Interestingly enough, the Scandinavian countries of Denmark, Norway, and Sweden eradicated rabies over a century ago.

One of the most characteristic diagnostic features of rabies is the pres-ence of oval or spherical-shaped **Negri bodies** produced within the nerve cells of the hippocampus and the Purkinje cells of the cerebellum. It is not fully agreed whether these acidophilic inclusion bodies are masses of virus particles or the result of a counter-response on the part of nerve cells to the presence of virus. In about 10 per cent of the brains of known rabid animals that are examined, however, Negri bodies are absent, but intracerebral injections of mice with portions of these brains will invari-ably cause death of the inoculated animals within twelve days.

Rabies is generally believed to be transmitted primarily through the bite of rabid dogs in the United States. However the disease may be trans-mitted by other animals—wolves in Russia, bats in Trinidad, and foxes in New York State. The vampire bat of South America has been found capable of transmitting rabies virus for 90 days before dying itself from the disease. It was reported in 1953 that insect-eating bats in the southern United States may be infected, and this is explained on the basis of the overlap in migration of northern bats and intermingling with more south-ern vampire species. The first documented case of human rabies from a bat bite was in 1958, but even healthy bats have been found harboring the virus in their saliva.

Treatment of a wound inflicted by any animal suspected of being rabid should be prompt and extremely thorough. In addition to the use of strong soap and water, a 1 per cent solution of Zephirin chloride is highly recommended. Most antiseptics will slowly inactivate the virus, and out-side of the body rabies viruses are also sensitive to ultraviolet light, desic-cation, formalin, and a temperature of 56°C for 30 minutes. Deep wounds should be thoroughly cleansed, and the lacerated tissues should also be cauterized with fuming nitric acid. Injections of antibodies in the form of gamma globulin in a dose of 0.5 ml per kilogram of body weight is strongly recommended immediately after a bite by a rabid, or suspected rabid, animal, and the combination of vaccine, gamma globulin, and antibiotics seems to hold more promise at this writing than any single procedure by itself.

The name *street virus* is given to those strains recovered from "naturally" infected animals, but after the organisms have been cultivated artificially in tissue cultures (generally embryo brain plus human or animal serum) or in embryonated chick or duck eggs, they are known as *fixed viruses*. These latter strains possess a shorter incubation period upon injection than is true for street viruses, and they also fail to produce Negri bodies. In fact, some fixed viruses may be so attenuated through multiple passages that they are incapable of producing clinical rabies even when administered in large doses, but they are nevertheless antigenic.

Of all of Pasteur's accomplishments in science he is probably best known to many of his countrymen for his studies on rabies. A statue has been erected in Paris to commemorate his contribution to this area of medicine. The original virus vaccines prepared by Pasteur were made from dried spinal cords of infected rabbits. His series of injections was long and painful, and some of his patients felt compelled to express the opinion that having the disease itself probably could be no worse than the discomfort and pain produced by the prophylactic injections! This pioneer vaccine preparation has largely been replaced with Semple's phenol-inactivated brain tissue vaccine, and the modern *Pasteur treatment* for prevention of rabies consists of daily subcutaneous injections into the abdominal wall for from 14 to 21 days, the length of the series depending upon the location and the severity of the animal bites.

This is not exactly a harmless or a painless procedure. Severe reactions can and do occur, especially in that segment of the population that is allergy-prone. About one patient in 2000 develops a neuroparalysis from such brain tissue suspensions, and a duck embryo vaccine is being studied for its efficacy as a possible replacement. Formalin, mustard gas, and high-intensity electrons have been employed to eliminate infectivity without impairing antigenicity of the rabies virus, and research in this area continues. An effective preparation is considered to be one which will impart sufficient immunity to a mouse to protect it from 1000 standard challenge doses (LD_{50}) of rabies virus. This means that at least 50 per cent of the injected mice should survive when their immunity is challenged with what is considered to be 1000 lethal doses of virus.

A strain of rabies virus designated *Flury* (isolated from a girl of the same name) is a living "avianized" virus passed from 176 to 182 times through chick embryos. This passage program causes the virus to change into a form that is nonpathogenic for adult mice, and it displays no tendency to revert. Studies have indicated that dogs can be actively immunized with Flury vaccine for periods up to three years, and varying levels of immunity have been attained in calves, cattle, monkeys, and chimpanzees. The Flury vaccine appears to be particularly valuable in protecting cattle where the vampire bat population is heavily infected with rabies.

The early symptoms of rabies in dogs generally include an alteration in the disposition of an otherwise calm animal to one displaying a nervous, restless type of fear. Apprehension usually makes the animal unusually affectionate at this stage. This phase is followed by a change in the dog's bark to more of a wolf-like howl with a tendency of the animal to snap at people, friend or stranger. At this point the dog may disappear for days on end, and during his absence he is likely to bite people or other animals indiscriminately. Eating loses its appeal, swallowing becomes difficult and painful, the mouth tends to remain open, and saliva drools out most of the time until paralysis and death finally step in. Infected cats, on the other hand, do not display an affectionate stage. They become wild, mean, furious, have dilated pupils, extend their claws, drool with their mouth open, become paralyzed, and die. A scratch at this stage may be just as serious as a bite since the cat's claws so frequently are contaminated with virus-laden saliva.

Medical personnel must be made aware that rabies can be spread from the saliva of infected human beings or animals to individuals who have breaks in their skin. Rubber gloves are a suitable protection when handling anything that might be contaminated with saliva or droplets from infected patients. Kissing is absolutely forbidden, and all glasses, dishes, and eating utensils must be scalded thoroughly to inactivate any rabies virus present.

Viscerotropic Viruses

Yellow Fever

Yellow fever gains its name from the jaundice of the eyes and skin so characteristic of liver damage caused by one of the smaller viruses whose particles measure less than 25 millimicrons in diameter. Although this is considered to be a viscerotropic virus, neurotropic properties are also evident. These infectious agents are inactivated at 55°C in five minutes, and their viability deteriorates rapidly in saline, Tyrode's solution, and Ringer's solution. However, they remain active for weeks in a frozen state and for years when lyophilized.

This disease entered the Western Hemisphere from Africa as early as 1500, probably through slave traders, and it has had a decided effect on the course of history, directly or indirectly. Carlos Finlay, a Cuban physician, in 1881 first suggested the role of a mosquito in the spread of yellow fever, and he even accurately pinpointed the species involved. But his announcement stirred little interest until the Spanish-American War (1898–1900) when American troops in Cuba were confronted with alarming morbidity and mortality rates which nearly cost them the victory.

Major Walter Reed was put in charge of a U.S. Army Commission to study the problem with the expectation of finding the cause and a remedy for yellow fever. After elimination of bacteria as possible etiological agents, the pioneer reports of Finlay were next examined, and through keen observation and the sacrifice of a long list of medical martyrs—doctors, nurses, technicians, and attendants, some acting willingly as human guinea pigs and others through accidental infections during the course of their investigations—the curious mechanism of insect-borne yellow fever was firmly established in 1901. Methods of control of this disease were worked out before the etiological agent was finally demonstrated as being a virus.

The implicated mosquito was found to be *Aedes egypti,* a household pest that flourishes in a broad band around the world, including practically all well-watered areas in the tropics and subtropics. These insects breed in artificial bodies of water around dwellings: tin cans, rain gutters, artificial pools, cisterns, depressions in rocks, etc. Elimination of breeding spots was the initial step in eradication of yellow fever, and when the mosquito population was controlled, the number of cases of the disease dropped sharply.

An infected individual suffers from a viremia during the first four or five days of the disease, which has an incubation period of from three to six days following a bite by an infected female mosquito. The triad of albuminuria, hemorrhage (black vomit), and jaundice are typical symptoms of yellow fever which has a mortality rate of about 25 per cent. When *Aedes egypti* partake of a blood meal from an infected person during the viremia stage, twelve days must elapse before the insect can pass the viruses on to another individual, but the mosquito remains infected for the balance of her life. A blood meal after the fifth day of disease in a person does not render the mosquito infectious, nor does an infected insect pass the virus on to succeeding generations. This is an important consideration in control of the disease.

Through measures developed and put into effect by General Gorgas and his men, yellow fever was controlled in Cuba and construction of the Panama Canal, which had been abandoned by the French because of uncontrolled epidemics among the workers, was able to proceed to completion without the hindrance of insect-borne diseases.

In man yellow fever commences with a sudden elevation of temperature accompanied by shivering and headaches, and the patient may vomit a bloody black mixture. The febrile stage lasts about five days during which time the disease is most infectious. Jaundice occurs and death of those scheduled to die can be expected within six to eight days. The prognosis is good if the patient survives for ten days after onset of clinical symptoms. Children born and raised in endemic areas tend to develop a mild form of the disease rather early in life, but non-natives generally are struck down by the more severe type and they experience a high mortality rate. When *Aedes egypti* invade a new area where the majority of the population is composed of nonimmune individuals, an outbreak of yellow fever can be explosive and disastrous.

Persons entering the United States from countries where yellow fever is endemic, including Central America, parts of South America, and Africa, must show evidence of having been vaccinated. Certificates are valid for six years beginning ten or twelve days following a single injection of vaccine. Children may be actively immunized as early as six months of age.

The vaccine employed is a chick embryo preparation of a modified live culture of virus designated 17D. Attenuation is carried out by long cultivation in tissue cultures. The vaccine is prepared in fertile eggs and is harvested from pulped embryo juices, and a single dose has been found capable of yielding antibodies that may persist for at least nine years. One natural attack of the disease confers long-lasting immunity, probably for life.

Since *Aedes* mosquitoes are prevalent in our southern states, public health authorities must be on a constant alert to prevent entry into the country of any individuals suffering from yellow fever which could initiate serious epidemics. In years gone by cases have been reported as far north as Boston, and serious outbreaks have been recorded in Baltimore, Philadelphia, and New York. Thorough spraying of airplanes coming from endemic areas has become a routine practice, and this procedure coupled with strict enforcement of vaccination requirements has kept yellow fever from becoming a serious problem in the United States. The widespread use of DDT and various spraying oils in endemic areas of the world and extensive education of the population in these countries have successfully minimized yellow fever where epidemics in former years were considered normal and unavoidable. Much remains to be done, however.

The protection afforded by yellow fever vaccine has been amply demonstrated in thousands of military personnel and in civilians who live in endemic areas by choice or through duties which call for their visiting such countries. Personnel working on international airlines, for example, fall into the latter category. Unvaccinated individuals who may have been exposed to yellow fever may be treated with convalescent serum to moderate the disease or to ward it off completely, but active prophylactic immunization through vaccination with 17D is to be preferred if time is allowed for the individual to build up his antibodies.

Once a person develops yellow fever, he should be cared for in a mosquito-free room, especially during the first five days when the viruses are freely circulating in his blood stream (period of viremia) and can be picked up through the bite of mosquitoes for transmission to others. Administration of immune serum or employing other chemotherapeutic measures is practically useless once the clinical symptoms of the disease are evident.

In 1931 it was reported in Brazil that *sylvan* or *jungle yellow fever* could be transmitted by insects other than *Aedes egypti* in jungle areas, with wild animals—monkeys, in particular—serving as reservoirs for the parasites. It is virtually impossible to eradicate all of these sources of infection, and males whose occupation takes them to the fringes of such jungles tend to contract this type of yellow fever unless they have been actively immunized. Diagnosis of the disease is confirmed by cultivating the virus in white mice or in monkeys, or by demonstrating antibodies through serological procedures.

Review Questions

1. What are viruses? How did they get their name?
2. Can all types of tissue cells be grown in test tubes?
3. What is the advantage of using tissue cultures of established cell lines over embryonated eggs for the cultivation of viruses?
4. What serological tests may be employed to detect the presence of viruses and their antibodies?
5. Is there a theoretical limit to the number of vaccines a person may be given? Is it possible to develop a superimmunized population?
6. Is there any means by which rabies can be diagnosed without sacrificing the animal and making sections of the brain?

19 | RESISTANCE TO DISEASE

Introduction

ONE OF THE MOST INTRIGUING ASPECTS OF MICROBIOLOGY, ESPE-
cially to those engaged in the medical sciences, is a consideration of how
man and other living creatures are able to survive in an environment that
is in so many respects biologically hostile. We are surrounded by microscopic marauders whose principal aim appears to be survival, frequently
at the expense of living animals and plants that are millions or even
billions of times larger than they.

Great progress has been possible during this past century because of
pioneer efforts on the part of a handful of scientific giants whose influence
has spread to include thousands of disciples engaged in every facet of
public health work. In addition to the front-line workers in this area—
physicians, nurses, dentists, sanitarians, technologists, and others—a strong
research team whose primary aim is to push back the boundaries of ignorance is necessary. In order to disseminate the knowledge they unearth
we must have qualified educators at all levels to bring the simplified word
to the layman who in most cases is not equipped with the technical background to understand the scientific jargon. In many instances he is not
even interested in this phase of his personal well-being and survival.

In its broadest sense disease may be considered to be any departure
from health—anything that makes a living organism uncomfortable (disease). Not all illness by any stretch of the imagination can be attributed

to the actions of microorganisms, but great progress has been made in identifying microbes implicated in contagious diseases, and workable control measures have been instituted to control these living microscopic agents. The search must be intensified to find causes and cures for chronic, debilitating diseases of nonmicrobial origin including arthritis, rheumatism, circulatory disorders, etc. Living longer has little appeal if we are merely prolonging years of suffering with organic diseases for which we have no known cure.

Resistance is the ability of the body to prevent disease through retarding growth and development of microbes and their poisonous products within a living host. This phenomenon is not the result of action on the part of a single biological device or system; it is the combined effects of a number of processes—some known and some still unknown. When an animal is not susceptible to a given disease, this is termed *species resistance* or *immunity*. (Have you ever seen a horse with a full-blown case of whooping cough, a mouse with mumps, or a dog with classic chickenpox?)

Frequently immunity may be a matter of degree, such as differences exhibited between races and species of animals with respect to specific diseases. Chickens fail to contract anthrax not because their tissues are immune to these bacteria, but rather (according to Louis Pasteur) because the relatively warm body temperature does not permit *Bacillus anthracis* to grow within the birds. By lowering the temperature of the chickens in cool water to about 37°C, Pasteur was able to make the birds susceptible to anthrax. Yet these bacteria can be made to grow *in vitro* in chicken blood incubated at 43°C, so factors other than body temperature must be involved.

The reader is undoubtedly familiar with instances where in a family or other small group all members were apparently equally exposed to a given infectious agent, perhaps through intimate contact with a sick individual during the contagious phase of his disease, and not all contacts came down with the disease. Why should this be? Scientists feel they know *some* of the reasons, but they are far from having a complete explanation.

Any consideration of immunity to a microbial disease must include such factors as the number of infectious cells or particles involved, their relative potency or virulence, and the sum total of forces the host is able to muster against the invaders. This might be expressed as a formula: $D = NV/R$, where D is disease, N the number of infectious units, V their virulence, and R is the total resistance of the host. Whenever the numerator is greater than the denominator, illness can be expected, and the severity of the disease will be related to how great these differences are.

A special branch of science known as *immunology* concerns itself with matters relating to resistance. The theories of immunologists may be confirmed, at least in part, by *serologists* who conduct test tube reactions for measuring and evaluating responses in blood specimens, particularly in the gamma globulin fraction which contains immune substances called *antibodies.* Immunity is a relative thing; it depends upon what the opposing force is. In one instance an individual may be confronted with large numbers of relatively avirulent microbes which can be disposed of by various mechanisms built into human beings. But a few highly potent pathogens may be able to overcome all opposition within the body and cause disease. This all goes back to the formula presented earlier.

Theories of Immunity

Through the years during which microbiology has been developing as a biological science a number of interesting proposals attempting to explain the action of immunity have been put forth. A few of these will be discussed briefly, but the list here presented is by no means complete.

Pasteur's Exhaustion Theory

Pasteur was of the opinion that each pathogen possessed specific food requirements in order to exist within a living host. Once these food elements or mixtures became exhausted, the microbes disappeared, the individual recovered, and he was protected from these same organisms for varying periods of time. Although this belief is of historical interest, we know today that the explanation is not a sound one. However, Pasteur's beliefs did lead others to make counter-proposals and to offer additional theories. This is one of the real benefits arising from publication of scientific investigations, whether they are pure figments of imagination or the result of extensive experimentation. Wherever a sufficient number of small contributions fit into a logical pattern, science moves ahead in spurts or breakthroughs as men of vision fit the isolated pieces into a meaningful whole.

Metchnikoff's Cellular Theory

When pus taken from a localized infection is stained with suitable dyes and examined under a microscope, the curious bacteria-engulfing action of leucocytes, known as *phagocytosis,* can be observed. Metchnikoff, after investigating this power of white blood cells, was of the opinion that this must be the secret of bacterial destruction *in vivo* which eventually frees the body of infection and imparts a protective action against future attacks by these same organisms.

Pimples, boils, and carbuncles are expressions of this type of local "police action" on the part of polymorphonuclear leucocytes; it is nature's technique for localizing and eventually destroying some bacteria, particularly staphylococci. But phagocytosis is relatively ineffective with streptococci and some other types of infectious agents, so this process, though it may explain in part recovery from selected microbial diseases, is not in itself the complete answer to the mystery of immunity.

D'Herelle's Bacteriophage Theory

A bacteriophage is a virus that is parasitic for bacteria—and very specific strains of bacteria, at that. The virus is so exacting in its host requirements that the bursting and dissolving effect it produces on bacteria can serve as a reliable index for typing strain differences in cultures of a single species of bacteria. The epidemiology of staphylococcus infections is presently being studied using phage-typing techniques.

This interesting lysis of bacteria was observed independently about 1917 by D'Herelle and Twort, and the theory of immunity proposed by the first-named investigator postulated that as soon as the number of phage particles reach a critical level, the invading bacteria are dispatched and the patient recovers. Observations conducted *in vitro*, however, were not confirmed *in vivo*, and the use of bacteriophage for treatment of disease has never yielded encouraging results. Phage action may take place in the body, particularly in the intestines, but it is not a primary means by which immunity is built up in human beings.

Ehrlich's Side-Chain Theory

Each cell, according to Ehrlich, consists of a nucleus which controls the nature and properties of the cell, in addition to a large number of side-chains, or *receptors,* by which the cell joins chemically with other substances in its environment. Poisons attack only certain cells for which specific receptors are available, according to this belief, and it helped to explain species immunity and the mode of action of antitoxins, but a number of holes can be punched in this theory.

Bordet's Theory

Colloidal chemistry and adsorption are the background for Bordet's theory of immunity. The combination of toxin and antitoxin was likened by him to the affinity of starch for iodine. When only a small amount of iodine is available, starch granules take on a pale blue color, but with an abundance of iodine the starch becomes dark blue. In a similar manner if only limited quantities of antitoxin are available, toxin molecules merely become weakened rather than neutralized.

Humoral Theory

Immunity cannot be explained by any one theory, and a number of proposals may be plausible up to a point. The humoral theory which is based upon the existence in body fluids of specific immune substances must be added to the rest. *Antigens* are usually proteins, although some polysaccharides may also serve in a similar capacity, especially in combination with other chemical structures. When antigens are introduced into an animal they cause, after a suitable interval, the formation of *immune substances* or *antibodies* which react with the provoking substance. The antigen functions as a foreign agent which the animal tries to overpower through formation of antibodies. Both antigens and antibodies are highly specific, and techniques for detecting and measuring specific responses within the body will be discussed later in this chapter.

Factors Influencing Resistance

Heredity

If the meaning of heredity is to be taken in a narrow sense—the transmission of characteristics of parents to their offspring through chromosomes —then it should become clear that microbial diseases are not inherited. It is true that infants may be born with bacterial or viral diseases, but such infections are acquired *after* fertilization of the egg by a sperm, and the disease thus becomes *congenital,* not hereditary. This is true when a mother has an active case of syphilis, for example, and *Treponema pallidum* is capable of attacking the developing fetus, or when an infant picks up *Neisseria gonorrheae* while passing through the birth canal of an infected mother. But this is not inheritance.

An individual might be born with an organically weak lung structure which could make him an easy target for tuberculosis, but he does not inherit tuberculosis in the true sense of the word. Allergy seems to run in families, as does the tendency for development of cancer, but this mechanism is still not well understood.

Age

It has been customary to speak of childhood diseases and illnesses of the elderly, but the reader should understand that almost any age group can contract almost any disease when conditions are favorable. Statistically there may be more cases of a given disease in a specified age group, and the designation therefore may be a convenient one for discussion purposes.

One of the primary reasons why particular infections are found more frequently in children than in older folks is because at the time of initial contact with the microbe the child lacks sufficient immunity to ward off infection, whereas adults have either had clinical cases in their childhood or have come in contact with a sufficient number of stray organisms to trigger their antibody-forming mechanism into action, with a resultant build-up of protection to ward off an active case of the disease in older life. Newborn infants and very old individuals are unable to produce antibodies at levels anywhere near those of the in-between age group.

Diphtheria formerly was considered to be a disease particularly of children under the age of five years, but as the result of long-range massive immunization programs, mothers today can rest easy with the assurance that this microbial killer has little or no opportunity to strike down their properly immunized youngsters. Whooping cough is another disease of childhood that effective vaccines have successfully held in check. But some of the other diseases, including measles and mumps, still flourish because reliable vaccination procedures have not yet reached the point of common usage, although at this writing measles vaccines appear to be emerging from preliminary experimental trials and, before long, should be in wide use.

Some childhood diseases can precipitate serious complications in susceptible older individuals. The virus of German measles, for example, is known to cause serious defects in babies if the mother contracts the infection during pregnancy. The microorganisms have a particular predilection for developing embryos, and pregnant women should make every effort to avoid all direct or even indirect contact with those who have this disease. Mumps in males after the age of puberty may cause orchitis, which in severe cases leads to sterility. Some investigators are of the opinion that if young boys have not had mumps by the time they reach the age of ten years, an effort should be made by their parents to expose them to the disease through contact with active cases. This proposal is not universally accepted, but it is interesting!

Cancer is generally thought of as being more commonly a disease of people past the age of forty, but this depends somewhat upon the type and site of the cancer involved. Young children may contract a cancer of the blood cells termed *leukemia,* while young adults appear to have more stomach cancer than other age groups. Breast and lung cancers strike older members of a population, and this writer is completely convinced by available statistics that the relationship between cigarette smoking and the incidence of lung cancer can no longer be doubted. He is also just as certain that unfortunately this knowledge will not serve to deter many otherwise intelligent individuals from smoking.

Sex

There is evidence, at least in syphilis, that some infections may be more benign in females than in males. Perhaps females possess a greater ability to acquire immunity by producing antibodies to *Treponema pallidum.* Morbidity and mortality due to whooping cough are higher in females, and this also holds true for infectious hepatitis. Death rates from tuberculosis is higher in females between the ages of about ten to thirty, but thereafter the rate for males exceeds that for females by a wide margin.

Mental State

There are no accurate measuring sticks for proving that an optimistic person with a positive approach to life tends to be not only a happier individual but also a healthier one, but the impression persists and is undoubtedly true up to a point. The pessimist too often becomes convinced that he or she has ailments, and the imaginary diseases become very real. Physicians must find it much easier to treat patients who think positively than those who assume a Gloomy Gus attitude and are willing to give up without a struggle; attitude can aid or impede recovery. Worry, according to Lord Dewar, is interest paid on trouble before it becomes due. Someone else has stated that a pessimist is one who worries that perhaps the optimist might be right!

The mushrooming of psychosomatic medicine and psychiatry can be attributed to an increasing awareness on the part of at least some of these persons who have a negative approach to life that a change in their attitude is necessary. They are willing to pay to have someone tell them what in many instances they already know! The writer has no quarrel with this as long as positive results are being accomplished. Anyone who is dedicated to improving the health of his fellow creatures should be interested in all phases of well-being, and psychology is an important tool for those whose occupation lies in the area of the paramedical sciences.

Living Conditions

Attempting to correlate living conditions with resistance to disease is no simple task, but it is probably a fair statement that crowding under unhygienic conditions affords a greater opportunity for infectious agents to be transferred from one individual to another. However, to try to stipulate what "crowding" is or just where it ends may be difficult.

The Army seeks to minimize the spread of upper respiratory infections by allocating about 60 square feet of floor space per man in a barracks and through inauguration of head-to-foot sleeping. But on troop ships transporting men during the pressures and shortages of war canvas bunks may be stacked four or five high with just enough aisle room to permit necessary movement between the tiers.

It is somewhat of a paradox to find that frequently the dirty little urchin who either loathes soap and water or who may not have ready access to them remains "healthy as sin," while the youngster who is kept spick and span may fall heir to whatever disease is making the circuit at the moment. Is it possible to be too clean? It is recognized that some contact with minimal numbers of microbes keeps our defense mechanisms stimulated and operational, and as long as the exposure is not overdone this type of active immunity serves a useful function in maintaining our resistance. As was pointed out in the previous chapter, the number of cases of poliomyelitis actually increased with improvements in sanitation.

Occupation

There are a number of occupations that are hazardous to human health, and Industrial Hygiene Divisions were created in many of our State Health Departments to deal with these problems. Stone cutters, for example, while carving names of the dead on tombstones will be etching their own inscriptions unless they protect themselves from inhalation of millions of sharp-edged particles of stone by using protective breathing devices or conducting the grinding operation under oil or other fluids to trap the dust. Silicosis is not only harmful in itself, but the damage inflicted on lung tissue can in addition predispose an individual to pneumonic infections.

Lead is another substance that can do serious damage to an individual's health, and persons engaged in industries including those dealing with paint, leaded gasoline, and battery manufacture must be protected from this poisonous element. A number of solvents are also dangerous when inhaled, and adequate ventilation must be provided to prevent illnesses from these sources.

Fatigue

A tired person cannot be expected to ward off an infection as readily as a well-rested and otherwise healthy individual. Here again it is difficult, if not impossible, to measure the exact effect that fatigue has on health. We do not all require the same number of hours of sleep each 24-hour period to maintain ourselves at peak performance during waking hours, but we should attempt to gear our rest to suit our optimum personal needs.

It is true that as we go from infancy to childhood our bodies do not need as much sleep, but most adults find that 7 to 8 hours makes them feel their best. In the twilight years of our lives the sleep requirement tends to rise for most individuals. The fuel we feed our biological engine will determine to a great extent how efficiently the complex system is going to operate, but even if we feed our bodies the most nutritious food available, we cannot operate indefinitely without allowing cells, tissues, and organs to rid themselves of accumulating wastes on an orderly basis. Rest and sleep provide the interludes necessary to fulfill these aims.

Portal of Entry

One of the reasons we are healthy as much of the time as we are can be attributed to restrictive requirements of some pathogens as far as entry into our body is concerned. Typhoid cells find their way in through the respiratory or alimentary tract, and when they set up housekeeping in the intestines and produce sufficient numbers of offspring to tip the scales in their favor we become ill. *Clostridium tetani* find deep, dirty, closed-over wounds particularly favorable for their anaerobic development. Staphylococci which utilize our outer skin surfaces as a natural habitat wait for breaks in this protective body covering through which they can pass and initiate their sometimes fatal infections. These special portal requirements limit the number of opportunities provided for pathogens to cause damage to tissues, and once they breach the outer defenses, the invaders must then contend with powerful internal forces that will be discussed later in this chapter.

Species Resistance

One of the segments of immunology that is less well understood is that concerned with species resistance to selected microbial diseases. There are some microbial diseases that can be contracted by both man and certain lower animals; tuberculosis and rabies are examples of such diseases. Brucellosis, on the other hand, may produce one set of clinical symptoms in man (undulant fever) and other responses (contagious abortion) in cattle. Household pets are undoubtedly grateful that they do not pick up the common cold from man, at least with the same symptoms, and there are a number of animal diseases that human beings are unable to contract.

We know that the antigenic make-up of the tissues of animals is sufficiently different to permit their being detected by serological techniques, and microbes through their specialized enzyme systems can differentiate tissues, attacking some cells and ignoring others. This area of science needs considerably more clarification.

Irradiation

Moderate exposure of human beings to sunshine is generally accepted as being beneficial to health, but conflicting reports make this observation somewhat questionable. It has been found that prolonged contact with ultraviolet light may actually make some animals more susceptible to certain infections, but whether such findings are applicable to human beings is not clear.

Race and Nationality

Variations in resistance exhibited between races and even between nationalities afford an interesting study in immunity that exists within a single species, and this is representative of *iso-immunity*. We are all human beings (*Homo sapiens*) and yet decided differences in susceptibility to pathogens are demonstrable. Part of the explanation undoubtedly lies in the cumulative effects brought about through generations of exposure to particular endemic infectious agents and their vectors. The exposure in many instances has been in subclinical amounts which have forced an active immunity to be built up within a given population. Other individuals having the same skin pigmentation but residing in areas somewhat remote from their fellow racial members frequently fail to exhibit these same quantitative differences, thus lending some support to the belief that immunity may not be so much a matter of race as perhaps the influence of environmental stimuli over extended periods of time.

Miscellaneous Factors

A number of other influences, including nutrition, economic status, and climate might affect an individual's resistance to disease, but it is difficult to pinpoint and to measure their effects on immunity. Diet naturally will affect the general health of the body, and a lack of specific food requirements will lead to deficiency diseases which in turn could predispose an individual to microbial afflictions. Persons in the lower economic brackets may actually choose their foods more wisely on limited budgets than some who have no ceiling on what they may spend for food, and this may distort the picture somewhat.

Insofar as climate is concerned, there are a number of seasonal diseases as well as climatic conditions that may favor growth and development of vectors of specific diseases such as mosquitoes and the spread of malaria or yellow fever. These are more obvious climatic factors; in addition, some investigators lean to the opinion that a feeling of well-being may be closely correlated with temperature, humidity, and atmospheric pressure

—even phases of the moon are said to influence the actions of some individuals. Prolonged periods of unpleasant weather—rain, extreme heat or cold, etc.—can affect work efficiency and attitudes of workers, and may affect their resistance to disease.

Tissue Factors in Resistance

Nature has built into our bodies remarkable barriers to invasion by undesirable organisms. Some of these shields are physical, whereas others are chemical. A few of these considerations will be discussed briefly.

Skin

Skin is a tissue that serves as a firm deterrent to uncountable hordes of microorganisms, particularly staphylococci that are a part of the normal flora of the outer surfaces of our body. So long as skin remains intact, such infections are prevented from becoming established, but pockets of infection in the form of pimples, boils, and carbuncles represent local weak points or breaks where leucocytes are called into play to reduce in number or to destroy the invaders through phagocytosis. Pus production is one of the stages in this struggle, with white cells comprising a substantial proportion of this pus.

Because of the physical make-up of skin it is virtually impossible to free the tissue of all microbes even by use of the best disinfectants available. The presence of occasional stitch abscesses following a surgical procedure should not be looked upon as poor technique on the part of the attending surgeon or members of his medical team. In suturing wounds it is not uncommon to disturb a focus of bacteria in the underlayers of skin that have escaped the killing action of the chemical employed to disinfect the area, and minute pus pockets may eventually appear at the point where the sutures enter or leave the skin.

In addition to the physical barrier thrown up by the skin there are also chemical factors involved in the destruction of microbes that come in contact with the body cells. Freshly liberated perspiration may exhibit an antibacterial action for a short time, but after being allowed to remain on the skin for a matter of hours, the fluid may actually serve to stimulate bacterial growth, leading ultimately to the production of unpleasant body odors.

Germicidal soaps, particularly those containing hexachlorophene, yield promising results insofar as reducing bacterial populations on skin surfaces is concerned. In fact, thin films of residual soap may be sufficient to maintain a reduced microbial flora for some hours after application.

The unattractive blemishes of acne and similar disorders on the skin of adolescents appear to represent a combination of physical and chemical alterations in the make-up of skin during puberty which permit the access of troublesome staphylococci. As teenagers grow older skin blemishes tend to disappear except in severe cases where the skin disease is more pronounced and tends to persist, and in such cases individuals should seek medical treatment from a dermatologist.

Mucous Membranes

The vascular nature of this type of tissue permits a bathing action with fluids and the antibodies they contain as a result of their release through the thin walls of capillaries. A bacteriological examination of the mucous membranes of the nasopharynx will reveal an extremely high microbial population. Many of these organisms, including pneumococci, meningococci, and streptococci, are potentially dangerous, but they are normally held in check by repelling forces existing in the area.

There is no question that upper respiratory infections increase materially with the arrival of cold weather when people spend more time in close contact with others in overheated rooms with low humidity. Mouth breathers appear to suffer from more colds than persons who normally take air through their nostrils where it is first warmed and moistened before passing into the lungs. Perhaps some readers may have noticed that after spending an evening in front of a hot fireplace, sore throats and colds are not an uncommon aftermath. Inhaling hot dry air may have something to do with this, especially in climates where the humidity normally is high. Saliva has been reported to be somewhat germicidal, but if this is so, the antimicrobial action is probably a minor one.

Lungs

Any organism that reaches the lungs by way of the respiratory tract has had to overcome enormous odds in its passage from the air. First of all the hairy lining of the nostrils serves as a physical trap along with the moist membranes lining the entire nasopharynx. The very nature of the tortuous passage in itself presents a significant barrier, and once the organisms get by these hurdles they are confronted with the antibodies that are constantly bathing the lung surfaces. The fact that lung infections do occur, however, indicates the highly aggressive nature of some microbes.

Stomach

We consume in our food and drink relatively large numbers of bacteria each day, but our digestive system destroys the great majority of them through the action of powerful gastric juices and the low pH created by the hydrochloric acid found in the stomach. The length of time that food remains in this portion of the digestive tract will naturally influence contact with destructive juices, and if considerable quantities of water are ingested, not only are the digestive juices diluted, but the food material passes through the stomach relatively quickly before too much harm can come to the included microbes. Stomach tissue in itself is remarkably resistant to microbial invasion and this presents a physical as well as a chemical obstacle to organisms. But enteric pathogens (typhoid, cholera, dysentery, etc.), because of characteristics peculiar to their members, are able to get through the stomach into the intestines where they carry out most of their destructive activity.

Intestines

Slightly below the point where bile enters the intestines there can be found an almost pure culture of *Escherichia coli,* suggesting that bile may be extremely germicidal to many species of bacteria with little or no harmful effects on *coli* which might even thrive in its presence. As mentioned earlier, enteric pathogens eventually gain access to the intestines where the walls of these organs frequently become the target for microbial action. Owing to differences between individuals, the number of pathogenic cells or virus particles required to initiate an infection must vary widely. A minimum infecting dose for one individual may be tolerated with no clinical manifestations in other persons who possess a relatively high degree of immunity to the organisms in question.

Body Fluids and Their Relationship to Immunity

Even after pathogenic organisms have managed to breach the external body defenses, they must be capable of surviving their bout with antibody-containing fluids (blood, lymph, etc.) which are in continuous contact with every cell of the body. The exact mechanism by which pathogens are able to overpower the active body defenses is not well understood, but no doubt exo- and endotoxins play some role in preparing tissues for invasion and destruction by additional microbes. The spreading factor of staphylococci and the lysins of streptococci must be added to the list of techniques employed by microorganisms to aid their own cause. Immunochemistry should eventually explain more about these processes.

Types of Immunity

Active immunity implies that the individual plays an active part in the build-up of a defense mechanism, through the stimulus of an antigen. The substances produced are antibodies and specific organs of the body—

liver, spleen, bone marrow, etc.—are sites for the manufacture of these protective substances. Generally a week or more may be required before a sufficient quantity of antibodies appears in the gamma globulin fraction of the blood to be measurable by serological means. In general, this type of immunity is designated as a prophylactic measure rather than as a therapeutic procedure. Time is the limiting factor in deciding which technique should be employed.

Passive immunity involves the injection into the patient of immune bodies produced in another person or in a lower animal. There is no substantial delay before the protective substances circulate and become effective, and this procedure is designed to be curative rather than prophylactic. Since the host is not actively engaged in manufacturing his own antibodies, the protection afforded through passive immunity is transitory.

A brief summary of the major types of immunity should help the reader to understand natural and artificial means by which man acquires resistance to microbes and their metabolic products.

Natural Immunity
>   Inherited (active)—by being an individual member of a given species or race
>   Congenital (passive)—from antibodies passed on to a fetus from the mother's
>   circulation

Acquired Immunity
>   Natural active—by recovering from a disease
>   Artificial active—through vaccination with dead or attenuated organisms
>   Artificial passive—through injections of immune serum produced in another
>   person or in an artificially immunized animal

Types of Antibodies

Because of the specificity of antigens and antibodies, serological reactions provide a valuable tool for the identification of some bacterial diseases and for the evaluation of measurable resistance of an individual to given pathogens.

Serologists have at their command a number of different *in vitro* techniques for detecting both qualitatively and quantitatively antibodies produced as a consequence of antigenic stimulation. A discussion of a few representative examples should provide the reader with a workable knowledge with which to gain some understanding of fundamental principles underlying serological reactions.

Agglutinins

An agglutination reaction involves the clumping of whole cells. Before such a serological reaction can take place, three main ingredients are required:

Antigen (*agglutinogen*)—whole cells
Antibody (*agglutinin*)—blood serum from an individual or an immunized
            lower animal
Electrolyte—usually physiological saline to serve as a diluent and to carry elec-
            trical charges

The agglutination reaction is perhaps one of the simplest and most widely employed of the serological tests. Not only is it a technique for identifying bacteria, but it is also employed to detect the immunological marks left in the body as the result of bacterial stimulation, either naturally through having the disease or artificially through vaccination. Agglutination tests also form the basis for typing blood and for determining Rh factors that have become of such wide interest and medical importance in recent years.

In conducting a quantitative bacterial agglutination test a standardized suspension of organisms is prepared in saline; graded amounts of diluted blood serum containing specific antibodies are blended with the cells before the mixture is incubated at a prescribed temperature (usually 37°C, although somewhat higher temperatures may be optimum for selected agglutination tests, including Rh determinations). If antibodies in the serum are specific for the antigens, cells tend to adhere to one another until the clumps become of sufficient size and weight to settle to the bottom of the tube under the influence of gravity. Chilling the tubes in a refrigerator overnight will serve to sharpen the readings still further. The highest dilution of serum that causes clumping of the suspended cells is called the *titer*, and the higher this figure, the more antibodies are present and the greater is the relative immunity of the person or animal for the particular organisms in question.

Transfusions on a truly scientific basis were not introduced into medicine until about the turn of the twentieth century when Karl Landsteiner reported the results of his findings on a relatively small sampling of individuals. When some blood specimens were placed in contact with the serum of other individuals, he observed a clumping reaction. Further studies uncovered three different human blood types, which were eventually expanded to include a fourth group. Other research workers reported similar findings, but unfortunately the Roman numeral designations for the four types varied among investigators and resulted in considerable confusion. An agreement was finally reached on an international or universal system of designations employing the capital letters O, A, B, and AB.

Two isoagglutinogens in human red blood cells and two corresponding isoagglutinins in the plasma are used to determine blood groups with antibodies against A and B factors occurring in reciprocal relationship to the antigen. Antibodies responsible for clumping A cells are called *alpha,* and *beta* antibodies react with the antigen of B cells. The following summary shows these relationships.

THE OAB SYSTEM OF ANTIGENS AND ANTIBODIES

Blood Type and Red Blood Cell Antigens	Blood Plasma Isoantibodies
O	Anti-A (alpha) and anti-B (beta)
A	Anti-B (beta)
B	Anti-A (alpha)
AB	Neither alpha nor beta

It can be determined which blood types can be employed for transfusions if the following cardinal principle is followed: *Never inject red blood cells for which the recipient possesses specific antibodies!* Remembering this rule of thumb it becomes clear that persons with type O cells can donate their blood to individuals with any of the four blood types, and for this reason they are known as *universal donors.* In like manner, type AB individuals having neither alpha nor beta antibodies are *universal recipients* since they can receive blood from donors representing any of the blood types.

When universal type blood is administered to a recipient other than type O, the rapid speed of blood circulation coupled with dilution ordinarily takes care of antibodies in the donated blood with little or no deleterious effect on the patient. However, in cases where patients are extremely ill, every attempt should be made to minimize even minor transfusion reactions by injecting only the exact blood type (*homologous*) rather than *heterologous* (type O into type A, for example). When incompatible cells are introduced into the circulation, clumping takes place and capillaries in the brain, lungs, and other vital organs are occluded, with disastrous consequences.

In typing blood a suspension of cells is prepared in physiological saline, and measured amounts of serum containing specific antibodies are blended with these erythrocytes. Either a rapid slide or a tube test may be employed. Antisera may be prepared in rabbits by hyperimmunizing them with selected human red cells, or human blood serum may be employed as a source of antibodies in the determination. When a rabbit is injected with type A human cells, for example, it builds up antibodies capable of causing such cells to agglutinate, just as serum from a type B person containing alpha antibodies causes A cells to clump.

The rapid slide test is conducted by placing on a clean slide two large separate drops of a saline suspension of blood cells to be tested. Into one drop is introduced anti-A serum; anti-B serum is added to the second drop on the slide. After the contents of the individual suspensions are mixed with a toothpick or by rotation of the slide, macroscopic clumping should become evident within less than a minute if antigens and antibodies are specific for one another. All negative reactions should be confirmed under the low power objective of a microscope to detect possible weak reactions that might otherwise be overlooked. Blood types are determined on the basis of the following findings:

No clumping of cells with either antiserum	Type O
Clumping with anti-A but not with anti-B serum	Type A
Clumping with anti-B but not with anti-A serum	Type B
Clumping with both anti-A and anti-B sera	Type AB

Blood typing determinations may be more accurate when suspensions of cells and antisera are placed in small tubes and centrifuged for two minutes at 1000 revolutions per minute to insure intimate contact of erythrocytes and antibodies. By resuspension of the spun cells, clumping action is readily observed and even weak reactions are accentuated.

Distribution of blood types varies from one country to another and with different races, and such findings have intriguing implications for anthropologists and others in allied fields of study. Students interested in pursuing this phase of science further are referred to advanced textbooks in immunology. To cite one example, it is interesting to compare the distribution of blood types of North American Indians with those of the rest of the inhabitants of the United States—a population which is sometimes referred to as the "melting pot" of the world.

Blood Type	General U.S. Population	North American Indians
O	45%	91%
A	42%	8%
B	10%	1%
AB	3%	0

Before a transfusion is carried out with what would appear to be homologous blood with respect to the OAB system, a *cross-match* is set up and confirmed by the physician who is to effect the blood transfer. In many hospitals the final decision relative to whether a bottle of blood is suitable for a given patient rests in the hands of the physician, which is probably as it should be.

In the cross-match technique two separate tests are made. The so-called *minor side* of a cross-match entails appropriate mixing of recipient's cells with donor's serum; the *major side*, which is the more critical of the two, involves mixing donor's cells with serum from the blood of the recipient. No clumping, either macroscopically or microscopically, should be visible on the major side, but slight agglutination may be permitted on the minor side since dilution *in vivo* will compensate for it.

Cross-matching is valuable for picking up any errors in preliminary grouping, as well as for detecting the presence of any other agglutinins (such as Rh) which could cause transfusion reactions and possible serious effects in the patient. There are a number of technical details about these procedures that might better be left for discussion and elaboration by individual instructors.

Landsteiner and Weiner in 1940 reported a major system of blood cell antigens that may have a profound effect in cases of multiple transfusions and in certain pregnancies. They discovered that the red blood cells of the rhesus monkey evoked antibodies in rabbits and in guinea pigs which agglutinated not only the erythrocytes of the monkey but also those of about 85 per cent of human beings. This came to be known as the *Rh factor*. Further investigations revealed the complexity of what appeared initially to be a case of clear-cut Rh positiveness or negativeness, and to-day there are increasing numbers of subgroups and genetic implications too extensive to be reviewed here. But for all practical purposes the Rh factor is usually referred to simply as positive or negative. A positive sample possesses at least one gene for a factor designated as D which is the most commonly occurring and strongest antigen discovered.

The technique for conducting an Rh test is similar to that employed for the OAB determination, but the blood samples are collected in tubes containing oxalate which prevents the blood from clotting. Saline must not be used in this test since it interferes with the Rh reaction.

Distribution of Rh factors varies in different groups just as is true with the OAB antigens, with the D fraction found almost always in the red blood cells of Chinese, Japanese, American Indians, and Negroes. Caucasians are Rh positive to the extent of about 85 per cent, whereas the factor is present in only about 65–70 per cent of Basques.

Rh positive cells, since they are antigenic for Rh negative individuals, should not be transfused into negative recipients. When a sufficient titer is built up by the Rh negative person, not only will subsequent transfusions do the Rh negative recipient no good, but actual harm will result when the injected cells are attacked and must be disposed of, putting an

acute burden on the kidneys and other waste-removing organs. This precaution in transfusions is particularly pertinent for females before and
during the child-bearing age. Rh negative women who have children with
an Rh positive father run a certain risk of encountering serological difficulties. This combination of Rh factors should be considered as *potentially* troublesome in causing hemolytic jaundice of the newborn called
erythroblastosis fetalis which may take on several forms. Infants may de-

FIG. 19.1. Blood refractioning laboratory. (Courtesy Armour Pharmaceutical
Company, Chicago, Illinois.)

velop jaundice of the basal nuclei of the brain, generalized edema, or
varying degrees of hemolytic anemia.

Rh positiveness is a dominant characteristic, hence an Rh positive man
is likely to father an Rh positive child who develops within an Rh negative mother. The cellular elements of the two circulatory systems are independent, but the fluid portions may pass back and forth across membranes
impermeable to cells. As long as the cells of the embryo are kept out of the
mother's circulation, where they would act as undesirable antigens, little
or no antibody against Rh positive cells can develop. Any weaknesses in

the separating membranes may provide one means by which intermingling of blood cells may occur. Accidents during pregnancy with injury to the developing fetus may be another, and a third possibility might take place during labor and delivery. Rh difficulties, therefore, generally are experienced after the first pregnancy, but contrary to popular belief not all couples with potentially dangerous Rh combinations experience such difficulties. Statistically about 13 per cent of marriages may be incompatible with respect to Rh factors, and only about one in nineteen of these couples ever has offspring with hemolytic jaundice, according to one survey involving 3940 pregnant women.

Obstetricians caring for Rh negative women where this type of problem might arise should have on hand at the time of delivery an adequate supply of Rh negative type O blood for transfusion to the newborn child. Through gradual withdrawal of the infant's blood and replacement with a new supply, antibodies passively transferred to the infant from the mother's circulation are diluted, and thus an adequate supply of oxygen-bearing red blood cells that will not be attacked by circulating antibodies is eventually made available to the newborn child. Any prolonged period of oxygen lack will cause irreparable damage to the brain cells with effects that can lead to all types of permanent mental disorders. This must be avoided.

As research continues in the area of hematology additional antigenic components are being uncovered including such designations as MNS, P, Kidd, Duffy, Lewis, Kell, and Lutheran. These blood fractions play a major role in determining questions of disputed parentage in legal cases and in occasional mixups of infants in nurseries, but they will not be discussed here.

An interesting correlation appears to exist between blood types and the frequency of certain diseases, although there is no evidence of linked genetic association. Duodenal ulcers, for example, are found in a disproportionately high percentage of individuals with type O blood, while gastric carcinoma appears more frequently among group A blood types than any other on a statistical basis. Other similar findings are being uncovered, but to date their meaning is not well understood.

Precipitins

As with the agglutination reaction, three principal ingredients are required for conducting a precipitation test:

Antigen (*precipitinogen*)—extracts of cells or soluble antigens
Antibody (*precipitin*)—blood serum from a patient or an immunized animal
Electrolyte—physiological saline

Precipitin is another humoral antibody and it causes aggregation of unorganized protein molecules or soluble antigens. When antibody is placed in contact with its specific soluble antigen a precipitation or flocculation takes place at the juncture or the interface where optimum conditions exist. Such a test may be performed in narrow test tubes, in capillary tubes when amounts of the test material are limited, or within marked areas in slides which may be examined microscopically or with the unaided eye.

In agglutination reactions the antibody-containing serum is diluted and the antigen held constant. In contrast, many technicians conducting precipitin tests erroneously vary the antigen concentration and keep the antibody constant when attempting to measure the titer of precipitin in a serum sample. Authorities justifiably criticize this technique and point out that if the antigen concentration is not excessive, the reason for diluting this ingredient in a serological test becomes unnecessary. This reaction is a surface type of phenomenon, and since more surface area per weight becomes available when a cell is broken up, it stands to reason that too great a concentration of antigen can operate adversely in such a system. Even though antibody may be present, it will not be detected unless a great deal of the antigen surface becomes sensitized by the antibody, and a false end point may be reached.

By diluting the antigen and holding the serum concentration constant one measures the potency and purity of the antigen but not the titer of the antibody, and this is the fallacy in the commonly employed procedure for conducting precipitin tests. It should be mentioned, however, that this antigen-diluting procedure is still useful in the identification of blood, particularly where the amount of blood is limited. Dilutions as high as 1:50,000 may be detected by precipitation tests in the hands of experienced operators. The ideal proportion between antigen and antibody can also be determined by employing decreasing amounts of antigen. The tube that first shows flocculation is the *optimal mixture,* or the *immunologically equivalent proportions,* and tubes on either side of it will generally flocculate successively with the passage of time.

Precipitin reactions are generally more sensitive than agglutination tests and they are of particular importance in medical–legal cases *(forensic medicine)* involving such determinations as the identification of blood stains. Even minute flecks of dried blood can be identified as being of human origin, and the "Dick Tracy" type of sleuthing may rely upon precipitation reactions to assist in arriving at decisions, some of which may determine a finding of guilty or innocent in murder cases. The Lancefield procedure for grouping beta hemolytic streptococci discussed in an earlier chapter (see p. 278) is also based upon this serological principle, as are certain tests for syphilis including the Kahn flocculation test.

The specificity of precipitins is such that they can be relied upon for sharply differentiating between unrelated soluble antigens. Adulteration of meat products (horse meat in hamburger or in sausage, for example), or the use of various substitutes for eggs in pastries can readily be detected by employing these antigen-antibody tests.

Opsonins

The Greek word *opsonin* means "to prepare food for," and this is exactly what this antibody does when it makes bacterial cells attractive to leucocytes by "sensitizing" the microbes prior to their being taken up by the white blood cells in the process of phagocytosis. Polymorphonuclear leucocytes can engulf inanimate objects without prior action by opsonins, but the repelling action exhibited by some pathogenic bacteria impedes their engulfment unless opsonin first acts upon them. Some serologists and immunologists prefer not to think of opsonin as a particular, distinct antibody, but believe rather that opsonization is merely a manifestation of general antibody activity.

Titration of opsonic activity is a common procedure in diagnostic laboratories, particularly in serological studies of blood serum of suspected undulant fever cases which often may be difficult to diagnose. This is not a simple procedure to conduct nor are the results always easy to evaluate, but the technique involved is a comparison of the average number of bacteria taken in by polymorphonuclear leucocytes using "normal" blood serum and serum from a patient suspected of having the disease. The *opsonic index* is the ratio of immune to normal phagocytic activity. If the patient's blood shows an average of thirty bacteria per leucocyte, for example, and the control specimen has an average of only five organisms per white cell, the opsonic index should be thirty divided by five, indicating a sixfold increase in phagocytosis in the presence of antibodies. In the absence of any positive bacterial cultures from patients, an opsonic index furnishes additional information to the clinician.

In setting up such an *in vitro* determination it is necessary to have whole bacterial cells, antiserum from the patient (in addition to normal serum as a control), plus added leucocytes. A fourth component called *complement,* a heat-labile unstable substance of mixed globulin composition and a constituent of plasma in all normal warm-blooded animals, apparently stimulates opsonic activity, but the mechanism by which it operates is far from clear. Although complement does not combine individually with either antigen or antibody, it does have an affinity for combinations of the two and it reacts with the complex.

Complement may in some manner be instrumental in helping to protect us from infections, but it is nonspecific and unrelated to the usual immune responses. When stored at room temperature complement loses its activity rather quickly; shaking will also cause some deterioration, but part of the lost activity may be restored if it is left standing in a cool environment. Refrigeration retards inactivation and lyophilization may be employed to prolong for months the activity of this labile ingredient.

After suitable incubation of an opsonic index setup, samples are removed, placed on a slide, stained with appropriate dyes, and the polymorphonuclear leucocytes are examined under the oil immersion objective. The average number of ingested bacteria is determined and compared with "normal" serum in calculating the index which may bear some relationship to the over-all degree of acquired resistance of a given individual.

Lysins

In conducting a determination for lysis (dissolving action) four major ingredients are required:

> Antigen—whole cells, either bacteria or red blood cells
> Antibody (lysin)—serum from a patient or from an immunized animal
> Complement—fresh serum usually derived from a guinea pig
> Electrolyte—physiological saline

Dissolving action does not take place under the influence of the antibody lysin unless complement is present, and not all bacteria are thus affected. Gram positive organisms fail to lyse as a rule, and of the gram negative species only the cholera vibrio, typhoid, some of the paratyphoid members, colon and dysentery organisms, *Brucella,* and *H. influenzae* are susceptible to lysin and complement.

The Wassermann test for syphilis, developed in 1906, is based on the principle of lysis, employing two antigen–antibody systems for determination of antibodies against *Treponema pallidum* in a patient. This is one of the most exacting and unwieldy of the serological tests, but it does provide valuable information that other reactions may not supply.

All of the minute details of complement fixation, and the Wassermann test in particular, will not be outlined here, but sufficient background material will be presented to enable the reader to gain some concept of underlying principles, since the findings of such determinations represent an important consideration not only for physicians but also for those engaged in the paramedical sciences.

Wassermann initially employed a watery extract of *T. pallidum* as his antigen, but a satisfactory substitute was found to be an alcoholic extract of beef heart muscle that had previously been extracted with ether. The active principle in this preparation is a cardiolipin which is reinforced with lecithin and cholesterol to improve its sensitivity and specificity.

As stated earlier in this chapter, complement has the facility of combining with specific antigen–antibody complexes, but in the Wassermann test it becomes necessary to employ a second antigen–antibody indicator system to give visible evidence of what has occurred in the primary reaction with the patient's serum.

Ingredients derived from five different animals are necessary for such a test for syphilis:

<table>
<tr><td>Beef Heart Extract
(Antigen)</td><td>Patient's Serum
(Antibody)</td></tr>
<tr><td colspan="2" align="center">Guinea Pig Serum
(Complement)</td></tr>
<tr><td>Sheep Red Blood Cells
(Antigen)</td><td>Rabbit Hemolysin
(Antibody)</td></tr>
</table>

When carefully measured, standardized amounts of beef heart extract and patient's serum are combined with guinea pig complement and the mixture is incubated in a 37°C water bath. If the serum contains antibodies specific for the syphilis spirochete, the antibodies will attach themselves to the antigen and complement will combine with the beef heart–serum complex thus formed. At this point no readily visible reaction has taken place and a second specific antigen–antibody system must be added to the tubes to serve as an indicator of the primary reaction.

Sheep red blood cells serve as the second antigen and blood serum obtained from a rabbit that has been hyperimmunized with sheep erythrocytes provides the specific antibody. Lysis of the sheep cells will not occur, however, unless sufficient complement is present to complete the reaction. If, therefore, the measured amount of complement has been bound by the first system, none remains for the indicator system and hemolysis of the sheep red blood cells will fail to take place. No dissolving of the erythrocytes, in other words, indicates that the patient's serum contained antibodies for *T. pallidum* and the Wassermann test is positive for syphilis. This can be a quantitative as well as a qualitative determination with a so-called four plus Wassermann representing a strong reaction and fewer pluses indicating lesser amounts of syphilis antibody in the patient's serum.

The lipoidal suspension of beef heart is not an antigen in the true sense, since it is incapable of inciting production of antibodies when introduced into an animal. However since this nonspecific extract is capable of binding antibodies in the serum of a syphilitic individual, the beef heart extract serves in the capacity of an antigen in this respect.

Antitoxins

From discussions in previous chapters the reader may recall that if bacteria liberate toxins (soluble poisons) during their active metabolism, such substances are termed true toxins or *exotoxins,* but when disruption of the bacteria must occur before bound poisons are liberated, then the toxic fractions are *endotoxins.* Effective antitoxins can be produced to counteract only soluble poisons, and some of the more notorious exotoxin-producing organisms are those causing diphtheria, tetanus, scarlet fever, and botulism.

We do not yet know whether antitoxins merely combine with the toxic fraction of such a poison and neutralize it, or whether (as is more likely) the mechanism is more complex, but such combinations prove effective both *in vitro* and *in vivo.* Exotoxins are nitrogenous substances that are thermolabile. The bacteria that form them usually remain more or less localized within the body, while their toxins may be carried through body fluids and the circulatory system to distant areas where they usually exhibit a strong affinity for particular tissues on which they inflict their characteristic damage. As is true for all antibodies, antitoxins are specific for the antigen which stimulated their production.

Endotoxins, which are heat-stable, remain fixed within a cell until the bacteria disintegrate either by biological or by physical means, and if they produce any antitoxin, it must be extremely weak and certainly of no consequence in therapy. Typhoid, paratyphoid, cholera, and dysentery organisms are examples of bacteria that produce endotoxins, and the diseases these microbes cause are customarily combatted through the use of prophylactic vaccination procedures, except for the dysentery bacteria that do not appear to possess strong antigenic qualities.

Neutralizing Antibodies

When some viruses are mixed with serum obtained from a vaccinated or previously infected individual it is possible to demonstrate a virus-neutralizing effect when the combination is introduced into susceptible hosts. The microorganisms apparently are not killed by the antiserum and viable viruses may be liberated through dilution or filtration of the mixture. Such viruses generally remain relatively infective, but with tobacco mosaic viruses the inactivation tends to persist following contact with specific antiserum. *In vivo* tests may not always parallel *in vitro* findings, and just what takes place in a host when viruses and their specific anti-serum come in contact is not understood.

The use of gamma globulin to modify the course of measles, polio, mumps, chickenpox, and other virus diseases through inducing acquired immunity lends support to the belief that neutralization of viruses, at least in part, does take place within a living host. Congenital immunity passed on to a developing embryo through the mother's circulation is further evidence of humoral passive protection during the initial stages of life after the birth of an individual.

Although the exact mechanism of virus inhibition may not be clear, the fact remains that the course of virus diseases may be altered through employing specific antibodies which may either neutralize the viruses themselves or modify the host target cells, perhaps through a form of physicochemical union.

Other antibodies have been described in the literature, but the six examples that have been discussed represent the better-known substances that are commonly measured in response to antigen stimulation.

Common Skin Tests

Schick Test

During impending outbreaks of diphtheria the work of health officers, physicians, and epidemiologists can be aided considerably if the most susceptible members of a given population are known to them. The Schick test was devised in 1913 by a man whose name the test bears, in order to provide this type of information. The reaction is an *in vivo* demonstration of the neutralizing effect of an antitoxin on its specific toxin.

One-fiftieth of a guinea pig minimal lethal dose (MLD) of diphtheria toxin contained in a volume of 0.1 ml is injected intradermally in the flexor surface of the forearm. Certain international health organizations are advocating somewhat stronger doses of test toxin which they feel might reduce the number of false positive and doubtful readings.

Individuals who are susceptible to diphtheria will exhibit a raised area of redness measuring between one and two centimeters in diameter. Inflammation that persists longer than five days is generally considered to represent susceptibility to diphtheria since it excludes any local irritation that might be due to substances other than the toxin in the injected material. A positive reaction will gradually fade, leaving a brownish discoloration with eventual peeling away of the skin in a matter of weeks. No permanent scar remains, however.

Persons who possess sufficient circulating antitoxin to make them relatively immune to diphtheria will show little more than a slight irritation reaction at the site of injection and it will generally disappear within a day or two.

In conducting a Schick test it is advisable to run a parallel control on the other forearm using a sample of toxin that previously has been heated to inactivate the toxic fraction of the mixture. This does not alter the other antigenic substances which in some sensitive individuals might cause local reddening which could yield false or questionable interpretations of susceptibility. A comparison of the responses at the two sites of injection should be made, and a trained observer generally has little difficulty in determining a positive Schick reaction.

Dick Test

The Dick reaction is identical to the Schick test in every respect except that it measures susceptibility of a person to the exotoxin of scarlet fever streptococci.

Tuberculin Test

In contrast to Schick and Dick determinations, the tuberculin test does not measure susceptibility, but rather detects in individuals an allergic response to specific proteins found in *M. tuberculosis*. Once a person has been infected with tuberculosis he becomes allergic, or hypersensitive, to tuberculo-protein even though the microbes may be completely walled off as calcified tubercles in the lungs or elsewhere in the body.

The tuberculin test has its greatest value as a screening check on adolescents and young adults. Those exhibiting positive skin findings should be followed up by chest X-ray examinations to determine the nature and the extent of the infection. Such findings may call for additional laboratory tests, including microscopic examination of sputum specimens for the presence of acid-fast rods and also guinea pig inoculations with sputum for further confirmation of active cases of tuberculosis.

A number of techniques have been described through the years for conducting tuberculin tests, and these have been described in Chapter 15 and need not be repeated.

Man has been endowed with an almost unbelievable resistance to disease. His body is much more than just an intricate plumbing system controlled by an efficient pump that might run for a hundred years or more without repair. In spite of all that has been learned to date about our biological machine the surface of knowledge has hardly been scratched, and the next hundred years should unlock many mysteries of paramount importance to understanding what makes us tick and what makes the living spring lose its tension in later years of life. The search for eternal youth continues in uncounted laboratories, though it may masquerade under various disguises. Perhaps the most vigorous search is being conducted by individuals who feel the bounce and enthusiasm of their own youth slowly slipping away with each passing year. These investigations may hit upon additional answers to the mysteries of our resistance to disease.

Review Questions

1. What part does heredity play in susceptibility to disease?
2. Are there many hypochondriacs, or do you believe most illnesses are caused by definite organic disturbances?
3. What differences, if any, exist between agglutinins and precipitins?
4. Which is more important, passive or active immunity? Defend your answer.
5. Is there any potential danger in a universal recipient (type AB) being transfused with type AB blood? Why?
6. What role is played by complement in the Wassermann test for syphilis?
7. With the development of more powerful antibiotics, is microbiology on the way out? Explain.

APPENDIX

The Metric System

Length

Linear measurements are based upon a unit called a *meter,* which is a ten-millionth part of the distance from the Equator to the North Pole. The actual standard unit is the distance between two lines on a platinum–iridium rod kept in the archives of the International Metric Commission in Paris, and the unit is equivalent to 39.37079 inches.

The metric system provides a convenient scale based upon decimals. Multiples of units are designated by the suffixes *deca* (10), *hecto* (100), and *kilo* (1000), and subdivisions of the meter are given the prefixes *deci* (tenth), *centi* (hundredth), *milli* (thousandth), and *micro* (millionth).

The size of microorganisms is expressed in terms of a *micron,* abbreviated as the Greek letter *mu* (μ), and microbes generally studied in an elementary course in microbiology fall within the range of about 1.0 to 5.0 microns (or *micra*) in length and about 1 micron or less in width.

1 meter	= 10 decimeters
1 decimeter	= 10 centimeters
1 centimeter	= 10 millimeters
1 millimeter	= 1000 microns
1 micron	= about 1/25,000 of an inch

431

Weight

The unit of weight in the metric system is a *gram*. To put this into familiar terms, there are about 454 grams in one pound.

$$
\begin{array}{ll}
1 \text{ kilogram} & = 1000 \text{ grams} \\
1 \text{ gram} & = 1000 \text{ milligrams} \\
1 \text{ microgram} & = \text{one millionth of a gram}
\end{array}
$$

Volume

When measuring volumes the unit is a *liter,* which is slightly greater than a quart. A liter may be defined as the volume of pure water which weighs one kilogram at 4°C and at 760 millimeters of mercury. Therefore when measuring water in most laboratory experiments it can be assumed for all practical purposes that each gram of water occupies a volume equivalent to one-thousandth of a liter, and this unit is called a *milliliter* (ml) or a *cubic centimeter* (cc).

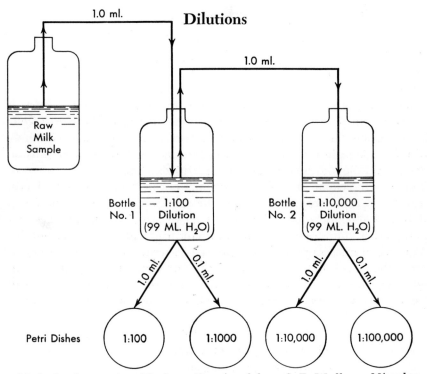

Methods of preparing dilutions. (Reprinted from S. E. Wedberg, *Microbes and You,* 1954, with permission of The Macmillan Company, New York, N. Y.)

Temperature Conversion

There are a number of methods for converting temperatures from one scale to another, and instructors may wish to introduce their students to one or more of these procedures in addition to the scheme outlined below.

To convert centigrade readings into degrees Fahrenheit, the following formula may be employed:

(Degrees C × 9/5) + 32 = degrees Fahrenheit.

To convert from the Fahrenheit scale to centigrade:

(Degrees F − 32) × 5/9 = degrees centigrade.

REFERENCES

American Public Health Association, 1955. *Standard Methods for the Examination of Water, Sewage, and Industrial Wastes,* 10th ed., American Public Health Association, New York.

Bausch and Lomb Optical Company, 1936. *The Use and Care of the Microscope,* Bausch and Lomb Optical Company, Rochester.

Bitter, R. S., and Williams, O. B., 1949. "Enteric Organisms from the American Cockroach," *Journal of Infectious Diseases,* **85,** 87.

Breed, R. S., Murray, E. G. D., Smith, N. R., *et al.,* 1957. *Bergey's Manual of Determinative Bacteriology,* 7th ed., The Williams and Wilkins Company, Baltimore.

Buchanan, R. E., and Buchanan, E. D., 1951. *Bacteriology,* 5th ed., The Macmillan Company, New York.

Burnet, F. M., 1955. *Viruses and Man,* 2d ed., Penguin Books, Baltimore, Md.

Burrows, W., 1959. *Textbook of Microbiology,* 17th ed., W. B. Saunders Company, Philadelphia.

Carpenter, P. L., 1961. *Microbiology,* W. B. Saunders Company, Philadelphia.

Clifton, C. E., 1950. *Introduction to the Bacteria,* McGraw-Hill Book Company, Inc., New York.

Conn, H. J., 1948. "The Most Abundant Groups of Bacteria in Soil," *Bacteriological Reviews,* **12,** 257–273.

Dack, G. M., 1949. *Food Poisoning,* 2d ed., The University of Chicago Press, Chicago.

DeKruif, P., 1926. *Microbe Hunters,* Harcourt, Brace and World, New York.

Departments of the Army and the Air Force, 1951. *Methods for Medical Laboratory Technicians* (TM 8-227, AFM 160-14), U. S. Government Printing Office, Washington, D. C.

Frobisher, M., 1957. *Fundamentals of Micriobiology,* 6th ed., W. B. Saunders Company, Philadelphia.

———— and Sommermeyer, L., 1960. *Microbiology for Nurses,* 10th ed., W. B. Saunders Company, Philadelphia.

Garrod, L. P., Perkins, J. J., Phillips, C. R., and Spaulding, E. H., 1957. "Becton, Dickinson Lectures on Sterilization," Seton Hall College of Medicine and Dentistry, Jersey City, N. J.

Hahn, E., 1959. "Temperature and Temperament," *Woman's Day* (Feb.), p. 30.

Hawley, J. E., Penner, L. R., Wedberg, S. E., and Kulp, W. L., 1951. "The Role of the House Fly, *Musca domestica,* in the Multiplication of Certain Enteric Bacteria," *American Journal of Tropical Medicine,* **31,** 572–582.

Hilleboe, H. E., and Larimore, G. W., 1959. *Preventive Medicine,* W. B. Saunders Company, Philadelphia.

Hirst, G. K., 1941. "The Agglutination of Red Cells by Allantoic Fluid of Chick Embryos Infected with Influenza Virus," *Science,* **94,** 22–23.

Kellert, E., 1959. "Chester Averill and the Chlorination of Drinking Water," *New York State Journal of Medicine,* **59** (15), 2947.

Krueger, W. W., and Johansson, K. R., 1959. *Principles of Microbiology,* W. B. Saunders Company, Philadelphia.

Kulp, W. L., 1961. "Laboratory Manual for the Fundamentals of Microbiology" (Mimeographed Exercises Used at the University of Connecticut).

Luria, S. E., 1956. *General Virology,* 2d ed., John Wiley & Sons, Inc., New York.

Neter, E., 1949. *Medical Microbiology for Nurses,* F. A. Davis Company, Philadelphia.

Pelczar, M. J., and Reid, R. D., 1958. *Microbiology,* McGraw-Hill Book Company, Inc., New York.

Raffel, S., 1961. *Immunity,* 2d ed., Appleton-Century-Crofts, Inc., New York.

Remington, J. P., 1956. *Practice of Pharmacy,* 11th ed., Mack Printing Company, Easton, Pa., p. 256.

Rose, A. H., 1960. "Yeasts," *Scientific American,* **202** (2), 136–149.

Ruehle, G. L. A., and Brewer, C. M., 1931. "United States Food and Drug Administration Methods of Testing Antiseptics and Disinfectants," U. S. Department of Agriculture Circular 198.

Salle, A. J., 1954. *Fundamental Principles of Bacteriology,* 4th ed., McGraw-Hill Book Company, Inc., New York.

Smith, D. T., and Conant, N. F., 1960. *Microbiology,* 12th ed., Appleton-Century-Crofts, Inc., New York.

Steel, H. H., Schreck, K. M., Caswell, T. T., Learner, N., Tyson, R. R., and Carrington, E. R. *Staphylococcal Hospital Infections,* Temple University Medical Center, Philadelphia.

Steinhaus, E. A., 1947. *Insect Microbiology,* Comstock Publishing Company, Ithaca, N. Y.

Stodola, F. H., 1958. *Chemical Transformation by Microorganisms,* John Wiley & Sons, Inc., New York.

Strother, R. S., 1959. "The Case of the Rabid Bats," *Reader's Digest* (Jan.), pp. 187–190.

Taylor, N. B., and Taylor, A. E., 1957. *Stedman's Medical Dictionary,* 19th ed., The Williams and Wilkins Company, Baltimore.

Wedberg, S. E., 1954. *Microbes and You,* The Macmillan Company, New York.

———, 1958. "Microbiology for Nurses" (Mimeographed Laboratory Exercises Used at the University of Connecticut).

Wright, E. S., and Mundy, R. A., 1958. "Studies on Disinfection of Clinical Thermometers," *Applied Microbiology,* **6** (6), 381–383.

Zinsser, H., 1935. *Rats, Lice, and History,* Little, Brown and Company, Boston.

GLOSSARY

Abiogenesis: Spontaneous generation. Life arising without some previous life.

Acid-fast: Not readily decolorized by acids, or by acid-alcohol in the case of mycobacteria.

Actinomycosis: Chronic infection caused by actinomyces. Lumpy jaw.

Activated sludge: Liquid sewage through which air is bubbled.

Active immunity: Resistance built up by a person or an animal.

Adaptive enzyme: An enzyme produced only when specific substrates are present in a medium.

Aerobe: An organism that lives in the presence of free oxygen.

Aerosol: A liquid agent or solution dispersed in air in the form of a fine mist.

Agar slant (or slope): A medium that has been allowed to harden in a slanting position within a test tube.

Agglutination: Clumping of microorganisms in the presence of specific immune serum.

Agglutinin: A substance causing agglutination. An antibody.

Agglutinogen: An antigen which stimulates production of agglutinins.

Alpha hemolysis: Partial destruction of erythrocytes. A greenish zone surrounding a colony growing on a blood agar medium.

Alveoli: Small cells or cavities. An air cell, one of the terminal dilatations of the bronchioles in the lungs.

Anaerobe: An organism which thrives without air or free oxygen.

Anamnestic reaction: A recall response. A booster vaccination resulting in a prompt increase in measurable antibodies.

Andrade's indicator: An acid indicator that may be added to fermentation media to detect a lowering of pH below neutrality.

439

Aneurism: A blood-containing tumor connecting directly with the lumen of an artery or formed by a circumscribed enlargement of an artery.

Anion: An ion which carries a charge of negative electricity. Electronegative with respect to cations.

Antibiotic: Metabolic product liberated by a living organism and which reacts adversely on other organisms.

Antibodies: Gamma globulins (protective bodies) produced in response to specific stimulus by an antigen.

Antigen: Any substance, usually a protein, which when introduced into the body incites formation of specific antibodies.

Antisepsis: Destruction of microorganisms that produce sepsis or septic diseases.

Antiseptic: A substance which prevents formation of infective matter; destroys microbes.

Antitoxin: A substance which is antagonistic to a specific toxin. An antibody.

Aqueous: Watery or a water solution.

Ascospore: A spore contained within an ascus.

Ascus: A sac or bladder containing spores.

Asepsis: Condition free from pathogenic microorganisms.

Autoclave: Apparatus for sterilizing by steam under pressure.

Autogenous vaccine: A suspension of microorganisms freshly isolated from a patient who is to be treated with the vaccine after inactivation of the living material.

Autotrophic: Self-nourishing. Organisms which form protein and carbohydrates from inorganic salts and carbon dioxide.

Bacillus: A gram positive, spore-forming rod. A genus of rod-shaped facultative bacteria.

Bacteremia: The presence of bacteria in the blood stream.

Bacteriolysis: Disintegration or dissolving of bacteria, usually by a specific antibody.

Bacteriophage: An ultramicroscopic agent (a virus) which causes dissolution of bacteria.

Bacteriostat: Anything which retards or inhibits bacterial growth.

Bacterium: A gram negative, non-spore-forming rod. Singular of bacteria.

B.C.P.: From brom cresol purple, a pH indicator with an effective color range of 5.2 (yellow) to 6.8 (purple).

Beta hemolysis: Dissolving effect on red blood cells resulting in a clear zone around a colony growing on a blood agar medium.

Binary fission: Splitting in two. Method by which bacteria divide.

Bioluminescence: Production of cold light by organisms.

Biolysis: Dissolving by biological means. The anaerobic and aerobic decomposition of sewage.

Boil: A circumscribed inflammation in the skin commonly caused by staphylococci.

Bordeaux mixture: Lime and copper sulfate.

Brom thymol blue: A pH indicator with an effective color range from 6.0 (yellow) to 7.6 (blue).

Brownian movement: Rapid vibration of microscopic particles suspended in a fluid.

Bubo: Suppuration of a lymphatic gland, especially one in the axilla or groin.

Buffer: A substance that tends to prevent rapid changes in hydrogen ion concentration upon the addition of small quantities of acid or base.

Calcified tubercle: A firm nodule or swelling. A characteristic lesion in tuberculosis in which calcium has been deposited around the lesion.

Carboxide: A mixture of ethylene oxide and carbon dioxide.

Carbuncle: A circumscribed inflammation of the skin and deeper tissues which terminates in a slough and suppuration. Frequently caused by staphylococci but larger and more serious than a boil.

Carrier: An individual who harbors specific organisms and who, though often immune to the agent harbored, may transmit the disease to others.

Catalase: An enzyme that splits hydrogen peroxide into water and nascent oxygen.

Catalyst: A substance which modifies the velocity of a chemical or physical process.

Cation: Product evolved at the cathode in electrolysis. A positive ion.

Cavitation: The rapid formation and collapse of vapor pockets.

Chancre: An ulcer-like lesion in the primary stage of syphilis.

Chemotherapy: The treatment of disease with chemical substances or drugs.

Chlamydospores: A variety of arthrospore which becomes encysted in a chitin-like envelope. Is composed of cytoplasm and contains food material.

Chocolate agar: A blood-containing medium in which the blood turns brown when heated.

C HOPKINS CaFe Mg: A "crutch" to remember the chemical elements required for growth of cells.

Chromogenic: Color-producing.

Cidal: Suffix forming adjectives signifying killing or having power to kill, e.g., germicidal.

Coagulase: An enzyme responsible for coagulation.

Coccobacteria: Short rods almost spherical in shape.

Coccus: A spherical-shaped bacterial cell form.

Collagenase: An enzyme capable of breaking down collagen, a protein contained in connective tissue and bones.

Colloid: Gluelike. A substance which, by reason of the size of its molecules, is slowly diffusable rather than soluble in water. Incapable of passing through an animal membrane.

Colony: A visible mass of microorganisms growing on a solid medium.

Color comparator block: A device employed for determining the pH of liquids by means of indicator dyes.

Commensalism: Literally, "eating at the same table." An organism living in, with, or on another, but not truly parasitic.

Complement: A thermolabile constituent of blood necessary for lysin to dissolve bacterial and blood cells.

Complement fixation reaction: The combination of a thermolabile constituent of the blood with an antigen–antibody complex. The basis of the Wassermann test for syphilis.

Congenital: Existing at or dating from birth.

Conidia: Free bodies on fertile hyphae. Not enclosed within sporangia.

Conjunctivitis: Inflammation of the membranes lining the eyelids.

Constitutive enzyme: An enzyme constantly present regardless of substrate in a medium.

Contact bed: A water-tight tank filled with crushed rock for aerobic breakdown of sewage.

Coverslip: A thin piece of glass employed with a hanging drop slide to study motility and arrangement of microbes.

Cross-match: The mixing of blood serum of a donor with blood cells of a recipient, and the mixing of blood cells of a donor with blood serum of the recipient.

Cryophilic: Cold-loving.

Cultural characteristics: Visible characteristics of colonies or growths in media.

Cystitis: Inflammation of the urinary bladder.

Cytologist: One who studies the science of cells with reference to their structure, function, multiplication, and life history.

Dark field illumination: Microscopic illumination in which the center rays are blacked out and the peripheral rays are directed against the object from the side. The object being viewed thus appears bright upon a dark background.

Decay: Aerobic breakdown.

Denitrification: Reduction of nitrates to nitrites, ammonia, and free nitrogen.

Dermotropic: Having a selective affinity for the skin and mucous membranes.

Dextran: Capsular material produced by certain species of bacteria and useful as a blood extender in the absence of plasma.

Diastase: A ferment occurring in plants, which has the property of converting starch into sugar.

Diatomaceous earth: A fine siliceous earth composed chiefly of diatoms.

Differential staining: A technique designed to bring out specific structures within cells.

Diplobacillus: A pair of rod-shaped spore-forming bacteria.

Diplobacterium: A pair of gram negative rods.

Diplococcus: A pair of spherical-shaped bacteria.

Disease: Discomfort. Any departure from health. An illness.

Disinfectant: An agent which destroys microbes of putrefaction or disease, or inhibits their action.

Droplet nuclei: Minute residues remaining when droplets dry out. They frequently contain microorganisms.

Durham fermentation tube: A vial inverted within a test tube for collecting gas liberated during fermentation.

Edema: A swelling due to the effusion of a watery fluid from the blood vessels into the intercellular spaces of the connective tissue.

Edematous: Marked by edema. An excessive accumulation of clear watery fluid in the tissue spaces. Dropsy.

Electrophoresis: The movement of particles in an electric field toward an anode or a cathode.

Empyema: Pus in a body cavity, especially in the pleural cavity.

Emulsify: To make into the form of an emulsion, which is a suspension of a solid, usually fatty or resinous substance, divided into very fine particles.

Endocellular: Within a cell.

Endotoxin: Bacterial poison released only when an organism is disintegrated.

Enteric organisms: Microbes whose natural habitat is the enteron, or digestive tract.

Enterotoxin: A poison that acts within the digestive tract.

Enzyme: A complex organic substance produced by plants and animals acting upon other substances and causing them to split into simpler substances. Capable of accelerating greatly the course of specific chemical reactions.

Eschar: A slough following a burn or cauterization of the skin or by infection.

Ethylene oxide: An organic microbicide employed in gaseous sterilization. Chemical formula C_2H_4O.

Exocellular: Released from cells.

Exotoxin: A poison liberated into the medium during active metabolism of cells.

False yeasts: Do not form ascospores. Ferment lactose.

Fermentation: An energy-yielding reaction. Anaerobic or intramolecular respiration.

Fibrinolysis: An enzyme which causes destruction of fibrin. Fibrin dissolving.

Fixed virus: Strains that have been propagated by serial intracerebral passage in some experimental animal in which the incubation period has become short and constant.

Flagella: Hairlike projections on bacteria used to propel the organisms through liquids.

Floc: A tuftlike mass, as in a chemical precipitate.

Fomite: Any inanimate object other than food that may harbor or transmit microorganisms.

Forensic medicine: Medical science in its relation to the law.

Formalin: An aqueous solution of formaldehyde.

Gamete: A sexual cell or germ cell.

Gamma colony: Visible growth of bacteria on a blood agar medium displaying no macroscopic breakdown of the erythrocytes in the medium adjacent to the colony.

Gelatinase: An enzyme responsible for hydrolysis of gelatin.

Gram negative cells: Cells that lose the violet color when placed in acetone in the gram staining procedure.

Gram positive cells: Cells that retain the violet color in the gram staining procedure.

Gram stain: A differential stain used to divide bacteria into two major groups. Gram positive cells retain the primary stain; gram negative cells lose the primary stain when decolorized with alcohol or with acetone under specified conditions.

Green soap: Potassium soap and alcohol. Eosin may be present.

Halogen: One of the chlorine group (bromine, chlorine, fluorine, iodine) of metalloids.

Hanging drop: Suspension of a liquid over a concavity for microscopic examination of motility and arrangement of cells.

Haptene: An incomplete antigen incapable of producing antibodies but capable of neutralizing specific antibodies *in vitro*.

Hauch: German word for "film" to describe characteristic development of *Proteus* growth on solid media.

HeLa cells: Cells obtained from a human carcinoma of the cervix.

Hemagglutination: Clumping of blood cells.

Hemolysis: Dissolving or rupturing of blood cells.

Heterogamete: A gamete (a sexual cell or germ cell) of a type exhibiting sexual or other differentiation.

Heterologous: Derived from a different species, or not corresponding to a particular antigen or antibody.

Heterotroph: An organism that derives its energy through breakdown of complex organic matter.

Holding method: A technique of pasteurizing milk and other dairy products by holding them at 145°F for 30 minutes to destroy pathogenic organisms.

Holophytic feeding: Taking in dissolved food through the cell wall and cytoplasmic membrane.

Homologous: Of similar structure. In immunity, the term refers to specific antigens and antibodies.

Humus: Dark organic material in soils, produced by the decomposition of vegetable or animal matter.

Hydrolysis: Chemical decomposition involving addition of water to a molecule followed by splitting at the point of linkage where the water is introduced.

Hydrophobia: Fear or morbid dread of water. Rabies.

Hypertonic: Having a greater degree of tension or osmotic pressure than the blood. More concentrated than physiological saline.

Hypha: One of the filaments comprising the mycelium of a fungus.

Hypotonic: Having a lower degree of tension or osmotic pressure than the blood. Less concentrated than physiological saline.

Imhoff tank: A large tank for sedimentation and digestion of sewage.

Immunity: State of being resistant to disease.

Incubation period: The interval between exposure to infection and the appearance of the first symptom.

Indole: A compound derived from decomposition of tryptophane.

Infusorial: Containing or consisting of members of the class *Infusoria*.

Intradermal: Into the skin.

Intramuscular: Into the muscle.

Intrathecal: Into the spinal cord or canal.

Involution: Retrograde development or degeneration.

Iso-gametes: One of two or more similar cells by the conjugation or fusion of which, with subsequent division, reproduction occurs. Similar sexual cells.

Iso-immunity: Resistance within a species.

Isotonic: Solutions having the same or equal tension or osmotic pressure.

Kinase: Colloidal substance which activates the enzymes with which it comes in contact.

Kopeloff-Beerman method: One of the modifications of the gram staining procedure.

Koplik's spots: Small red spots on the buccal mucous membrane, in the center of which may be seen a minute bluish white speck. Occur only in measles before the skin eruption.

Leuco (Leuko): White or colorless.

Leucocyte: A white blood corpuscle. Unpigmented ameboid cells in the blood.

Leukemia: Cancer of the blood.

Limber neck: Characteristic symptoms in poultry following ingestion of *Cl. botulinum* toxin.

Lipoprotein: Fat-protein complex.

Lumen: The space in a tubular structure.

Lyophilization: Freeze-drying employing high vacuum and sublimation. A method employed for preserving cultures.

Malignant pustule: Primary lesion in anthrax.

Medium: A nutritive substance for microbes.

Membranous croup: Disease characterized by difficult breathing due in part to the formation of a membrane in the air passage.

Meningitis: Inflammation of the membranes of the spinal cord or brain.

Mesophilic: Growing at a middle range. Usually refers to temperature.

Metabiosis: A condition in which an organism produces conditions or growth substances favorable to another organism.

Metachromatic granules: Deeply staining bodies seen in cells, especially *C. diphtheriae*.

Metric system: A decimal system of weights and measures.

Microaerophilic: Growing at low oxygen tension. Usually require increased levels of carbon dioxide.

Micron: One-millionth part of a meter. About 1/25,000 of an inch.

Milk sickness: Trembles. Poisoning due to trematol acquired by domestic animals after eating white snakeroot. Transmitted to man through milk.

Milliliter: One-thousandth part of a liter, or 1.0567 U.S. liquid quarts.

Millimeter: One-thousandth part of a meter.

Mordant: A substance employed to fix a dye.

Morphology: Science which treats with external configuration or structure of plants and animals.

Much's granules: Gram positive, non-acid-fast granules found in pus or cold abscesses associated with tuberculosis.

Mutagenic agent: Any agent that induces mutation.

Mutant: In heredity, a variation or sport which breeds true.

Mutation: Sudden permanent change or transformation.

Mycelium: The vegetative body of a fungus composed of a mass of filaments called hyphae.

Negri bodies: Minute bodies found as cell inclusions in the Purkinje cells of the cerebellum in rabies.

Nitrogen fixation: Conversion of atmospheric nitrogen into nitrates by selected bacteria.

Nucleoprotein: One of a group of conjugated proteins consisting of a compound of simple protein with nucleic acid. An important constituent of a cell nucleus.

Nucleus: The controlling mechanism of a cell. Contains nucleoprotein.

Ohne hauch: German, "without film." Descriptive term with respect to colonial growth of *Proteus* species.

Oidium: An oval or rectangular body (egg) on septate fertile hyphae of *Geotrichum*.

Oligodynamic action: The inhibitory effect on microbes displayed by certain heavy metals, especially silver.

Opsonic index: The ratio of the phagocytic index of immune serum to that of normal serum.

Opsonin: An antibody which prepares cells for phagocytosis.

Organic: Pertaining to or derived from living matter.

Organoleptic: Affecting or making an impression upon an organ or the whole organism.

Osmosis: Phenomenon of passage of certain fluids and solutions through a membrane or other porous substance.

Osmotic pressure: The pressure built up on one side when two miscible fluids of different concentrations are separated by a permeable membrane.

Otitis media: Inflammation of the middle ear.

Oxidase: An enzyme responsible for oxidation.

Oxidation: A chemical process by which organisms secure energy for growth.

Oxidation–reduction: An enzyme system in tissues by which oxidation and reduction proceed simultaneously through transference of hydrogen or of one or more electrons from one metabolite to another. Redox system.

Panacea: A remedy for all diseases. A cure-all.

Pandemic: A disease that is epidemic at the same time in many parts of the world.

Passive immunity: Resistance acquired by defense factors not originating within the protected individual.

Pathogenic: Giving origin to disease or to morbid symptoms.

Penicillin: An antibiotic produced by selected species of the mold *Penicillium*.

Peritonitis: Inflammation of the peritoneum.

Petechiae: Small crimson, purple, or livid spots due to extravasation of blood in the skin.

Pfeiffer phenomenon: Bacteriolysis of vibrios in the peritoneal cavity of immunized guinea pigs.

Phagocytic index: The average number of phagocytized bacteria per leucocyte.

Phagocytosis: Ingestion of microbes by leucocytes.

Phenol coefficient test: Quantitative technique for evaluating the effectiveness *in vitro* of antiseptics and disinfectants.

Photodynamic action: Related to the energy or force exerted by light.

Photogenesis: Production of light. Bioluminescence. Phosphorescence.

Photophosphorescence: Production of light. Photogenesis.

Photoreactivation: Reversal of injury to cells caused by ultraviolet light through post-irradiation exposure to light waves larger than the inactivating waves.

Photosynthesis: A process of constructive metabolism in chlorophyll-containing plants exposed to light.

Physiological: Pertaining to cells, tissues, and organs of living things.

Plaque: A patch or differentiated area exhibited by a culture growing in a solid medium as the result of bacteriophage action.

Plasma: The fluid portion of blood.

Plasmolysis: The shrinking of cells as the result of their being placed in a solution above isotonic.

Plasmoptysis: The swelling of cells as the result of their being placed in a solution less than isotonic.

Pleomorphism: Having many shapes.

Pock: A skin pustule in smallpox or a similar disease.

Potentiometer: An instrument for measuring electrical potentials.

Prognosis: Forecast or outlook of the course and termination of a disease.

Proteolytic: Effecting digestion of proteins.

Protoplasm: The form of matter in which life is manifested.

Psychrophilic: Cold-loving.

Ptomaine: Any class of alkaloids formed by the action of putrefactive bacteria on nitrogenous matter.

Putrefaction: Anaerobic breakdown.

Pyelitis: Inflammation of the kidney.

Pyocyanase: A by-product of *Pseudomonas* species capable of displaying antagonistic action against other organisms.

Pyrogenic: Fever-producing.

Rennet curd: A sweet curd brought about by the action of the enzyme rennin.

Respiration: Energy-yielding reactions occurring within a cell.

Rh factor: Rhesus factor. Antigens present in the blood of rhesus monkeys and in the erythrocytes of the majority of human beings.

Ribonucleic acid: A polynucleotide containing the pentose sugar d-ribose.

Sandwich plate: A type of streak plate on top of which is poured a thin cap layer of blood-containing agar.

Sanitize: To make clean, free of pathogens, but not necessarily sterile.

Saprophyte: An organism living upon dead or decaying organic matter.

Selective medium: A medium which permits the growth of certain species and simultaneously suppresses that of others.

Septa: Cross walls on septate hyphae.

Septicemia: The presence of pathogenic organisms in the blood.

Serology: The study of test tube reactions using blood serum.

Short time high temperature pasteurization: Heating to 160°F (71°C) for from 15 to 17 seconds, followed by rapid cooling to below 50°F.

Silicosis: The condition resulting from the inhalation of particles of silica or stone.

Sludge: A muddy or slimy deposit from sewage.

Sporangium: A structure housing asexual spores.

Spore: The reproductive element of one of the lower organisms. In contrast, spores of bacteria are inactive resting or resistant forms.

Spot plate: A white porcelain plate containing depressions. Employed in colorimetric determination of pH.

Spreading factor: A substance produced by some bacteria which affects the permeability of tissues. Hyaluronidase.

Static: In a state of equilibrium or rest. Not in action.

Sterilization: The act or process of killing or freeing from life.

Stormy fermentation: A characteristic breakdown and shredding of milk proteins under the influence of rapid gas formation by *Cl. perfringens*.

Streak plate: A technique of spreading organisms over the surface of a solid medium for the purpose of isolating organisms.

Street virus: A virus encountered in nature.

Streptobacillus: A chain of rods, specifically gram positive, sporing rods.

Streptobacterium: A chain of gram negative rods.

Streptokinase: An enzyme produced by streptococci capable of lysing plasma clots.

Stricture: A circumscribed narrowing or stenosis of a tubular structure.

Subcutaneous: Below the skin.

Supernatant: That which floats on the surface.

Swarming reaction: A characteristic film or "Hauch" associated with colony growth of *Proteus* species.

Sweet curd: A rennet curd. A soft curd that occurs in milk in the absence of acidity.

Symbiosis: Living together of two species of organisms for mutual benefit.

Synergism: A cooperative effort producing a reaction that no single organism can accomplish independently.

Taxonomy: Classification, especially of plants and animals, according to natural relationships.

Tetanolysin: A hemolysin formed by *Cl. tetani.*

Tetanospasmin: The poison produced by *Cl. tetani* responsible for contraction of skeletal muscles.

Tetanus: A disease with spasmodic and continuous contractions of the muscles. Lockjaw.

Thallus: The plant body of typical thallophytes.

Thermal death point: The lowest temperature that kills all cells in ten minutes.

Thermal death time: The maximum time required at a given temperature to destroy all cells in a given material.

Thermoduric: Heat-enduring.

Thermogenic: Heat-producing.

Thermophilic: Heat-loving.

Thrombus: A clot composed of blood elements.

Tincture: An alcoholic solution.

Titer: The highest dilution of serum that will give an antibody response with its specific antigen.

Toxicity index: The ratio of the highest dilution of a germicide required to kill tissue in ten minutes to the highest dilution required to kill the test organism in the same time and under the same conditions.

Toxoid: A poison treated so as to inactivate its toxicity. A detoxified toxin.

True toxin: An exotoxin against which an antitoxin can be produced.

Tubercle: A small morbid growth, especially the specific lesion of tuberculosis.

Tyndallization: Fractional sterilization. Steaming for a few minutes at 100°C on three or four successive days, separated by 24-hour intervals at a temperature favorable to spore germination.

Universal donor: An individual with type O blood. One who is able to donate blood to all four blood type recipients.

Universal recipient: An individual with type AB blood. One who can receive blood from all four blood types.

Urease: An enzyme that attacks urea with the release of ammonia.

Vaccine: A suspension of microorganisms employed for creating artificial active immunity.

Vacuole: A minute space in any tissue. A clear space in the substance of a cell.

Virulence: Quality of being poisonous. Relative power possessed by organisms to produce disease.

Volutin: Nucleoprotein found in certain bacteria and yeasts. Metachromatic bodies, Babes-Ernst granules, intracellular material present in certain bacterial species, especially *C. diphtheriae.*

Water-insoluble pigment: Color that remains within cells and fails to diffuse into the surrounding medium.

Water-soluble pigment: Color that diffuses from cells into the surrounding medium.

Wort: An infusion of malt.

Yeast: The common name of *Saccharomyces*. Single-celled, non-chlorophyll-containing plants which multiply by budding and ferment simple sugars.

Zygospore: A spore formed by the conjugation of two other spores.

Zymase: An enzyme of yeast which promotes alcoholic fermentation.

INDEX

Abiogenesis, 55
Acetobacter, 347
Acid-fast organisms, 288, 289
Acquired immunity, 415
Actinomyces bovis, 293–295
         israeli, 294
Actinomycosis, 293–295
Activated sludge, 180
Active immunity, 287, 384, 414, 415
Aedes cinereus, 320
    egypti, 257, 258, 399–401
Aerobacter aerogenes, 167, 170
Aerobes, 64, 79
Aerosols, 134
Agar
  chocolate, 60, 308
  composition, 49
  plate technique, 139
  slants or slopes, 70
Age and resistance, 406, 407
Agglutination
  with *Proteus,* 326
  test for *Brucella,* 311
Agglutinins, 311, 416–421
Agglutinogen, 416
Air, 196–208
  analysis of, 206
  composition of, 196–198
  conditioning, 74, 201

pollution, 198
  treatment of, 205–208
Air-borne infections, 203
Alcaligenes viscolactis, 12
Alcohol as a disinfectant, 118, 119
Ale, 349
Alexander the Great, 31
Alimentary anthrax, 283
Alizarine yellow, 48
Allodermanyssus sanguineus, 370
Alpha antibodies, 417
Alpha hemolysis, 60
Altitude and boiling point, 91
Aluminum pans, 224
American spotted fever, 364
Amoebic dysentery, 161
Anaerobes, 21, 64, 77
  fermentation by, 26
  reduction of methylene blue by, 77
  techniques for growing, 63–65
Anamnestic reaction, 302
Andrade's indicator, 78
Aneurism, 341
Ångstrom unit, 147
Aniline dyes, 133
Animal poisonings, 227–229
Anionic detergents, 132
Anopheles mosquitoes, 197, 258
Antagonism of microbes, 36–39

451

Anthrax, description of, 280–284
Antibiotics, 37, 108, 193, 230, 233–243
Antibodies, 415–427
    agglutinins, 416
    antitoxins, 34, 287, 426
    heterologous, 417
    homologous, 417
    lysins, 424–426
    neutralizing, 426, 427
    opsonins, 423, 424
    precipitins, 421–423
Antigens, 33, 416
Antimicrobial agents, 119–137
    alcohol, 118
    dyes, 133, 134
    fumigants, 134, 136
    halogens, 119–124
    heavy metals, 124–126
    inorganic acids and alkalies, 137
    oxidizing agents, 128, 129
    phenolic compounds, 129, 130
    soaps and detergents, 130, 131
Antimony poisoning, 224, 225
Antiseptics, 39, 109
Antitoxins, 34, 287, 426
Aqueous solutions, 151
Argyrol, 126
Arrangements of bacteria, 8, 9
Arsenic poisoning, 225
Arthropods, 256–258
Artificial immunity, 415
Ascitic fluid, 60
Ascomycetes, 345
Ascospores, 345
Asepsis, 39, 83
Asiatic cholera, 333
Aspergillosis of birds, 358
Aspergillus niger, 357
              oryzae, 357
Atabrine, 241
Athlete's foot, 358
Atmosphere, microbiology of, 196–208
Autoclave, 52, 93–98
    diagram of, 53
Autogenous vaccine, 270
Autotrophic organisms, 27, 186
Azide agar, 63
Azotobacter, 188

Babes-Ernst granules, 285
Bacillus, 8
              anthracis, 21, 144, 280–284, 403
              cereus, 16
Bacteria
    identification of, 67–82

pathogenic, 265–343
sizes, shapes, and arrangements of, 6–11
Bacterial cell, 5–24
Bacterial metabolism, 25–41
Bacteriology, *see* Microbiology
Bacteriolysis, 336
Bacteriophage
    theory of immunity, 405
    typing, 272, 273
Bacteriostasis, 61, 108
Bacterium, 8
Bandycoot, 367
Barnum, P. T., 107
B.C.G. vaccine, 290
Bedding as a fomite, 261
Bed pans as fomites, 260
Beef heart extract, 425
Beer yeasts, 348, 349
*Bergey's Manual of Determinative Bacteri-
    ology,* 73, 194, 265, 292, 322, 323, 329,
    330, 361, 373
Berkefeld filters, 86, 100
Beta antibodies in blood, 417
Beta-propiolactone, 137
Binary fission, 8
Biochemical oxygen demand, 181
Biological methods of anaerobiosis, 65
Biological oxygen demand, 181
Bioluminescence, 28, 29
Bismuth sulfite agar, 63
Blaberus craniifer, 257
Black death, 315
Blood
    agar plates, 59
    fractionating, 420
    serum media, 61
    type distribution, 418
    typing, 417–419
B.O.D., 181
Body fluids in immunity, 414
Body wastes, disposal of, 252
Boiling, 86, 91, 92
    effect of altitude on, 91
Books as fomites, 260
Bordeaux mixture, 127
Bordet-Gengou medium, 313, 314
Bordet's theory of immunity, 405
Bordetella pertussis, 312–314
Borrelia recurrentis, 258
              vincentii, 336, 337
Botulism, 34, 218–220
Bound water, 22
Brilliant green bile medium, 63
Brill's disease, 363
Broadstreet pump, 335

Brom cresol green, 48
Brom cresol purple, 48
  milk, 76
Bromine, 124
Brom phenol blue, 48
Brom thymol blue, 48
Broth cultures, 75
Broth turbidity tests, 242
Brownian movement, 13
Bruce, David, 308
Brucella abortus, 308, 309
           melitensis, 308, 309
           suis, 308, 309
Brucellergin, 311
Brucellin, 312
Brunhilda virus, 392
Bubo, 317
Buffer, 18

Cadmium poisoning, 225
Calcified turbercle, 289
Calmette-Guerin, 290
Candida, 345
           albicans, 351–352
Capsules, 10, 74
Carbon cycle, 190, 191
Carboxide gas, 102
Carriers, 242–247, 329
Carbuncle, 282
Catalase, 128
Catalyst, 25
Cathode rays, 150
Cationic detergents, 132
Cavitation, 152
Cell
  plant vs. animal, 6
  wall, 11, 16
Cesspools, 178
Chancre
  hard, 341
  soft, 255
Chancroid, 255
Chamberland filter, 86, 100
Chart, descriptive for bacteria, 80
Chemical analysis of water, 170, 171
Chemical methods
  of anaerobiosis, 64
  of control of microbes, 106–142
Chemical poisoning, 224–227
Chemical reactions in disinfection, 116–118
Chemotherapy, 194, 230–243
  in malaria, 240, 241
Chicken pox, 314, 374, 380–382, 427
Chlamydospores, 355

Chloramine, 141
Chloramphenicol, 194
Chlorination of water, 160, 161
Chlorine, 119–121
  residual in water, 173, 174
Chlorophenol red, 48
Chocolate agar, 60, 308
Cholera, 333–336
Chromogenesis, 30, 31, 56, 75
Chrysops discalis, 320
Cisterns, 159
Citrate test, 169, 170
Citric acid production, 357
Clark and Lubs broth, 169
Classification
  of bacteria, 6
  of yeasts, 345
Clostridium botulinum, 193, 218–220, 295–297
           histolyticum, 298
           novyi, 298
           pasteurianum, 189
           perfringens, 45, 145, 192, 297
           tetani, 45, 110, 192, 299, 410
Coagulase test, 271
Coagulation
  in disinfection, 116
  of egg albumin, 88
Coccobacteria, 9
Coccus, 9
Coins as fomites, 259, 260
Coliform bacteria, 62, 170
Collodion filter, 86, 102
Colloid, 5
Colony, appearance of, 9, 74
Color comparator block, 51
Columbus, Christopher, 202, 340
Commensalism, 40
Complement, 336, 423
  fixation reaction, 326, 364, 424–426
Completed water test, 168
Composition
  of sewage, 176
  of soil, 185
Compound microscope, 7
Confirmed water test, 167
Congenital immunity, 415, 427
Congo red, 48
Conidia, 355
Connecticut Advisory Committee, 107
Contact bed, 180
Control of microbes
  in air, 199
  by chemical means, 106–142
  by physical means, 143–154

Conversion of temperatures, 433
Cooperation of cells, 39
Copper sulfate, 127, 128
Corynebacterium diphtheriae, 20, 34, 62, 152, 284–287
Cough plate, 313
Counting colonies, 55
Cox, Herald R., 367
Coxiella burnetii, 258, 367
Credé process, 126, 306
Cresol, 130
Cresolphthalein, 48
Cresol red, 48
Criteria for ideal disinfectant, 110–113
Cross-matching of blood, 418, 419
Cryophilic bacteria, 143
Cryptococcus neoformans, 345, 349–351
Cups as fomites, 45, 261, 262
Cultivation
    of microbes, 42–66
    of rickettsiae, 361–362
    of viruses, 375–380
    of yeasts, 346
Cultural characteristics, 20, 74, 75
Cultures
    broth, 75
    transfer of, 67
Curds, acid, rennet, sweet, 76
Cyanide poisoning, 225
Cycles of elements, 35–36
    carbon, 190–191
    nitrogen, 187–190
Cylinder test for antibiotics, 241, 242
Cystitis, 79, 252, 324
Cytologist, 5
Cytoplasmic membrane, 11, 17
Czapek-Dox medium, 356

Da Rocha-Lima, 359
DDT, 318, 363, 401
Decay, 187
DeKruif, Paul, 367
Dengue fever, 258
Denitrification, 189
Dermacentor andersoni, 320, 364, 367
                variabilis, 364, 365
Dermonecrotizing toxin, 32
Dermotropic viruses, 374, 381–386
Descriptive chart for bacteria, 80
Detergents, 130–132
Desiccation on microbes, 144, 145
Dextran, 11
D'Herelle's phage theory of immunity, 405
Dick test, 277, 428

Differential stains, 71
Dilution technique, 432
para-Dimethylaminobenzaldehyde, 79, 168
Diphtheria, 20, 34, 62, 152, 427
Diplobacillus, 9
Diplobacterium, 9
Diplococcus, 9, 10
Diplococcus pneumoniae, 13, 60, 266–268
Disc technique for disinfectants, 138
Disease, 83, 233, 402
    transmission of, 244–264
Disinfectants
    chemical reactions of, 116–118
    criteria for, 110–113
    evaluation of, 137–142
    factors influencing, 113–116
Disinfection, 83, 109–118
Disposal of human wastes, 176
Drilled wells, 159
Drinking fountains, 172, 173
Driven wells, 159
Droplet nuclei, 247–251
Dropsy, 60, 146
Dry heat sterilization, 86–88
Dug wells, 158
Duran-Reynals factor, 277
Durham fermentation tube, 77
Dyes as bacteriostatic agents, 108, 133, 134
Dyne, 151

Eagle test, 342
Earth pit privy, 177
Eberthella typhosa, 330
Edema, 146, 335
Egg, culture of rickettsiae, 369
Egg-meat medium, 65
Ehrlich, Paul, 54, 231, 341
Electricity, effect of on microbes, 153
Electrophoresis, 153
Elements for cell growth, 46
E.M.B. agar, 62, 327, 332
Empyema, 266
Endamoeba histolytica, 161
Endemic typhus, 364
Endo agar, 61, 79, 167, 332
Endocellular enzymes, 26
Endomycetales, 345
Endospores, 21
Endotoxins, 33, 276, 426
    vs. exotoxins, 33, 34
Enteric organisms, 61
Enterotoxin, 272
Enzymes, 25–28
    adaptive, 27
    constitutive, 27

definition of, 25
endocellular, 26
exocellular, 26
naming of, 27
Eosine methylene blue agar, 62, 79, 167, 327, 332
Epidemic typhus, 362, 363
Epidermophyton, 358
Erythema of streptococci, 276
Erythroblastosis fetalis, 420
Erythrogenic toxin, 276
Erythromycin, 194
Escherichia coli, 62, 125, 166–170, 252, 253
Ethylene oxide, 102, 136, 137
Evaluation of disinfectants, 137–142
Evans, Alice, 309
Exocellular enzymes, 26
Exotoxins, 33, 426
    vs. endotoxins, 33, 34
Exposure time for sterilization, 95

Factors influencing disinfection, 113–116
Factors influencing resistance, 406–410
Facultative organisms, 80
Fahrenheit, Gabriel, 87
False yeasts, 345
Fatigue and resistance, 409, 410
Fava beans, 227
Feed supplements, 239, 240
Fermentation, 26, 77, 78
Fertile eggs, 376
Fertile hyphae, 353
Fibrinolysin test, 271, 272
Filter paper discs, 138, 242
Filters
    intermittent, 180
    pressure, 163
    rapid sand, 162
    slow sand, 162
    trickling, 180
Filtration techniques, 99–102, 161–164
    Berkefeld, 86, 100
    Chamberland, 86, 100
    collodion, 86, 102
    Seitz, 86, 100
    sintered glass, 86, 101
Fingers in disease transmission, 244–247
Finlay, Carlos, 398
Fish, tolerance of to copper sulfate, 128
Fixation of nitrogen, 188
Fixed virus, 397
Flagella, 11, 13
    arrangement of, 15
Flander's Fields, 301

Fleas as vectors, 257
Fleming, Alexander, 37, 234
Flies, 214, 215, 393
Floors as fomites, 261
Flowing steam, 86, 93
Fluoridation of water, 164
Fluorine, 122
Flury rabies virus, 397, 398
Fomites, 45, 258–264
Food
    for energy, 264
    handlers, 213, 214
    infections, 217
    in media, 46
    microbiology of, 209–229
    poisoning, 215–229
    preservation by antibiotics, 240
Formaldehyde, 134
Formalin, 134
Formation of salts with proteins, 117, 118
Four Horsemen of the Apocalypse, 359
Fumigants, 134–137
    beta-propiolactone, 137
    ethylene oxide, 136, 137
    formaldehyde, 134
    glycol vapors, 135
    hydrogen cyanide, 135
    sulfur dioxide, 135
Fungi, 344–358
Fungi Imperfecti, 345, 358
Furniture as fomites, 261
Fusobacterium fusiforme, 336

Gaffkya tetragena, 279, 280
Gallons of water in a well, 159
Gametes, 355
Gamma colonies, 60
Gamma globulin, 427
Garbage, disposal of, 215
Gas gangrene, 45, 145, 192, 297–299
Gas sterilization, 86, 102
Gelatin, nutrient, 75, 81
Gelatinase, 75
German measles, 386, 387
Giemsa stain, 361
Gin, manufacture of, 349
Glasses as fomites, 261, 262
Glossary, 439–450
Glycol vapors, 135
Gonorrhea, 253, 254
Gonyaulax catenella, 227
Gram negative bacteria, 302–343
Gram positive bacteria, 266–302
Gram stain, 8, 22–24, 72, 73

Granules, 11
    metachromatic, 19, 285
    Much's, 19
Green soap, 245
Growth curve, 43

Halogens, 119–124
Hands in disease spread, 244–247
Hanging drop, diagram of, 15
Hansen's disease, 292
H antigens, 325, 330
Haptene, 267
Hard chancre, 341
Hauch, 325
Health, defined, 106, 197
Heat
    dry, in sterilization, 86–88
    moist, in sterilization, 86, 89–98
    production by microbes, 29, 30
Heavy metals, 124–128
HeLa cells, 377, 393
Hemagglutination-inhibition, 360
Hemlock, water, 228
Hemolysins, 277, 278
Hemolysis, alpha and beta, 60
Hemophilus ducreyi, 253, 255
                    influenzae, 314, 388, 424
                    pertussis, 59, 312
Hemotoxin, 32
Heredity and resistance, 406
Herpes zoster, 380–382
Heterogametes, 355
Heterologous antibodies, 417
Heterotrophic organisms, 186
Hexachlorophene, 131
Hexyl resorcinol, 141
Hinton test, 342
Hippocrates, 196, 209
Hirst test, 390
Holding method of pasteurization, 90
Holophytic feeding, 17
Homologous antibodies, 417
Homo sapiens, 411
Honey poisoning, 228
Hot air sterilization, 86, 88
Humoral theory of immunity, 406
Humus, 185
Hyaluronidase, 277
Hydrogen cyanide, 135
Hydrogen ion concentration, 47
Hydrogen peroxide, 128, 141
Hydrolysis in disinfection, 117
Hydrophobia, 395–398
Hydrophobic organisms, 152
Hypertonic solution, 17, 147

Hyphae, 352, 353
    fertile, 353
    vegetative, 353
Hypotonic solution, 147

Ice, microbiology of, 171, 172
Identification of bacteria, 67–82
    cultural characteristics, 74, 75
    morphology, 72–74
    physiology, 75–80
Imhoff tanks, 179
Immune response in smallpox, 385
Immunity
    theories of, 404–406
        Bordet's, 405, 406
        D'Herelle's bacteriophage, 405
        Ehrlich's side chain, 405
        humoral, 406
        Metchnikoff's cellular, 404
        Pasteur's exhaustion, 404
    types of, 414, 415
        acquired, 415
        active, 287, 384, 414, 415
        artificial, 415
        congenital, 415
        inherited, 415
        natural, 415
        passive, 287, 384, 415
        species, 403
Immunology, 404
IMVIC reactions, 168–170
Incineration, 86, 87
Incubation period, 43, 331
Indicators
    of pH, 48
    of sterility, 103, 104
Indole test, 78, 79, 168, 169
Industrial wastes, 181
Infantile paralysis, 391–395
Infections, air-borne, 203
Infectious jaundice, 337
Influenza, 387–391
    virus, 374, 388, 389
Influenzae, Hemophilus, 314, 388, 424
Inherited immunity, 415
Inhibitory media, 61–63
Inoculation of subcultures, 54
Inorganic acids and alkalies, 137
Insect-borne diseases, 361
Intermittent filters, 180
Intermittent heating, 86, 93
Intestines and resistance, 414
Iodine, 121, 122, 141
Irradiation and resistance, 411
Isoantibodies, 417

Isogametes, 355
Isoimmunity, 411
Isoodon macrourus, 367
Isotonic solution, 45, 146

Jaundice, infectious, 337–339
Jefferson, Thomas, 384
Jenner, Edward, 383, 384
Jungle yellow fever, 401

Kahn test, 342
Kauffman and White schema, 330
Klebs-Löffler organisms, 285
Kline test, 342
Koch, Robert, 54, 126
Koch's postulates, 280, 281
Kopeloff-Beerman stain, 23
Koplik's spots, 386
Koser, Stewart, 169

Lactobacillus acidophilus, 211
              bulgaricus, 212
LaMotte sulfo orange, 48
Lancefield's typing of streptococci, 278
Landsteiner, Karl, 416, 419
Lansing virus, 392
Lead poisoning, 225, 226
Leeuwenhoek, Antony van, 54
Leon virus, 392
Leprosy, 292
Leptospira canicola, 338
              icterohaemorrhagiae, 173, 337
Lethal toxin, 32
Leucocidin, 279
Leucocytes, 12, 37
Leucocytic toxin, 32
Leuco methylene blue milk, 77
Leuconostoc dextranicum, 12
Leukemia, 407
Lice as vectors, 257
Light
   effects of on microbes, 147, 148
   production, 29
Limberneck, 297
Lipoproteins, 18
Lister, Joseph, 54, 85, 205
Litmus, pH range of, 48
Live steam, 86, 92
Living conditions and resistance, 408, 409
Lockjaw, 21, 45, 110, 192, 299–302
Löffler's medium, 61, 285
Lumpy jaw, 293
Lungs and resistance, 413
Lymphogranuloma inguinale, 255, 256
              venereum, 253, 255, 256

Lyophilization, 145, 304
Lysins, 424–426
Lysol, 130, 141

Magic bullets (606), 231
Major side of crossmatch, 419
Malaria, 196, 258
   chemotherapy for, 89
Malignant pustule, 283
Mallon, Mary, 92
Man Against Death, 367
Maneval's agar, 346
Mantoux test, 291
Mazzini test, 342
Measles, 385–387, 427
   German, 387
Meat extract, 49
Mechanical pressure on bacteria, 145, 146
Media, selective, 61–63
Medium, requisites for, 44
Membranous croup, 285
Meningitis, 65, 79, 266, 302–305
Mental state and resistance, 408
Menthol, 141
Mercuric chloride, 126, 127, 141
Mercurochrome, 126, 141
Mercury, 126
Merthiolate, 127, 141
Mesophiles, 144
Metabiosis, 40
Metabolism, 25–41
Metachromatic granules, 285
Metaphen, 141
Metchnikoff's cellular theory, 404
Methylene blue milk, 77
Methyl orange, 48
Methyl red, 48
   test, 169
Metric system, 431, 432
Mice as vectors, 215, 331
Microaerophile, 80
Microaerophilic techniques, 65
Microbe-free animals, 206
Microbiology
   of atmosphere, 196–208
   of food, 209–229
   of ice, 171, 172
   of sewage, 175–182
   of soil, 183–195
   of water, 155–174
Micron, 7, 431
Microscope, figure of, 7
Microsporum, 358
Microtatobiotes, 361, 373
Milk sickness, 227

Minor side of crossmatch, 419
Mites as vectors, 257, 361, 369
M.L.D. of toxin, 427
Moist heat sterilization, 86, 89–98
Moisture in media, 44, 45
Molds, 353–358
Money as a fomite, 260
Monilia albicans, 351, 352
Moniliales, 345
Mordant, 14
Morphology, 20, 72–74, 80
Moses, 57
Mosquitoes, 258, 393
Motility determination, 74
Much's granules, 19, 289
Mucor, 130, 131
Mucous membranes and resistance, 413
Multiple pressure tuberculin test, 385
Murine typhus, 364
Mushroom poisoning, 227, 228
Mus musculis, 370
Mutagenic agents, 149, 150
Mutations, 149, 238
Mycelium, 353
Mycobacterium leprae, 281
                    tuberculosis, 19, 43, 151,
                    288

Napoleon's retreat, 362
Nationality and resistance, 411
Natural bodies of water, 157
Natural immunity, 415
Negri bodies, 396, 397
Neisseria gonorrheae, 45, 65, 144, 152, 253,
                    305, 406
                    meningitidis, 65, 79, 302
Neomycin, 194
Neufeld reaction, 100, 267, 268
Neurotropic viruses, 374, 391–398
Neutralizing antibodies, 426, 427
Nitrobacter species, 187
Nitrogen cycle, 187–190
Nitrogen fixation, 188
Nitrosomonas species, 187
Nostoc muscorum, 70
Novobiocin, 194
Nucleoprotein, 19
Nucleus, 5, 11, 18
Nutrient gelatin, 75

OAB blood types, 417–420
O antigens, 325, 330
Occupation and resistance, 409
Oculoglandular tularemia, 321
Oidia, 355

Oligodynamic action, 125, 163
Ophthalmia neonatorum, 126, 307
Opsonins, 423, 424
Opsonocytophagic test, 311
Osmosis, 17
Osmotic pressure, 108, 146, 147
Otitis media, 266
Oxidase test for gonococci, 308
Oxidation in disinfection, 117
Oxidation-reduction, 77
Oxidizing agents, 128
OX-2, Proteus, 326, 363, 364, 367
OX-19, Proteus, 325, 326, 363, 364, 367
OX-K, Proteus, 326, 363, 367
Ozone, 128

Pandemic, 315
Paper money as a fomite, 260
Paradimethylaminobenzaldehyde, 79, 168
Paratyphoid fever, 34
Paroxysmal stage, 313
Parrot fever, 255
Passive immunity, 287, 384, 415
Pasteur, Louis, 287, 315, 382, 403
Pasteur treatment, 397, 398
Pasteurella avicida, 315
                    pestis, 20, 257, 315
                    tularensis, 257, 258, 319–321
Pasteurization, 86, 89, 90, 367
Pasteur's exhaustion theory, 404
Pathogeinc bacteria, 265–343
Pathogenic molds, 357, 358
Pathogens, 42
    in soil, 191
Pediculous capitus, 362
                    corporis, 362
Penicillin, 37, 85
Penicillinase, 271
Penicillium camemberti, 131, 212, 357
                    chrysogenum, 131, 237, 357
                    notatum, 38, 194, 234, 357
                    roqueforti, 212, 356
Penicylinder cup technique, 139
Pepion Adventure, 38
Peptone, 49
Peritonitis, 266
Personal hygiene, 213
Petechiae, 302
Pfeiffer phenomenon, 336
pH, 47–52
Phage typing, 272, 273
Phagocytosis, 12, 404, 405
Phenol, 129
Phenol coefficient of compounds, 129, 141
Phenol coefficient test, 140

Phenolic compounds, 45
Phenolphthalein, 48
Phenol red indicator, 48
Phipps, James, 383
Phosphorescence, 28, 29
Photodynamic action, 134
Photogenesis, 28, 29
Photoreactivation, 148
Photosynthesis, 36
Phycomycetes, 354
Physical forces on microbes, 143–154
Physical methods for anaerobiosis, 64
Physical properties of media, 54
Physiological solution, 45
Physiology, 20, 75–81
Pigment production, 30, 31
Piroplasma species, 258
Pit privy, 65
Plague, 315, 316
Plant and animal cells, 6
Plants, poisonous, 227–229
Plaques of phage, 273, 274
Plasmolysis, 17, 147
Plasmoptysis, 147
Pleomorphism, 20
Pneumonia, 251, 266–268
   virus, 374
Pneumotropic viruses, 374, 387–391
Pocks, 381
Poisoning
   bacterial, 215–224
   chemical, 224–229
Poisonous plants and animals, 227–229
Poliomyelitis, 374, 391–395, 427
Pollution of air, 198
Pools, swimming, 173
Portal of entry, 410
Postulates of Koch, 280, 281
Potassium permanganate, 129
Potentiometer, 48
Precipitinogen, 421
Precipitins, 421–423
Preservatives in food, 226, 227
Pressure filters, 163, 164
Pressure on microbes, 145, 146
Presumptive water test, 166, 167
Primary smallpox reaction, 385
Prontosil, 232
beta-Propiolactone, 137
Propionibacteria, 212
Proteolysis, 32, 77
Proteus OX-2, 326, 363, 364, 367
   OX-19, 325, 326, 363, 364, 367
   OX-K, 326, 363, 367
Proteus reactions with rickettsiae, 326, 363

Proteus species, 35, 79, 224
Protoplasm, 5
Pseudomonas, 31, 173
   aeruginosa, 322, 323, 338
Psittacosis, 255
Psychrophilic organisms, 143
Ptomaine poisoning, 216
Public drinking cups, 172, 173
Pulmonary anthrax, 283
Pustule, malignant, 283
Putrefaction, 187
Pyelitis, 79, 252
Pyocyanase, 322
Pyrogen, 30

Q fever, 258, 326, 361, 367, 368
Quaternary ammonium compounds, 132
Quellung reaction, 267
Quinine in malaria, 240

Rabbit fever, 319–321
Rabies, 395-398
   vaccine, 397, 398
   virus, 374
Race in resistance, 411
Radiation on microbes, 147–151
Rapid sand filter, 162
Rats in disease spread, 317, 318, 331
Rats, Lice, and History, 359
Reductase, 77
Reduction of methylene blue, 77
Reed, Walter, 373, 399
Relapsing fever, 258
Rennet curd, 76
Reproductive hyphae, 353
Resistance
   to antibiotics, 237, 238
   to disease, 402–429
Resistance factors, 406–410
Respiration, 26
Rh factor, 416, 418, 421
Rhizobium leguminosarum, 39, 40, 273
Rhizopus nigricans, 355
Rhubarb poisoning, 228
Ribonucleic acid, 24
Ricketts, Howard, 359
Rickettsia akari, 257, 370
   prowazekii, 257, 359
   quintana, 257, 360
   rickettsii, 257, 258, 364, 366, 370
   tsutsugamushi, 257
   typhi, 257, 364
Rickettsiae, 359–371
Rickettsial pox, 361, 370, 371
Roaches, 393

Rocky Mountain spotted fever, 258, 326, 359, 361, 364–367
Rod-shaped bacteria, 280–302, 308–333
Roentgen, Wilhelm K., 149
Roentgen rays, 149, 150
Rotation of elements, 187
Rubella, 387
Rubeola, 385–387

Sabin vaccine, 394
Sabouraud's medium, 346
Saccharomyces, 211, 345
            carlsbergensis, 349
            cereviseae, 347
            ellipsoideus, 347, 349
Salk, Jonas, 394
Salk vaccine, 394
Salmon, D. E., 330
Salmonella, 215, 217, 330–333
            california, 330
            cholerasuis, 330
            enteritidis, 217
            food infection, 217, 331, 333
            hartford, 330
            hirschfeldii, 218, 331
            paratyphi, 218, 331
            schottmuelleri, 218, 330, 331
            thompson, 330
            typhimurium, 215, 217, 331
            typhosa, 61, 62, 140, 141, 331, 332
Salmonella-Shigella agar, 62, 327, 332
Salts with proteins, 117
Salvarsan, 232
Sanitize, 21, 86, 132
Sand filters
    rapid, 162, 163
    slow, 162
Sandwich plates, 60
Sanitation
    in the home, 213–215
    in restaurants, 213–215
Saprophytes, 42
Sarcina lutea, 10
Scarlet fever, 34, 428
Schick test, 427, 428
Schizosaccharomyces, 345
Schmutzdecke, 162
Scrub typhus, 326, 361, 368, 369
Sedimentation tanks, 179
Seitz filter, 86, 100
Selective media, 61, 325
Semple rabies vaccine, 397
Septa in fungi, 353

Septicemia, 109, 266
Septic tanks, 178
Serology, 20, 404
Serratia, Serafino, 32
Serratia marcescens, 31, 32
Sewage, microbiology of, 175–182
Sex and resistance, 408
Shadowing technique, 375
Shapes and arrangements of bacteria, 8–10
Shellfish poisoning, 227
Shigella, 326–330
            ambigua, 120
            boydii, 328
            dysenteriae, 61, 328
            flexneri, 328
            paradysenteriae, 328
            shigae, 328, 329
Shingles, 380–382
Short time high temperature pasteurization, 90
Side chain theory, 405
Silicosis, 151
Silver, 125
Silver nitrate, 125, 126
Sintered glass filter, 86, 101
Sizes of bacteria, 6
Skin anthrax, 283
Skin and resistance, 412
Skin test for *Brucella*, 311–312
Slants, 70, 75
Slime layer on bacteria, 11
Slow sand filter, 162
Sludge, activated, 180, 181
Smallpox virus, 374, 382, 385
Smoking and health, 201
Snakeroot poisoning, 227
Sneeze, 247–251
Snow, John, 335
Soap, 45
Sodium azide agar, 63
Sodium benzoate preservative, 226
Sodium lauryl sulfate, 46
Sodium thioglycollate, 64
Soft chancre, 255
Soil
    composition of, 185
    microbiology of, 183–195
    as a vehicle for pathogens, 191
Soluble specific substance, 267
Sonic waves, 152
Species resistance, 403, 410
Spheres, arrangements of, 9
Spirillum, 10
Spirochete, 10
Spontaneous generation, 55

Sporangium, 354
Spores, 21, 73
Spore staining, 73
Spot plate, 49, 50
Spreading factor, 277
Springs, 159
Sprue, 351
S.S. agar, 62, 327
S.S.S. in capsules, 267
Staining procedures, 70–74
Standard nutrient agar, 49–54
Staphylococcus aureus, 31, 38, 125, 139, 140, 141, 269–275
Staphylococcus food poisoning, 220–224
Steam
    flowing, 86, 93
    intermittent, 86, 93
    live, 86, 92
    under pressure, 86, 93–98
Steam sterilization, 52–54, 93–98
Sterility indicators, 103, 104
Sterility of media, 52, 53
Sterilization, 21, 83–106
    gas, 86, 102
    hot air, 86, 88
    moist heat, 86, 89–98
Stomach and resistance, 413
Stormy fermentation, 298
Streak plates, 56–59
Street virus, 397
Streptobacillus, 8
Streptobacterium, 8
Streptococcus pyogenes, 275–279
Streptokinase, 278
Streptomyces species, 194
Streptomycin, 194, 321
Subcultures, inoculation of, 54–65
Suitable foods for microbes, 46
Sulfa drugs, 232, 233, 321
Sulfur, melting point of, 105
Sulfur dioxide, 135
Sumner, James, 27
Surface tension, 118, 151, 152
Swarming reaction of *Proteus,* 324
Swimming pools, 163, 173
Sylvan yellow fever, 401
Symbiosis, 39
Synergism, 39
Syphilis, 254, 339–342
    screening tests for, 342
    Wassermann test for, 424–426

T.A.B. vaccine, 332
Taxonomy, 6

Tellurite agar, 62
Temperature
    conversion table, 433
    as a physical force, 143, 144
    and steam pressure, 93
Tetanolysin, 300
Tetanospasmin, 300
Tetanus, 110
Texas fever, 258
Thallophyta, 345
Thallus, 353
Theories of immunity, 404–406
Thermal death point, 89
Thermal death time, 90
Thermogenesis, 29
Thermometers as fomites, 260, 261
Thermophiles, 29, 144
Thrombi, 271
Thrush, 351, 352
Thymol blue, 48
Ticks as vectors, 258, 361
Tin poisoning, 226
Tincture, 151
Tissue culture, 362, 377–380
Tissue factors in resistance, 412–414
Tissue toxicity tests, 141
Titer, 311, 369
Torula histolytica, 349
Towels as fomites, 261
Toxicity index, 141
Toxins, 32–34
    endo-, 33, 276, 426
    erythrogenic, 276
    exo-, 33, 426
    M.L.D. of, 427
    of streptococci, 276
Toxoid, 34, 287
Transfer of cultures, 67–70
Transmission of diseases, 244–264
Treatment
    of air, 205
    of water, 160–164
Trematol, 227
Trench fever, 360
Trenchmouth, 133, 336, 337
Treponema pallidum, 45, 144, 231, 253, 339–342, 406, 408, 424, 425
Trichophyton, 358
Trickling filters, 180
Tricresol, 130, 141
Trombicula, 369
Tsutsugamushi disease, 326, 361, 369
Tubercle, 289
Tuberculin tests, 291, 292, 428, 429
    Mantoux, 291

Tuberculin tests (*cont.*)
  Vollmer, 291
  Von Pirquet, 291
Tuberculosis, 288
Tularemia, 258
Twain, Mark, 107
Twort-D'Herelle phenomenon, 272
Tyndallization, 93
Types
  of antibodies, 415–427
  of immunity, 414–415
Typhoidal tularemia, 321
Typhoid fever, 34, 61, 62, 140, 141, 410
Typhoid Mary, 246, 247
Typhus fever, 326, 361
  endemic, 364
  epidemic, 362, 363
  scrub, 368, 369
  vaccine, 362

Ulceroglandular tularemia, 321
Ultrasonic vibrations, 152
Undulant fever, 308–312
Universal donor, 417
Universal recipient, 417
Urease, 27, 325
  test for, 79, 325
Uses
  of antibiotics, 239, 240
  of molds, 356
  of yeasts, 346–348

Vaccine, 34
  autogenous, 270
  rabies, 146
  T.A.B., 333
Vaccinoid reactions, 385
Varicella, 314, 380–382
Variola, 382–385
Vegetative cells, 21, 353
Vegetative hyphae, 353
Venereal disease transmission, 253, 339–341
Vermin, 214, 215, 256–258
Vibrations, sonic, 152
Vibrio, 10, 34
        comma, 333
Vincent's angina, 133, 336, 337
Vinegar, 347
Virology, uses of antibiotics in, 240

Virulence, 10
Viruses, 372–401
Viscerotropic viruses, 374, 398–401
Vitamins from yeasts, 348
Voges-Proskauer test, 169
Volutin, 20
Vollmer test, 291
Von Pirquet test, 291
Von Prowazek, 359

Walls as fomites, 261
Washcloths as fomites, 261
Wassermann test, 424–426
Wastes, human, disposal of, 179, 180
Water, 264
  bacteriological testing of, 165–170
  chemical testing of, 170, 171
  in media, 49
  supplies, 155–174
  treatment, 160–164
Water hemlock, 228
Waterhouse, Benjamin, 384
Waterhouse-Friderichsen syndrome, 303
Water-insoluble pigment, 31
Water-soluble pigments, 31
Weil-Felix reaction, 363, 370
Weil's disease, 337
Wells
  drilled, 158
  dug, 159
Whey, 76
Whooping cough, 312–314
Wilson-Blair medium, 332
Wool-sorter's disease, 283
World Health Organization, 282, 290, 382, 389
Wort, 349

Xenopsylla cheopis, 364

Yeasts, 344–352
Yellow fever virus, 258, 374, 399–401

Zephiran, 132
Ziehl-Neelsen stain, 288, 289
Zinsser, Hans, 359
Zygospores, 355
Zymase, 348

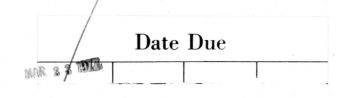